PRAISE F(
A NEW REPL
OF THE HEART

For the full text of these and other endorsements, see the book's website:
anewrepublicoftheheart.org.

"In a world of exploding crises, we are all called to contribute. But how do we find our unique contributions, make them most effectively, and bring out the best in all whose lives we touch? These are among the most crucial questions of our time, and Terry Patten beautifully elicits the wisdom with which we can find our answers."

—ROGER WALSH, MD, PhD, University of California,
author of *Essential Spirituality: The Seven Central Practices*

"*A New Republic of the Heart* is THE manual for all who want to meet this moment as the historical call to action that it is. Combining brilliant social commentary with a step-by-step blueprint for catalyzing whole-system change from the inside out, it shows us the way to rise into our personal and collective destiny."

—CLAIRE ZAMMIT, PhD, founder of FemininePower.com

"With deep caring and illuminating insights, Patten unfolds an integrative analysis of our impending crisis of civilization, offering a valuable handbook for those trying to make sense of what's happening and—most importantly—what they can do about it. Even those of us who don't subscribe to integral theory can benefit greatly from his investigation of an 'activist spirituality,' his recognition of political engagement as love in action, and his astute explanation of how we can become effective agents of change through self-transforming communities."

—JEREMY LENT, author of *The Patterning Instinct: A*
Cultural History of Humanity's Search for Meaning

"*A New Republic of the Heart* provides practical imperatives for gathering our collective strength, intelligence, and spirit into powerful strategies that can change the course of our future. Each page is filled with insights and recommendations that have personal, community and global significance. A must-read for those who know that together we can be catalysts of change."

—CONNIE BUFFALO, president of Renaissance
Project International

"Confronting the myriad challenges facing us and our planet is a delicate endeavor. Terry Patten invites us to step with both feet into the center of this complex terrain and then hands us an empowering map for not only finding our way through it, but truly being part of the solution."

—CRAIG HAMILTON, founder of Integral Enlightenment

"With extraordinary eloquence, Terry Patten integrates integral theory, social commentary, and true humanity, laying out a new path for how spiritual practice cannot just come fully online in our hearts but deeper into our world. May this groundbreaking book help you navigate changing times with grace."

—MIRANDA MACPHERSON, author of *Boundless Love*

"Patten marries brilliant big-picture analysis and heartfelt soul practices to chart an evolutionary path forward for humanity that accelerates our spiritual growth and awakens our deepest service. Just the medicine we need!"

—STEPHEN DINAN, CEO of The Shift Network and author of *Sacred America, Sacred World*

"In a time when too many of us are closing our eyes and ears to reality, Terry Patten has braved the harrowing passage necessary to grapple deeply and authentically with our ecological predicament and why we keep making it worse. This book deserves a wide readership."

—MICHAEL DOWD, author of *Thank God for Evolution* and host of "The Future Is Calling Us to Greatness"

"With a rare combination of spiritual depth and razor sharp intellect, Terry Patten weaves together social justice, environmentalism, and a sober look at today's multifaceted crises into a true marriage of spirit and action. A lifetime's worth of spiritual practice radiates through every paragraph."

—DUSTIN DIPERNA, author of *Streams of Wisdom*

"*A New Republic of the Heart* is a potent revolutionary guide for twenty-first century activists. Expect to be inspired by a clear vision and a call to coalesce innovators, ecologists, and evolutionaries and awaken their heart intelligence."

—MARILYN HAMILTON, PhD, founder of Integral City Meshworks and author of *Integral City*

"In *A New Republic of the Heart*, Terry Patten shares the fruit of his decades of intense inner work—a new toolkit for a whole-system change."

—JOSH BARAN, author of *The Tao of Now*

"Like all true spiritual guides, Terry Patten shows us how to open our hearts and respond to this suffering world. His book is thoughtful, careful, and joyful."

—DIANE MUSHO HAMILTON SENSEI, author of *The Zen of You and Me*

"Terry Patten has followed his deep inner calling as inseparable from the calling to contribute to the health of our burning world. *A New Republic of the Heart* communicates the evolutionary activism it takes to walk paths that lead to the answers we need."

—THOMAS HÜBL, international teacher and founder of the Academy of Inner Science

"Without mincing words about what humanity is facing, this guide to spiritual activism gives direction for a sane and sustainable, heart-based paradigm."

—ANODEA JUDITH, PhD, author of *The Global Heart Awakens* and *Eastern Body, Western Mind*

"As an evangelical Christian and social conservative, I am repeatedly surprised by the deeper truths here with which I agree. These include the belief that this is indeed a defining moment for humanity, and that the solution, while seemingly beyond reach, is in fact both close and personal; that we have within us the potential to be and to do far more than we ever previously imagined; that the necessary change begins within the very heart and soul of every person—from the bottom up, so to speak; that the times call for a kind of mindfulness and intentionality that humankind has never collectively achieved in the past; and that as we turn inwardly to tap our true human potential, we must also turn outward in a spirit of tireless and selfless servanthood.

We must urgently resume the great dialogue of civilization in a way that will lift us beyond the boundaries of our sectarian and political differences toward the embrace of a better future for our endangered world. Whatever your party or religion, read this book, and for the sake of everything that is true, good, and beautiful, let's talk about it—together."

—EMERSON ALLEN JOSLYN, MD, High Point, North Carolina

"The depth of this book is astounding. *A New Republic of the Heart* is for anyone drawn to thinking deeply, feeling fully, and acting boldly on behalf of the planet and all life."

—J. MANUEL HERRERA, Silicon Valley elected official

"Piece by piece, Terry Patten dismantles our comfortable, well-trod positions on the global future. He invites us into a bigger space, one that includes all positions yet transcends position-holding. From here we have access to not just facts but wisdom; we are able to accommodate more of what wants to be seen and felt, and we can act in a way that brings into being a healthier, more sacred world."

—JEFF SALZMAN, "The Daily Evolver"

"Terry Patten's book unearths a practical wisdom that unites the causes of the world with the deeper causes of our being. *A New Republic of the Heart* extends both frontiers of activism and consciousness, serving humanity collectively with helpful insight into what is needed currently and in the years ahead."

—OLEN GUNNLAUGSON, editor of *The Intersubjective Turn* and *Wisdom Learning*

"In *A New Republic of the Heart*, Terry Patten combines his brilliant mind and deeply compassionate heart to demonstrate a path to awakened activism. This important book connects pragmatic practices for individual activism with a visionary blueprint for a broad transformation of human civilization. It will show you how to become the change you want to see."

—STEVE MCINTOSH, president of the Institute for Cultural Evolution and author of *The Presence of the Infinite*

A NEW REPUBLIC OF THE HEART

AN ETHOS FOR REVOLUTIONARIES

TERRY PATTEN

FOREWORD BY ANDREW HARVEY

North Atlantic Books
Berkeley, California

Published by
North Atlantic Books
Berkeley, California

Cover design by Howie Severson
Book design by Happenstance Type-O-Rama
Printed in the United States of America

A New Republic of the Heart: An Ethos for Revolutionaries is sponsored and published by the Society for the Study of Native Arts and Sciences (dba North Atlantic Books), an educational nonprofit based in Berkeley, California, that collaborates with partners to develop cross-cultural perspectives, nurture holistic views of art, science, the humanities, and healing, and seed personal and global transformation by publishing work on the relationship of body, spirit, and nature.

North Atlantic Books' publications are available through most bookstores. For further information, visit our website at www.northatlanticbooks.com or call 800-733-3000.

Library of Congress Cataloging-in-Publication Data

Names: Patten, Terry, author
Title: A new republic of the heart : an ethos for revolutionaries / Terry
   Patten ; foreword by Andrew Harvey.
Description: New York : North Atlantic Books, 2018.
Identifiers: LCCN 2017036209 | ISBN 9781623170479 (paperback)
Subjects: LCSH: New Thought. | Self-actualization (Psychology) | Spiritual
   life—New Age movement. | BISAC: BODY, MIND & SPIRIT / New Thought. |
   RELIGION / Spirituality.
Classification: LCC BF639 .P148 2018 | DDC 158—dc23
LC record available at https://lccn.loc.gov/2017036209

1 2 3 4 5 6 7 8 9 United 22 21 20 19 18

Printed on recycled paper.

North Atlantic Books is committed to the protection of our environment. We partner with FSC-certified printers using soy-based inks and print on recycled paper whenever possible.

CONTENTS

FOREWORD

by Andrew Harvey

The book you hold in your hands will take you on a journey that will awaken and liberate you. And it will empower you to change the world.

I'm delighted to welcome you to a rare, sober, deep, spacious, seriously humorous conversation—a conversation many of us are longing for and trying to have. Terry Patten's passionate intelligence calmly cuts through our consensus trance and speaks directly to what really matters right now. The voice of this book penetrates our collective sleep and awakens us from the dream.

It comes just in time. This is a time when most of us are hypnotized by our screens, small and large, when our ears are closed to voices that challenge our refusal to feel our actual situation. There is an alarming tendency in spiritual circles to resort to easy answers to hard questions, to dwell in superficial compassion, cheerfulness, and premature forgiveness, but with no willingness to understand or confront our ecological and spiritual emergency, or the dire structural injustice that supports it. Thousands of well-meaning people have gone unconscious, entrained into habits they imagine are "spiritual" but that actually reinforce irresponsible bypassing and dissociation.

In this din, amidst the babel of what some Native American traditions call "pretender voices," it is very difficult to speak the truth in a way that can be heard and integrated. Because he actually *practices* the humility he advocates, Terry Patten dwells in the innocent "don't-know mind" of an undefended, intelligent heart, with the openness and curiosity that makes possible endless learning and growth. This makes him a credible guide to the conversation we so desperately need, the one we keep inadvertently avoiding, the conversation that could catalyze us back into responsible adulthood in the greater human family.

Many people are just now waking up to the truly horrifying, even unbelievable severity of our ecological, social, economic, and cultural crisis. Please listen to what this book has to say, and let it bridge you into a powerful, dynamic relationship to the horror and wonder of our time. It will help you navigate the winds of fear and your desire to turn away from what is now before us. It won't stigmatize those reactions; after all, such feelings are entirely human. Instead, it will help you be shattered in all the ways that are appropriate, and also to rest in the deeper, more spacious container in which you can become strong enough to bear the stark news. It will help you be simply present as an intelligent heart, not overcome by the devouring madness of our time. And it invites you to discover your place in the ongoing conversations among people committed to inspired action.

This book defines a new genre—it is a work of social commentary and a deep practice book; it is a brilliant synthesis of evolutionary neuroscience, integral theory, deep ecology, and spiritual wisdom. And it is a compelling call to inspired social activism. This is a truly consequential conversation about what is really happening, and what most matters in our time.

It proceeds in four movements.

First, you are led through an unblinking tour of our holistic crisis and the obstacles to clear understanding, helping you recognize our seemingly insurmountable dilemma as a demand for growth, awakening, and activism. Terry Patten helps you to become activated as you fully apprehend exactly how our sacred, catalytic existential and spiritual challenges and opportunities require our service.

Second, you will explore the territory of paradox: of how wholeness expresses itself in every facet of not just the natural, more-than-human world, but of our hypercomplex, fast-changing human civilization. This book helps you to be transformed, by looking and seeing with evolutionary eyes, noticing how a nuanced, integral perspective can reveal the hidden patterns behind our minds, our subcultures, our culture wars, and our inspiring evolutionary opportunities.

Third, Terry Patten unpacks how our radical urgency and wholeness imply a whole life of practice, and how every day and every moment are implicated. And he offers an integral view that unites transcendental spirituality with immanent earth-based spirituality, expressing itself in each soul's unique journey, and the stories that illuminate them. And he vividly illustrates this by sharing the details of his own soul journey and the archetypes that resonate in his personal experience.

Fourth, this book connects that practice to creative activism: both to "outward" activism—in-the-system, against-the-system, and around-the-system—and to "intimate" holistic activism, in our relationships and conversations. It offers a revelatory introduction to catalytic experiments in dialogue and "we-space" and the future of friendship—into becoming the kinds of spiritual friends, the kinds of sangha that might evolve the next Buddha. It even explores a series of very specific conversations that are needed if we are to transform the suicidal trajectory of industrial civilized culture.

This book concludes by addressing us very directly about the open-ended nature of its sacred call. It is an initiation into a never-ending commitment and a never-ending cooperative adventure in becoming "the ones we are waiting for." It acknowledges that many of us are already doing this work. And yet it also sees into and calls forth a future of integration that is still unrealized.

The intelligence of the heart cannot be asked to wait any longer. It must now reclaim the whole human world. This is what Patten calls an "integral revolution," a process of growing into a new structure and stage of human evolution. That's both necessary and unavoidable. Whether our future is a great hospice project or a great process of bringing wisdom to a new cycle of technological, social, and economic innovation, it needs our highest heart intelligence. That must be enacted in every heart, in every relationship, in every organization, in every fiber of our body politic.

This broad cultural awareness is emerging spontaneously, expressing a dawning universal intuition of what Charles Eisenstein evocatively calls "the more beautiful world our hearts know is possible." This intuition is arriving in the hearts of millions of people all over the world. It expresses a new patriotism, a civic responsibility to bring into being "a new republic of the heart."

This compelling prophecy rests upon an enormously significant reality. A new republic of the heart is already coming into being. It is happening in my heart-mind—and yours—through our committed activism, and in the hearts and minds and hands and feet of hundreds, and thousands, and millions of others. This book is important because it builds a bridge from our fragmented confusion to a happy recognition of what it will be to arrive, together, as novitiate citizens of our next evolutionary stage and structure, illumined by the transmissive intensity of higher, divinely inspired states of consciousness.

If you read this book, and feel it with an open mind and heart, you will be changed irrevocably. You'll be drawn into brokenhearted, joyous commitment to the great work, the only thing that means anything after all our structures of human-created meaning are burned through.

You will arrive in the dawning awareness that at a deep level you are already growing in loyalty to an emergent new republic of the heart. It already exists. Paradoxically, it also needs us to bring it into being. This new republic may become our homeland, and there the divisive battles of our current politics may become unnecessary. But in the meantime, this great undertaking asks everything of us—a whole life of practice and growth and friendship and service and courageous creativity.

So read on, and receive an initiatory vision. In this stunning marriage of wild heart and cool mind, Terry Patten turns the black diamond of our global darkness to illuminate our hearts, hone our capacity for selfless service, and resplendently deepen our commitment to enact our divine identity and its joy, whatever happens.

This is a major work of pioneering originality, accomplished with great intellectual grace and profound sacred passion. Enjoy it and be changed.

ACKNOWLEDGMENTS

I t took a village to write this book; I would like to express my deepest gratitude to a few of the many people who provided support and encouragement from its inception to completion.

Thanks especially to Larry Boggs, my primary final editor, cocreator, and sounding board, whose tireless dedication to clarity of understanding and impeccability I will forever be grateful for; Elizabeth Debold, a brilliant and incisive coconspirator in clarifying the structure that has brought the ideas of this book into fruition; and several dear friends who have provided crucial reflection and editorial help at various stages in this project—including Deborah Boyar, Rebecca Baum, and my longtime collaborator Marco Morelli, with whom I brainstormed and refined these ideas and how to communicate them from 2011 to 2016. Thanks also to Brad Reynolds, who expertly created the Four Quadrants figure.

Profound gratitude to Andrew Harvey for his encouragement and for championing this project and to Jim Willems for being my companion in the vision and passion that birthed it. Deep thanks to Rafael Cushnir, Gene Dunaway, Roger Walsh, Sean Esbjörn-Hargens, Dustin DiPerna, Jeremy Lent, Bill Kauth, and Andrew Gaines, who have read drafts or sections and were excited enough by the book's vision to help me improve it.

Deep appreciation to Frank Marrero, Grant Hunter, Lisa McKay, JoAnn Lovascio, Tom Steininger, Ellen Daly, Carter Phipps, Michael Dowd, Connie Barlow, Jean Houston, Jeff Salzman, Diane Hamilton, Ken Wilber, and Adi Da Samraj, who have gracefully influenced me with their original ideas and/or inspired (or shared) this vision in various, sometimes profound, ways. And a broad thank you (and apology) to the many people *not* named here who have supported, inspired and accompanied me and contributed over the years.

This book has evolved the thinking I embodied in an unpublished manuscript from 2004: *The Terrible Truth and the Wonderful Secret: Answering the Call of Our Evolutionary Emergency.* I am grateful to everyone who helped that early work come into being, especially Deborah Boyar and Frank Marrero and also Larry Boggs and Julia Gilden. I also benefited from the thoughtful reflections I received from Raphael Cushnir, Sean Esbjörn-Hargens, Geoff Fitch, Terri O'Fallon, Ken Wilber, and Steve McIntosh.

Sincere thanks to everyone at North Atlantic Books, particularly Tim McKee for his wise, gracious patience, counsel and faith; Alison Knowles for her enthusiastic support and guidance; Ebonie Ledbetter for her careful dedication; and Bevin Donohue and Doug Reil for their energetic belief in a new republic of the heart.

INTRODUCTION

What's Really Happening?

Our times are strange and wondrous—so strange and so wondrous that they far outstrip our comprehension! Even as we are verging on world-changing breakthroughs in science, technology, consciousness, cooperation, and leadership, we're also verging on catastrophic breakdowns of our planetary ecology, as well as our cultural cohesion, economic and social order, and, of course, our politics. It is wild, significant, inspiring, and terrifying that this is all happening *simultaneously*. We are clearly approaching a moment of truth.

We need the guidance of higher wisdom. Fortunately, all of humanity's highest wisdom traditions are in conversation as never before. And yet the circumstances that have sometimes enabled wisdom to guide the human future seem to be eroding underneath our feet. Our collective nervous system is surging with adrenaline, jolted again and again by breaking news and visions of apocalypse as well as technological utopias and dystopias.

What's really happening? Where are we headed? Is human civilization really coming apart? Will we all come together as never before? What does that mean for us personally? What can we do? How can we "be the change we want to see in the world"?

In 2016, while I was writing early drafts of this book, the average planet-wide surface air and ocean temperatures were the warmest ever recorded for sixteen consecutive months—and extreme weather events continued to increase in size and frequency. At the same time, a backlash against liberal democracy, immigration, and globalization spawned a worldwide political crisis, and our planetary ecology and climate were (to put it mildly) not the dominant popular priorities.

Although I feel chilled to the bone by some of what we might be facing, I am also uplifted and inspired to behold our most dramatically positive possibilities. It is becoming a cliché to state that we're in a race between consciousness and catastrophe. So my focus is not on laying odds. It is on the inner work that can enable us to do the outer work of navigating this time of transition in the best ways possible.

Some colleagues and I have discovered some crucially helpful insights and practices. I believe they can lead us to a grounded, positive, authentic way of relating to our predicament and our opportunities. These insights and practices might help get us through the years ahead. More important, they might even help us take giant steps into a collective transformational process that can actually change the human game in the ways many of us have sought to all our lives.

Such a game-changing transformation would be something like what was, in ancient times, symbolized by a precious jewel. Buddhists have called it a "wish-fulfilling gem." Such a diamond cannot be formed except under titanic pressures. Sudden, dramatic evolutionary progress often takes place under conditions of extreme tension, when pressures require rapid and dramatic adaptation. When new conditions disrupt ecological balance, other crucial environmental factors change, and they force new faculties and behaviors to emerge.

We are seeing this happen to the planet—but the same thing is happening to us. As the planet is pushed to its limits, so too are we. While the changes being triggered ecologically are threatening in many ways, their effects on us, even when they do harm, may well also produce the evolutionary pressures that will form something like a diamond, a qualitative structural transformation of the elements of our very character. It will demand everything of us. That means we must accept responsibility for human evolution itself—and that this evolutionary transformation must take place not over eons, but rather as an accelerated "punctuated" sociocultural transformation.

Evolution has shown its ability to find astonishing expressions under the right circumstances. It has always proceeded against overwhelming life-and-death odds, but right now we are in the midst of a collection of interconnected challenges and opportunities of unprecedented scope and intensity. If evolution proceeds in fits and starts, with long periods of relative "equilibrium" punctuated by turbulent periods of rapid evolutionary innovation, those of us alive today are right in the center of the action.

BOOM OR DOOM?

Two compelling and mutually conflicting metanarratives, each with conflicting views of our predicament, are in competition among intelligent observers. The first is optimistic. It is a narrative of continual survival, adaptation, transcendence, and progression. In this view, our technological and cultural advances are entering a period of game-changing exponential acceleration. Our increasing collisions with planetary limits, and the unfolding catastrophic consequences of our unsustainable behaviors, though very real, will finally sober us and force us to change our collective habits, and we will have new means to ease the transition. Circumstances will teach us wisdom and set us firmly back on a positive evolutionary path into a marvelous unchartable future.

An evolutionary version of this narrative sees our precarious global predicament as an important transition but a temporary bottleneck in our upward evolutionary trajectory. It sees a powerful creative drive, native to every morsel of reality, driving our evolution. This dominant creative factor will be key to ensuring our continued survival and progress in ecology, science, culture, ethics, technology, politics, economics, and consciousness.

In the version of this narrative that inspires me, humankind will eventually establish a metacommunity, or *metasangha,* of "communities of practice," expressing our highest ethics and values. And this future civilization will eventually manifest a new stage in the evolution of the human race—a new adulthood for the species—perhaps even a unified and transcendent super-organism that some see as the next Buddha, or as the true meaning of the second coming of Christ.

The second, equally influential metanarrative is pessimistic and socio-ecological. It sees a more primitive and instinctual power as the dominant force driving both our development and our degeneration, and ultimately determining our fate. This darker side of that raw evolutionary energy or *Eros* manifests as an unquenchable and compulsive drive for survival, dominance, adventure, acquisition, conquest, consumption, and control. We have long been in the grip of this power-Eros, and look at what has happened. We've nearly exhausted Earth's resources, enormously overshot its carrying capacity, and are now on the verge of an age of contraction, scarcity, environmental degradation, social upheaval, and economic collapse—and these dangers appear more likely with every passing year.

In this narrative, humankind's unbridled drives will inexorably lead to the collapse of civilization and the planetary biosphere, resulting in mass species extinctions—and, in time, scenarios that may well lead to a dystopian, nearly uninhabitable planet and perhaps the end of the human race. Many deep ecologists say we have already entered the early stages of the collapse of human civilization.

My life and work have been fueled and inspired by the optimistic evolutionary metanarrative. But I've been shaken, sobered, and educated by my intensive study of the science and journalism supporting the pessimistic metanarrative, which more realistically accounts for the latest current data. The history and evolution of humankind, and even of each individual life, reveals a struggle between the forces and effects of the evolutionary-creative Eros and the instinctual-power Eros. And while we may place our hopes in the first narrative, we cannot dismiss the mounting evidence that supports the second. No one can know for sure which of these metanarratives will shape our future. We are suspended between two antithetical possibilities, as well as a spectrum of possibilities between the two extremes. I believe that even though certainty is beyond our grasp, we are the prime actors in the drama. And even without any certainty, we can greatly influence the outcomes.

I take this to heart, and I suggest we all do, because we're each partially in charge. The locus of control of human civilization—this vast and hypercomplex system—is distributed, nonlinear, and unpredictable. It is no more conscious, no more able to choose its direction, anywhere else than it is right here, right now. That implicates me, and you, at least in some small but potentially significant way. If humanity is to wake up to its predicament and choose a sustainable future, millions of people will necessarily participate. And where might that awakening and participation begin? When? I can't expect it to be the exclusive responsibility of someone else—of some political or spiritual leader or expert or philanthropist or celebrity. It must also depend on me, if I am aware enough to sense and feel that I can make some small difference—and the same goes for you.

That means that I must remain "in conversation with" the leading edges of the dark ecological narrative, *and* with the leading edges of the humanistic technological narrative of progress. At the same time, I do well to stay close to the insight that even though I care deeply about the future of life, I can trust reality itself (however much death and loss it may contain) never to really be a "problem." Regardless of its nature, the future is not a dilemma, and it doesn't need to be solved. And this does not change another truth: I want to pay attention when what I love is threatened.

I am honor-bound to remember that I don't know what will happen, and that no one else knows either. Wisdom requires being *epistemically humble* enough ("knowing that you don't know," rather than epistemically closed, or "thinking you know") to learn what is revealed by a wide range of perspectives. The interaction between us and these perspectives and the scenarios they imply will create the future into which we all will live. I can hold the question much better if I don't close myself off to any part of what human intelligence sees. And so I become a multiperspectival participant in the affair of our common life, fully aware that we must act decisively and effectively in the midst of great uncertainties. After all, we do know the dire consequences of not acting.

WHAT WE CAN DO

We know that both the worst and the best in human beings, and our potential for rapid radical change, all emerge in times of crisis.

This crisis will require very different tools than anything we've relied on in the past to dig ourselves out of holes and harrowing emergencies. This is a new kind of challenge. Technological and scientific breakthroughs will create openings for fundamental change. They will be a necessary part of the path forward, *but they are not sufficient.* The same is true of the wisdom born of high states of consciousness. And it is true of enlightened organizational practices. Leadership in any of the ways we have understood it until now will be crucial, but it too will not be enough.

What will be required is "whole system change"—a broad transformation of all human civilization. That's enormous and unprecedented, so of course it will take a while. It implies *constant* transformation and aliveness, inner and outer. To take this seriously on a personal level is to confront an impossibly grand imperative. In effect, our predicament is calling on us to simultaneously volunteer for the supreme commando raid behind enemy lines and to join a metaphorical monastery and give up our lives to the wholeness that sustains us. And we are asked to renew these commitments again and again, in every new moment. We are called to a robust and dynamic new form of spiritual activism—or activist spirituality—that fuses the "inner work" of personal transformation and awakening with the "outer work" of service, social entrepreneurship, and activism.

Our relationships, our communities, our connectedness to others, our ability to be resourceful and resilient—these are likely to be our most meaningful security under the extreme circumstances that are increasingly likely. And our psychological and spiritual resilience will become our most essential capital. Our thriving may depend most of all on our courage and generosity, our ability to defy our fear, to be happy for no reason at all, to cooperate with others locally in our community, and to bounce back creatively after traumatic setbacks. These are the kinds of virtues—and the kinds of bonds—that will probably really matter.

The balance could quite possibly tip toward survival and evolution. A large part of me—the greater part—still believes it will. But no one knows the future. In the process of writing this book I have faced the futures I feared facing, and it took me through a disorienting, months-long plunge into a "dark night of the soul." I wouldn't have been true to myself if I had refused to consider the darker possibilities—and their transformative gift of a different kind of hope, and gravitas, on the far side of despair. Even if global catastrophes and planetary extinction are our inescapable fate, how our souls respond, transform, and reveal their character are matters of utmost significance. And besides, every day is a gift.

No matter what lies ahead, it is tremendously important that we participate in ways that express our highest character and values. We can choose to act on the basis of what is best in ourselves. We can try to engineer and serve a comparatively "soft landing" to our overheated, turbulent trajectory, a benign transition from gross unsustainability to a sustainable human presence on our planet. And we can care for one another, even under the worst-case scenarios. In any event, we can wake up together into responsibility instead of sleepwalking into apocalypse.

LET'S TALK

In this pivotal moment of truth for our species, a whole wave of radical conversations is inevitable. For these conversations to really make a difference, we must break through our personas and our inauthentic poses. This is a deeper level of discourse than has hitherto seemed thinkable in public—disarming, tender, and authentic. To my knowledge, we have never had such public conversations. Any such conversation requires an extraordinary degree of intelligence, freedom, clarity, and intimacy—and perhaps it can only take place in a moment of supreme urgency like this one. But now the stakes for humankind are our collective fate—a life-and-death choice. As Samuel Johnson noted, "Nothing clarifies a man's mind so much as the knowledge that he shall be hanged in the morning."

We are in territory that can clarify our minds—perhaps the calm before the storm. This historical moment may be the last window when we can initiate such a conversation in an environment of relative tranquility. Such a conversation requires a level of trust, vulnerability, and truthfulness that our culture seems to preclude, and we tend to shy away from it. It isn't easy to examine and feel our deepest fears, or to acknowledge our unsustainable, addictive way of life. In a way, it is like a twelve-step "moment of clarity," out of which unexpected changes of habit and character become mysteriously possible through "a power greater than ourselves." That power may be the pressure of evolution itself.

Important conversations will refine practical solutions to our current social, political, economic, and environmental crises. Some among us have already been having those conversations for years. But they haven't yet produced the urgently needed outcomes. Those conversations will deepen, extend, and continue.

A new, soul-level conversation is called for. It can only occur in a very different state of consciousness. It also requires new, more spacious and holistic and dimensional and nuanced structures of mind. It requires integral consciousness and the integrated intelligence of our whole being—what I call *integral heart intelligence* (which integrates mental intelligence and a powerful will with intuitive wisdom).

These collective evolutionary capacities emerge when individuals consistently practice transformative inner disciplines, individually and with each other, with the united intention to serve a greater good.

We are going to be drawn out of our comfort zones, but perhaps into something deeper and more real, meaningful, and rewarding. Periods of great adversity often produce exciting and satisfying lives. There is a kind of love possible during times of war or natural disasters, a kind of vivacity and authenticity.

In this way, we might actually do something even better than surviving the coming crises and catastrophes that might await us. We might learn to thrive in a way that perhaps we were not before our runaway planetary emergency began to threaten every comfortable structure of existence.

We might become something so far beyond what we are, who we have been, and how we have thought and lived and loved and spoken and treated one another and our planet, that we might for all practical purposes be a new species.

This is a grand idea, and yet it is reasoned from evidence. And it is simple. It is the basis for the vision, motivation, and practices presented in this book.

When we emerge from the isolating trance of our fragmented subcultures and begin to act with others with the understanding that we really are all in this together, something important happens. We enter together into a profound shared experience. We enter into a new consciousness and creativity that are not available to lone individuals. No one, regardless of their enlightenment, can be what many of us can be when we are awake together, united in consciousness, vision, fellowship, care, and purpose.

Intimate, candid, catalytic soul conversation can open a doorway out of our collective trance, our conditioned alienation, our collective bad dream. It is a cluster of conversations that lead into an integral culture and consciousness: the next stage in our evolution. And in that consciousness, all our other necessary conversations about practical and political solutions to urgent problems can be fruitful in a way they have never been until now.

Writing this book has been profoundly humbling. I don't imagine I stand on some superior moral or spiritual ground. I am a student of this process and these ideas a teacher who teaches what he most needs to learn. I need this soul conversation as much as you do. And this book is my attempt to begin the conversation with you, and with as many people as possible.

This book represents my attempt to complete the enormous unfinished work of my generation. We may not be able to leave behind as healthy a planet as we were given. But I wish to bequeath to my son, and all our daughters and sons, a supremely valuable legacy. I hope this book can be a catalyst—one of many—to help us grow into the new version of humankind that is envisioned here.

My hope is that, having read this far, you will choose to enter this conversation. For me it is a first step in a process of building connections, conversations, relationships, and communities that both nourish and embody the higher potentials of our species—one that will provide a solid integral foundation on which we may begin to build together, in the clear, pure words of Charles Eisenstein, "the more beautiful world our hearts know is possible."

A BRIEF TOUR THROUGH THE BOOK

This book reflects my own process of coming to terms with our current planetary crisis in all its complexity and uncertainty, exploring the nature and implications of global citizenship, and clarifying a radical new understanding of practice and activism. It addresses not only the external crisis but all the internal processes by which we understand—or fall short of understanding—what is truly going on, and by which we become the change we want to see in the world.

Part One establishes the multidimensional context. It summarizes our cataclysmic ecological predicament, the wholeness underlying our interconnected, more-than-human world, and the evolutionary and integral visions that establish a basis for a more integrated consideration of how we live meaningful lives in a time of crisis. It synthesizes important insights and ideas that readers can also find in other contexts.

Chapter One surveys our critical evolutionary predicament and crisis, including both its perils and promises—from the state of Earth itself to the trickiness of understanding our situation clearly, including the wickedness of the problems themselves as well as how our own brains and psyches make it maddeningly hard to fully understand and effectively respond to them.

Chapter Two faces the sober facts, and responds with activism. Appreciating the gift of life, and loving life, we allow our hearts to be pierced by the maddening situation we find ourselves in; we consider how we can ground ourselves in an unconditional happiness that doesn't depend on "reasons" to be happy; and, finally, we consider the esoteric anatomy of activism—the absolutely complementary nature of inner and outer work.

Chapter Three considers reality's undivided wholeness—the most basic, obvious, and elusive truth about ourselves and our environment—and how our usual approach (especially in "civilized" societies) is to bypass this perspective in favor of endless fragmentation and analysis, which contributes to the pathology by which we have wrought ecological havoc on our whole planet.

Chapter Four views humans in the context of our sweeping evolutionary story and sees into this pivotal moment when we shift into a much accelerated evolutionary future.

Chapter Five introduces an integral way of understanding our multidimensional reality, appreciating how all human perspectives are partial views of a larger truth. Beyond the cognitive, emotional, and spiritual limitations of our typical fragmented thinking are more holistic perspectives that offer a basis for a "radical integral ecology."

My original thinking is largely concentrated in *Part Two*, which explores an integral understanding of the nature of individual and collective spiritual practice, purpose, social responsibility, and evolutionary activism. These explorations point the way toward an integrated practice that is both personal and social and that enacts *whole-system change*—a process that is profound, radical, and all-inclusive. I explore how we can begin right where we are, in our relationships with one another—and in our conversations—to seed a broad-based cultural transformation.

Chapter Six describes integral practice grounded in the awakening of free consciousness and love. It unpacks the holistic understanding of life, the humble, curious, joyous disposition, and the flexible improvisational disciplines of a comprehensive, integral spiritual practice—and how it becomes a creative relationship to life's unfolding that can inform every new moment.

Chapter Seven explores the unique adventure of practice that unfolds for each individual soul, and how it can enable us to live our deepest purpose, which we can often best understand through old stories, archetypes, and metaphors.

Chapter Eight shows how such holistic inner work expresses itself creatively in all kinds of outer work that creatively address the need for whole-system change and the multidimensional nature of culture and society. Evolutionary activism can take a multitude of forms, including in-the-system political activism, protest against the system, and activism that obviates government, going around the system. We look at four specific examples, and consider a broad range of integral approaches to political change.

Chapter Nine looks at the powerful synergies activated by communities of practice, as a source of hope for the future, and describes the tender, fierce, passionate nature of authentic communication, as well as the lessons learned through the integral community's experiments with "we-space." Here we begin to speculate about how this new tribalism will shape our near future.

Chapter Ten explores the nature and effectiveness of conversations, and the structures and boundaries that attend to them. It considers what it takes to engage deep, generative mutual exchanges, and explores significant conversations about the human future that are taking place within three groups of leading-edge thinkers—but that need to be happening *between* the groups.

Chapter Eleven is about our unique role in this place and time for transforming civilization and planetary life. We are "it," whether we like it or not, and it is up to us—through our inner and outer work—to enact all necessary changes for creating a living, sustainable, exciting future. This work expresses who we truly are and it will go on forever, even "after it's too late"—which it never is.

PART ONE

Fragmentation and Wholeness

Our Wicked Predicament and the Consensus Trance

Facts do not cease to exist because they are ignored.
—ALDOUS HUXLEY

The most radical thing any of us can do at this time is to be fully present to what is happening in the world.
—JOANNA MACY

Our loyalties are to the species and the planet. We speak for Earth. Our obligation to survive and flourish is owed not just to ourselves, but also to that Cosmos, ancient and vast, from which we spring.
—CARL SAGAN

It is hard to imagine a threat that is better able to elude our understanding and response—one that is more abstract, insidious, inconvenient, and spectral—than the presence of too much human-originating carbon dioxide (CO_2) in the air. It is colorless and odorless—utterly invisible. The biggest sources are distant from our own locus of control. The worst effects are still in the relatively distant future. The identities of the victims and their dates of reckoning are unknown, yet we need to act now if they are to be spared. Full understanding of the problem requires scientific sophistication far beyond that of most citizens, politicians, and journalists—and any action taken against this threat will require the agreement and understanding of politicians, business interests, and the electorate. Meanwhile, amidst simmering culture wars, vested interests are already using and will continue to use sophisticated disinformation campaigns to turn voters and decision makers against such actions, intensifying polarization and gridlock, and blocking our collective capacity to comprehend and respond proactively to *any* aspect of our ecological predicament (which, as we'll see, goes well beyond climate).

At the same time, there are real reasons for hope. Solar and wind power and electric vehicles are enjoying an enormous boom. The majority of the world's nations have expressed commitments to counter climate change, and public opinion around the world supports strong action. Humans have already devised and begun implementing technological and policy initiatives that, if widely implemented, could—according to scientific experts from multiple disciplines—not only halt the growth of carbon emissions but actually begin to *reverse* global warming within a generation.

Some of the most promising initiatives were recently analyzed by Project Drawdown, which quantified the hundred most effective *currently existing* solutions to address climate change. (The findings are described in the book *Drawdown: The Most Comprehensive Plan Ever Proposed to Reverse Global Warming,* edited by Paul Hawken.[1])An international team of researchers identified promising solutions, conducted research into their viability and modeled them, quantifying their costs and benefits and how much each can contribute to "drawing down" atmospheric carbon levels by 2050. Each of these solutions requires enormous projects or social transformations, but they are not pie in the sky; each of them is at least beginning to be implemented. They encompass such widely diverse projects as large-scale conversions to solar and wind power, reducing food waste, converting refrigeration technology, and reducing livestock emissions (responsible for up to 20 percent of greenhouse gases annually) by transitioning to plant-rich diets. These solutions taken together can (this project calculates) not just halt increases in atmospheric carbon, but *roll them back*—and this can begin within thirty years! All of this can be done by scaling up current proven technologies.

But these are each massive projects, and even efforts to implement demonstrably effective existing solutions are meeting formidable resistance. We don't have agreements—the political and popular will—to enact all those solutions on the scale and schedule called for. Instead, cultural wars and political conflict are intensifying. Wars and economic instability threaten to further disrupt progress. And climate change is only one facet of our enormous ecological predicament. Meanwhile, contemporary culture is focused on more "immediate" concerns.

In addition to the elusive nature of global warming, a tangle of additional causes and effects conspires to further distract, divert, numb, or dull human beings into incomprehension of our actual situation and of the full scope of our wickedly complex challenges. These factors are so numerous and appear in so many guises that here we can only offer a general survey of a few of the critical hidden causes.

In broad terms, these impediments to understanding fall into two categories. One is the elusive nature of the problem itself, and the other relates to glitches in human nature, affecting both individuals and collectives. These two types of impediments affect all of us—not just "climate deniers" and the scientifically ignorant. Every one of us is playing our part in what often appears to be a slow-motion train wreck.

A GLOBAL TIPPING POINT

There is overwhelming evidence that we are living at an enormous global tipping point—"the moment of critical mass, the threshold, the boiling point."[2] There are many signs—from actual weather and ecological events to volumes of shocking data—that point to the conclusion that our planet and biosphere, our life-support system, is in deep trouble. The consensus of the world's environmental scientists is that our species is encountering an epochal array of global and environmental challenges that threaten the future of industrial civilization and human-friendly planetary conditions.

In a 2009 article in *Nature,*[3] a team of natural scientists tried to quantify our overall situation. They identified nine interconnected planetary thresholds that, if crossed, risk disrupting the "unusual" ecological and climatic stability that has marked the last ten thousand years. We've already passed three of the boundaries, are close to crossing four, and two can't really be measured. We may be approaching multiple tipping points that may affect Earth's capacity to support human life.

As of this writing, our most accurate measurements of atmospheric carbon dioxide (CO_2) are 400–410 parts per million (far above the presumably "safe" level of 350 ppm, and inexorably climbing). Serious environmental scientists believe it is too late to prevent the dramatic changes associated with at least a two-degree Celsius increase in global temperatures, and that it will take a huge breakthrough in public awareness and enormous changes in our lifestyles to keep increases from rising much further.

What does this imply? The climate is already warming even faster than early predictions regarded as "worst-case," and given the potential for runaway effects as tundra thaws and methane is released, some scientists believe warming is likely to accelerate. We are already seeing extreme weather events. More big storms and floods and droughts are likely, as well as major crop failures and famine, millions of deaths from heat waves, and even more massive refugee influxes. These and other potential impacts are likely to continue to send shock waves and a cascade of chain reactions through our already vulnerable economic, social, and political systems.

But this tipping point does not just relate to climate and the biosphere; it relates to every arena of human and nonhuman life on Earth.

As if that weren't enough, there's a dimension of our predicament as fundamental as ecology—the fact that acceleration itself is unsustainable. Human civilization is addicted to growth, and that growth has been steadily accelerating. Physicist Geoffrey West, in his book *Scale,* studied organisms and cities to discover the ratios and patterns that show up when biological and social sciences are approached through the lens of physics. West observes that patterns of growth and change are self-accelerating, with cycles of innovation shortening, and that these bear toward a mathematical singularity (or evolutionary deadline) in time. He concludes that present trends, if extended, would lead to an economic crash and the collapse of the social fabric. But, he says, this crisis is not inevitable. For this to be averted, we would need a grand unified theory of sustainability "bringing together the multiple studies, simulations, databases, models, theories and speculations, concerning global warming, the environment, financial markets, risk, economies, health care, social conflict, and the myriad other characteristics of man, as a social being interacting with his environment."[4]

Even before West's book appeared, Peter Russell quietly published an essay expressing similar conclusions by reasoning inferentially from the patterns of history and current events:

However fast we find the pace of life today, one thing is sure, twenty years from now it is going to be much faster, and twenty years after that much faster still, and twenty years after that... almost unimaginable.

Some look at where this acceleration is taking us technologically; to the so-called singularity when computers surpass human intelligence. We would then move into a new era of development unlike anything we have seen so far. But whatever may transpire in a post-singularity world, one thing is certain: The acceleration in the rate of development will not stop. Quite the opposite; it will leap upwards even steeper.

Herein lies our blind spot on the future. Continued acceleration is inevitable, and is winding us up faster and faster in a whirlwind of change from which there is no way out. Yet any notion of a long-term future for humanity implies the acceleration has ceased. You cannot have it both ways.

In addition, accelerating change puts ever-increasing stress on the systems involved—human, social, economic, and planetary. Stress stems from failure to adapt. And failure to adapt leads ultimately to breakdown of these systems.[5]

Russell concludes that long-term human survival is highly improbable, but that in the generations we have left, we have an amazing opportunity to grow spiritually and to incarnate what is best in our human character. We can make eternal contributions to what Kabbalists call "the book of life." The logic of acceleration seems to clearly imply an inevitable end to the human experiment. However, West and Russell admit they don't know for sure. The future is indeterminate. Unpredictable change is perhaps the only sure thing.

For three decades I have been deeply contemplating exactly what we know and what we don't know (and there is a *lot* we don't know), and what this crisis or tipping point means for each of us, and what we can and must do about it. Like many others, I have passed through periods of disorienting despair, feeling—on the basis of persuasive evidence—that human civilization has likely passed the point of no return and is in the process of collapse. Along the way, I encountered the invisible fraternity of brave souls who have endured a dark initiation into these disorienting prospects, and I've benefited from their fellowship and counsel.

I have also been heartened by the fact that people have wrongly imagined doomsday since the beginning of time, and by the fact that Earth and its biosphere are so alive, dynamic, and unpredictable that no one knows exactly how things will unfold—which leaves us ample room for hope. A crisis, says one dictionary, is "the point in the progress of a disease when a change takes place which is decisive of either recovery or death." And principles of physics offer another hopeful analogy. Nobel physicist Ilya Prigogine studied the levels of order in open systems, and discovered that as they become more and more chaotic, they reach a bifurcation point, where they either collapse into chaos, or spontaneously reorder themselves, *"escaping to a higher order."* Prigogine believed human societies were reaching a bifurcation point.[6]

So I've been contemplating the multitude of fronts on which we are simultaneously arriving at the threshold of radically transformative breakthroughs offering promise for a disruptively wondrous future—including almost unimaginable, revolutionary scientific and technological advances, but particularly focusing on transformative advances in human consciousness and culture. And, as you will see, I have not only come to believe in our potential to evolve into a life-sustaining society, I have made it my life's commitment to help bring that into being. But a serious conversation cannot begin, especially among people steeped in a cultural climate permeated by denial, without the proverbial "two-by-four across the forehead." So let's begin this journey into hope and inspiration by facing the reality of our sobering, shocking predicament.

A LIFE-SUPPORT SYSTEM IS NOT OPTIONAL

Let's look for a moment at how we got to this state of affairs. Although we've approached these critical thresholds only recently, the basic recipe that has gotten us here has been cooking for centuries. For the past five hundred years, Western civilization has grown by expanding into new frontiers—first by colonizing the New World, and then through new levels of technological, industrial, and agricultural efficiency, powered by fossil fuels and other nonrenewable resources. We have consumed a great proportion of the nonrenewable resources we can efficiently mine or drill for (including metals, minerals, and especially fossil fuels). Meanwhile, we are each personally and collectively embedded in a capitalist industrial economy that requires perpetual growth.

A healthy future for humanity requires a healthy living planet.[7] And a growth economy based on constant material expansion eventually becomes incompatible with the health of a finite planet. To radically re-engineer the system, we will have to simultaneously re-engineer ourselves. This requires whole system transformation—including a healthier, more creative, more compassionate and engaged humanity than we have ever seen up to now. Both of these together—our Earth and its biosphere, and our own inner lives and life choices, individually and in community—constitute our life-support system.

The nature and unprecedented seriousness of our predicament presents us not only with great challenges but with a basis for radical hope ("radical" in a sense that I will explain fully later in this chapter). The more I have learned, the more I have found myself moving in two directions simultaneously—grieving more profoundly for the worsening state of the planet, and opening to radical inspiration about what we can do on behalf of our future, even amidst great uncertainty.

Much of what I am sharing here is not news. Books and media have educated us about our climate and ecological predicament for decades. They also report innovative technologies—actual and anticipated—with transformational potential. Learning to absorb the true implications of these apparently contradictory realities and to respond effectively to the urgency of our predicament calls for us to develop and deepen our capacity to hold contradictions—and discomfort. But for this to begin to happen, we need to bring our hearts to the material, not just our minds.

In our explorations we will encounter much that seems contradictory. The way to take all of this in is to contemplate its implications at a deeper level than we are accustomed to doing—to feel it as well as conceptualize it. Take it slow, imagining the impact on your life, on everything you love, on your favorite places, and on your beloveds in the generations to come. This might bring you more in touch with the reality and seriousness of this conversation.

Let's take an unflinching look at the ways that we humans are hardwired to engage in modes of denial or disoriented states of upset. By understanding these issues, we can get past the state of gridlock that paralyzes us, individually and collectively.

WHY IS ADDRESSING THIS PROBLEM SO DIFFICULT?

There are two kinds of factors that obstruct our ability to grapple with the human predicament. On the one hand, there are the defenses and other mechanisms (largely fear-based, as we will discuss later) within human psychology and consciousness that result not only in widespread denial—which has done so much to paralyze effective action in relation to our ecological and evolutionary emergency—but in less obvious (and often quite unconscious) forms of resistance to facing other inconvenient or complex truths. But there are also "external" factors—the confounding elements in the situation itself that impact our ability to take it all in fully and objectively.

The complexity and enormity of our current predicament set it apart from any other problem humanity has faced in its history. Every systemic challenge is intertwined with a host of others, all highly dynamic. Ecological problems are intertwined with economic, political, social, and cultural dynamics. For a committed activist, even deciding where to focus first is daunting enough. Without an understanding of the nature of this territory, we run the great risk of assuming we can solve our current problems in the same ways—and as easily—as we've eventually solved most of our other challenges historically. That would be a grave mistake.

So let's look more closely at some of the confounding factors that make our current predicament so difficult to face and understand.

WICKED PROBLEMS AND BLACK SWAN EVENTS

There is a technical term in the social sciences for the kind of problem (or suite of problems) we now face. They are referred to as *wicked problems* (so named because they are wickedly hard to solve). This term was created to describe problems—along with the challenges of addressing them—at the level often faced by world leaders, military planners, and corporate leaders. But at this unique time, arguably, all of us—not just world leaders—face a slew of such problems.

Social science theorists define a problem as "wicked"[8,9,10] when it:

- is multidimensional; has multiple causes, symptoms, and potential solutions;

- cannot be definitively delineated or demarcated because its many stakeholders frame it within different worldviews;

- can be considered a symptom, as well as a cause, of other problems;

- is unprecedented, complex, and consequential, yet solutions are hard or impossible to test accurately;

- and has a tendency to fester or get more severe, with nothing automatically stopping the vicious cycle or intensifying feedback loop.

Some have categorized climate change as "*super*-wicked"[11] because, additionally:

- there is no central authority;
- those seeking to solve the problem are also causing it;
- current policies have increasingly negative future implications;
- and time is running out.

Additionally, we are increasingly aware that the whole landscape will probably be periodically transformed—dramatically and suddenly—by events we have little hope of predicting. Unpredictable and seemingly unlikely events—sometimes with positive and sometimes with negative cascading effects—periodically transform everything. These have been called *black swans*[12] because of their unpredictability. (At one time all swans were presumed to be white, and sighting the first rare "impossible" black swan defied all expectations.)

There are many examples, negative and positive, of black swan events—from World War I to the impacts of the internet and the rapid dissolution of the Soviet bloc, and, more recently, the 2016 U.S. election cycle.

A black swan, according to Nassim Nicholas Taleb, is defined by three criteria:

- It is an outlier, far outside the realm of regular expectations. Nothing in the past pointed clearly to its possibility.
- It has extreme consequences and impact.
- Human nature leads us to concoct explanations for its occurrence *after the fact*, creating the *illusion* that it was explainable and predictable.[13]

This has further confounding implications for planners, including activists: the future is quite likely to be shaped to a significant degree by events that are right now beyond our imagination. The wicked problem/black swan convergence describes conditions that bring to mind another term used by military and corporate planners—an acronym for a special category of planning challenges: VUCA, which stands for Volatile,

Unpredictable, Complex, and Ambiguous.[14] These are among the most difficult circumstances in which to plan and strategize, and they apply fully to our ecological predicament. Action is clearly urgent, and yet finely refined strategies need to be constantly adjusted; because the situation is VUCA, strategies are wickedly difficult to keep on target.

Of course, it is still necessary to do our best to anticipate future conditions. But clearly, our ability to foresee the future is going to be severely limited by these unpredictable factors. These dynamics call for forms of activism rooted in something much more profound than prediction and strategy. The nature of the problem demands a kind of thinking that we mostly don't yet know how to do. As Einstein is quoted as saying, "We can't solve our most pressing problems with the kind of thinking that created them."

We are being called to make a transformative leap to a whole new paradigm not only of thinking but of *being human*—a new consciousness and a whole new stage in the evolutionary trajectory of our species. This great transition, which requires "whole system change," is probably necessary for sustainably resolving any of the many facets of our larger predicament. Therefore, this is what I focus on here—along with the life practices that can midwife and nourish the consciousness and culture of the human beings who will enact it.

DATA SMOG AND APERSPECTIVAL MADNESS

The wicked nature of our predicament is further complicated by what has been dubbed *data smog*. More than ever in our history, today we are all inundated by an avalanche of information. Ironically, today's unprecedented quantity and ubiquity of information have obscured what is important, rather than making it obvious. The result is *less* certainty about our world and even about ourselves. More information usually means more conflicting information. So rather than settling things, information is now leaving many of us more up in the air.

We must remember that all the information we receive daily (whether "news" or "science") goes through many hands, many "editors" and algorithms, before reaching us. We are at the far end of a great game of Telephone. By the time we find out about a news event on television or radio, in newspapers or magazines, online, or from friends and peers, it may have been unrecognizably altered out of context, oversimplified, and "spun," perhaps even to the point of being downright false. In fact, increasingly, it may actually have been false to begin with!

Some of our confusion is manufactured via intentional disinformation, but much of it comes innocently, courtesy of the postmodern explosion of "many valid perspectives." Gradually, in the eyes of many, this has relativized all truths. Amidst this cognitive imbroglio we can find evidence to justify any opinion, to fan the passion of every prejudice. This has led to our becoming more committed to our preconceptions, more polarized, and less certain of any objective truth. The slippery, fragmented, and superficial nature of our cultural discourse—what integral philosopher Ken Wilber has called "aperspectival madness"—is a recipe for confusion, paralysis, and disaster.

Although some research seems to show that our multimedia culture can accelerate development of certain cognitive capacities, other evidence seems to indicate that the never-ending avalanche of information may, in important respects, be actually making us *dumber*, eroding attention spans, memory, and judgment. More and more social critics are coming to the conclusion that this trend is far more consequential and pernicious than we generally have suspected. Many believe, in fact, that it represents an unnoticed cultural crisis that has sapped the basic health of our whole society.

Moreover, thinking more, even in the ways that build capacities, doesn't necessarily make us more insightful. Incessant cogitation may make us smarter in certain ways, but it certainly doesn't automatically make us wiser—or even better able to see what is in front of our faces.

More significantly, under these conditions we tend not to contemplate the questions that ultimately matter, which can be truly explored only in *slow time*—questions such as those concerning the mystery of being, the nature of love, what makes a human life truly meaningful, or, in the context of this consideration, *what is to be done.*

Too often, the sensational and banal hold sway. A sad consequence is that, numbed by a constant drumbeat of grim warnings, we sometimes tend to dissociate from everything except our most immediate experience. Our daily "hands-on" experience of life and our network of trusted friends and associates may seem to be the only trustworthy sources; everything else may seem profoundly suspect, because it is always contradicted by another bit of news or opinion, and because it is not part of our direct experience. So many overwhelming threats loom on all sides that there often seems little to be gained from thinking about the world's urgent problems, or life's deep questions—or from preparing, materially and spiritually, for potential disruptions of our current lifestyle.

This particular kind of overload creates both confusion and paralysis. Amid the cacophony of clashing opinions about the nature or extent of our predicament, how do we winnow out the false, overblown, distorted, or oversimplified assertions and discern the underlying reality? How do we discover what is real and important to us now?

CORNUCOPIANS, MALTHUSIANS, AND A GROWTH ECONOMY

Our ecological predicament and the prospect of collective peril are so emotionally upsetting that most people flinch and automatically gravitate toward the public consensus that we need not allow the news to register. Any contradictory "good news," on the other hand, feels so profoundly relieving that we gravitate toward it as well. Most discussions of our ecological predicament are not actually real considerations of the facts about our situation and opportunities; the real discussion is the subtext, which is all about emotions—hope versus despair. If that is our only choice, of course we'll choose hope. But what is that choice really based on?

The tension between hope and fear—between facing stark ecological limits and the belief that technology, ingenuity, or innovation will save the day—is not new; in fact, it has been debated for centuries. These two poles of thought and belief have been referred to as the *Cornucopian* (optimistic) and *Malthusian* (pessimistic) perspectives.

The term "cornucopia" is derived from the "horn of plenty" of Greek mythology. *Cornucopians* generally argue against limiting economic and population growth. They believe that advances in technology can take care of society's needs. An increase in population is good because it drives economic growth and generates more creative ideas. These ideas drive new technology, procedures, systems, and models that will address any problems associated with sustaining human life on the planet.

Malthusians are named for Thomas Malthus (1766–1834), an influential British cleric and economist who popularized a pessimistic view of population growth and its associated problems. Malthusian theory is predicated largely upon the idea that exponential growth, in population and consumption, demands more and more of certain inherently finite resources, eventually leading to collapse. The ultimate Malthusian scenario predicts that the exhaustion of resources will result in wars, famine, and environmental degradation or destruction—hardly foreign or unthinkable ideas today.

At their extremes, the two theories propose either that the end is near, or that we don't need to worry at all. Of course, there are more cranks at the extremes than there are in the middle. And yet those holding the middle ground are not necessarily taking everything into account either. You will find people arguing every position between the extremes—and all the internal and external influences we have just examined are pulling on anyone who attempts to parse this equation.

This debate has gone on for hundreds of years. In the history of Western civilization (ignoring for now Easter Island, the Mayans, and even the Roman Empire), the Cornucopians have always been right. Every time people have argued that we were coming upon a limit, we have engineered our way beyond it.

But while the Cornucopians have been historically vindicated, the Malthusian perspective, refined and upgraded, may be ultimately relevant again. Geoffrey West points to superlinear scaling and a finite time singularity as new emergent dynamics that seem likely to put an end to our recent cornucopian era.[15]

In his classic 1982 book, *Overshoot: The Ecological Basis of Revolutionary Change,* William Catton described the Cornucopian myth as the belief that resources are unlimited. He described our last five hundred years of history as a period of unique discoveries—first of the "new world," and then of coal and oil and natural gas—that created functionally unlimited resources to power ever-expanding Western economies. But with the exhausting of all unexplored terrestrial frontiers and the advent of "peak oil" (the migration to extracting inaccessible, offshore, and inefficient tar sands and shale fuels), we are now encountering the beginning of the end of our era of unlimited cheap resources.

Those facts are persuasive. And yet the much more palatable Cornucopian viewpoint is also powerfully persuasive, not only because it is comforting, not only because it fits nicely with all of the other tendencies and social pressures previously described—but also because proponents can point to so much history during which it has proved true. And it's true that brilliant scientists are hard at work on breakthrough technologies they hope can open up yet another era of expansion.

The optimism of Cornucopians has been a driving force in Western civilization. In more recent times—powering the beginning of the Industrial Revolution—coal, then oil, offered nearly unlimited quantities of extra energy that we could exploit. For two hundred years, everything that has happened in Western history has been based on this constant increase. We have been able to keep growing during all of this time.

Growth is necessary in an economy based on interest-bearing currency, but it also has become a deep psychological and cultural presumption: "We have always grown, and we need to keep growing." If we can't keep growing, we're in trouble. Theoretically, to live sustainably shouldn't require any growth at all. Same number of people; same need for food; same number of pesos/dollars. Nothing has to increase. Yet because of the nature of our money, because of the nature of our history, because of the nature of our marketplace, we are forced to increase. And we *want* to increase, because we think increase equals success.

This presumption about growth—this association of growth with thriving and success—functions in the lives of every individual, every country, and every culture: as a bribe. If you participate, you can have wealth and respect. There is comfort. There is convenience. There is mobility. But a civilization so addicted to growth that it cannot slow down without crashing is caught in an unsolvable predicament if there are *any* limits to *any* aspect of growth. And yet the gospel of growth is now extending to everybody. "Let's educate everybody. Let's raise the standard of living of everybody"—as if it were possible to guarantee this. This is the promise of modernity. Postmodern pluralistic idealism wants to promise this possibility universally.

This idealism ignores something big. Like a scuba diver neglecting her air line, it forgets our dependence upon our ecological foundations. And the enormous consensus around the presumption that we all *can* thrive without a great reckoning—a presumption of even those (including politicians and policymakers) who warn of limits and demand climate action—is a mighty and nearly invisible undertow that can pull us into the kind of hope that blinds us to reality.

Global capitalism has worked miracle after miracle, and continues to be our most prolific mechanism for manifesting the new miracles we so badly need. And yet it has also been a blind "machine of more," consistently wreaking terrible destruction across modern history, and has not proved quick or efficient about cleaning up its own messes. A transition to a radically new economic model (perhaps neocapitalist or post-capitalist) will clearly be necessary. And yet it is almost impossible for most of us to imagine how that can happen, short of a global collapse.

ULTIMATE HOPE VERSUS FALSE HOPE

If the measure of a human life is its significance, its ability to have positive effects much larger than itself, then all of us alive now have hit the jackpot. We are the lucky ones who have been born "where the action is," in a time when we have the potential to make a difference on an evolutionary scale. And we have unprecedented access to, and the ability to draw on, the highest accumulated knowledge and wisdom of all cultures across all ages.

Even deeper than our anxiety, and buried below our unspoken fears, I believe many of us sense this. And many of us also feel what might be described as a radical, defiant, unreasonable hope.

Here I am not speaking of the commonplace "hope" that rests on denial or rationalization. I am speaking of something more difficult to articulate, yet discernible by one who resonates with the music of the soul. It is a hope born of faith in the process of life itself, in the human spirit, in sacredness—or in an intuited sense that, in spite of everything, reality is whole and holy. However we describe it, most of us have at some point glimpsed a wondrous power beyond the mere observable mechanics of things, and we know it can work miracles. When we keep showing up in the next moment with openness, intelligence, positive expectancy, generosity, the desire to be of benefit, and the courage to throw ourselves into life completely—that is when we participate in miracles. The virtue of hope confers the courage it takes to lean forward into the future. That is what we intuitively choose; we recognize that this positive orientation to life is healthy, whatever the prognosis of experts may be.

With this hope, therefore, we place our intuitive bet on life and the creativity of evolution. When hope is powered by this kind of faith or intuition—our sense of the ultimate wholeness and beauty of things and our own power to meet real challenges—it is actually not irrational at all.

But we must not confuse the ultimate hope we may have in the goodness or rightness of things with the false hope that they will automatically turn out well for us and for our world. A radical, robust hope lies *on the other side* of despair. It can energize and sustain us, inspire our highest capacities, make us a powerful positive force in the world, and help us to effectively address our inconceivably vast challenges. False hope anesthetizes us, not only against unpalatable truths, but against the direct perception of the challenges necessary to address them creatively and dynamically. In order to productively address and adapt to our global predicament, we need to face the facts, and we need to act.

In the face of these wicked global challenges, the temptation to space out, or to narrow our view down to a single limited perspective that we can imagine accounts for them, is nearly overwhelming. That is why climate denial has so much political and cultural force. In order to discover the truth about our world, we need to notice the deep ways that our social practices are reverse-engineering our brains and nervous systems, enabling us to systematically deceive ourselves.

THE SEDUCTION—AND POWER—OF HOPE

Belief in technological progress, and general optimism that things will turn out well, are both essential and dangerous. On the one hand, commitment and positive thinking have tremendous self-fulfilling prophetic power. Henry Ford's one-liner is justly famous: "Whether you think you can, or you think you can't—you're right." On the other hand, as we've seen, hope functions to justify denial or feel-goodism, and can be an excuse for doing nothing—or for being so focused on certain solutions that the downsides (which can prove deadly) get played down or ignored.

It is not hard to see the value of optimism. People frequently succeed by imagining positive outcomes and working hard, often while also making creative use of advanced technical skills. The energy of optimism and positivity is infectious and unmistakable. The enormous body of literature devoted to personal growth, self-help, and success is itself evidence of the creative power of positive attitudes—and the vast majority of men and women in positions of prominence and power affirm similar sentiments. Optimism is a great unspoken agreement, and absolutely necessary if we are to attract and inspire others.

But blind optimism ignores the damage caused by cheerful denialism. We have conducted a centuries-long experiment in techno-optimism that has produced both wonders and horrors, doing grievous damage to the family of life. But perhaps if our innovative spirit is chastened by sober prudence, we can now help turn things around for the better. Let's take a brief look at some promising possibilities in this direction.

Where Radical Hope and Conventional Hope Meet

As we have seen, there are solid reasons to believe we can meet today's challenges. But not as we are. The challenges call for changing the character of human societies around the world, and the human beings who comprise them. The needed changes are so complex and comprehensive that they have multiple causes and effects and logical starting points and bottom lines. Is it "really" about policies, or economics, or technological advances, or human values, or culture, or consciousness? The answer is yes to all of those. But it doesn't stop there. We're being called to undertake a great transition of the whole human system, even while we are living within its old patterns.

To me the greatest grounds for hope are in the resilience and creativity that have emerged many times before in human history and prehistory when we have been faced with unprecedented challenges. This is a key meeting place between radical hope and *realistic* forms of conventional hope. There is ample good news, as the abovementioned Project Drawdown has fully analyzed and documented. The success of these present and future efforts, however, will depend on our ability to take in (emotionally as well as intellectually) the dark scenarios implied by current scientific data.

Some of this good news involves the use of clean, renewable energy. In addition to the possibility of massively scaling up wind and solar, we will develop additional renewable energy sources. Perhaps researchers will even discover the hoped-for godsend—a new source of energy that's radically clean and efficient, and that's scalable and practical.

Another crucial and miraculous breakthrough would cheaply, cleanly capture and sequester greenhouse gases, drawing carbon out of our atmosphere, and potentially reversing human-caused climate change. It seems unlikely, but human knowledge is too limited for us to be certain it won't happen.

Some experts suggest that we could learn new ways to enhance natural ecological processes, speeding up the ability of the natural world to restore its health.

But all technologies, present or future, miraculous or not, need to be not just invented but also implemented on a wide scale, and implementation requires political will and tremendous resources. That means a series of *social* transformations—some of which we will discuss more deeply in the latter portion of the book—will be the sine qua non for efforts such as those mentioned above to be successful. These cultural and social projects can take place on many different scales, but they could perhaps be accelerated through large-scale mobilization efforts—think of what that level of mobilization did for the U.S. during the Great Depression and then during World War II.

Radical hope is based partly on an awareness that there is much we don't and can't know. Therein lies an opening for possibility. We might even contemplate another opening: Maybe future "solutions" don't depend entirely on human agency. Perhaps the processes governing the dynamics of the biosphere are even more nonlinear than we realize, and just a few of these human-caused breakthroughs will enable our planetary living system to self-regulate and tip the scales back toward restoration of natural balances.

There are also numerous futuristic scenarios that are taken seriously by scientists, such as those involving machine-based ethical "superintelligence." These speculative possibilities range from realistic (but far from fait accompli) to fantastical. But we cannot blindly put our faith in any of them. As I've repeatedly stated, *all* of these depend on what we choose to do, individually and collectively. Paradoxically, these optimistic scenarios are much more likely to become reality if people cut through denial and soberly take in the magnitude of our ever-intensifying predicament.

Profound large-scale transformations at every level—physical, behavioral, technological, scientific, economic, political, social, cultural, and personal—are implied here. We are talking about profound "whole system change." Can it happen? Critical masses of people rising up as one have made positive differences (as well as negative ones) many times throughout history. But in this case, more is required than simply winning some political and technological victories; it will also require quantum leaps in human maturity and spiritual vision. It will take a new structure of consciousness to catalyze many other cultural and societal breakthroughs, and a new kind of politics in which wisdom can increasingly guide human affairs.

One of the foundations for that innovation in consciousness, and for the relationships and communities that would express and embody it, would be *radical honesty and basic shared agreement about at least certain aspects of reality.* We will need to penetrate or cleanse everything that veils and distorts our personal and cultural doors of perception in order to achieve such a clear view.

The Shadow Side of the "Light"

The pull toward continuing our habitual business of growth as usual is so much a part of our ordinary habit that it will take enormous pressure—or enormous insight—for radical changes to take effect. Each new technological innovation, whether necessary or not to our quality of life, tends to mesmerize and distract us. A new gadget or vehicle or weapon or other technology is something we can create quickly and successfully. We can see the results directly—right before our eyes. Our minds are not challenged to imagine abstract, distant, or ominous implications.

In addition to the fact that hope feels like both a core human value and a national one, the prospect of a grim human future tends to evade cool rational assessment and consideration. The subject of our predicament is avoided like kryptonite—because we recoil in pain from what we believe are its profoundly debilitating psychological and emotional effects.

Human beings, myself included, find much of our strength by being motivated toward hoped-for futures. Our psychological need to maintain an optimistic perspective on life is so deeply ingrained that it colors all our thoughts, actions, and decisions.

People make decisions emotionally; afterward, we rationalize them with logic. Factual evidence rarely persuades people to change their attitudes and beliefs—on the contrary, research shows human beings more commonly harden their attitudes when confronted by evidence that seems to undermine their pre-existing beliefs. So we respond instinctively, deflecting instead of absorbing objective facts if their implications challenge our attitudes, especially if we fear they might cause us to lose heart.

Studies in neuroscience, psychology, and social science keep underlining this reality. So it is extremely hard to sort out how our own emotions are influencing our assessment of the real facts of our human situation.

Mainstream culture reflects individuals' fierce tendency to imagine a future much like the present, one that denies any reckoning with its own unsustainability. As social creatures, we can't help but participate in this mass illusion, or at least in some parts of it. It is so easy to go with the flow of conventional expectations, most human beings actively dismiss and exclude much of what we know at some deeper level to be true. We censor our own thoughts. We change the subject.

Denial-based hope makes us feel good, and it pulls us more and more into its fantasy world, which allows us to become more and more oblivious to the fragility of our situation. Beneath this false hope—looming large and yet hidden from us, like an elephant in the room—lies *fear.*

THE ELEPHANT IN THE ROOM—
THE HIDDEN FEAR AGENDA

In order to function, human societies must agree on a consensus reality. Without it we lack a social common ground. But the agreements we have are of a "lowest common denominator" variety, which critically limits our ability to picture reality in a way that's adequate to the complexity of our current dynamics. Some of us want to revise the old social agreements while others cling to them, and our common ground is increasingly unstable.

Not everyone thinks alike; there are seemingly unbridgeable gulfs between the ways different individuals think about complex issues such as climate change. These differences are not arbitrary and are not easily solved. They are not only matters of cultural identity; they reflect deep developmental and educational differences. They not only make it hard to understand each other; it also becomes very hard for most of us *not* to begin to relate to our divisions as if we were facing a competing tribe. So our mutual distrust grows, resulting in our civic dysfunction.

We critically need conversations that build connections across all the world's subcultures. But a shadow falls across all these urgent, crucial conversations and keeps even the most climate-savvy among us in a state of cognitive dissonance: the shadow of fear. Fear overtakes and overpowers all other agendas.

We fear the disruption of our lives. If our predicament threatens the future of human civilization, it jeopardizes everything that gives our lives a sense of meaning. It implies a bleak or nonexistent future for our grandchildren, friends, students, and all legacies we might hope to leave behind. It is the death, not just of us, but of the whole world we know. It is the most terrible scenario we can imagine. If we allow ourselves to imagine it as a realistic prospect, we fear being immobilized by depression. But we also fear what would happen if we took the predicament to heart and began to do everything we could to address it. In that case, the obligation and sacrifices of our activism would upend our lives and comforts and identities—and maybe, when all is said and done, no good would come of it anyway.

The subtle shadows of all these fears are operating invisibly in the background, distorting all supposedly rational conversations about our civilizational predicament. Fear and our inability to face it give rise to denial of the scope and urgency of our predicament, and reflexive faith in imagined technological salvation. This is made worse by the many "experts" who try to persuade us (at least implicitly) to think of this subject as if it were only a matter of politics and economics, rather than physics and ecology. Our individual and collective psyches function very differently, depending on whether we are emotionally dominated by hope or fear. These powerful unacknowledged emotional responses are the subtext that usually dominates every attempt at objective discussion. A dark synergy operates between hardwired denial (which we also see in the face of atrocities, especially those in which people are complicit) and the extremely complex, elusive nature of this whole subject.

Sometimes we humans have to hit bottom before we wake up and really change. This is the language of addiction and recovery. We are nearing that moment in the human story.

Much like a family sitting down with an addict for an intervention, it seems to me that our whole species is being commanded "Halt!" by the scientific evidence of our planet's ecological crisis. We have a destructive addiction—and we are ruining our home and destroying the lives of our family members. We are hearing, in no uncertain terms—from the rising CO_2 levels, mass species extinctions, melting glaciers, dying coral reefs, and rising seas—that we have to stop what we are doing *right now*, and go into radical rehab. And the voices are only getting louder.

Even so, many leaders—not to mention regular folk, including my own peers—seem to close our ears to these voices. And part of the issue is that, as addictions and their dynamics go, this one is a whopper—in size, momentum, and complexity.

The immobilizing potential of fear is magnified by our sense of personal impotence. It is simply easier to block out horrible realities if we seem to have little ability to affect them. We'd rather be resigned to it as one of "the things we cannot change" and choose serenity. We like to focus on the things we can change—on our personal goals, dramas, trials, and satisfactions. And our personal lives always demand constant and immediate attention. So, many people confidently assert that our "emergency" is an unhealthy preoccupation—a distraction.

Instead of changing the world, many of us simply change the subject. After all, if we can't actually improve our situation, what's the point of getting worked up? Both reflexive optimism and learned helplessness are based on deep-rooted cultural agreements as well as subtle but very effective personal indoctrination. The idea of the "consensus trance"—which we will now examine—does much to explain both of these behavioral root factors.

CONSENSUS TRANCE: HOW WE PERCEIVE (AND DENY) REALITY

I was an undergraduate in Ann Arbor, Michigan, when I first encountered experimental psychologist Charles Tart's powerful idea that what is usually called "normal" consciousness may also function as a "consensus trance."[16] This idea explained why my inherited cultural assumptions about what is true and how we come to find the truth had begun to ring hollow. It also goes a long way toward explaining why "climate denial" is so pervasive in politics, corporate culture, talk radio, and among ordinary people.

Simplified, the premise of consensus trance is that "normal" waking consciousness is actually a trance state. One of its implications is that people believe what they are indoctrinated to believe—and that this mass hallucination is powerful, often impervious to our own direct experience and critical thinking.

This concept defines the psychology of social consensus and conformity, and helps explain why the collective agreement related to our predicament can be so fierce. Consensus trance supports the tacit acceptance of "official" narratives (however unfounded they may be), and encourages us to unconsciously repress, deny, or reject unpalatable truths.

Like Freud's initial insights, Tart's thesis about the consensus trance emerged from his study of hypnosis. He saw that the process of drawing children into a sense of "the right way to do and see things" functioned very much like a hypnotic induction. Particular views are reinforced again and again throughout our lives, starting in childhood, via countless social cues.

Tart connected this with the implications of research into how beliefs influence perceptions, and proposed that normal waking consciousness is actually the product of an extensive collective hypnotic induction. This induction is practiced consistently by parents and teachers, and reinforced by every social interaction. It is sometimes brutally enforced via powerful taboos.

While a requisite amount of this kind of "training" helps uplift a child's primitive, unformed awareness, it also tends to inhibit free, expansive, and critical perceptions of reality in those who don't outgrow it.

Tart describes the effects of this induction not just in terms of behavioral shaping but in terms of consciousness itself. In Tart's view, our *entire state of consciousness* is indistinguishable from a trance. Tart proposed that we are inhabiting this trance together, and we have even been given hypnotic suggestions to ignore the evidence that we are in a trance.

This explains in part why the "consensus reality" about which almost everyone agrees rarely corresponds to objective reality. Groups of people gradually come to agree on which perceptions should be allowed into their awareness, and then quite spontaneously and automatically train one another to see the world in only in that way.

Tart's insights, grounded in experimental psychology, explained for me the mechanism behind so many of the hidden contradictions I had noticed in my everyday life since adolescence. And today, they continue to inform me about why it is so difficult for the perils of climate change to gain traction in our society—even among those individuals who acknowledge its reality at some level.

Tart's findings became a focus of lifelong investigation for me, and perhaps laid an important foundation for my enduring passion for spiritual practice. After all, a very common and enduring metaphor in world mysticism is that of awakening from a dream. Almost 2,500 years ago, the great Taoist sage Chuang Tzu wrote, "While…dreaming [the dreamer] does not know it is a dream…. Only after he wakes does he know it was a dream. And someday there will be a great awakening when we know that this is all a great dream. Yet the stupid believe they are awake, busily and brightly assuming they understand things…how dense!"[17]

Tart's insight extends not just into spirituality but also into social and political theory. Noam Chomsky's book *Manufacturing Consent* traces how Freud's nephew, Edward Bernays, extended principles of psychology to the new field of public relations. It demonstrates how intentional manipulation has exploited the habitual tendencies of the human nervous system to manipulate public opinion. In a sense, public relations (and today, many other forms of media, marketing, and other methods of communicating news, advertising, and sociocultural trends) continues the hypnotic induction that begins in school, advancing and deepening the indoctrination.

Back in the 1960s and 1970s, the mechanisms responsible for "manufacturing consent" were rather crude by contemporary standards. We didn't have neurohacking, micro-targeting, digital content optimization techniques, bots, or fake news to influence public consciousness. The world of mass media was relatively new and innocent; consequently, it was perhaps a little easier to see what was really going on. Today, the sophistication and volume of the mechanisms responsible for manufacturing consent make it at once more powerful and more insidious.

The hypnotic power of the consensus trance explains and affects many of the other challenges to our full, open, objective perception of our planetary crisis. It has played—and will continue to play— a central role in our collective response to the predicaments at hand. It shapes and anchors in place our collective agreements about technology and about hope; it encourages denial. The consensus trance is not easily penetrated, even by the reality that our home is on fire.

THE CHALLENGE AND THE OPPORTUNITY

We have seen how several factors—the wickedly complex nature of our current set of problems, combined with the illusion of technology's limitless resources, and finally the consensus trance into which we have all been inducted—have made it dramatically difficult for any individual or group to know exactly what is happening, let alone for a whole *society* to understand and agree on what is happening and what to do about it. And we have seen that what we over-simplistically call "climate change" is itself only one facet of a larger ecological and cultural predicament that is the most "wicked" and elusive problem we have ever faced, because it reveals or hides itself in so many ways, and it affects literally everything.

How do we get from where we are now to where we are required to be? That is the issue we will briefly return to now.

As we have seen, none of the great issues of our time can be effectively solved without acknowledging and then meaningfully addressing our climate emergency and broader ecological predicament. But those issues are intertwined with the whole structure of our lives, of our societies, and of human civilization. They challenge our whole way of life. And, as we have also seen, we cannot fully accept this challenge until we begin to understand and change the circumstances—both external and internal to us—that have kept this urgent imperative off our radar.

Whole-systems change is required, and in a real sense it must begin inside ourselves.

But how to begin? Nothing could be more confounding! Facing the impossible questions that our predicament asks of us is like confronting a multidimensional koan, an impossible Zen riddle that has no direct answer the mind can devise and understand, but which must nonetheless be answered.

Classically, a koan is pondered for minutes, hours, days, years, or even a lifetime. Eventually it confounds the conventional mind, awakening insight and transforming one's whole way of being. The question transforms the questioner, awakening at least a glimpse of higher consciousness. The practitioner stays present to the koan by "living the questions" and "loving the questions" over time, until they reveal their answers (and then even deeper questions), as Rilke wrote to his young poet friend Franz Kappus.

Among the most famous classic koans are "What is the sound of one hand clapping?" and "Show me your original face, the one you had before your parents were born!"

Dogen, the founder of Zen Buddhism and koan practice in Japan, wrote Genjo Koan, a monograph in which he pointed to the inseparability of life and practice, and called for recognizing the koans given to us by life itself. He might have called our world crisis the great Genjo Koan of our time, the existential Genjo Koan of humanity's whole evolutionary trajectory.

Our mission, if we choose to accept it, is to face these impossible questions, this Genjo Koan. If we face the questions of our time; if we recognize that they really cannot be avoided; and if we acknowledge how important, real, and existential they are, we will have accepted our mission. If we don't numb and distract ourselves, these deep questions will inevitably affect us. Facing them will deepen, awaken, and transform our consciousness, our whole way of being, and our behavior.

Once this challenge is accepted, the real work begins—and this work takes place both inside and outside of us. It requires quantum leaps in consciousness, community, and dedication, as well as in technological and social innovation. It requires new creativity at the levels of the individual, the local community, the virtual community, institutions, corporations, cities, and nations. It requires us to develop and express creative potential that has been virtually untapped—or, all too often, sabotaged—until now. It involves, in countless ways, the need to translate abstract ideas into concrete terms, and to discover what mandates such knowledge creates. And—starting at the level of every individual—it involves taking stock of where we are, and *who* we ultimately are.

I believe the only way we can come to terms with the many dimensions of our ecological crisis—and with all of our built-in resistance to acknowledging and acting upon it—is to become a conscious, effective, connected community, and act together. And that is wise in any case, regardless of our future. Our best security will be our families, our friendships, our communities, our ability to be self-responsible, resourceful, and resilient—and these connections are also how we reweave the social fabric, at a new level. Our psychological, social, and spiritual resilience will become our most essential capital. More important, our thriving may depend on our ability to work with our fear, find happiness and peace amidst sorrows and difficulties, and bounce back creatively after traumatic setbacks.

When he was in his eighties, James Hillman wrote *The Force of Character,*[18] in which he identified the soul work of his moment in the life cycle, which is to withstand the ultimate ordeal of decline and death with grace and grit, and to put "finishing touches" on one's life's main creative product—one's own character. If "it's too late," we can at least write the end of the human story well, through self-understanding, love in action, brother-sisterhood, elegance, and genius.

That is why it's so crucial, regardless of ultimate outcome, that we cultivate our best capacities and form intimate spiritual friendships that can grow into a broader social movement inspired by a grounded, healthy, and responsive spiritual vision. I believe such responses will emerge organically from practices and activities you and I can engage in. Having spent a lifetime exploring and facilitating and collaborating in such practice, I will be sharing here what are, for me, revelatory insights.

By acting together in the ways this book suggests, a truly auspicious future could well await us, as well as a deeply meaningful relationship to apparently "dark" times. Together, we can forge a productive path through a landscape that will undoubtedly be forever altered, literally and figuratively. It will be a future of joy and wonders as well as destruction and heartbreak—as is our present moment. It will be shaped by human beings, and by what is best in our collective character and imagination—if, that is, we grow up and show up at our very best.

Translating Heartbreak
into Action

The work we have to do can be seen as a kind of coming alive. More than some moral imperative, it's an awakening to our true nature, a releasing of our gifts.

—JOANNA MACY

Without inner change there can be no outer change. Without collective change, no change matters.

—ANGEL KYODO WILLIAMS

No one can say with certainty how our civilizational crisis will play out. We don't know how much suffering and destruction—human and nonhuman—might lie ahead, or how soon. But we do know, with increasing certainty, that the actions of human beings have created an existential predicament; and we also know that the actions of human beings—for good or for ill—will determine the future of our great grandchildren and most other living beings. The stakes could scarcely be higher. We cannot wait to "see what happens" before we act on this awareness. Rather, we are obliged right now to do whatever we can to help prevent or mitigate the horrific scenarios that we may have set in motion. What could be a greater moral imperative?

Only human beings can protect and defend the future of life on Earth from human beings. It will take conscious individuals making deliberate choices based on the best information available—people presuming responsibility to make a difference. Nothing could be more honorable and worthwhile.

The word "activist" conjures images of sit-ins, people circulating petitions and raising money and marching and organizing and meeting, and getting people to the polls. But it also means doing research, starting businesses, making loans, and changing one's diet. When people creatively act on their moral intuition, all kinds of things happen. The world of activism is very big, diverse, and dynamic. And it requires— and helps us along in—transcending the collective trance.

GRATITUDE, GRIEF, AND SPIRITUAL ACTIVISM

Spiritual life involves growing into a wise and healthy relationship to reality. The word "spiritual" points to the deepest level of being—essential and existential. Spiritual growth and development enable us to glimpse the bountiful grace in which we live—the beauty of the world, and the privilege of conscious embodied existence. Gratitude is universal spiritual wisdom, and it is sufficient.

Such gratitude is awake. It is realistically in touch with loss and death and threat—not in denial. Saints are grateful even while resonating empathically with suffering. Everything we love is mortal, even the living Earth. Everything regenerates, and yet is also wounded and under threat. The heart breaks to see the destruction of vulnerable people, living creatures, and wild places. We want to protect them. We want to help. As Joanna Macy so sagely puts it, "If everyone I love is in danger, I want to be here, so I can do what I can." Activism is simply acting on the impulse to "be of benefit" to something greater than yourself, in a whole variety of ways. Not all of them look like overt "activism," but many do. All are natural expressions of human maturity.

But exactly how can we effectively address the totality of this crisis? If addressing it requires knowing exactly how the crisis will unfold and exactly what it will take to prevent it, then we can't. As we have seen, no one, not even the best of scientists, has that degree of omniscience, especially with the kind of wicked predicament we are facing. There is no way that we can address the whole tangle of causes and consequences—everything is connected to everything else. Our predicament requires a revolutionary transformation of every aspect of human life—a "Great Transition" or "Great Turning." It will ultimately require revolutionary changes in human consciousness, behavior, culture, and the physical, economic, and political infrastructure of our whole civilization. It is so vast and intricate, it easily seems impossible. We might be tempted to despair, but despair easily becomes a self-fulfilling prophecy. And yet, because this huge transformation has so many aspects, every one of us can readily find ways to magnify love and sanity and beauty and truth and human connection. Every one of us can find many things we can actually *do*.

Paradoxically, the many little things we can do—each of which may seem in itself woefully insufficient to our total predicament—may well be a good start. We will continue to see the endings of life all around us, and we will grieve for all of the losses we witness. Our spirit and consciousness will go through a transformative ordeal as we take in new terrible truths about our predicament. But many actions on many levels, when collectively engaged (and perhaps further catalyzed by positive black swan breakthroughs) may ultimately add up into a single great action. At our micro level, there are many things we *can* do, and *are doing*, to address even our mega crisis.

To be an effective agent of change does not mean we have to know everything. But it does require opening to another level of transformation and creativity. Our predicament presents us with a vast demand and limitless opportunity for growth. Our crisis seems overwhelming, and yet we live in a universe of awe-inspiring creative potential—in nature, in our fellow humans, in the evolutionary process, and certainly in ourselves. The story of evolution is a story of miracle after miracle. We must simultaneously take in the magnitude of the problem—grieve for much inevitable suffering—and do what we can on behalf of creative solutions, on every scale. To do both requires great openness on our part—openness to growth and to creative responses that we didn't know were possible. We give ourselves over to something that feels true. We magnify health and wholeness, even in the face of fragmentation—and in our trust of the larger process, we also become more effective. Our souls are positively stirred, and conscripted. This process of growth is clearly never-ending.

The first stage of the journey into spiritual activism is grounded robustly in gratitude and appreciation. In the second stage, we awaken from denial, apprehend the enormity of the challenge before us, and allow a great grieving process to transform the soul. We benefit even from the awful moments of hopelessness—because despair is not just the end of our conventional hope. It is also the beginning point for a new possibility, a third stage—perhaps a kind of *unreasonable* affirmation.

The Wisdom of Grieving

Not only is grieving a stage of the spiritual activist's journey, but the grieving process *itself* often unfolds in stages, which can be described using Elizabeth Kubler-Ross's famous five stages of grief. These five stages—*denial, anger, bargaining, depression,* and *acceptance*—describe the process of psychologically responding to the prospect and reality of any catastrophic loss.

Denial can be said to be a defense against suffering and grieving. If reality is too painful, don't face it. Maintain equilibrium and good humor by closing the metaphorical eyes, or the mind. Turn off the news, doubt its veracity, change the channel.

While we can certainly criticize people's motivations for disengagement, it is also true that the attitudes communicated in media are often reactive and draining. So there are good reasons to practice skillful, selective disengagement from the 24/7 news cycle. Making intelligent and economical use of media and politics disciplines tendencies toward both mindless addiction and reactive avoidance.

Anger easily becomes a habitual defense against feeling loss, sadness, and fear. There are very good reasons to be angry. Anger is the energy to change what needs to be changed. But healthy anger rises and falls, rather than becoming a chronic state, and it stays in touch with grief.

The next stage is *bargaining,* an attempt to regain lost equanimity, perhaps by imagining alternative scenarios that mitigate the sense of loss. Whereas true equanimity is based on opening up to all of reality, including its darkness, bargaining seeks to keep painful realities at bay. It is a more sophisticated form of denial.

The fourth stage is *depression.* When it is clear that heartbreaking loss cannot be avoided, the being is at least temporarily shattered. We begin to fear losing something we have always depended upon and taken for granted—such as the company of a loved one, the restorative and healing grace of Mother Earth, or the ability to live in a prosperous, secure, open liberal society without doing anything to protect or defend it.

Mature, responsible adults are charged with staying intelligently related to the realities of our lives. But that requires us to pass through all the harrowing stages of grief into acceptance.

True *acceptance* recognizes the reality of our situation and accepts responsibility to arrive in basic equanimity and a capacity to act. We find a way to choose life, even in a world that includes horrific losses. We choose engagement with reality, including the gritty and not always pleasant involvements with people we may not like and in situations we would prefer to avoid. We know we have arrived in acceptance when we are in motion, doing what we can to make a positive difference. We find deep equanimity in activism itself.

Grief as Gateway

Grief is not weakness—it is a form of moral intelligence and even wisdom. It takes us through a necessary gateway.

It took me decades to fully appreciate how holy it is. And then, in 2016, the gates swung wide open. I had for so long lived such a blessed and joyous existence, I was a bit unprepared for what I would feel. But for me 2016 was not just an election year with all the shock many of us felt about the outcome; it was also a year of an alarming series of record-high global temperatures and extreme weather events, and deep grieving over the grave damage we are doing to our living planet.

One of grief's great lessons is patience—an attitude of self-compassion. Under these kinds of circumstances, my imperfections rise to be noticed. Even under the most serious circumstances, I will be imperfect, maybe a bit of a klutz or unconscious in some moments, or seeking what cannot be found. Those limitations don't simply go away—not for me, nor for you, nor for anyone. But we are privileged (even if awed) to be present in these very interesting times, facing realities that people before us couldn't countenance without horrified despair. It may take us many tries to get this right (and even then, we are never perfect), and our failures may even be costly. But, with self-compassion, self-forgiveness, and generosity, we can see our way through.

On the other side of all disillusionment and even despair, there will also be joy, and goodness, and beauty. Gratefulness and celebration have always sprung from the soil of loss and grief. We will be alive, and life will be good. However difficult circumstances become, we will be able to savor the beauty of life in each present moment.

Seeing an overwhelming army massed on the horizon was anciently seen as the test of a soldier's mettle—it was the time to get strong, fierce, and inspired. The battle was coming. And in the meantime it was wonderful to be alive. The "meantime" is all any of us has ever had anyway.

May we all be instructed by William Blake's beautiful quatrain:

> *He who binds to himself a joy*
> *Does the winged life destroy*
> *He who kisses the joy as it flies*
> *Lives in eternity's sunrise.*

FINDING YOUR "YES"

Activism emerges from the stark recognition that we really are the cocreators of our world. We wake up from the trance in which we had imagined ourselves to be passive observers of the world, standing somehow apart from it. We recognize that we are not "in the stands" watching the action from an objective vantage point, and we never have been. We have always been on the field, and the ball is in play. When we realize we are full participants, we awaken into activism, and our practice becomes to engage with the game completely, holding nothing back.

One reason we give it all we've got is that nobody knows what will come. "It's hard to make predictions," Yogi Berra famously said, "especially about the future." The future is indeterminate. It will emerge, and we have a part to play in determining *what* exactly will emerge. This uncertainty calls for sobriety, humility—and the aliveness of unreasonable hope. We do not and cannot know enough to justify despair and passivity.

Scientists and environmentalists have sometimes predicted that we have twenty, or ten, or five years to turn things around, to launch a society-wide mobilization to convert our presence on the planet into a sustainable trajectory. These estimates were not just wild guesses. They were based on real data, and I respect and learn from them. But it doesn't serve to relate to them credulously.

Human knowledge is far too incomplete to quantify our opportunities. The real bottom line is that even though the world may be seriously out of balance, we just don't know—and can't know—exactly how bad (and good) things really are. We don't know how severe or sudden climate changes will really be. We don't know how soon and how much sea levels will rise. We don't know how disruptive the transition will be from our unsustainable global financial, food, and transportation systems to sustainable ones. We cannot and will not be able to know how much (or how little) disruption, pain, loss, and degradation are in store for us.

But we don't have to figure it all out. We don't have to become tangled up in our unknowable future as if it were an unsolvable dilemma. We don't have to handicap the odds in this high-stakes evolutionary horse-race in order to respond. We can cut through all the mind chatter by asking a deeper and more essential question:

Can I find in myself a no-matter-what commitment? Under the worst-case scenario, can I still tap into the well of uncaused, unreasonable happiness? Can I still relate to my fellow humans, and to all of life, with care and love? Can I still, to the fullest extent possible, remain present as a force for good in every moment?

A no-matter-what commitment resolves all dilemmas. Even if our predicament is hopeless, incapable of being turned around, we are still capable of loving one another, capable of enjoyment, capable of doing whatever we can to make life better, and capable of surrendering to the unknown. Ultimately, we cannot know what lies on the other side of our predicament. But we can still be happy, because our happiness is not based on external certainties (or "reasons"), but rather on our ultimate connectedness with the source of all life. And this noncontingent happiness is free to express itself in the service of others and of creation. If we do these things, we are saying a resounding "Yes!" to life. And that "Yes!" makes all the difference.

Seen from another angle, this great "Yes!" is also a great "No!"

When we see an approaching slow-motion train wreck, we yell out a warning. A scream issues forth that refuses to stand idly by and allow the destruction to take place. We can feel a great "No!" shouting forth from our own hearts. It is deeper than our feelings and even our understanding. Something much bigger than us is finding its way into life through us. And it expresses as much urgency, right now, as the most pressing deadline ever could.

Life wants to keep living. Insists on it, even. Evolution wants to keep evolving, and simply will not be refused. It comes forward with ancient, revolutionary fervor.

That is what has been surfacing and circulating. This impulse toward activism is the sound of love when it roars—when it demands to be heard. The universal is deeply personal.

THE HIT IS A GIFT

Affirmation is primal and necessary and reflects a deep truth about us, but it doesn't hide the fact that we live in shocking times. Traumatic events can jolt and debilitate us. We can be traumatized not only by our personal experiences but also by political setbacks and shocks suffered by others in our network of care and concern. Our circumstances require us to get serious about how we are managing our attention and conducting our energy, especially when we, or those we care about, take a real "hit."

We can learn from George Leonard's teachings on mastery, where he used an apt phrase to convey a principle from aikido: "Take the hit as a gift."[19] It means that when your sparring partner hits you, he gives you energy, energy you can use in several ways.

First, the hit can awaken you, so you can relate to it as a teacher. Second, in the dance of the martial art, the movement to hit you will to some degree unbalance your opponent, which can give you an opportunity and advantage. Third, even if they land a solid blow, it will stimulate your life energy, your *ch'i*, so the hit is itself a source of energy.

The new energy stimulated by the hit is often at first inflamed and reactive. The hit is intended to force you to react, and when reactive you are weakened. You really have to stay present (which usually means, breathe and feel and notice) in order for the hit to become a conscious experience. It is important to get in touch with the totality of the hit, including how it hurts, how you are reacting, even how it may have injured you—or others, or values you care about. But when you find your way entirely into the present moment, you discover that the hit has activated your whole being. It has awakened you, and it is a source of energy.

Sometimes we must respond to old hits that have already overwhelmed and depleted us. We feel emptied by pain and loss. We are exhausted, and we don't want to deal with it. The hit is still a gift, but it asks us for an entirely different move. We have to find our way to a heart of compassion for ourselves. Noticing our own inseparable divinity and humanity, we can metaphorically take our inner child in our arms. Our self-care and self-compassion flow. They restore our felt connection to whatever we cared about that was attacked in the first place—and that is another source of strength.

Care is not fast-moving like anger. Anger is suddenly right there, ready to mobilize and move—now! Care is a warm, deep reservoir of comforting strength and sanity that you can steadily draw upon over time. Care for yourself is the foundation. Many of us need to restore our self-care. Without a foundation of self-care, our care for others and the whole easily gets out of whack, becoming unhealthy and draining us.

On the basis of taking good care of yourself, your care for others and for the whole organically flows. When you find your way into sincere care, breathing and feeling and resting in your felt connection to everything you care for, you tap into a source of steady, stable power. It can take you wherever you need to go.

If the hit is immediate and fast-moving, analogous to anger, recognize it as a gift right away and conduct its energy intelligently. If the hit is deeper and slower-moving, more like grief, find your way to a healthy caring for yourself, others, and the whole. Doing this deliberately and somatically is wise. When you are feeling that shock, take a few minutes, close your eyes, go inside, and really feel what's going on. Remember that it is possible to discover the gift in the hit. Such resilience is crucial to sustainable activism.

GOOD AND EVIL

My friends Michael Dowd and Connie Barlow use the word "evil" to mean "self-interest that pursues its own financial or pleasurable self-interest, knowing that in doing so it is harming the future or harming others or harming the body of life." Much rational discourse eschews normative judgments, hesitating to cross from "what is" to "what ought to be," but I think Dowd and Barlow's definition is a widely acceptable, durable, and useful working definition of "evil" that can ground rational decision making in a universal morality.

It is a deep truth that when we join in battle, we tend to become like our opponents. Evolution and the course of life would be served if we could learn to fight such "evil" in a different way—such as Gandhi and other nonviolent resisters have discovered—so that we can prevail without becoming like what we oppose. It is critically important that we forge new ways of coming together with one another in the service of our larger health and wholeness. That means creating a space for all people and creatures—and even wisely and compassionately accounting for those who lack empathy and compassion, including those we may perceive as evil and threatening.

Taking a systems view of this pattern, we look to find resources for healthy change that are already right here at hand. Where is the unused energy that is ready to come forward to create wholeness?

This energy may be in our capacity for friendship. It is my experience that there is a fundamental goodness, even some latent heroism, in almost every human heart. There is a willingness to go beyond narrow self-interest in a spirit of courage and generosity. We have the potential to form relationships that can function differently, less constrained by our fear and mistrust of one another. In our friendships and families, we can build new, stronger bonds of love and trust—bonds that can withstand the tests of our evolutionary life-and-death challenges. We will also have to develop a social immune system, so that our trusting social organism isn't hijacked by charismatic psychopaths.

THE HIGHEST CALLING OF OUR CHARACTER

Think of the American Revolution's Founding Fathers, the patrons, artists, intellectuals, and scientists of the Renaissance and the Western Enlightenment. Think of Mahatma Gandhi, Martin Luther King, Nelson Mandela, Mother Teresa of Calcutta, Desmond Tutu, the fourteenth Dalai Lama (Tenzin Gyatso), Aung Saan Suu Kyi, and Pope Francis.

Think of Jesus. Or Socrates. Or Gautama Buddha.

Realize they are the saints, saviors, prophets, and nobles of a broader, universal activist spirit—the soul of the universal impulse that has activated every big step we have taken in our evolutionary journey. This is the same spirit that also animated many early Christians and early Buddhists. It can be seen in the philosophers and prophets of the Western Enlightenment, and in the Magna Carta and the Declaration of Independence.

It is worth considering three individuals particularly: Mahatma Gandhi, Martin Luther King, Jr., and Nelson Mandela. Each of them catalyzed great societal shifts whose time had come. These leaders were able to rise above and harmonize the negativity, reactivity, and conflict that tended to compromise others. Their appearance coincided with great cultural changes; historical forces organized themselves around them, moving history forward. And they helped reweave the social fabric. They did this in part by their words and deeds and ideas and policies. But they especially led *by their example.* These three iconic figures are almost universally acknowledged as "saints with *cojones,*" world-transforming servant-leaders, the exemplars of the highest potential of leadership and greatness.

Gandhi and King in particular were career-long advocates of nonviolent resistance, a strategy that can not only be extraordinarily effective, but can actually transform one's adversaries—or weaken them, but based on the adversaries' own responses. In one of his studies of exceptional individuals, psychologist and educator Howard Gardner saw Gandhi as a particularly outstanding exemplar of a class of individuals he refers to as "influencers." On a large scale, Gandhi's activities eventually led to Indian independence from Britain. But these large-scale changes only happened because of his ability to "become an educator, instructing his audience over time to think in a subtler manner," convincing multitudes of people to "think differently about the most important issues…. All assumed that the struggle would eventually have to be engaged violently—with English arms and prestige being arrayed against Indian numbers and nationalistic zeal. Gandhi succeeded in convincing people the world over to reconceptualize matters"—including judging people as fellow human beings and keeping disagreements nonviolent. But, "most stirringly, both parties in a conflict can be strengthened if they handle themselves with dignity in the course of nonviolent confrontations."[20]

The greatest of the great men and women of history—the ones we revere most highly—are the dedicated *activists*. Over the past five hundred years, our great historical advances have been championed by such activists. Giordano Bruno, Voltaire, and countless others had to defy the Catholic Church to usher in the Enlightenment. The American Founding Fathers, including Benjamin Franklin, George Washington, and Thomas Jefferson, had to defy the British monarchy to found the United States. Countless other activists had to struggle to establish, in nation after nation, the foundations of liberal democracy that make our current culture, including the shape of contemporary activism, possible.

We have all heard many stories of heroic activism. Sometimes the fights are for basic rights, such as (in the U.S.) the abolition of slavery, the right to vote (among women and people of color), or (up to a century after slavery ended) the rights of African Americans to use all public accommodations. The heroic efforts of women to claim their equal humanity have been unending throughout history. Workers, indigenous people, LGBTQ people, and even consumers have had to fight for basic rights. Today's activism ranges through such diverse areas as access to medical care, privacy protections, and protection of the biosphere.

Activists have an irreplaceable cultural role, helping societies to evolve. It is undeniable that societies transform through many diverse processes. But historically, many of our most important transformations, the key historical advances, have required struggle. In order for history to proceed, people have had to *advocate* for the new. They have had to criticize old, outmoded customs and policies, recognize the next possibility, speak up, join together, act upon that recognition, and exert influence. Activists have moved history forward.

Notwithstanding a long list of strategic mistakes and setbacks and losses, activists have been on the right side of history again and again. We have a vital role and responsibility, and we feel the weight of it. History proves that we have a mandate and a central role, even if we are perpetually working at the margins of the dominant power structure.

THE SOUL OF ACTIVISM

We become activists after we notice suffering and destruction, cruelty and indifference, waste and peril, and the harm in which we are living—and heed the biblical injunction to "not stand idly by." The injustice may be done to us, or to friends or strangers or other forms of life, or even to values. When we see such injustice, we feel absolutely compelled to act.

We speak up. We listen to the stories of others who have been through similar experiences, or whose own experiences inform us and rouse us to action. When a group of us agrees, and we dare to believe we can make a difference in some way, and we cooperate to make something happen, we have become activists. Sometimes we are acting on our own behalf, or on behalf of our group, and sometimes on behalf of others.

It can be scary to defy the norm, to dare to attempt to exert influence. You must be willing to take risks. Sometimes they are just the "opportunity costs" of giving your energy to a cause instead of investing in yourself. Sometimes they are risks of ridicule, rejection, and retribution. And sometimes they are big risks—risks of real losses to one's job, career, community standing, and personal comfort. Sometimes there are even risks of imprisonment, violence, torture, death, or retribution against loved ones.

Wherever we may be on the spectrum of activism, to become an activist takes courage. Activists are those who dare to go against the grain of what people around them are doing. They speak truths that others do not want to hear. They defy the norm in service of a higher principle.

Activism expresses a heroic impulse. But activists need not appear extraordinary. The values that inspire activism are the same values that drive the classic stories of literature, art, and popular entertainment. Everyone who begins as an underdog, or as an ordinary individual who leads an ordinary life, and then becomes challenged or moved to stand for higher values on behalf of a community or principle, is expressing the heroic qualities of the activist. These implicit values have been imparted, via parables and stories and poetry, to all of us, from the time we were children.

Activism expresses fellowship, connection, relationship, a sense of brotherhood and sisterhood. When we act on our connectedness to others, we heal something essential in ourselves. We locate ourselves in something deeper than our postmodern alienation. Our connectedness in the service of larger things transcends the superficiality of many relationships and associations. In this era when traditional communities and extended families are the exception, the community of like-minded and heart-based activists can be an essential healing and grounding force. This is all the more true because as activists we are, to a degree, voluntary outcasts from some elements of mainstream society.

Activism is sometimes characterized as angry and strident. And sometimes it is. Sometimes anger is necessary and appropriate. Healthy anger has an essential function in advancing history. But anger tends to summon fear, and it easily becomes destructive. Healthy activism is most fundamentally an expression of care rather than anger. It is love in action.

The soul of activism was captured by Pope Francis's invocation, "Let us be 'protectors' of creation, protectors of God's plan inscribed in nature, protectors of one another and of the environment."[21] This is an inherently rewarding and blessed state. As Marianne Williamson succinctly put it, "A life of love and effort on behalf of the collective good promises the satisfaction of knowing that you are doing what you were born to do."[22]

History is replete with horrible human suffering—from plagues to wars to holocausts to unspeakable cruelties against women, slaves, adulterers, gays, heretics, infidels, people of color (and those who consorted with them), aboriginals, foreigners, animals, and the natural environment. And it *is only because these horrors were witnessed and addressed by activists (humanitarians, prophets, saints, scientists, physicians, abolitionists, political dissidents) that even more unspeakable atrocities or more horrific scenarios were avoided.* In a similar fashion, it will take activism to avoid or mitigate the worst-case scenarios that our own prophets—often our scientists—are warning against.

Our creative powers—the very creativity that enables us to realize more positive outcomes—are mobilized by taking our threats seriously and doing all we can.

Middle-class citizens of imperfect Western democracies benefit from science and technology and rational discourse, privy to all the converging streams of human culture, including our highest wisdom traditions.

We have a chance to live lives that are extraordinarily comfortable, safe, free, and creative. In these times, if we have the opportunity to live extraordinarily meaningful lives, I feel we have an *obligation* to do so. If the measure of a human life is its chance to have significance that extends beyond itself, then we've hit the jackpot. We are alive at game time on the planet, when everything that we value is genuinely threatened, when it's time for all hands on deck.

When we see one another, realizing that we are in this together, and that the situation requires our collective responses, something happens. Our eyes meet; our different ways of being inspired and activated coincide. That higher purpose exalts our friendship and cooperative synergy, imbuing our connection with potential significance.

THE SHADOW SIDE OF ACTIVISM

Meaningful service gives activists' lives deep purpose and significance. And solidarity and fellowship can be gratifying and nurturing. Our sincere care can feed us, generating healthy neurochemicals. And we experience great joy in our victories, even small ones.

And yet we also endure much frustration. Overall, the concerns that motivate activists have also tended to drain us. Any innovative social initiative must overcome tremendous inertia. Institutional change tends to take place very slowly, with victories coming only after many years of very little apparent progress. And there is little funding for it, so activists often make personal sacrifices in service of a cause—and then we rarely see quick successes. Even when we do, we often see our gains brutally reversed. Environmental destruction, bad policies, suffering, injustice, hatred—it all persists, even as we work passionately. Meanwhile, all lives, activists' included, are visited by what Buddhists call the "heavenly messengers" of sickness, old age, and death. *Activism requires enduring through difficulty.*

Activists take on an extra commitment. In addition to the need to survive and thrive personally, we are committed to making a difference at the level of society. So we experience the ongoing progress of our causes as our own advances and setbacks. This can add to our stress.

And we often find ourselves competing, at a disadvantage, with people who don't take on these extra responsibilities. Even the most heart-centered, healthy, joyful activists feel these stresses. How many activists talk about burnout? It's no wonder most people do not choose this path, even though the highest foundational values that our greatest literature inspires in every child imply the courage to take a social stand.

It takes real wisdom and skill to keep our hearts open without letting the suffering in the world drain and deplete us. This is one of the most important capacities activists must build. We have to learn to put on our own oxygen mask first—silently, internally, many times a day. The most basic level of the inner work is an absolute requirement: we must learn to manage our own emotions and motivations. If we develop the knack for caring for ourselves and allowing ourselves to be fed by the regenerative dynamics of our sincere care for the planet, the people, and the cause, we can learn to counteract the tendency to be depleted and drained by unproductive "overcare."

Of course, that's easier said than done. Many activists do get drained, and then live in stress, with a deep underlying sense of alarm, grief, or dread. This can go on for years, even decades. It eventually degrades our immune system and neurology. In such states, judgment tends to be distorted. If the outer work is always prioritized over the inner work, personal needs go unmet. This inevitably undermines well-being and effectiveness, and often creates a subtle residue of resentment and righteousness. Activists sometimes lose humor and perspective. We become grim and pessimistic, or resentful and impatient, or sad and depleted, or righteously judgmental.

If we have been injured by systemic corruption or oppression or other gross injustices, we may also have good reason to be angry. In that case, our task is to develop an intelligent relationship with our anger. Anger is very tricky—it's a source of great power, but it can undermine everything it is trying to accomplish. Our job is to learn how to use the energy of that anger intelligently, so that we can thrive and create real change.

Meanwhile, our trauma and emotions deserve respect, sincere care, and compassion from others. Even more important, we need self-respect and self-compassion. We generally have legitimate grievances that need to be addressed. However, the attitudes of victimhood and grievance do not empower us, they are not psychologically healthy, and they certainly don't help us communicate effectively. The people we are communicating with, even those we must oppose, cannot effectively be addressed as if they were the perpetrators of our trauma, who owe us a remedy. To the degree that our trauma has impaired us, it is imperative that we recover enough to end the cycle of injury and trauma. And that requires healing, new self-awareness, humility, and the courage to understand ourselves and engage life in positive terms. Then we can channel our energy in service of higher values, rather than recycling our unconscious compensatory motivations.

That is why inner work is so necessary. Practitioners must reconnect to the deeper meanings of their lives, and to their deepest sources of joy and inspiration. In communities of practice, they can do this together. They can support one another, and be buoyed by the awakened clarity, love, courage, and insight of their fellow practitioners. We must remember that self-care is the foundation for all healthy care. Inner work is often the remedy to the ailments common to activists.

THE OUTER WORK IMPLIES THE INNER WORK

What will it take to cocreate a new way of being human, and a new world? How do we get started? How do we transform what we are already doing (and how we are already being) so that we can actually achieve new results?

Clearly we must move toward a convergence of the "inner work" and the "outer work." This implies a life of practice and a truly integral revolution of the being.

As we'll soon see, this is already underway. We are awakening to a deeper, more spiritually grounded awareness, and being restored and inspired by insights and intuitions borne by higher states of consciousness. We are awakening to new ways of seeing our work and the world. And we are awakening to new forms of outside-the-box thinking, with higher-order metaperspectives on the issues facing our planet.

Meanwhile, more and more spiritual practitioners are coming to recognize that our impulse toward awakening and self-actualization can be fulfilled only by being of real benefit to others. As we in the practicing community awaken to a new sense of urgency, our inner work begins expressing itself in more and more consequential outer work, service, social enterprise, volunteerism, and other good works that make a meaningful impact on people's lives. *As we awaken, a new kind of activist is awakening within us.*

Finally, as we increasingly understand the inseparability of the inner and outer work, we are realizing that an important part of our work is to awaken ourselves and others into love and freedom and clarity. This is the "activism of awakening." And we are beginning to see how such awakening—far from taking us away from the "on-the-ground" work—is actually a crucial dimension of even the most grounded initiatives focused on tangible benefits to systems, structures, people, and the planet.

Wholeness and Fragmentation

A human being is a part of the whole, called by us "Universe," a part limited in time and space. He experiences himself, his thoughts and feelings as something separate from the rest—a kind of optical illusion of his consciousness. The striving to free oneself from this delusion is the one issue of true religion.

—ALBERT EINSTEIN

The word "whole" derives from the same etymological root as do the words "hale," "heal," and "health." It may even share the same proto-Indo-Aryan root syllable with its homonym "holy." In the context of this book, the most meaningful synonyms for "wholeness" are "integrity," "coherence," and "health," and its most meaningful antonyms would be "fragmentation," "corruption," "incoherence," and "disease."

But, beyond those definitions, wholeness is radical. It might even be said to be the most essential nature of reality. Contemporary science points us in that direction. Matter and energy are not separate, nor are space and time, we are told. All living things are family, says our DNA. But even

If we could define it, that would not boundaries it and it would no longer be whole.

those observations don't capture the radical nature of wholeness—or its slipperiness.

Above all, we might say that wholeness is elusive. No definition is sufficient. We cannot think our way into it. It is not something we can wrap our brain around—not the brain we have now, at least. But a consideration and contemplation of wholeness can be very revealing. And this consideration is absolutely essential not only for any spiritual or sacred activist, but for anyone wishing to understand the multifaceted nature of reality, or of what's really happening in our world.

An idea commonly spoken of is that "the whole is greater than the sum of its parts." That conveys some of the flavor of wholeness. The word "synergy," which means "working together," refers to holistic dynamics that are greater than the sum of the parts. Activism requires synergy. Although synergy has many definitions and applications in the sciences, it points to the fact that the interaction of seemingly separate processes can create results that are utterly unpredictable if we simply examine the parts themselves. Activism is a multifaceted process involving many people, many parts—and so is all of reality. This is all the more true when one considers the elusiveness of the Whole itself, in its most radical sense. Everything is related, everything is contained in the Whole, and we do not even know what "everything" consists of!

Today's society—and even today's greatest scientific and technological successes—all express fragmentation, which, as we've said, is the antonym for wholeness. Above all, today's culture and mindset reflect fragmentation. We learn how things work by fragmenting them, taking them apart. Kids, at least in the predigital generations, would take things apart to find out "what makes them tick," and with skill, persistence, and luck, would find out how they worked, or be able to fix them. Science works along the same principles: it digs in and analyzes the parts. Western medicine also works along these same lines; this is especially epitomized in the principle of surgery. Find the offending organ or system in the body, and deal with that.

The problem with fragmentation at any level—whether in science, academic studies, politics, culture, or even the ways we use language—is that it can make the Whole not only elusive but invisible. It is a separative approach rather than a holistic (or "wholistic") one. It breaks things down into their component parts and mechanisms, and learns a great deal— including gaining the reintegrative vision of our evolving cosmos, and the revolutionary powers of science and technology. But analysis only takes a given part and studies it. The fragmented approach often forgets the larger context of the item studied—so it examines and reifies its understanding of it apart from its relationships. And yet nothing exists in isolation.

Even the way we speak of ourselves and others betrays the sense of isolation and fragmentation that colors our "consensus trance." It has often been pointed out by mystics and philosophers, and even some scientists, that our self-identity is a construct based on conventions of thought, memory, and language. "I" am thought to end at the surface of my skin, yet everything about me is utterly dependent on and related to my surroundings. If the environment were withdrawn for a moment, "my" body/mind would cease to exist. To ignore this is to ignore that all of life is a massive global ecosystem, a living system in a dynamic universe.

Once we acknowledge our interdependence in its totality—of being contained in the unimaginable context of the whole—certain things become obvious. One is that the "us versus them" mentality in *all* its myriad forms—"them" referring to people we view as other, or an environment or biosphere we view as other than ourselves—is not only unhelpful but is based on an illusion. Another is that our situation vis-à-vis the Whole is inconceivably more vast and mysterious and awe-inspiring than our minds can imagine. We cannot "know" it, but we can apprehend it, and our intuition of wholeness takes the form of awe, wonder, or love. Fear, hatred, discord, and often certitude itself are the products of obsessive fragmentation. If we choose our intuition of wholeness— whether through contemplative and meditative practices, or through opening the doors of relationship to others, or through study—we usually become better able to face all the more conditional, limited realities of our lives. We even become better able to make a positive difference by acting in constructive, synergistic ways.

One result of looking at our situation—at our planet's situation—more holistically is that we can more clearly see how a greater wholeness holds the human prospect. And that wholeness is not and could not be endangered. In fact, it is ever resurgent, no matter what. But we can also see that industrial human civilization—and even human-friendly planetary conditions—are endangered indeed. The data on which we base these findings are, of course, products of analysis—and fragmentation is absolutely necessary to help us know facts and act on them. But today's earth and climate science, with all their data and analysis, point to a nonfragmented totality. Scientists today see, as never before, just how interdependent everything is.

While apprehending the fragility of our situation can be fragmenting, terrifying, and depressing, the lesson of interdependence also points to something from which we can draw hope and confidence—a deeper dimension of things; the natural *telos,* or attractive power, of wholeness.

Even while things are very noisily falling apart, they are always also silently coming together, in diverse, remarkably inexorable ways. Wholeness is dynamic. Although "wholeness" is a noun, it refers to an active *process*—a natural tendency for fragmented or distorted energy to restore its natural, more coherent flow. We heal from illness and from wounds. Life restores and reasserts itself every spring.

Interdependence also points to how awesome and unfathomable the universe is—not just the observable, physical universe, but all of life, all of experience. We do not know and *cannot* know ultimately what the Whole "consists of." This is both humbling and inspiring. We are not separate from anything, and yet all the "anythings"—the totality of everything—can never be counted and measured. That means we can relax our fears. We can know that we are not separate and can never be separated from wholeness.

We can open our imagination to be instructed by the great saints and other individuals who have appeared in our midst, who have understood and told us about these wondrous paradoxes. If the world is big enough for great teachers and great activists, and even great enlightened sages who have understood the mystery of existence, then wholeness must be able to find its way into the inner lives of human beings. If it finds its way into the inner life of human beings in general, then it will be expressed in our outer works, and no consequence will vanquish us. At the same time, there is more reason than ever to be committed to embodying love in action, to take care of what we love. Activism simply becomes, as Joanna Macy has said, something we naturally do.

FACETS OF WHOLENESS

Aside from the infinitely vast totality of life and of possibilities, we can make other interesting observations. Buckminster Fuller famously pointed out that "I seem to be a verb." And as we've just pointed out, wholeness is a dynamic activity, always in process. Wholeness naturally reasserts itself, in ways we know and, undoubtedly, in ways we don't know. Wholeness has agency. Things *want* to move toward wholeness. "Immune responses" are observed not only in biological organisms, but in social and cultural ones. We see similar processes throughout the natural world. And we see them in the human psyche and spirit.

We can think of wholeness in many ways, and none are final or complete. We have considered it as the *boundless totality* of everything. We can also think of it as *source*—that from which all of life, all existence, springs. Or, borrowing more from Western thought, we can think of it in a *teleological* sense—as that final omega point toward which everything is heading. We can consider its *integrative* qualities of bringing everything together (much as integral theory attempts to do). And we can certainly think of it as *radical,* meaning literally at the root.

Perhaps wholeness is so paradoxically *all of the above at once* that it interrupts every distinction with a reunification. Therefore, by its nature it can never be fully known in the terms of conventional subject-object consciousness. It is a radical mystery, perhaps intuitively grokkable only when there is no difference between the knower and that which is known.

Our mind tends to want to "grasp" things. But it can only relax in the presence of radical wholeness—in a state of "mind-blown" amazement. Once the whole is apprehended to that degree, perhaps we might begin to learn to think "*from* the whole *to* the parts" in a way that gives birth to a very different worldview.

Mysteriously, we could say that wholeness has a kind of purpose: wholeness, already self-complete, seemingly wants to be felt and lived more fully, known more completely, articulated and expressed more richly, and enacted with more power and integrity and grace. We will see more about that in the next chapter on evolutionary consciousness. It is a process that has no end.

It should be obvious from what has been said that wholeness is not synonymous with any one idea, system, framework, philosophy, or pattern of understanding; it resists being "owned" by any school of thought. Rather, it is a *context* for such systems, frameworks, and philosophies. Wholeness transcends all perspectives, and is owned by no particular perspective.

WHOLENESS, SCIENCE, AND SPIRITUALITY

Wholeness is the central principle of humankind's most ancient wisdom, pointed to (but not captured) by many names—from the "unspeakable Tao" of ancient China to the indivisible Brahman-Atman of the Vedas to the "being" ascribed by Pre-Socratic Greek philosophers to the God (Yahweh, or YHWH) of the Abrahamic religions. Wholeness is signaled indirectly in much of the world's spiritual wisdom—apophatically invoked in the agnostic psychology of Buddhism as well as in the "cloud of unknowing" of Christian mysticism.

Modern secular readers may need to translate, because wholeness was most often signified by the ancient texts with religious words like "God" that pose challenges not only to our knowing but to modern scientific beliefs. However, the divine was not always conceived of as an anthropomorphic mythic deity; the wisest esoteric mystics of every great tradition have long understood divinity in transpersonal and usually transcendent terms.

That higher wholeness, or God, was the source of the most profound inspiration. But it tended to be conflated socially with mythic religious dogma, and then to function as a kind of "final word," stifling doubt and innovation. Only by freely examining, measuring, testing, and analyzing the component parts of things have we known them rigorously enough to discern the physical laws of nature, and to translate them as physics, chemistry, and biology.

That kind of "knowledge of the parts" is the source of the world-transforming power of Western humanistic science. We have analyzed the particular dynamics of the apparently separate phenomena comprising wholeness, and integrated the fragments of our hard-won knowledge into a series of increasingly sophisticated and comprehensive theories that have increased our powers to understand and control those phenomena.

But all along, even as some human beings harnessed the power of knowledge by slicing reality into ever-tinier slivers, others were trying to glean its deepest meanings by integrating those fragments into a clearer perception of its seamless totality—sometimes in ways that reintegrate science and religion.

In the late eighteenth and early nineteenth centuries, one of the first scientifically informed Western descriptions of wholeness emerged among German idealist philosophers like Fichte, Schelling, and Hegel. Although they used the theological language of their day, their perspective can be stated something like this:

While transcending all its parts, God (our original wholeness and divinity) has manifested itself through the physical world. Evolution—the often meandering but steady and inexorable emergence of new and "higher" forms of existence, from matter to life to human beings—is how the spirit of that wholeness and divinity has unfolded in time and space. And that spirit is still unfolding. The implicit potential of that wholeness and divinity are gradually made explicit through evolution.

Michael Murphy, a founder of Esalen and the human potential movement, describes this worldview as an "emerging canon" that—although currently mostly surviving and thriving only on the margins of the academic, scientific, and religious mainstream—will eventually capture the world's imagination. He also points out that it is already a more satisfying integration of our most essential inner and outer data than naive scientific materialistic positivism or traditional religious belief.

Not that we will ever abandon the incredibly useful, subject-object, parts-to-whole analyses of science. My spiritual experiences have transfigured my worldview, but not in a way that exempts me from rational accountability to the evidence, or that disconnects me from the scientific mode of testing and validating knowledge. I recognize the necessity to closely read the facts and evidence around our rapidly evolving world.

We can apply "both/and" thinking. On the one hand, I can appreciate that it is important not to confuse facts with theories, documented evidence with elegant syntheses, or scientific knowledge with mystical vision. On the other hand, I can appreciate the power and value of intuition and vision, and the moral importance of human growth and transformation. There's no need to marginalize any kind of valid human experience or knowledge. Wholeness, by its nature, does not exclude any perspective; it invites us to inquire into how they can all coexist.

Certain aggressive "skeptics" zealously guard the citadel of science as if it were threatened by this whole realm of discourse, deriding it (and even the most meticulous, rigorous, hard-headed research into supernormal human capacities) as "woo-woo," "fuzzy-headed," or "pseudoscience." The skeptical enterprises sometimes make valid and important points, especially when attacking superstitions, sloppy thinking, and careless statements. But they often attack "straw men" with an excess of righteous contempt, acting as though materialists are incapable of errors or biases.

There is an important distinction between engaging in measurement-based science and intuitively synthesizing a more adequate, inclusive, nuanced worldview. Or between evidence-based science and preliminary research to explain paradigm-defying phenomena or anomalies. These activities should not be conflated or confused. It is valid to critique the naive enthusiasm of unsophisticated people who appropriate scientific ideas in support of idealistic wishful thinking. But there is an equally valid critique to be made of the attempt to delegitimize sophisticated discourse that appreciates intuitive insights and higher states of consciousness, or that intends to learn from the implications of mystical experiences.

The project of integrating human knowledge includes a great body of work that inspects the evolution of the states and structures of interior consciousness, sometimes correlating them with the evolution of exterior physical structures. This work validates the potential for—and, indeed, supports the importance of—awakening into higher states and stages of consciousness.

In this context it is useful to distinguish prerationality from transrationality. Archaic consciousness was prerational; it had not yet become capable of applying reason with rigor. Transrational consciousness is not only capable of using reason, it has developed enough to be awake to and interested in realities beyond the reach of reason. It is able to accept that there are dimensions and dynamics of reality that have not yet been (and some that may never be) fully measured, validated, or described by the physical sciences. It even allows that these are potentially important. Quite a few distinct transrational fields of study have now emerged (from the noetic sciences to transpersonal psychology to contemplative neuroscience to integral philosophy), and practitioners in these fields have entered into conversation with experiential explorers of the experience of wholeness—*contemplative* practitioners.

In part, what these new fields of study have done is to embody a new kind of intelligence, grounded in intuitive wholeness and expressing its health. Where is its point of view located? Where exactly does wholeness stand? Wholeness cannot really be visualized, except perhaps as an exploded sphere "whose circumference is nowhere and whose center is everywhere."[23]

The center may be everywhere, and yet it is also at the heart. Subjectively, wholeness is most readily intuited by our heart intelligence (to which we will return in chapter 6). It is felt at the heart, and can be most readily experienced via the breath. Wholeness is transmuted at the heart into our wisest feeling-impulses—like care, appreciation, well-being, affection, strength, generosity, and courage.

Thus, wholeness is infinitely profound. High mystical states are experiences of wholeness. In these states, divisions fall away—between self and other, matter and energy, experience and experiencer, consciousness and phenomena. With no knower there can be no known, no subject and no object, no boundary of any kind. A self-validating sense of wonder, joy, bliss, and love subsumes everything. This radical wholeness is "prior" to the experience of divisions that appear to subject-object consciousness. The most profound utterances of ancient scriptures, of mystics, of poets and philosophers are often infused with the spiritual fragrance of the presence of this felt wholeness. It is, indeed, the essence of sacredness and holiness.

This urge toward wholeness also expresses itself in our era's renaissance of a living, more than merely rational spirituality. Perhaps the greatest experts on paradoxical wholeness—this totality that simply cannot be grasped with subject-object thinking—have been humankind's great mystics and spiritual masters. Wholeness goes by many different names: "suchness" or "Buddha nature" or "the Self" or "awareness" or "open intelligence" or "spirit" or "God" or "love" or "wonder," to name just a few. Whatever name they give it, millions of spiritual practitioners are now students of wholeness in one way or another.

Because it takes one to know one, there is a backlash too. From the perspective of subject-object consciousness (the mode of science and most rational discourse), this unitive apprehension of wholeness is an entirely subjective experience—even perhaps a hallucination with no intrinsic meaning—rather than valid "knowledge" of the nature of reality. It cannot be tested and verified or falsified, like valid scientific knowledge. So it tends to be excluded from "mainstream" rational public discourse.

Wholeness may be ignored or denied, but it doesn't go away. It is self-validating and resurgent—in part because it not only carries with it a sense of peaceful clarity about the nature of things, it sometimes seems to elicit wise behavior, and even a kind of "grace" or good luck, which enables people with such an intuition to be a harmonious influence on others. Although many people these days report achieving these states of consciousness, at least for brief moments, it is still extremely rare for someone to stabilize a powerful direct intuition of such wholeness consistently and to sustain it over time.

Increasingly, however, intuitions of wholeness have begun penetrating mainstream culture. This trend is inexorable. It will ultimately breed broad recognition that intuitions of wholeness can coincide with "attention to the parts," informing and uplifting the dispositions of scientists and researchers.

CONTRACTING FROM WHOLENESS

The world's ancient mystical traditions tell the story of wholeness and fragmentation in esoteric terms, in terms of consciousness and energy. This account directly tackles the paradox that even though our underlying reality is wholeness, the predominant experience of human beings is one of fragmentation.

These traditions all suggest that divine wholeness is the most fundamental nature of reality, and it is unbroken and unblemished—and yet human beings separate themselves, becoming "egos" instead of harmonious expressions of and participants in that original wholeness. This is the ancient esoteric meaning of "sin"—in Greek *hamartia*, "to miss the mark" by losing touch with and denying wholeness itself. A nuanced process-oriented version of this primal narrative holds that the ego is less an entity than a *present activity*. All conscious embodied beings experience reflexive shock at their mortality and vulnerability, and keep recoiling into separation, presuming the position of a separate self in a world of separate entities and processes. This present activity takes place at an "extremely subtle" or "causal" level of being, entirely invisible to ordinary conscious awareness. Wholeness, although unbroken, is not an object in our field of vision and so escapes our notice. From the perspective of mortal beings, wholeness is always being fragmented by this activity of self-contraction—so consistently that separation does not seem to be an activity at all; it just seems to be "the way things are."

This whole event of contraction is a process within a continuous field of potency or energy—the vibratory substrate (called "conscious light" by mystics) that contemporary physics tells us is the "stuff" of all matter and energy. The divisions that are experienced take place in a field of force or energy, and so do the reactions or results. So wholeness is constantly being fragmented. And yet that's only half the story—*wholeness is also always reasserting itself.*

There is a tendency for disturbed energy to regain the continuous flow or circuit that is original to it. Thus, the innate wholeness that is the nature and form of reality always tends to reassert, resume, or reinforce itself. This tendency is experienced subjectively in individuals as a desire for health, awareness, love, or wholesomeness. The pressure of this desire opposes the tendency toward contraction, fragmentation, division, solidity, and separation—the dualistic mind of "me and that" that results from the activity of contraction.

Things don't only keep loudly falling apart; they are also always quietly coming together. Wounds heal. The immune system mobilizes and the disease runs its course and health is returned. And we can participate consciously in this process, intensifying it. The reassertion of health and wholeness is stronger when it is supported by a strong sympathetic intuition of the prior unity or wholeness of existence. The intensifying fragmentation around us summons an intensifying subjective impulse to join with others out of care for the whole, restoring wholeness when we can.

The most radical teaching about wholeness and fragmentation can be found simply in the prior unity of all opposites and conditional experiences. Contraction creates the experience of separation and division and dilemma. Problem or dilemma, then, is the essential structure of human suffering. Subtly, it is presumed by all individual egos, in every ordinary activity, and even by traditional mystical and spiritual paths that strategize ways to reunite with a wholeness that has somehow been "lost." But the problem cannot be radically solved from the perspective of the separation it presumes in the first place. Seeking relief from separation doesn't work. We can only awaken from the dream of separation and recognize that it isn't true, and never has been.

And, in the meantime, entirely apart from our seeking to escape separation, health and wholeness and integrity keep reasserting themselves. Our attraction to wholeness drives our healthiest and noblest choices and aspirations. Even more fundamental than seeking, it is woven through our character. So, when we are healthiest and most conscious, we live a wholesome life.

CHALLENGES TO LIVING A LIFE OF WHOLENESS

Wholeness is the simplest and most fundamental of all values and properties. And the burgeoning, evolving transrational worldview described earlier, embracing all expressions of wholeness, should support us in this quest to live those values.

Yet a contemporary life that embodies wholeness is stubbornly elusive, especially when our world is complexifying and fragmenting so rapidly.

Human life and consciousness are enormously complex. We experience ourselves as individual and apparently separate human beings composed of many subpersonalities and drives and faculties and levels of capacity. We are always finding ourselves in contexts that require us to account for ourselves as separate individuals—like relational exchanges where we have distinct roles and are guided by rules. But the wholeness of the natural world inexorably evolves, seemingly indifferent to our apparently separate identities.

How can we account for all the fast-moving complexity? We can't. And there is no pause button—our lives keep confronting us with discrete, specific challenges that require timely responses. So we act, react, or fail to act. Have we adequately accounted for wholeness? There is no source of objective feedback.

And as profoundly as we have evolved on all levels, the habits of our neurological hardwiring still retain a deep thread of primitive conditioning that tends to cognize big abstractions like "the whole" as something "out there"—separate from the self, and thus not important to our lives, at least for now. For the vast majority, even among apparently "highly evolved" people, the good of the individual, family, group, tribe, political party, city, or nation trumps the good of the Whole (which, again, is viewed as a separate "thing," apart from us). This helps explain the contempt of many politicians as well as ordinary citizens for our climate and environment; the mind of parts doesn't notice that the economy is a subset of the ecology. This thinking encourages separate selves and separate groups to compete against "the other" for limited resources. It encourages and rewards our cannibalization of the commons and of Earth.

But a system, culture, or civilization built on this model will eventually fall apart. Because *everything* is a part of the Whole, the well-being of all parts depends on the health of the Whole. The failure of humans to see and embody this has resulted in a chaos of disconnection, in which most individuals and organizations "game the system" in one way or another, gaining advantage for themselves at the expense of the collective. Corporations are incentivized to maximize their shareholders' advantages, and they often do so at the expense of the commons. Citizens game corporations and governments if they can. In this respect, we enable one another to degrade our shared well-being. Each of us then functions something like cancer cells or tumors, sapping the health of the larger body politic. We have recently reached a level of social complexity that has created countless hiding places for such cancerous "memes." This is what has produced the chaos, fragmentation, conflict, and disintegration now occurring all around us.

Our looming crises, likely centuries in the making, are a result of this mind of separation—countless generations of humans living, striving, and creating from a consciousness partially defined and compromised by fear, separation, division, conflict, and competition.

What is ironic and can seem vexing is that separative thinking (also often called "subject-object consciousness") is so damn productive. The symbols and ideas that are creating so much confusion, division, conflict, and fragmentation are the very mental tools that have paradoxically made possible the advance of human knowledge and progress. We separate our "subjective" awareness from the "objects" we perceive, notice differences, identify our preferences, and exert our efforts to achieve effects. By separating wholeness into component parts, we perceive, distinguish, analyze, measure, and increasingly comprehend these parts. This allows us to construct frameworks, categories, and criteria for knowledge; protocols for rigor, observation, and investigation; and techniques to apply knowledge in ways that, over time, have given us enormous powers.

The cognition of separate parts has been an immensely potent move. It has enabled us to discern and manipulate the laws of physics, the structures of matter and living organisms, the underlying principles and dynamics of energy, and the relationships and interactions among infinitesimal particles in the subatomic realm. It has enabled us to understand the structures of living organisms; the fossil record of biological evolution; and the secrets of the atom, relativity, galaxies, deep space-time, and the quantum universe. It has empowered our engineering of all the innovations that have transformed human life over the past five hundred years.

The power acquired through "knowledge of the parts" has been an enormous blessing. But it has also been a curse. On one hand, it has been the key to most human creativity and progress, through the world-transforming power of Western humanistic sciences. And yet it has become an unconscious habit that has estranged us from the Source of our very being. We are addicted to it, and often reflexively drawn into it. It is part-and-parcel of the "consensus trance." It is a continual source of reinforcement for a particular and limited way of being, and often leads to a contracted, reductive, narrowed view of the world, through which lazy minds cognize separation, division, conflict, and destruction—not only among men and women, but between humans and nature.

But the mind of science has long been confronting the implications of a multidimensional, evolving, integrated reality, grounded in wholeness and expressing it. Wholeness is not in tension with science; it is the message of our best scientific understanding of life. Science is in the process of recontextualizing and ultimately contradicting the story of separation, even though the separative habit remains strong in the minds of many, including many scientists.

In hindsight, we can see how much cultural evolution has unfolded out of separative consciousness. Out of this consciousness, and with the powers it has given us, we have created a complex global civilization that expresses a "consensus reality" that dreams up more radical separation, division, conflict, and competition than our science tells us is real and natural.

And we have created a vast web of rapidly deteriorating and unsustainable institutions and social and environmental conditions, which now threaten the future of our civilization and a human-friendly biosphere.

This habit-based separative consciousness is now *itself* tending to become a real danger to our survival. It has already led us to an evolutionary impasse. Acting from this consciousness cannot be ultimately effective. Such actions reinforce their own operating assumptions, habits, and patterns. "Good works" done from this state of consciousness will not ultimately save us. Whether it's more educating, innovating, recycling, conserving and legislating; more donating, volunteering, protesting, organizing, and demonstrating; more good intentions and great ideas; trying harder, being smarter; knowing what's wrong and what's possible—none of these things can ultimately succeed. If we act from separative consciousness, even all the good things we do will inadvertently reinforce the separation we presume, so our good deeds will inevitably spawn additional problems.

Advances in technology, scientific knowledge, cultural values, spiritual vision, and psychological sophistication are remaking the world so rapidly that there is ample reason for hope. Yet it is this lower, primitive structure—this consciousness rooted in separation rather than wholeness—that responds unskillfully and even destructively to evolutionary challenges. It must be alchemically transformed if we are to rise to a new evolutionary octave.

The most cutting-edge sciences in every field, the deepest psychological insights and spiritual teachings in human history—these will not save us until we *integrate* them into our selves, our institutions, and our cultures. Otherwise they will remain like unread books on library shelves. They only come alive when they live in us and we live them in life.

Something unprecedented is required from us now if we are to survive and thrive. And that something new must be grounded in wholeness and in consciousness. It is *who we are and how we see* that holds the potential for the necessary radical leap. That is why, in the next two chapters, we explore how an evolutionary perspective and an integral framework provide foundation and fuel for this increasingly urgent imperative.

CARE FOR THE WHOLE: INTEGRATING ACTIVISM AND AWAKENING

How can we remain consciously rooted in a deep, unifying intuition of prior wholeness—and live from there? How can we be the very presence of that wholeness in action? How can we be the agency of wholeness that heals division?

It is perhaps *the* question of our time. Activism and awakening are two great projects with the potential to be integrated in a way that can liberate a profound, hidden, and world-changing synergy. There is deep kinship between our urge to awaken to Reality and our impulses to make the world better through our dedicated service. When they connect deeply, our public life is uplifted and energized. A higher integration of awakening and activism might have the potential to generate a movement of wholeness adequate to address our current challenges of fragmentation.

But shadows too often fall upon both of these great purposes. Both activism and inner awakening intuit a higher wholeness and intend to bring it to life. But it is profoundly difficult to embody activism *or* awakening in our complex, fast-moving contemporary world in a way that is not in some way subtly naive, incomplete, avoidant, self-serving, or otherwise ineffective—sometimes even destructive.

Our resonance with wholeness is fundamental to our urges toward both activism and awakening. Whether we know it or not, most of us are inspired to penetrate the illusion of separation, and yearn at some level to integrate everything healthy and noble and holy in ourselves and in the world.

And yet even "awakeners" and activists commonly picture themselves as separate and estranged in the way I described above. The habit of human thought and speech is simply to imagine ourselves separate from and independent of what we think about and describe. The mind imagines that every object of attention exists by itself, separate and independent from other objects and from us.

In a universe of more than three hundred sextillion suns, and mind-boggling numbers of atoms, subatomic particles, and, supposedly, unimaginably greater amounts of "dark matter" and energy, we see a world of separate entities, and we ourselves feel separate, discrete. From there, the full integration of everything can begin to seem like a mystical abstraction or a utopian ideal, rather than inherent and obvious and heartening.

We've thus tended to leave wholeness and integration out of our activism and awakening. Our energies tend to flow in one direction or the other, at least in each moment of experience—inner or outer, activism or awakening. Yet recognizing and intuiting the underlying wholeness of existence is essential to the kind of intelligence that our predicament—and potential—demands.

Activism and awakening each aspire in some way to heal the fragmentation of human experience. And they each partially achieve this. Awakening cultivates a wholeness in our personal awareness and life that puts us profoundly in touch with our moment-to-moment experience. It restores our relationship to wonder, to the essence of life and death, and to all sentient beings.

Activism strives for a wholeness in our social relations, our political and economic systems, our institutions, and our structures of power.

These expressions of inner work and outer work are complementary, but each is, in its own way, incomplete. The obvious thing to do is to bring them together in a greater wholeness that draws on the strengths of each of these two great purposes, finds common cause, and innovates new synergies and greater efficacy. A "movement of movements," if you will—an ecosystem of wholeness.

Of course, there are and have been great spiritual activists—from Jesus of Nazareth to Mahatma Gandhi to Mother Teresa to Martin Luther King—who have exemplified some integration of these two purposes, of the inner and outer work, as we saw in the last chapter. And vital public conversations have continually emerged among spiritually inspired activists, from the students of Gandhi and King, to Quaker peace initiatives, to Catholic liberation theology.

Wholeness is also expressed in the modern work of those attempting awakened activism—including engaged Buddhists like Joanna Macy, deep ecologists like Thomas Berry and Brian Swimme, compassionate climate activists like Paul Hawken, Bill McKibben, Michael Dowd, and Connie Barlow, and sacred activists like Andrew Harvey, Marianne Williamson, and Charles Eisenstein. All of these individuals seek to evolve activism and advance social change in service of wholeness.

We also know that there are countless unrecognized "awakening activists" doing good work every day. The more we look, the more we find these everyday heroes and exemplars of wholeness in action.

There is a resurgence of wholeness wherever science and spirituality find ways to be in authentic dialogue, such as the Mind and Life Institute conferences on neuroscience and dharma involving the Dalai Lama. There is wholeness in Pope Francis's climate encyclical, arguing for "integral ecology." There is an opening into wholeness in the attempts to integrate our knowledge about the evolution of matter, life, and mind as chapters in a single story, the "Big History" championed by David Christian and Bill Gates.

Nonetheless, a *movement*—a broad, self-aware, culturally effective arising of awakening activism—has yet to truly take root. The discourse, practices, institutions, narratives, values, and cultural structures and agreements of a greater integral wholeness are only just beginning to appear.

CULTIVATING WHOLENESS: A PRACTICE, A PROJECT, AND AN EVOLUTIONARY IMPERATIVE

Once we become attuned to wholeness, we can begin to see it showing up everywhere around us. And once we seriously commit to and intentionally orient ourselves toward wholeness, we can embody a deliberately more inclusive and expansive approach to every aspect of our lives. We can cultivate a more wholesome and essential relationship to life. We can evaluate our actions by more holistic standards. We can create new practices, unfold new strategies, and form new organizations explicitly oriented toward emergent wholeness.

We can call such a bias toward and attention and commitment to wholeness—with the potential to counteract and transcend the fragmentation of our postmodern world—an *integral impulse,* and those who express it *integralists.* This orientation is part of the answer to that urgent, rubber-meets-the-road question of our moment: How can wholeness be *lived?*

Thankfully, although an enormous transformation—still in the future—is called for, this orientation is already emerging in many corners of contemporary culture.

I have had the privilege and fortune to participate in a number of specifically integral initiatives over the past forty years—from my life in a profoundly integrative spiritual ashram to my work as an integral teacher, coach, and cultural leader. I've witnessed the birth of what I call the *integral evolutionary ecosystem,* comprising many such initiatives and practitioners. Yet, viewed alongside the scale and complex dynamics of our challenges, all such projects are obviously early versions of something much more powerful that has yet to fully emerge.

Despite our present cultures of separation, polarization, and alienation, we are not separate or disconnected. An integral transformation of *ourselves* and our relationship to this larger web, and the discovery and development of new, holistic ways of being and doing, are becoming evolutionary imperatives.

We are being called to our next stage of evolution and to a new level of consciousness. We are being called to evolve beyond the exploitive, cannibalizing behaviors arising from narrow self-interest, and to embody values that serve the greater good of the whole. We are being called to develop a new revolutionary framework for our global culture, based in a profound realization of our interdependence, our prior and ultimate wholeness and unity.

This evolution of human nature can be nurtured by an integral practice that combines inner work with altruistic service and action in the world. In the next two chapters we will explore both an evolutionary perspective (chapter 4) and an integral framework (chapter 5) that will allow us to understand and arrive at a simplicity on the other side of complexity, from which we can express wholeness in just this way.

The Evolutionary Perspective

The conflict dates from the day when one man, flying in the face of appearance, perceived that the forces of nature are no more unalterably fixed in their orbits than the stars themselves, but that their serene arrangement around us depicts the flow of a tremendous tide—the day on which a first voice rang out, crying to Mankind peacefully slumbering on the raft of earth, "We are moving! We are going forward!"

It is a pleasant and dramatic spectacle, that of Mankind divided to its very depths into two irrevocably opposed camps—one looking toward the horizon and proclaiming with all its newfound faith, "We are moving," and the other, without shifting its position, obstinately maintaining, "Nothing changes. We are not moving at all."

—PIERRE TEILHARD DE CHARDIN,
THE FUTURE OF MAN

If one of the things that ails us is fragmentation of perspective and constriction of vision, one antidote is to step back, take a deep breath, and consider our situation from a wider, more integrated vantage point—an evolutionary perspective. This helps us frame our current circumstances within a much larger trajectory of time and life.

Evolutionary theory, in strictly biological terms, is grounded in many specific observations about the fossil record, genetic mutations, and adaptations to changing environments. But the larger pattern of discoveries consistently paints an arc of development—over the longest spans of time—from simpler, less conscious and cooperative life forms to more conscious, complex, and cooperative ones.

Thus far, we have only observed life on planet Earth. But we know that the planet itself displays its own evolutionary arc—from simpler to more complex combinations of matter and energy.

Today's scientific consensus is that there was a "Big Bang" some 13.8 billion years ago, as space, time, matter, and energy exploded into existence. Over vast eons, this matter/energy self-organized into atoms, molecules, stars, planets, and other celestial entities. It formed large communities of star systems called galaxies; some of these galaxies are centered on black holes that resemble a photonegative of the singularity we fathom was at the heart of the Big Bang, swallowing matter and light into nonexistence. All this displays both a remarkable order and a mysterious chaos that we have only begun to comprehend at a physical level very recently.

We also know that human civilization has evolved. While any particular epoch involves many advances and regressions, when we consider the last 120,000 years (starting in the Stone Age and extending to our postmodern age), we notice the same evolutionary arc—from simpler to more complex and cooperative forms of organization.

And when we discuss human civilization, we must consider not only biological adaptations, but also technological innovations, sociocultural change, and the emergence of higher consciousness. That higher consciousness has likewise evolved cognitively, morally, aesthetically, and spiritually.

If we piece together these multiple evolutionary trajectories, it becomes clear that the process of evolution cannot be reduced to cosmic, biological, or cultural evolution—it is more fundamental than any particular scientific or humanistic discipline can capture. The story encompasses everything, from the birth of the cosmos, to the agricultural, scientific, and cultural revolutions of recent history, to our individual attempts to understand reality, or to awaken into higher awareness.

The story of evolution is so vast and all-encompassing that it would be foolish to purport to explain it or claim to know what is supposed to happen next, except in the broadest terms. But while we can't predict exactly where it is going, we can begin—for the first time in this great story—to consciously participate in it.

THE EVOLUTIONARY IMPULSE

We are among the first generations of human beings who are able to contemplate the scientific story of our origins. And this story tells us something deeper than merely material scientific facts.

We can now recognize and contemplate that complexity and consciousness and cooperation have been favored over thousands of millions of years by the "random" processes of biological evolution. At a minimum, they have been favored by natural selection. Without imputing magical powers to a nonordinary force, we can rationally posit that there is significant meaning in that directionality. On that basis it's worth synthesizing the implications of the evidence and stepping beyond it to speculate.

There is no scientific proof for our speculations. But I join a great many other people who find it useful to speak of an "evolutionary impulse" that is active across every domain of existence—from matter to life to mind and spirit. It is significant that this impulse operates not only through natural selection (which includes "survival of the fittest" in the strictest neo-Darwinian terms), but also toward the seemingly miraculous emergence of new potentials—tending over time toward greater complexity, more sophisticated forms of intelligence, and more powerful forms of cooperation.

In its tendency toward complexity and consciousness, we can infer that the universe has been "heading somewhere," in the words of Pierre Teilhard de Chardin. All along it has, metaphorically, been wanting to do something. What is this something? What is the purpose of becoming more complex and conscious and fully articulated and interconnected and cooperative?

It is as though evolution, all along, has been working to create a way of seeing and knowing itself—and now, in our lifetimes, the universe is seeing itself for the first time with a new, more granular clarity. It is as though you and I are the eyes of the universe as it suddenly glimpses its own image. In an awe-inspiring "coincidence," we're also just now, at the very same time, seeing that we must cooperate to change our behavior on a massive scale if we're going to be able to keep evolving. This ancient evolutionary trajectory, which has all along been moving toward more complexity, consciousness, and cooperation, is facing a need to manifest a quantum leap in consciousness and cooperation in order to keep the evolutionary process moving ahead in a healthy way.

Another implication of this story has to do with the way evolution has sped up more and more across these billions of years. From the perspective of a single human lifetime, evolution has always been imperceptible. But this gradual acceleration of biological and then cultural evolution has reached a speed in our lifetimes in which cultural evolution, for the first time, is visible to human beings. We are the first generations of human beings who are seeing these changes unfolding before us in a time frame that we can directly experience. And there's an inspiring and truly spiritual message in this evolutionary perspective.

This shift to evolving consciously (instead of unconsciously) is momentous. How dramatic that we are just beginning to glimpse it at the very time when, for our survival, we have to see and understand and respond to its implications.

We can see from the above that evolution is more than a theory or a system of ideas; it is the natural context of all manifest existence, a "curve all lines must follow" in the lovely words of Pierre Teilhard de Chardin. It is the grandest metanarrative—the story into which all other narratives must fit themselves.

This understanding of evolution, tracing the deepest patterns not just of adaptation but of emergence, points to ways in which we—collectively and as individuals—can actively and consciously participate in this deep movement of Great Unfolding. Rather than merely being pushed and pulled by the surface currents of the day, we have the capacity to intentionally influence the course of this emergence.

If there was ever a time to develop, advance, and use that capacity, it surely is now.

THE EVOLUTION OF THE EVOLUTIONARY WORLDVIEW

Many of the greatest philosophical thinkers of the last three hundred years were pioneers in learning to see ourselves through the eyes of evolution—from Georg Hegel and Friedrich Schelling to Ralph Waldo Emerson, Walt Whitman, and Henry James Sr.; from Sri Aurobindo and Pierre Teilhard de Chardin to Ken Wilber. This is now continuing via the Big History project, as taught by David Christian and promulgated by Bill Gates.

This process of awakening to and assimilating an evolutionary worldview has been rippling through every aspect of human culture in a series of revolutionary changes over the last two centuries of Western history. This process is now affecting—and often transforming—every field of human knowledge. But the widespread acceptance of evolution as our context, and the process of absorbing its wide-ranging implications in our lived experience, is still in its relative infancy. Not everyone sees or accepts this worldview; not everyone is an "evolutionary" (yet).

Disagreement is predictable and inherent to the process. Of course, the emergence of a truly evolutionary worldview would be as messy as the process of cultural evolution itself. It is partly through controversy that it evolves. Creative tension, differentiation, conflict, negotiation, cooperation, mutual influence, and synthesis advance and deepen the process. Similar patterns can be discerned in biological evolution.

Historically significant worldviews are powerful, multigenerational, large-scale systems of agreement. Such systems, when we inhabit them, tend to dictate how we frame reality and our own identities. And though these agreements live in the subjective consciousness of individuals, they are neither wholly subjective nor completely objective. Worldview structures are also "intersubjective." They occupy what integral philosopher Steve McIntosh has called the "agreement space" that exists *in between* individuals. And they too are always evolving.

New cultural advances emerge in response to the inadequacies of whatever shared agreements have gone before. We push off against limitations, usually either differentiating something brand-new or reintegrating something we temporarily left behind that now needs to be reincluded. This powers evolutionary progress. As each successive wave of new understanding is revealed to be incomplete, it is followed by another wave, and our worldview is again further reshaped.

Consider, for example, that Isaac Newton—by far the most advanced scientist of the early eighteenth century—publicly supported the calculation that God created the world on Sunday, October 23, 4004 BCE. In less than 150 additional years of scientific observation, enough geological, fossil, anthropological, zoological, and astronomical evidence had accumulated to radically change the scientific consensus. In that relatively brief span, it became clear to the scientists of the mid-nineteenth century that our planet's history stretched back not for thousands but for many millions of years.

After Darwin's *On the Origin of Species* appeared in 1859, the theory of evolution quickly began morphing—even in popular perception—from a scandalous heresy into an incontrovertible (if still popularly controversial) scientific fact. A whole new world began to come into view. Instead of imagining ourselves created by God in his image, dwelling in a pregiven world of fixed forms, educated, rational people began emerging into an evolutionary view of reality.

We could see and accept that we (and all living things) descended with tiny modifications, generation by generation, from the simplest life forms over billions of years. Human beings, we realized, were not just the distant cousins of the apes and dogs, but also of ants, ferns, jellyfish, and bacteria. And our brains and bodies are the creative recombinations of the dust of long-extinct stars.

Across the decades that followed Darwin, discoveries in astrophysics and the social sciences also began to make clear that biology is not the only domain of evolution. These discoveries revealed that cosmic evolution gave rise to biological evolution, which in turn gave rise to cultural evolution.

While all these implications have been assimilated to a certain degree in our culture, we are still early in the process of accepting other evolutionary implications: that the evolution of consciousness is as real and significant as biological evolution; that we can consciously participate in evolution; and that evolution can become aware of itself. As consciousness evolves, these newer understandings of evolution might one day be as widely understood and accepted as biological evolution is now.

Models of reality in which human beings are seen as discrete, separate entities—which seem all but universally accepted today—may at some point be considered as outdated as the biblical world-creation myth that was still in effect even in scientific circles three hundred years ago. In the current evolutionary worldview, many of us already understand that we are, in fact, constantly changing creative *processes,* participating in a vast drama of constantly changing patterns. We are *activities.* In the words of Carter Phipps, an evolutionary worldview continues to "break the spell of solidity."

But human beings have barely begun to fully absorb and internalize the implications of this "process view." And we have barely begun learning to think with a "deep time" perspective that can imagine slow changes over millions and billions of years. The pervasive human tendency is still to reduce our dynamic evolutionary processes to a stick-figure narrative populated by solid, fixed, discrete, separate "things." It is also much easier to grasp. And, practically speaking, this understanding of ourselves and life has been mostly adequate to how we have lived until now. But that thinking has helped bring about our predicament, and will greatly limit our ability to accurately comprehend and effectively address it.

Internalizing all the implications of an evolutionary worldview will continue to be a complex cultural process. To define, refine, inhabit, and explore this worldview is a huge, ongoing collective project. It knits together many disciplines and a remarkable series of epiphanies into a profoundly illuminating and inspiring vision. That vision—perhaps especially now—holds not only explanatory and predictive potentials, but creative and developmental ones.

To fulfill those potentials, the human imagination will be asked to make enormous, expansive jumps beyond our current habits of thinking. But it will serve us to do so; we are urged, even required to do so now, by evolution itself.

EVOLUTION'S INHERENT OPTIMISM

Philosopher of science Holmes Rolston[24] points out that our "big history" includes "three Big Bangs." The first Big Bang, the one we know by that name, took place—according to our current best science—13.8 billion years ago. It gave birth to space-time and to matter and energy and our universe of billions of galaxies—what we can call the physiosphere. The second Big Bang, through which life emerged from matter, is now dated at about 3.8 billion years ago, when the first one-celled prokaryotes emerged from the primordial soup, giving birth to what we call the biosphere. The third Big Bang took place somewhere between one million and 120,000 years ago, with the first emergence of human consciousness, language, and collective learning—what we call culture.

In the first Big Bang, as the physiosphere came into being, it manifested photons and the first atoms of hydrogen and helium, and then the first stars and galaxies, and then planets and some additional elements—and eventually, via supernovas, it manifested heavier elements and more complex planets. But all these evolutionary changes appeared only *very* gradually, over hundreds of millions or billions of years.

On our planet this pattern was abruptly transformed about 3.8 billion years ago, when the first living cells appeared during what Rolston refers to as the second Big Bang. As these cells evolved, they eventually gained nuclei, began to sexually reproduce, and became multicelled organisms; they differentiated, and in time manifested ecosystems that pervaded not just the oceans but also the land and even the atmosphere. Evolution speeded up to the point where great transformations could be measured in mere millions and even hundreds of thousands of years. Microbes and algae appeared, then mollusks and grasses and ferns, and insects and amphibians and fish, and primeval forests and reptiles—and eventually primates—all coevolving in myriad complex ecosystems, each of which themselves evolved. All of this took place across epochs that included dramatic extinction events and cataclysms, but also more and more complex and cooperative and interconnected—and eventually more conscious—forms of life.

The third Big Bang was the appearance of humans and consciousness and culture on Earth, which took place somewhere between one million and 120,000 years ago. This Big Bang gave birth to the inner universe of thought and language and meaning—what is sometimes referred to as the "noosphere." Human beings began a process of collective learning, wherein we refined our ability to make tools and clothing, use fire, store food, create language and ritual—and eventually grow crops, domesticate animals, and live together in towns and cities. And this cultural evolution took place much more quickly than previous evolutionary advances, with big changes occurring in mere tens of thousands of years, and eventually in just a thousand years or so—and, in recent times, dramatically accelerating, with huge changes taking place in just hundreds of years and then decades.

This has transformed our relationship to evolutionary changes. Until very recently all of them—cosmic, biological, and cultural—have proceeded so slowly that they have eluded direct human perception until long after the fact. But cultural evolution is moving quickly enough now to be directly perceptible during a human lifetime—even as it is happening. This is radical, and new.

Meanwhile, human culture has begun to reshape the biosphere and the physiosphere. Today, the future of thousands of species of life will be determined by human behavior—by what happens in the evolution of human culture. At the same time, human consciousness and culture have continued to grow more complex and interconnected, and more conscious, cooperative, and fully articulated—now with breathtaking speed.

EVOLUTION'S METHOD:
DIFFERENTIATION AND INTEGRATION

In each of these Big Bangs, some universal principles apply. On every scale, we see the articulation of new, unique forms and behaviors, which interact and conflict and negotiate tensions. Their resolution leads to new forms of cooperation and integration and unity, which in turn give rise to new differentiation. This process refines progressively, through successive generations of differentiation and reintegration—the features we name when we look back on evolutionary history.

This process of "differentiation and integration," as it is often summarized, leads in virtually all directions, proceeding in a seemingly random fashion. But over time, the significant trend ("selected for" by the process itself) is the evolution from simpler, less intelligent entities and life forms to more conscious, complex, cooperative ones. We evolve upward.

This would seem to contradict the retro-romantic idealism that modern human technological advances are simply a wrong turn along our evolutionary trajectory. As already discussed, there is no denying the enormously toxic pathologies of our contemporary human footprint on the biosphere. But it is also important to note that there were ugly imbalances at every stage of our evolutionary journey—along with unique beauty. Every new stage of evolution has brought into being both "dignities and disasters."

There is enormous hope in the creativity of evolutionary emergence. Because the hope and promise provided by the evolutionary story is so compelling, so inspiring, and so ultimately positive (if inherently messy in the process), it can take some effort and rigor to hold our present uncertainties in *wholeness*—especially for those who have internalized an evolutionary worldview.

Notwithstanding the wisdom, curiosity, perspective, and resilience the evolutionary worldview might bring, it could also lead us to rely too much on the inherent creativity of evolution in a way that subtly (or not so subtly) leads to complacency or abstraction. We might run into a fine line between optimism and denial. Certainly, to walk a path between hope and denial requires a finely tuned consciousness. Nonetheless, an evolutionary awareness is characterized by grounded optimism. It is one of several key characteristics of a disposition that could serve us well in navigating the "wicked problem" future that likely awaits us.

From an evolutionary perspective we can see that any future is unlikely to be an extension of past trends, and that wildly creative new emergent possibilities will probably astonish us, more often positively than negatively. (Who could have predicted the emergence of mind from life, or life from matter?)

Likewise, any time we try to apply measurement to violence or depravity, we are confronted with evidence that human history has displayed a far more benign and comforting trajectory than we ordinarily realize. Brutishness has declined consistently and dramatically. This is especially obvious when we view it across any recent millennium, but it is also distinct across most centuries. Instances of horrific cultural regression to brutishness cannot be denied, but there are also persistent and often wondrous advances. Our *evolutionary* context is nothing like the frightening world-in-trouble we tend too often to imagine and communicate to one another.

This does *not* discount the very real and epochal perils we face. There will inevitably be much to grieve in the coming years, decades, and longer. But a grim sense of impending doom, *unmitigated by a sense of evolutionary possibility,* is not only inaccurate, it clearly won't elicit our best. I have long argued that, whether or not it can be confirmed by data, a kind of basic optimism—at least a positive orientation to each moment of living—is a moral imperative.

Simultaneously, it really *is* urgent that human societies transition to energy sources that don't spew carbon into the atmosphere; that we lighten our footprint so that healthy natural habitats can regenerate or thrive; and that we minimize our lasting and even temporary damage to the living body of our mother planet. Those things too are moral imperatives. And it is also imperative that we stay related to all informed and intelligent perspectives on our ecological predicament—and that we grow, change, relate, and connect in ways that take the predicament seriously and respond effectively.

The evolutionary perspective ultimately doesn't call for simple naive optimism, any more than it insists on a purely pessimistic take. It doesn't split off into declarative extremes; it calls for *wholeness*. It thus calls us to face the darkness without losing sight of the light—synthesizing credible bases for pessimism with optimism about the potentials of evolutionary emergence.

It does so in a spirit of radical faith—faith that what is most inspiring is *reality*, and that life and evolution will find astonishing expressions under any and all circumstances.

INSPIRED BY CONTACT WITH
THE IMPULSE OF EVOLUTION

Because the entire cosmos is always naturally manifesting its latent wholeness and divinity, and expressing them in many ways—everything always developing, progressing, and evolving—at some level, we can feel it. If we are awake and clear enough, each of us can intuit that universal impulse, experience the river that runs through everything (including us), and locate it in our subjective experience. It is evident in our highest aspirations—for awakening, illumination, love, freedom, and joy, and for making a positive difference in the world through our creativity, scholarship, industry, charity, and kindness. Those desires are healthy expressions of the greater wholeness that is our nature.

The potential, power, and leverage represented by the individual and collective experience of this "evolutionary impulse" has enormous potential. Some of us who are inspired by this larger story of evolution—and who see an opportunity for active and conscious participation, rather than merely witnessing and reporting—call ourselves "evolutionaries." Our ranks are growing, and so is our understanding of evolution's implications and potentials.

A sense of felt contact with the "evolutionary impulse," expressed in diverse ways, is a distinctive quality among evolutionaries. Many of us are working hard creating projects, furthering new organizations, initiatives, businesses, conferences, and websites; serving clients and students; or writing blogs, papers, and books. Some are pushing the boundaries by innovating new kinds of organizations and leadership, and coloring outside the lines that previously divided entrepreneurship, philanthropy, community organizing, international development, artistic inspiration, human empowerment, and reinventing government.

There is an innovative inspirational spirit alive in a growing community—a profound ambition to be of service. There is an openness to the "strange attractor" of an emergent higher wholeness—even a sense of contact with it. We seem to share the sense that we are cocreatively participating in what Alfred North Whitehead called "the creative advance into novelty."

Some version of this self-aware excitement and sense of purpose was present in the Italian Renaissance, and among the French Philosophes, the German Idealists, the continental Romantics, and the American Transcendentalists and the "New Thought" movement they birthed. *Felt contact with the spirit of evolution* is also a defining characteristic of evolutionary culture.

Some sense of the living impulse of evolution has been inspiring and driving me since I was a child. Paradoxically, it has driven me further now, to face the sobering implications of our ecological predicament.

And it is something that, in thoughtfully preparing for the most whole, generative, and constructive response to this unprecedented present and future, we can consciously draw from and build upon. What is already an emerging movement will be developed, expanded, and deepened. This evolutionary spirit and impulse can be purposefully brought to every effort to support or bring about a life-sustaining society. The individuals and communities who will survive, thrive, and create this new future will be those who not only share this connection to the impulse of evolution, but who consciously enact it.

AN EVOLUTIONARY LEAP

Our present crisis is not merely a historical but an evolutionary event, transcending historical change and affecting our species as a whole. Families, tribes, towns, and nations have been annihilated in our historical past, but other families, tribes, towns, and nations have carried on. Never before has global human civilization reckoned with threats to its survival. Never have we faced such serious and likely lasting changes in the planetary biosphere. Only recently have we become able to even conceive of such events.

Thousands of futurists, prophets, and visionaries agree that humanity faces radical transformation in our lifetimes and those of our children and grandchildren. Some imagine a golden-age "singularity" in which science, technology, and artificial intelligence will enable the human species to free itself from limits. Others think we're entering a period of ecological disruption that foreshadows an apocalyptic end of human civilization as we know it. But evolutionary theorists offer a model that accounts for both the light and dark of our current scenario: the concept of *punctuated equilibrium.*

According to paleontologist Stephen Jay Gould and others, the fossil record seems to show long periods of equilibrium, in which species go through very gradual evolutionary changes, punctuated by relatively short periods of time during which they undergo rapid dramatic changes. Often cultural evolution has followed a similar pattern.

It may be that the human species is now entering a period of such rapid new adaptation that we will undergo an evolutionary leap. These necessary changes will be psychological, cultural, social, technological, political, and even physical. *The leap may take place most deeply in human consciousness itself*—a leap in what it means to be a human being. The oncoming storm of global and personal disturbances will require dramatically different new choices and behaviors—in fact, whole new ways of being.

Sudden, dramatic evolutionary progress is thought to take place under conditions of extreme evolutionary tension. Although ordinary levels of evolutionary tension manifest slow, gradual shifts, intense pressures require rapid and radical emergence. Where a species might have thrived nearly unchanged in its old ecosystem for tens of thousands of generations, it must now change drastically—in relatively few generations—to survive and to thrive.

Many scientists and scholars agree that we are entering one of these "punctuated" eras of rapid change—and we must rapidly readapt, or disappear. In other words, it's game time on the planet—now! We will either evolve—quickly—or perish.

This demand that we transform or perish is a natural consequence of our own evolutionary success. Isn't it entirely natural that any intelligent, dexterous species that developed tools, language, writing, and technologies would eventually become successful—and that its success would increase and accelerate? Might it be natural for such a species to eventually overrun its limits until it overpopulated, polluted, and depleted its environment—all before it fully realized what it was doing?

William Catton's 1980 book *Overshoot* describes these dynamics precisely. He notes that if *any* species on *any* planet (or island, pond, or petri dish) discovers how to expand the planet's (or island's, etc.) carrying capacity in ways that are not permanently sustainable, it will overpopulate, overshooting that carrying capacity. If that happens, it will eventually degrade the renewable resources upon which it depends and exhaust key nonrenewable resources. It is also natural that even once the problem becomes evident, it takes significant time for the species to metabolize that information psychologically, culturally, and socially—and muster the coordinated will necessary to adapt on a species-wide level.

Our predicament is therefore perhaps best viewed as natural and, perhaps—to some extent, at least—inevitable. Our evolutionary emergency *might* be an entirely predictable phenomenon. This gives us an intelligent basis for relaxing the (rather useless) tendency to fret that humanity has somehow committed a terrible sin, or at least mistake. We can stop pointing our finger at a culprit, blaming others, or blaming *anything*—even human greed, laziness, or bullheadedness; even Cartesian paradigms of separation, or patriarchal social psychology, or mechanistic mindsets. We can instead arrive in the present moment, as an intelligent species—one that has traced a remarkable trajectory across human history and now has further to go.

After emerging from our crudest origins, we developed language, agriculture, writing, and literature, and built cathedrals. We then gained an understanding not only of Newtonian science, through which we industrialized, and then also of relativity and quantum theory, and then genetics, neuroscience, and information science, leading to the internet, nanotechnology, robotics, and an accelerating future of unimaginable technological breakthroughs. Now our knowledge—*and, more important, our consciousness*—is approaching a singularity too. It is not merely advancing, but accelerating at unimaginable speed toward radical change. A great transition is inevitable, either to a life-sustaining society or to a gritty, diminished human future.

The key to the future of human evolution cannot be reduced to any single factor or domain. It can't just be ecological, technological, cultural, physical, or social. It will certainly be all those things, but the transformations this evolutionary pressure elicits may also be—may *need* to be—spiritual, ontological, and psychological. We are talking about not just the evolution of the human mind or body, but the evolution of the human spirit.

Our entire way of being with ourselves and one another—individually, mutually, and collectively—is now under evolutionary pressure to manifest radical new emergent properties. This, I believe, creates the conditions for tremendous potential and hope.

The Integral Revolution

Everything that from eternity has happened in heaven and earth, the life of God and all the deeds of time simply are the struggles for Spirit to know itself, to find itself . . . and finally unite itself to itself; it is alienated and divided, but only so as to be able thus to find itself and return to itself.

—GEORG WILHELM FRIEDRICH HEGEL

With science we touch the True, the "It" of Spirit. With morals we touch the Good, the "We" of Spirit. What, then, would an integral approach have to say about the Beautiful, the "I" of Spirit itself? What is the Beauty that is in the eye of the Beholder? When we are in the eye of Spirit, the I of Spirit, what do we finally see?

—KEN WILBER, *THE EYE OF SPIRIT*

To make progress in addressing the crises imperiling humanity and Earth, we must find ways to effect radical transformations in our understanding and knowing. I will describe a way of understanding and knowing—often referred to as the *integral* approach—that I have found extremely valuable in my own trajectory of learning. My experience has shown me that this approach educates and enlarges our cognitive capacities for addressing many kinds of challenges—and for making fuller use (theoretical and practical) of the holistic, spiritual, scientific, and evolutionary perspectives.

Over the last two decades, one of the most significant trends in contemporary culture, and one of the most needed, has been the emergence of an *integral impulse*—an instinct to see through confused categories and myriad specialties to apprehend what's really happening as a whole. Our language, habits, and minds tend to draw lines dividing up reality in ways that are real only to our minds. Our specialized knowledge domains create fragmented perspectives on our world—which is incredibly complex and fast-moving, but in fact undivided and whole. Reality is an undivided whole in which we can discern a dance of whole systems that are themselves composed of smaller wholes, and so on, "all the way down" to our very cells, molecules, atoms, and quarks. One term for such an understanding of wholeness-in-diversity is the word "integral."

While we can call anyone who understands and practices wholeness an "integral" thinker and practitioner, or "integralist" (since integration is truly central to their work), there are also movements, communities, institutions, and individuals that explicitly understand what they are doing in terms of such greater integration, and some of them call themselves "integral." This is important, challenging, and paradoxical work, because wholeness is profoundly elusive, especially when our world is complexifying and fragmenting so rapidly. Once we seriously commit to and intentionally orient ourselves toward wholeness, we can embody a *deliberately* more inclusive and coherent approach to every aspect of our lives.

From 2004 to 2007 I participated in an extraordinary experiment in integral culture. In late 2003, integral philosopher Ken Wilber and his nascent organization, the Integral Institute (I-I), announced its first public seminar for early the following year. It felt like a historic moment. I had never spent so much money on a seminar before, but there was no question: I had to be there. And I was not disappointed; the seminar was astonishingly intelligent, open-hearted, multidimensional, and alive, and I found the people who gathered there entirely delightful.

Wilber's ideas had attracted thousands of intelligent and interesting people, and a community of discourse constellated around his work. I was almost immediately invited to join the core team he was assembling, and very quickly I was warmed and inspired not only by the level of depth and excellence of my colleagues and the way we engaged with our projects, but by the rich matrix of key "integral" and "evolutionary" insights, across a range of fields, that inspired so many of us. Moreover, we collaborated on a series of ambitious projects. We offered several dozen public seminars on Integral Life Practice, Integral Leadership, Integral Psychology, Integral Ecology and Sustainability, and Integral Spirituality. We developed rich integral practices and curricula for all these and many more fields of study.

Because the investigation was so alive, many of us were inspired to take the integral project into new frontiers, cooperating with scholars and practitioners in many fields, especially those working closely with the structures and stages of adult development. But the Integral Institute, after growing rapidly for a few years, never became fully sustainable. We managed many tensions and factors as well as we could, but our challenges ultimately proved too formidable. At the end of 2006 and the beginning of 2007, I-I essentially went into hibernation for a decade, while many of its initiatives were advanced by a great number of new, independent enterprises.

Much of I-I's original spirit survived, though. And it has matured, diversified, and found many new expressions. Alumni of that original effort have founded graduate-level programs, international conferences, businesses, workshops, schools, online communities, podcasts, and a whole ecosystem of diverse projects. The integral movement continues to grow, interpenetrating many other leading-edge initiatives. Instead of being focused only on furthering "the integral project," it has become an integral evolutionary ecosystem—a loose-knit network of practitioners, scholars, and communities who creatively cooperate with practitioners in many areas of culture and society. That mutual dynamism is lighting up new pixels of the next new emerging picture of human consciousness and culture. Since those early days other thinkers have brought additional rich distinctions that have added further levels of sophistication, such as Edgar Morin's "complex thought," Otto Laske's "dialectical thinking," and Steve McIntosh's integral philosophical work, as well as the metatheoretical critiques of Roy Bashkar, Sean Esbjörn-Hargens, Mark Edwards, Bonnita Roy, and others.

Wilber's integral philosophy is widely used, even at some of the highest levels of government and business. Although it has numerous detractors, it nonetheless provides critical attitudes, approaches, and analytic frameworks that make it possible to follow an evolutionary trajectory, grounded in wholeness, into—and, hopefully, through—the crises we face. I discuss Wilber in considerable detail here because he is by far the most influential and thorough integral theorist, as well as being a close colleague and a huge influence on my thinking. But integral consciousness is widely distributed. There are now many integral thinkers, philosophers, and cultural leaders, all of whom recognize a new worldview beyond postmodernism. Many embrace the label "integral"; but many other cultural innovators aren't self-consciously "integral," and yet reflect and express what I recognize as a growing integral awareness. A diverse body of lively discourse continues within and beyond the integral community, and that emergent conversation is critical to how I think it will play its full and absolutely critical cultural role.

THE INTEGRAL FLAVOR

When I first encountered Wilber's integral theory, it was hardly news to me that I live in a diverse world shaped by the interactions of contradictory perspectives. Phenomena really do appear to be different from different vantage points. But even people who know better are frequently drawn to "either/or" thinking. In that frame, one person or viewpoint is right and another is wrong. It is at these moments of impasse that integral theory illuminates new possibilities. Integral theory does not ask

"Who is right?" but "How do we make sense out of multiple apparently contradictory perspectives?" As Wilber has written, "Nobody is smart enough to be wrong 100 percent of the time," and, especially resonantly, "Every perspective is both true and partial."

It is impossible to overemphasize the significance of this insight. If every perspective is both true and partial, then there is real truth in what we see. And there is real truth seen by those who disagree with us. *And there is more to reality than anybody can see.* This insight frees us from the traps of false certainties, into a much wider awareness. It makes "epistemic closure"—the closed-minded certainty that we are right—yield to "epistemic humility"—the embodied understanding that knowledge is a process that is always evolving, so it is best to be curious and open and to always question our certainties. Fortunately, this is not the exclusive province of integral evolutionaries. It is also reflected in popular sentiments like "The more I learn, the more I realize I don't know." Such an attitude enables us to listen, and to hear, so that we can find ways to bridge the divides between us that are harming us all.

When you think about it, healthy, intelligent people naturally develop skepticism about their own views and evolve in their thinking. At some point in their maturation, what I would call a distinctly integral "flavor" begins to characterize their disposition. But this is raised to another level when it is informed by spiritual insight. In the Platform Sutra, a Buddhist scripture, the Sixth Patriarch instructed his disciples, "Should someone ask you about a dharma answer him with its opposite. If you always answer with the opposite, as [opposites] depend upon each other for their existence, both will be eliminated and nothing will be left behind." Thus, the radical wholeness of being is illuminated—form not separate from the formless, action not separate from nondoing, etc., across "the thirty-six pairs of opposites." And this illumination is central to the integral project, which is informed not just by higher cognitive complexity but also by higher states of consciousness.

Here I describe the ideal that tends to influence and organize integral sensibilities. It is rarely if ever realized fully, as I am describing it here. But this is the spirit that informs this emerging structure of consciousness.

This integral disposition, because it is essentially holistic at heart, tends not to get involved in the timeworn disputes between left and right, progress and nature, science and spirituality. It understands and appreciates the partial truths in the attitudes of conflicting worldviews. It is both serene and engaged. It is suspicious of antimodernist (or postmodern) angst and pessimism, even while appreciating the foundational importance of a healthy biosphere. It doesn't resonate with the politics of blind anger or knee-jerk reactivity. It can be intensely proscience without falling into rigid scientistic skepticism. It is rational, and yet is also emotionally connected and intuitively awake. It is spiritually awake without falling into magical thinking or naive belief. It consistently intends action without indulging reaction. It orients to possibility. And it takes the long view.

These qualities are beginning to surface in many places. Philosopher Jurgen Habermas expresses an integral flavor of consciousness without being associated with the word or with the "evolutionary" conversation. Some integral awareness has begun to color the thinking of mainstream figures from Pope Francis to Barack Obama to David Brooks. Futurists such as Stewart Brand, Kevin Kelley, Larry Page, Bill Gates, John Mackey, Nick Bostrom, and countless others imagine the trajectory of modern science and technology, occasionally veering into new, integrationist territory. Some European intellectuals, including Habermas, Peter Sloterdijk, Alain Badiou, and Bruno Latour, are bringing a more integral flavor into postmodern philosophical discourse. They are joined on this side of the Atlantic not just by explicitly integral theorists like Steve McIntosh, but also by diverse original thinkers from outside that ecosystem like Jeremy Lent (a postreductive cognitive historian) and Holmes Rolston III (a prominent philosopher of science and religion). Social entrepreneurs inspired by Muhammad Yunus, Paul Hawken, Van Jones, and Charles Eisenstein are expressing the beginnings of an integral flavor that is evolving among ecological activists and others on the American left. People with integral awareness are being attracted to political careers all around the world. There is integral and evolutionary consciousness appearing in the rising shamanic movement, characterized by embodied feeling-knowledge, rational scientific discernment, and multidimensional awareness. These represent only a tiny sample among hundreds of equally valid examples. If we choose to lean in and engage with their insights, we can discover some tangible hope for our collective future.

INTEGRAL ATTITUDES AND ALTITUDES

Wilber's integral theory not only invites an open and engaged attitude, it also offers some key "orienting generalizations" that reveal how different perspectives relate to each other. Wilber observes the universal structure of how the world's great spiritual traditions map the process of "waking up" from the dream of separated existence into wholeness and then into high meditative states of consciousness, and he recommends meditation as a central integral practice. He distinguishes this, however, from the equally important process of "growing up" into a more conscious and complex order of mind, which we will discuss here.

Shifts in how we think occur across the human life span in a remarkable process that builds in complexity and self-reflection. New capacities for understanding experience arise when one's very patterns of thought and perception can be contemplated. As developmentalist Robert Kegan says, new levels of cognition "make what was formerly subject object," turning what had been invisibly shaping our perception (subject) into a conscious object of awareness. So, for example, while an infant is completely subsumed in and identified with his feelings and sensations, like hunger, the developing child begins to observe those sensations and make choices in relation to them—deciding, for example, to postpone lunch in order to play.

New stages of development offer us greater degrees of freedom from instinctive responses, habits of thought, or patterns of feeling. Each new level *transcends and includes* what went before, so that the new capacities develop out of older ones. It's as if we have a higher altitude, a "bird's-eye view" from which to see it all. For instance, our capacity to read and understand abstract thought stands on the shoulders of our capacity for language—abstract thinking wouldn't be possible without language. Just as in material evolution, where atoms are the building blocks of molecules that are in turn the component parts of cells that together form organisms, human development is a holarchy[25] of "wholes within wholes within wholes," something quite distinct from a hierarchy of value. Atoms are not inferior to molecules. A five-year-old is not a defective twelve-year-old. But there are distinctions between their characteristics and capacities.

Integralists connect the insights of human development with cultural evolution. As we just saw, historically significant worldviews are powerful, multigenerational, large-scale systems of agreement that dictate how we frame reality and our own identities. They take root only over time. A truly integral worldview, according to Wilber, would necessarily embrace the enduring insights that come from each of the previous waves of cultural development. We can understand this by looking at just three major structures—the *premodern* (or *traditionalist*), *modern,* and *postmodern* worldviews.

The premodern worldview is authoritarian, religious, and traditional. The modern is achievement-oriented, egalitarian, and rational. Postmodern worldviews emphasize compassionate sensitivity to self and others, challenging objectivity and expressing liberal, pluralistic ideals. These worldviews exist in a historical relationship: premodern, traditionalist cultures began about five thousand years ago, modern about five hundred years ago, and the postmodern only 150 years ago—emerging more fully in the liberation movements of the 1960s. The tensions between these worldviews are the all-too-familiar stuff of our current "culture wars."

It is important to realize that individuals cannot be slotted into a single worldview; we usually express a unique mix of cognition, values, emotional maturity, interpersonal awareness, or any of several dozen other distinct lines of intelligence, each of which can express different levels of development. But all of us are deeply patterned by these dominant worldviews, and most often we primarily resonate with one of them.

Integral philosophy offers a potent potential synthesis that includes and transcends traditional, modern, and postmodern perspectives on reality. It recognizes that the later historical worldviews are built on the foundation of those that came before, and yet appreciates that even the more advanced perspectives tend to be blind to certain values and realities that the other worldviews see and care about strongly, and blind also to the critical interdependence of these worldviews. Because an integral disposition is able to contain and be comfortable with apparent contradictions, when fully mature it is able to naturally, spontaneously, and comfortably include certain aspects of the dispositions of all worldviews. This book often speaks in rational modern and pluralistic postmodern terms. In that language I am endeavoring to integrate the necessary foundational virtues of traditionalist people, values, and institutions, and also to learn from indigenous and tribal people.

An integral disposition understands that we will always be living in a world in which these apparently conflicting worldviews and identities (but potentially synergistic energies) coexist. In short, an integral perspective helps us to comprehend the problems that we face and to better understand and work with other human beings in all their diversity, thus contributing to a healthy culture. Each of these other worldviews, by its nature, tends to be locked in certain zero-sum certainties about the nature of reality in which their viewpoint is viewed as right and all others are wrong. Structures that cannot open to a higher integration underpin every side of our culture wars. A mature integral worldview has the potential to skillfully rise above the fray, accept the value of all the other viewpoints, and reweave the cultural fabric.

Integral theory has a paradoxical relationship to human development—and some of the critics of integral theory fail to see the rich two-sidedness of these developmental categories. Unlike many postmodernists and traditionalists, integralists appreciate and strongly advocate for development. On the other hand, integral theory's theoretical foundations show us a legitimate basis for the idea that wisdom and right relationship to things occurs at all levels—and that the "later" levels of development must learn from the "earlier" levels, as well as the other way around. For example, there is a valid basis for an integral valorization of the wisdom and leadership of indigenous peoples.

It is true that the "higher" we develop, the more complex, conscious, and interconnected our cognitive structures become, and the more adequately they can account for the complex nuances of our world. On the other hand, at an "earlier" moment in that developmental process, one is more firmly rooted in the body and the living earth and its psyche and *anima mundi,* and is less likely to become pathologically disconnected, lost in complexity. The "bottom" is the most basic and central, and deserving of profound respect and even reverence. So every developmental scale can also sometimes appropriately be inverted to value what is most important and appreciate the foundational nature of what preceded us.

THREE COMPETING WORLDVIEWS
AND FOUR QUADRANTS

Ken Wilber's philosophical distinctions have been widely influential—in part because of the way they understand and integrate the scientific, psychological, sociological, philosophical, and spiritual understandings of all worldviews. Such a synthesis allows us to see what we are facing from different angles in a way that makes a more comprehensive response possible. Although there are important worldviews—*archaic, magical,* and *warrior*—that came into human existence earlier than the "traditional" worldview, and even though new "integral" worldviews are emerging that go beyond the postmodern worldview, we will focus first on clarifying further the three competing points of view that are dominant among educated people: the *premodern* (or *traditional*), *modern,* and *postmodern* worldviews.

Integral theory emphasizes two key understandings that originated in the traditional, premodern worldview and yet are only now becoming explored more deeply by great numbers of people. First, the deeper, often secret, mystical traditions of the world's religions offer us an extraordinary map of the higher meditative states of human consciousness that shows remarkable consistency across mystical traditions. Second, the perennial philosophy, the common essence of the world's great ancient wisdom traditions, recognizes various levels of existence, of "being and knowing," from Matter to Life to Mind to Soul to Spirit. This spectrum can be found in Plotinus and it permeates the great traditions, including the writings of innumerable religious scholars. This "great chain (or nest) of being" was thought to have been "given" by God, expressing an inherent divine holarchy.[26]

The modern rational worldview is the lingua franca of the kind of serious scholarship and discourse that gave rise to integral philosophy. Wilber created his four-quadrant map of human knowledge by starting with the disciplines found in any modern university—for example, biology, physics, psychology, archaeology, literature, government, anthropology, and engineering. Wilber notes that each describes evolution moving through progressive stages or waves—but in entirely different terms.

Physics, chemistry, and biology focus on and measure different aspects of "exterior" material reality and derive understandings of the laws that govern the physiology and behavior of individual atoms, molecules, stars, galaxies, planets, and organisms. *Psychotherapy, spirituality, art, and literature* focus on the interior reality of individual human beings. *Systems sciences, including much of economics and ecology,* focus on understanding the dynamics of the collective exterior behaviors of people or of living or nonliving systems. *Ethics and many social sciences* focus on understanding the agreements that structure the interior lives of groups.

Just two fundamental distinctions—between interiors and exteriors, and between individuals and collectives—delineate these four domains. Each represents a fundamental dimension of reality, where we can see the evolution of intentions and values (interiors of individuals), of behavior (exteriors of individuals), of culture (interiors of collectives), and of systems (exteriors of collectives). Taken together, these four quadrants account for the relationship between the different dimensions of reality and areas of knowledge. This schema brings to light the unique and necessary perspective that each offers, and suggests that all four domains are needed to understand any important situation and to design adequate solutions. (See Figure 1.)

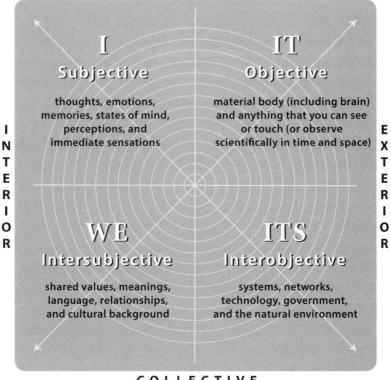

Figure 1: The Four Quadrants

Integral consciousness also values the sensitivity and awareness contained in the postmodern worldview, which appreciates the simultaneous validity of different cultures' ways of being, and of multiple perspectives in general, as well as the importance of our inner lives. By experimenting with different approaches to psychological research, psychotherapy, spiritual practice, alternative healing modalities, and psychedelics, adventurous postmoderns have explored many dimensions of human interiors, gaining knowledge central to the integral synthesis. Additionally, there is deep postmodern appreciation for the whole web of life and for ecological sustainability.

Nevertheless, as integral philosophers have pointed out, postmodernism has also—especially in academic circles—become a bastion of a "liberal" orthodoxy that has often stifled inquiry and dissent and contributed to cultural polarization. And yet integral consciousness matures out of the basic insights of postmodernism, recognizing that traditional perspectives, for example, reveal different partial truths. This complements the objective knowledge of modern rational science, permitting a holistic appreciation of the fullness of both objective and subjective dimensions of human experience, knowledge, inquiry, and progress.

Integralists understand that it is not possible to engage productively with the human predicament without accounting for these multiple dimensions of reality—all quadrants and all perspectives. And that means engaging with the hopes, needs, and desires of human beings who hold different worldviews and identities, and who speak different languages, and whose thinking emerges from different disciplines. We need to understand each perspective more fully—realizing that they each live in us. Our own unconscious desire to distance ourselves from elements of earlier worldviews creates blind spots, or shadows, that often make connection and creativity nearly impossible.

Human consciousness first emerged among people preoccupied with survival and focused on meeting very basic needs, expressing *archaic consciousness*. We matured into an ancient tribal *magical consciousness,* which was probably our first semicoherent worldview. Out of that consciousness, the power gods prevailed, and the *might-makes-right warrior consciousness* of our earliest kingdom societies emerged. These are the stages previous to the "traditional" consciousness described below. All these worldviews still hold sway over many individuals—and recently we have seen numerous examples on the world stage, where the "might makes right" position has waxed resurgent—even though, in the broader view, these forms of consciousness have waned in influence over the last five thousand years.

Now we will delve more deeply into the three major worldviews that dominate most of our world today, and explore the characteristics of individuals who most strongly hold each of these worldviews. A caveat is in order here: In real life, very few people express any of these worldviews in an entirely pure form. Most of us express a hybrid. But because the structures we are discussing are enormously powerful, we will take the liberty of talking about them using broad generalizations, because doing so illuminates even more than it obscures.

TRADITIONALISM TODAY

Traditionalists embody many of the premodern values that have always enabled human beings to bond and cooperate with other members of their ethnic and religious groups. Early on, human beings evolved powerful neurological mechanisms that hardwire us to our families and tribes. Within the "us" of our tribe, we know where we stand. We are also hardwired to appreciate the values of authority, conformity, loyalty, and perceived purity that align us with "our" goodness and order against "their" evil and chaos. The view is binary, absolute, black-and-white. Thus, at the dawn of the world's great religious traditions, the law was harsh, but people became able to nobly sacrifice themselves for God and country and other higher values. The capacity to subordinate one's self-interest for the sake of duty is the glue of every civilized society. Traditionalism is the foundation of civilization, and the context of the other values below.

Traditionalists are often easily recognizable. Their opinions in—and influence on—the public sphere, particularly in the United States, subject them to caricature, and their influence on almost all aspects of public life is often a cause for concern among modernists and postmodernists. But, while traditionalism is evidenced in members of all races and national-ities, when viewed in its more political aspects in the United States—including the "culture war" against political progressives, environmental activists, and the international neoliberal consensus—it is much more associated with white traditionalists than with African Americans, His-panics, Asians, or native peoples. (In fact, traditionalists among these other groups tend by and large to be fairly liberal politically, especially in areas of social justice, but also in other areas, including acceptance of environmental science. Here ethnic identity is the strongest governing factor.) Further, in spite of our tendency to think in terms of "red states" and "blue states," traditionalism is much more associated with rural or small-town life than with urban life. This distinction applies almost anywhere in the U.S. Small towns in inland California are generally much more conservative than large cities in the South or Midwest. Another characteristic of traditionalists—one that is true across the board—is a much stronger adherence to traditional religious faith.

Traditionalists continue to be very important players in contemporary society. Because of the virtues cultivated in traditional families, traditionalists are in many respects the finest among us. In America and all over the world, people who live in rural areas, people with a strong work ethic, people focused on the security of their family and its traditions, and people who attend church regularly are more likely to have traditional values and worldviews. The best of them are hardworking, resourceful, and resilient. In spite of their often politicized and negative views of such issues as climate science, many of these people are living with more direct contact with the living earth and nature than are many "green" city dwellers. They may get up before dawn to work, and go to bed early. Many have businesses; they are also often the soldiers, police, and firefighters, the first-responders who put their lives on the line to protect their communities and the nation. They are our cousins and neighbors, the people with whom we share this country. Ironically, traditionalists often embody the virtues that postmodernists put forth, such as care and a real sense of community. They prioritize their families and their church and neighborhood communities, and their levels of civic engagement are typically much higher than most urban nontraditionalists. Their experience of life is not as constantly mediated by mental and virtual abstractions as that of urban-dwelling knowledge workers.

In spite of their often holding rigid belief systems, in most cases beliefs do not define traditionalists as much as actions and behaviors. Traditionalists tend to be practical, direct, and focused on objective, tangible realities. So they work hard, emphasize self-responsibility, and deplore dependency. They hunt and fish and start their own businesses.

When they enter the political arena, and chant "drill, baby, drill" (and enlightened modern and postmodern minds take offense), it is often not based merely on a disregard for climate science and common sense (or whatever other factors apply). It might be, to a greater degree, because they resent the often less self-responsible lives of many postmoderns and moderns. That, combined with the righteous moral superiority and deconstructive relativism of contemporary postmodern culture, and the occasionally vindictive or suppressive excesses of those enforcing political correctness, are the factors that have made them angry, and account for the militancy of their anger—even the fortress mentality in which they pit themselves against overeducated urban "outsiders" who appear to be threatening their freedoms and traditions, forcing other lifestyles on them, and delivering their country to foreigners.

There is, of course, a big catch. The complexities of contemporary culture evolved more recently than traditional worldviews—they are the cultural extension of the mindsets of agrarian societies. Conformism doesn't encourage curiosity. So traditionalists are "over their heads" in our postmodern world. Traditionalists tend to interpret the experience in black-and-white terms that are most strongly dictated by the attitudes of the group with whom they identify, as handed down by established authorities. This enables them to march "in lockstep," which makes them more politically powerful.

Anciently, traditionalists knew what was true by looking to authorities—to the Bible or to Aristotle or to the edicts of the pope or king. The willingness to conform to authority was a hallmark of traditional morality. Even today, traditionalists often treat the theology, prescientific notions, and worldviews of ancient scriptures as more valid than the knowledge produced by the scientific method. In contemporary life, the leaders of traditional churches, political organizations, and partisan media serve this function, becoming enormously powerful. Their "rank and file" willingly embrace a shared social identity and easily conform to its norms. This means they are not really thinking rationally, in modern terms. They think their traditions and beliefs have proved more trustable over time than abstract scientific arguments.

Basic traditional patterns underlie the structure of every individual mind. We all can feel the powerful hardwired pull of the approval and disapproval of the communities and groups to which we belong. That is why traditionalism remains the most foundational "source code" for generating social agreements. These codes are how we most readily create strong families and sustainable communities. When sustainability is able to work *for* traditionalists, they will be powerful champions of the struggle for a human civilization that supports a healthy biosphere.

MODERN RATIONALITY

In school we learn the historical story of the Renaissance, the Age of Enlightenment, the scientific revolution, the industrial revolution, and now the digital revolution. This story is usually told as the victory of reason and its miraculous powers over primitive "superstition." The modern rational worldview champions universal values such as evidence-based scientific knowledge, individual rights, excellence and achievement, the rule of law, and meritocratic competition in a free market. It brings intelligent long-term strategic thinking, innovation, and nuanced accountability. Modernity is focused on material reality, regarding empirical scientific proof as the most important if not the only foundation for valid knowledge. (During the Enlightenment, modern thinkers called for Christians to "read the book of nature" rather than only consulting the Bible.)

Modernism ascended on the world scene about five hundred years ago, together with science and free markets, and it is still the dominant worldview in Western culture. Even though modern capitalist societies have famously disenchanted the world and devastated the biosphere, they also have radically expanded human knowledge, abolished slavery, recognized universal human rights, engendered democracy, and uplifted material conditions for the vast majority of human beings.

At its best, modernism is optimistic, industrious, intelligent, and able to achieve its goals. At its worst, it is arrogant, believing it knows *the* truth, dividing the world between "winners" and "losers," and losing track of larger concerns, including the deeper values of the human soul. Placing its faith in entrepreneurial capitalism and free markets, it tends to be highly competitive and driven to succeed. However, it is also capable of thinking long-term in world-centric rather than merely ethnocentric terms. Its "neoliberal consensus" has produced the technocratic regime of open markets in a global economy. This modernist project is personified by the Brussels bureaucrats leading the EU and by American coastal elites from the Ivy League to Wall Street to Silicon Valley.

Modernism is characterized by meritocratic ideals in which "the best and the brightest" are rewarded with money and prestige. A morality of proportionality (you should get what you deserve), also evident in traditionalism, takes strong hold in modernism. It also values personal effort and problem-solving for the greater good. The result is success begetting success—but the intoxication of repeated successes in one area can lead to a narrowness of vision, overconfidence, and addiction to technical fixes that may create or exacerbate destructive downstream results, or "unintended consequences."

The modern mind's intelligence and power come in part from the empowerment of individuality—the separation of the human individual's subjective consciousness from the objects he observes. The transition to modernity gave birth to an individuated self who could literally "think for himself" in the way that his or her predecessors could not. From that original separation or fragmentation, many more flowed. Traditional separations of human culture from nature and of mind from body were no longer expressions of divine order but were seen as expressions of objective reality and human physiology—the reality of a fragmented world of separate entities. Reason was exalted as superior to unreliable emotion and intuition. And further separation followed. The "knowledge disciplines" differentiated ever more areas of specialization, making distinctions between psychology and philosophy, endocrinology and medicine, cytology and biology, and human-computer interface design and computer science—and hyper-specialization is continuing apace.

Differentiation, however, easily slides into dissociation, which is another reason the great dignities of modernity have been accompanied by the disasters of the modern era. Science investigates only the observable exteriors of reality, the factors that can be sensed and measured, so it has come to dominate (or, as Habermas put it, to "colonize") the inner lives of human individuals, collectives, and all nonhuman life. Modern culture, in fact, through its power to objectify and differentiate, principally engages in *instrumental reason,* which looks to determine the most efficient means to an end—often disregarding costs to other human beings, the natural world and the web of life, and even one's own soul. A holistic "vision-logic" is required in order to reason beyond such short-sightedness and to advance practical wisdom, and this gap sows the seeds for a cognitive advance into postmodern structures of thought.

It is not appropriate to blame modernists for their limitations, any more than it is appropriate to blame traditionalists for theirs. It is not obvious to the modernist faculty of reason that it has itself developed or evolved. It confuses its newfound capability of reflecting on what it sees in a detached manner with literally standing apart from the world and seeing it for what it is. The illusion of objectivity can give rise to profound arrogance. Subjective psyche, soul, spirit, and life itself are then regarded as unreliable epiphenomena of material processes (which Wilber memorably describes as "frisky dirt"). Humanity's ancient wisdom in the domains of art, morals, and spirituality is seen as merely poetic and of no value in providing information, nor in unveiling truth and reality. Scientism usurps the actual practice of science. Modern culture gradually discarded what had been learned about the growth of the soul into higher levels of consciousness. Our traditional moral developmental curriculum was regarded as quaint and obsolete. The higher transrational dimensions of the human being were conflated with prerational "superstitions" and delegitimized.

While I think it is fair to critique modernism harshly, we must honor it and engage many of its terms of discourse. It is important not to throw the baby out with the bathwater. It is said, with real justification, that modernism went too far, and became emotionally dissociated, spiritually dead, and impoverished of compassion, feeling, and communitarian instincts. Modern rational discourse is, however, an enormous achievement. It is perhaps our irreplaceable common ground, the only way that human beings can talk with one another to adjudicate our disagreements peacefully.

We live in a world populated mostly by premodern minds but whose public and official center of gravity is modern. Traditional participants in the public sphere have learned its rules of discourse, as have postmodernists. Reason is the common language through which we can conduct public dialogue about our shared interests as human beings, and through which we can bring intelligence and wisdom to our collective decision making. We have enough of a cultural consensus around evidence, science, and reason that they provide the best common language through which we can reach our political, social, and collective decisions. Therefore, modernism provides the structure of meaning-making, the common language into which we must learn to translate whatever else we might want to say. We can bring in new values, ones that are not at the core of the preexisting neoliberal capitalist consensus; but if we justify them in rational terms, we can communicate with people who do not share our worldview. Communicating across these barriers is precious, and it may be the linchpin of our survival.

A crucial cultural task for all intelligent people is to revivify and raise the level of rational discourse, and make it relevant and potent in a whole new way. We will certainly need to allow it to include important dimensions of reality that it has until now tended to exclude, and to awaken it from unexamined assumptions and habits. But our crisis demands that we find ways to engage in real, vigorous, culture-wide inquiry. And rational public discourse must be refreshed and restored, not torn down by the cynical "post-truth" zero-sum ("I win—you lose") tactics of political and cultural factions. Our current task involves reknitting our social fabric, through principled appeals to reason and care for our common well-being.

POSTMODERN CONSCIOUSNESS

The limitations of the modern worldview could not be resolved except by evolving new awareness, which gave rise to the postmodern worldview. Postmodern consciousness notices the limitations of "objective" knowledge, seeing that there is no such thing as radical objectivity. Where you stand dictates what you can see. The language you speak determines the questions you can ask and the answers you can hear.

Postmodern consciousness also notices the limitations of knowledge and wealth, of science and progress. It notices the structural injustices built into the "meritocratic" marketplaces of the modern world, and advocates for marginalized groups—from indigenous people to those of color, to colonized subjects, to women, and now to gender-nonconforming individuals. And it is sensitive to the sated unhappiness that so often results from our consumer culture's "good life." It knows that "whoever dies with the most toys" wins only a soulless game. It pays attention to feelings, relationships, communication, psychology, and spirituality.

Postmodern sensibilities see and feel the spiritual bankruptcy of mere egoic competitive success, especially when it runs roughshod over the sensitivities of the human spirit and the ecological health of the natural world. The "sensitive self" that arises in postmodernity feels its relationship to all living creatures, the entire living Earth. Some of its most profound expressions are depth psychology and ecopsychology, which are rooted in the attitude of deep ecology. The mind awakens to a re-enchanted natural world and sees nature's *inherent* value, independent of its instrumental value to human beings.

The political thrust of postmodernism has been to deconstruct the narratives that have supported all forms of institutionalized injustice—racial, religious, gender-based, and ecological. It sees that scientific knowledge is never perfectly objective, and that it is sometimes characterized by myopia and arrogance. But it easily takes this too far. Extreme postmodern relativism deconstructs all knowledge, all truths, viewing them as nothing more than social constructions. Although this critique is very sophisticated, it has seeped into the larger culture, creating an opening that has been cynically exploited to produce our "post-truth" cultural moment. It is a distinctly *postmodern* rationale that apologists for *traditional* values have used to justify a rejection of any *modern* rational accountability. Postmodernism has inadvertently assisted in cultural regression.

The philosophical sophistication of the postmodern critique contrasts with the sclerotic nature of much postmodern discourse. It tends to be critically handicapped by "political correctness"—stuck in a cumbersome style of discourse characterized by enforced terminologies, reflexive acceptance of attitudes of victimization and grievance, and laborious consensus decision making. It is no wonder that postmodernism has never been able to marshal more than marginal cultural, social, and political power.

Many centers of postmodern culture have so completely lost touch with important traditional and modern virtues that they have been willing to judge and scorn vast swaths of people, asserting moral superiority. Ironically, given their concerns for the well-being and rights of others, they have not been aware of the ways in which they, as individuals, fail to embody some of the virtues of hardworking traditionalists. To traditionalists, postmoderns seem even more extreme, dissociated, and arrogant than the neoliberal elites. To traditionalists who appreciate, want, and need the stability of the values that have been the foundation of our social agreements for a long time, postmodernists seem like extreme modernists. In their most extreme expressions, they not only deny all traditional authorities, like the church and the state, but they seem bent on dynamiting them and the foundations of order in society. Postmodernists seem to want to release all the impulses, desires, and cravings that traditional religious morality has only barely managed to keep in check.

While rattling traditionalists, postmodern culture is often focused on battling modernism. (When new stages of consciousness arise in response to the limitations of the previous stage, there tends to be a hypersensitivity to those limitations.) Seeing that the modern mind has lost contact with higher states and stages of consciousness, the postmodern mind may idealize non-Western spirituality. Just as the modern mind cannot see how it has developed out of traditionalism, postmodern consciousness cannot see that it develops out of and depends on a foundation of modern rationality. It sees the modern mind as having separated itself from the great web of life so radically that it inherently tends to destroy it. In its eyes, the great "evil" is modernity—and those who pursue its agendas. Modernity's bias toward "doing," toward mascu-line agency in dominating the world, is another problem, one that needs to be balanced, postmodernists feel, by a return to feminine communion with nature.

Seeing how those at the bottom are victimized by hierarchies of dom-ination, postmodern consciousness tends to be instinctively hostile to all hierarchies. Many postmodern thinkers resist even the richly doc-umented stages of development that Wilber regards as fundamental. Wilber has written widely about how the relativism and aversion to hier-archy that characterize postmodern consciousness have tended to interact with the narcissism of the Boomer, Gen X, and millennial generations to produce a toxic stew of worldview pathologies—self-indulgence, self-righteousness, cynicism, dystopic ecology, and New Age wishful think-ing. Instead of leading cultural evolution, this postmodernist-influenced culture presents a barrier to individual and collective health and growth. By deconstructing all truths, unhealthy postmodernism often tends to obstruct rather than advance further cultural evolution. And by con-fusing the rigor and optimism of integral consciousness (more on this below) with the "evils" of modernism, it resists the truths described here.

However, there is an important area where postmodernity has it right, and that is in recognizing our ecological predicament as the defin-ing issue of our time. As previously discussed, current trends are as severe as the most extreme doom-saying environmental catastrophists ever prophesized. Worldviews arise in relation to changing life conditions—and the life conditions arising now in an era of rapid climate change are most directly addressed by the postmodern worldview.

If we want to navigate a world in ecological crisis, we need many of the insights and sensitivities of the postmodern mind. The more evolved worldview, beyond postmodernism, can itself be called "integral." Like every new stage of development, the integral viewpoint has come into being in response to the limitations of the previous stage, and it is highly sensitive to its pathologies. In distinguishing itself from postmodernism, integral culture has not yet asserted sufficiently effective moral leadership in relation to the ecological predicament. To perform its crucial cultural function it must not be locked in resistance to postmodern environmentalism and instead needs to uplift and energize the critical ecological agenda and empower the holistic transition it knows is necessary. Integral culture must be informed by the maturity inherent in integral consciousness itself, with its built-in inclusiveness and openness to each level of truth.

INTEGRAL CONSCIOUSNESS

Integral consciousness notices the fragmented world that postmodern "aperspectival madness" produces, and intuits that a deeper, unnoticed wholeness lies underneath. Spontaneously, it begins to integrate humankind's many valid but conflicting perspectives. It intuits the possibility of a comprehensive understanding of a reality in which everything, including consciousness and culture, is always evolving. Integral awareness appreciates that all worldviews—primitive, traditional, modern, postmodern—are each in close contact with different enduring truths. And it feels a need to emerge from the limitations of postmodern habits in order to coherently account for the full range of reality—encompassing not only divinity but dirt, all the way down to subatomic particles. Integral consciousness tries to account for and honor *every* dimension of development and evolution and experience.

This integral disposition must begin to find its way into the attitudes of those who are beginning to grow beyond the limitations of postmodernism. The integral disposition in its truest realization is able to contain contradictions. It is able to comfortably contain certain aspects of the dispositions of both rational modernism and pluralistic postmodernism, even while authentically valuing traditionalist people, values, and institutions. On the one hand it is characterized by modernist optimism, a pragmatic, "just-do-it" sense of personal agency and cultural progress, and keen interest in long-term, large-scale strategic analysis and execution. On the other hand, it is also characterized by pluralistic cultural sensitivity, ecological care for all planetary life, egalitarian concern for the whole human family, deep appreciation for feminine sensibilities, and a warm communal impulse grounded in empathy and a sense of mutual belonging. It is spiritually alive, inspired, and informed by intelligent awakening and inner work. It is not, however, "New Agey" in its flavor, or anti-intellectual. And it is unwilling to be held hostage by any form of political correctness.

Ken Wilber's far-reaching review of intellectual history attempts to systematically account for all humankind's conflicting perspectives using just five powerful distinctions—quadrants, levels, lines, states, and types. Wilber presents a comprehensible and orderly "theory of everything." "AQAL" theory (standing for All Quadrants/All Levels—or all lines/ all states/all types) offers a masterful rhetoric that has helped stimulate tremendous insight and vigorous scholarship, dialogue, practice innovations, and activism.[27] This synthesis is exciting because it is structured in a way that can honor every possible expression of human experience in a single, multidimensional holistic embrace.

Another way of clarifying the unique characteristics of integral consciousness is by identifying the kinds of thinking associated with each worldview. *Formal operational thinking* (originally described by Jean Piaget) is most often associated with modernist consciousness, and it tends to perceive reality as presenting clear correct or incorrect alternatives, within a closed, positivistic world of objective exterior realities. *Early vision-logic,* or *relativistic* thinking, is most often associated with postmodern consciousness. It can see the validity of many perspectives, but it has difficulty seeing how they can be integrated. It is better at opposing limited views than synthesizing a clear new vision. *Middle vision-logic,* or *dialectical* thinking, perceives reality as a hyper-complex "process of processes" of changing dynamic systems and relationships that naturally tend toward growth and development. Such dialectical vision-logic naturally allows for both spiritual and material realities, both progress and ecology. It gives rise to *integral consciousness,* which naturally intuits how conflicting worldviews and perspectives, even when in apparent conflict, actually support one another in their mutual evolution. It sees with eyes that can notice new dimensions of dynamic complexity while never losing sight of wholeness.

RADICAL INTEGRAL ECOLOGY

As we have seen, most human beings are locked in a consensus denial of the severity of our ecological crisis. Among those willing to puncture that denial we often hear a clear and simple, morally based explanation of the recent history of human violence against the natural world. This postmodern narrative holds that the arrogance of white European Christian men, powered by modern science, the free market, and the history of colonialism, has been the primary source of imbalance in our world. Its primal sin, rooted in a presumption of separation between man and nature, self and other, has given rise to the horrific predicament of having overshot Earth's carrying capacity. According to that narrative, the modern mind, science, technology, and capitalism are evil—they are the source of our "evolutionary wrong turn."

I believe there is valid insight to be found in this true-but-partial story—quite a bit more than some integralists admit—but there is enormous distortion too. The modern stage of development is the necessary foundation for postmodern and integral consciousness. And modernists are postmodernists' irreplaceable allies if they are to restore respect for scientific evidence and rational discourse—a necessary task if human civilization is to avoid destroying itself.

A radical integral ecology is called for—in other words, an integral worldview that encompasses and fully recognizes and *radically* values the interrelatedness of the whole living planet.[28] It expresses mature integral consciousness, which can make common cause with postmodern environmental consciousness, because both are willing to grapple with the moral implications of modernity's destructive arrogance. At the same time, it is ready to join with modernity's pragmatic, rational, and technical prowess in the service of more adequate and comprehensive solutions. It recognizes that our ecological and climate predicament is a four-quadrant affair. It poses a great series of technical problems, but it is more fundamentally a problem of consciousness and culture. A holistic transition is clearly necessary, but it poses a huge challenge, for reasons that have to do with the dynamics of cultural evolution itself. Humble, integral cultural leadership is required.

The crises of our time are chastening us and will in time require all of us to acknowledge the inarguable foundational truths of deep ecology (notwithstanding the common tendency for these truths to be conflated with other unfortunate postmodern excesses). "Conquering" nature was indeed a deluded goal that ultimately has been critically destructive to our own life-support system. The health of the "web of life" (which some deep ecologists imbue with a retro-romantic longing for some illusory pristine and sacred state of nature) really *is* the irreducible foundation for the health of all human existence. This cannot be theorized away. Where the biosphere goes, so goes humanity. And postmodernists are not mistaken in noticing an awe-inspiring degree of dynamic synergy among living things that is suggestive of the Gaia hypothesis and much more. Our biosphere has both exteriors and interiors. The interior, "spiritual" discovery of deep ecology is that the less-articulated consciousness of animals, plants, and the interrelated living planet is far wiser and more intelligent than modernists and traditionalists have imagined or been able to feel and see.

A radical integral understanding of ecology embodies a hidden synergy between deep ecology and integral philosophy. Deep ecology invites us into a shift in perspective about our place and purpose in the cosmos. The proper understanding and conduct of human culture and behavior, deep ecologists tell us, must be rooted in the perception of our limited place within the larger biosphere whose life and health is the foundation of our own.

Integralists can fundamentally agree: the holarchic nature of existence means that more complex forms of life are dependent on the prior, simpler ones. "Higher" levels have more depth or complexity, but "lower" levels are more fundamental. In a fragmented world, it is sometimes necessary to stand the hierarchy on its head and revere the "lower" as "more important." Truly integral consciousness values the whole spiral or spectrum of evolutionary development. Life has profound value beyond that of lifeless matter, for instance, but without matter there would be no life. This is also true for every stratum of life on Earth: each newly evolving form of life grows inextricably out of earlier life forms, with which they are interwoven. We are the sons and daughters of the trees.

Deep ecologists realize that human happiness, sanity, and fulfillment depend on a healthy natural world. They have come to recognize that there is a profound myopia in our historical anthropocentric arrogance. They spend time in nature and awaken to awe and wonder in relation to the whole family of life. Opening into communion with plants, animals, and natural places, they are relieved of an underlying stress they had not previously recognized. They realize that industrial human civilization's whole relationship to life is subtly painful, because it depends on separation, the effort to subdue and exploit nature, to stand apart and superior. This shift of perspective goes to the psychic roots of our environmental crisis, which is something we experience not just outwardly, in the form of imbalances in nature, but inwardly, as a subtle, craven, driven dissociation from our embodied relationship to the natural world. We are uplifted by recognizing and feeling that we have many relations in the larger family of life.

But deep ecology is, on its own, sorely incomplete. To fulfill its aspirations it will need to grow into integral consciousness. Both of these views recognize that human beings are part of a far larger, cosmic evolutionary process that gives our lives greater context and purpose, so both are inspired to commune with and care for the entire web of life. However, integral consciousness also recognizes that consciousness evolves, and that interior evolution is just as miraculous as biological evolution. Even while recognizing the immaturity of pathological anthropocentrism, integral consciousness deeply appreciates the unique creative potentials of human interiors, in individuals and in human collectives. Integral consciousness values the special depth that arises in human beings, including the dignities of modernity and the foundations of traditionalism.

Thus, unlike the postmodern mind of deep ecology, true integral consciousness recognizes sacredness in the highest interior human potentials, not just in the exterior web of life that is our foundation. It has the potential to appreciate the whole spectrum, empathizing with and, at least in principle, communicating respectfully and effectively with traditionalists and modernists; it can even contend successfully with the egocentric might-makes-right impulses of warrior consciousness. It outgrows postmodern impotence, which can "speak truth to power" but which cannot take and wield power effectively. It rests in a deeper trust of the process of cultural evolution, so it can imagine and participate in hybrid emergent solutions that combine technological advances with deep ecological reverence and restraint.

Thus, unlike weak relativistic postmodernism, integral consciousness has the potential to exert powerful cultural and social leadership and constructive (versus deconstructive) creativity. This can find expression in every realm of human affairs, from business to public policy, to twenty-first-century science and technology, to academic philosophy, to arts and literature, to popular culture. It can take us beyond the impotent "anti-heroes" of ironic postmodern art to a new full-throated "post-ironic" affirmation of human values and virtues that integrate with our whole natural world.

However, a radical integral ecology will also awaken beyond the immature tendencies of nascent integral culture, including reactive rejection of and distancing from the many valid dimensions of postmodern sensibilities and the tendency to naively imagine that evolution's creativity will automatically solve all problems. The evolution of human culture and human beings is not at all assured. The awe and sense of optimism that arises when we take in the glory and complexity of the evolutionary process is a powerful inspiration and it helps us awaken beyond simplistic materialistic models of cause-and-effect. Even so, evolution isn't simply a guaranteed linear path of increasing complexity and depth. The dinosaurs were an evolutionary cul-de-sac. They did not spawn the next phase of life's evolutionary expression. Humans must make many good choices if we are not to become another evolutionary dead end.

A radical integral ecology will also express a truly integral spirituality. It will integrate transcendental spirituality and intuitions of higher states of consciousness with reverent worship of the immanent sacred living earth. It will be awake to the divinity of what is "highest" and truly universal, the nondual consciousness that is the essence and very Mystery of existence. But it will be equally awake to what is "deepest" and most fundamental, the embodied ground of all human experience—earth and sky and the four directions worshipped by our most ancient earth-based spiritual traditions, through which we express our brotherhood and sisterhood with all our incarnate relations (the whole human and more-than-human family, including the plant spirits and fellow creatures). It will also acknowledge that the evolutionary process of "transcending and including" is disorderly and imperfect, as we are. What is "transcended and included" as we grow in awareness is not always mastered or retained in a whole or healthy way. It is not regressive to reengage and reemphasize aspects of prior states and structures of consciousness that have not been fully integrated. In fact, doing so is sometimes necessary to building a broader foundation for the pyramid of total personal development. This is especially true with regard to regaining a full and healthy relationship with the natural world.

Whether one begins with a sympathy for deep ecology or integral theory, any serious observer of this moment in human history should be able to acknowledge that we are facing a crisis that cannot be surmounted without leadership grounded in the enduring truths of both of these paradigms. And we cannot preserve what is best through technological innovation alone. A dramatic reduction of the pace of human consumption and destruction of the natural world is inevitable. The only benign scenario by which this can be accomplished is through a profound and comprehensive cultural turnaround, a great transition. We will need both interior and exterior change, including transformations of the psychology and behavior of individuals and societies. A radical integral ecology is thus necessary and inevitable.

CREATING AN INTEGRAL CULTURE

Radical integral ecology is characterized by solutions that are both "non-zero-sum" and "out of the box."

Non-zero-sum means win-win: that one party's gain is not another party's loss. We are called to take a more comprehensive view of who and what is involved in any solution, so that the impact on the commons—especially the air, water, forests, wildlife, and earth we share—is never neglected. Future solutions must actually be *win-win-win*—wins for both sides of whatever human interests are competing, and also a win for the health of the whole. But not dogmatically. Win-win solutions are not always possible; sometimes it is necessary to fight for a single position against others. At times an integral approach to ecology may simply need to engage a battle (for a carbon tax, for example, or other appropriate public policies). Knowing that the perfect is the enemy of the good, integralists won't be so paralyzed by the desire to create non-zero-sum transactions that they will miss opportunities to create positive change. The integral flavor takes righteousness out of the equation so that we can actually hear and respond humanely to one another, rather than be boxed in by identities or polarities.

An integral approach isn't going to think only in familiar "boxes" or categories, focused merely on how to improve our existing systems. Integral approaches will address these problems in a whole variety of ways that defy the frameworks through which we are used to seeing them. One out-of-the-box approach that has already caught the global imagination is to educate girls in the developing world. Another equally significant priority is to make fossil fuels noncompetitive. Many out-of-the-box approaches are bubbling up all through culture and the integral evolutionary community. Some integral initiatives make an entrepreneurial art form out of incubating new out-of-the-box communities, artistic creations, or ideas. New technologies will also be critical here: more efficient renewable energy sources, new types of batteries, and ideas that no one has thought of yet. Rather than merely incrementally tweaking the current system, we must also imagine how it can be bypassed. We are already creating more jobs in the United States with solar and wind than we are with coal; they could already outcompete fossil fuels in many situations if government subsidies for fossil fuels were eliminated. But even more radical changes are called for. Evolutionary tension is building for exponential advances, and so is the integral impulse to imagine them, and to extrapolate into the territory ahead.

Because these are *integral* approaches, they won't exclusively focus on such *exterior* technical solutions and systems upgrades (the right-hand quadrants), but also will take into account the *interiors* of the individuals and communities who must implement and sustain them (the left-hand quadrants). The integral four-quadrant matrix is out-of-the-box—it makes us think beyond any specialized area of expertise. Most people already understand that transitions to renewable energy in communities dependent on the coal economy will collide with the attitudes, needs, and identities of their workers and residents. What may be harder to imagine is the pervasive cultural transformation that will necessarily occur as human societies radically economize our consumption of non-renewable natural resources.

No matter how many great, out-of-the-box, non-zero-sum, techno-logically dazzling, socially minded, and economically generative innovations we develop, the true test of a Radical Integral Ecology will come from our capacity to communicate with, cooperate with, tolerate, and care for one another. Cultural fragmentation and conflict, and the cynicism and resentment that enable them, are environmental poisons. The real ecological crisis is not a merely practical and technical problem, but equally a crisis of collective will, a cultural crisis.

A 10 PERCENT TIPPING POINT?

Ken Wilber has pointed out that at the time of the American Revolution, about 10 percent of the colonists were educated people who actually thought of the world in rational modern terms like those the Founding Fathers imbued in our founding documents. He has also speculated that when 10 percent of its population grows into a new structure of meaning-making and values, a whole society is able to rewrite its public rules based on that new structure. Although this claim is by no means mainstream, it is an extremely interesting conjecture. A 10 percent tipping point is observed or theorized in several other sociocultural models.

Scientists at Rensselaer Polytechnic Institute reported in 2011 that when just 10 percent of a population holds an unshakable belief, their belief will always be adopted by the majority. Members of the Social Cognitive Networks Academic Research Center (SCNARC) at Rensselaer used computational and analytical methods to discover the tipping point where a minority belief becomes a majority opinion. The scientific press regarded this finding as having "implications for the study and influence of societal interactions ranging from the spread of innovations to the movement of political ideals." According to SCNARC Director Boleslaw Szymanski, "When the number of committed opinion holders is below 10 percent, there is no visible progress in the spread of ideas. It would literally take the amount of time comparable to the age of the universe for this size group to reach the majority. Once that number grows above 10 percent, the idea spreads like flame."[29] This research bolsters Wilber's "integral tipping point" conjecture. I find it entirely credible that a new stage of maturity, and a more integral worldview, might begin to reach critical mass at this 10 percent level.

In various places at various times, integral theorists, especially Wilber, have estimated the percentage of the population of the U.S., Europe, and the world who share various worldviews. It is estimated that between 2 percent and 7 percent of the populations of educated wealthy societies have adopted an integral worldview at some level. *If* this theory holds, and *if* general social forces are causing more and more people to mature into structures of awareness that are free of the limitations of postmodern presumptions, attitudes, habits, and beliefs, then a social transition might soon be possible. A transition into a new structure of meaning is an exciting time, a cultural renaissance. It can be seen in the Renaissance and the Enlightenment, and in what we often call the Sixties—the arrival of a significant cohort of people holding new postmodern values. Ahead of us might be another transition, this one to an integral consciousness—self-aware in important new respects, and capable of a new level of skillful and harmonious relating.

Maybe or maybe not. But it is good to know that there may be unexpected tailwinds ahead, for which the recent past is no prologue. It can be psychologically positive to expect good luck, to imagine "grace" is with us in the great enterprise this book points to. Perhaps cultural forces can catalyze nonlinear gains in our ability to wisely govern our collective affairs, even as technological advances make it critical to our collective survival.

Maybe radical integral ecology can play a role. After all, it is a holistic mode of being. It reflects a rooted integral consciousness with an innate telos toward the reweaving of our social fabric and the healing of our general inability to speak to and be heard by one another, intimately, socially, and across our cultural divides.

And yet even that is not dogma. There are lots of ways to do it. There are many early expressions of radical integral ecology. They can be found in communities of practice at the leading edge of culture, such as cohousing arrangements or eco-villages. In some of these communities, people are experimenting with cooperative and altruistic modes of being and living. The game we are playing is accomplished through self-transcending practice, powerful friendships, and deepening mutual trust. In order to become a cultural force, we must build powerful intragroup resonance and shared practice. That is why the radical implications of an integral ecology imply a revolution of the heart—a growing capacity for appreciation, care, generosity, courage, and creativity. It is both a solo and a team effort.

PART TWO

Being the Change

Life as Practice

What we call "mastery" can be defined as that mysterious process through which what is at first difficult or even impossible becomes easy and pleasurable through diligent, patient, long-term practice.
—GEORGE LEONARD, *THE WAY OF AIKIDO*

This is work that is alive, effervescent, free, liberated, gloriously enlightened, true, and great. Do you think it can be attained by people who shut the door and sit quietly with blank minds?
—LIU I-MING, *AWAKENING TO THE TAO*

As long as the sky exists and as long as there are sentient beings, may I remain to help relieve them of all their pain.
—DALAI LAMA XIV, THE BODHISATTVA VOW

Opening up to holistic, evolutionary, integral perspectives illuminates both the external and internal facets of our world, including our multidimensional crises. But, as we've already seen, to actualize these perspectives we need to become responsible for creating our personal and collective futures—and that goes far beyond merely thinking differently, and far beyond piecemeal involvement in various causes. Evolution into our full human and spiritual potential cannot be separated from creating the conditions that make such evolution possible. And that requires a healthy life-support system—our living planet. Each of these—our evolution and our life-support system—is utterly dependent on the other. Human life is dependent on a healthy planet, and the living Earth now depends on what humans will do.

Knowing how difficult it is to apprehend a hypercomplex reality accurately, and seeing that we have certain limited and deeply habitual ways of thinking and feeling, we can only learn the new requisite skills and ways of being in the same way that anyone—from athletes to artists and musicians to engineers—learns new skills: *through committed practice.* From an integral evolutionary perspective, practice consists of many things, from meditation to physical disciplines to attitudinal choices. And a crucial emerging element of practice is to practice *in community*; in other words, to create a community and extended network of practitioners with similar intentions (regardless of our universal human foibles) who can be mutually supportive—and whose relationships with each other can grow and develop.

Practice in community involves cultivation of higher states and structures of consciousness and awareness, and breaking out of the habits of the "consensus trance." Based on an apprehension of the innate wholeness of reality, an integral framework and understanding is helpful. We can see all points of view and all worldviews in an intuitively accessible holistic context, and thus transcend the reflexive, familiar mindsets that are nearly universal in our public discourse. And practice in community also implies shared values—particularly an appreciation for development on every scale, extending to each of us individually—and a "growth mindset," a sense that we can always learn and change and grow. This means striving for and encouraging as much clarity and excellence and generosity and creativity as we can. And, by intending to live a life of continual growth and transformation, and encouraging that in others, we create conditions for actual cultural advancement.

At the root of all such change is *practice,* both individual and collective. In my passion to get to the essential marrow of transformation, I've directly specialized in teaching practice for many years. The following summary of practice is couched in the terms that relate directly to fulfilling the call of our evolutionary emergency.

Practice is commonly defined as the "repeated exercise or performance of an activity so as to develop greater proficiency or capacity." And, as we've seen, all forms of practice certainly involve these things. But I often find another definition more useful: "Waking up again and again, and choosing to show up in life in alignment with one's highest wholesome intelligence." Practice is what gives us the clarity, presence, intelligence, and empathy necessary to be fully given over to anything we do, including activism.

I was very fortunate that my first teacher, Adi Da Samraj, taught me to relate to *sadhana*—or spiritual practice—as a radical, global, and inclusive affair. I was brought to understand, in my bones, that practice is always immediate. It is about waking more fully into the reality of *this very moment.* Thus it includes not just *what* I am doing, but *how* I am relating to it (and to everything), and *why.* And it depends on my taking responsibility in every moment for serving wholeness, awareness, life, and love.

Of course, such training or teaching is much more the exception than the rule. But at a certain point in the journey of a life, many people begin to realize, at least at some level, that life is a school—or, put another way, a teacher. It keeps delivering the same lessons again and again, in new forms, until we really learn them and move on to *new* lessons and an ever more refined relationship to life.

WHOLENESS AND PRACTICE

In many ways, the early twenty-first century—this moment of crisis and predicament—is a time of fragmentation. It is a time of rapid change and turbulence, in which existing patterns are being disturbed more and more, creating reactions and confusion that result in incoherence

and even corruption in the public sphere, and also in the more intimate sphere of our relations. That calls for us to choose, practice, and
embody health, integrity, and wholeness. To stand whole, refusing to
believe the reactive mind of separation and fragmentation—that is
what's *truly* subversive, in the best sense. It is not only a spiritual act
but a revolutionary one.

— All conscious beings tend to contract, to recoil, to shut down and
close off from the challenges of mortal existence. We reenact our incomplete psychological processes, rooted in causes ranging from trauma, to
attachment wounds, to addiction. Contraction is a deep pattern, even
in the most well-adjusted individuals. And yet it is possible to observe
and recognize the activity of contraction. Based on such recognition,
with persistent, sustained practice, it becomes possible to relax the pattern—to open into greater awareness, freedom, courage, and functional
capacity.

The knowledge of wholeness is most directly cultivated in meditation.
In unitive states of consciousness people have direct intuitive experience
of the nonseparate wholeness of all objective and subjective realities, or
"awareness itself." These intuitions are much more than a simple cognitive insight. They are experienced energetically, kinesthetically, emotionally, and cognitively. And they can therefore inform people's ways
of navigating, behaving, and relating. This often results in a shift of perspective into one in which *life lives us,* rather than the other way around.
This depersonalization (recognizing that "I am awareness"), in which
awareness is most free, does not produce dissociation, but instead relaxes
resistance, completing a circuit back into an intimate, warm, personal,
embodied experience of living.

These dynamics of contraction and expansion, of consciousness and
unconsciousness, are always at play in life. This is true not just in individuals but in relationships and groups. Tendencies toward fragmentation contend with choices for integration. Tendencies toward disease
and death contend with cycles of resurgent vitality and health. Corrupt
impulses contend with aspirations to integrity. Courage contends with
fear. Humility contends with arrogance. Life wounds us, and the body

naturally heals. The universal principles of wholeness express themselves in every individual life, and in every moment.

The *practice of wholeness* is thus ongoing, and pervades every sphere of our lives. It means intending to enact the health and wholeness of the body, mind, emotions, relations, culture, society, and the entire natural world. It is also about participating consciously and constructively in every dimension of the larger whole. Most important, integral practice expresses what is called an "ontological" stance, or a "way of being"—a core commitment that organizes the whole life. In that fundamental intention, the inner work and the outer work converge. Commitments give rise to actions, which change us, making us more capable of fulfilling our commitments, which deepen and evolve.

What is involved in practicing wholeness? First, it calls on us to recognize, intuitively, the mysterious wholeness that is *already* our condition. On the basis of that understanding, and our natural attraction to greater wholeness, we practice by intending to more and more fully recognize and participate in (and *as*) that wondrous dynamic wholeness.

That which has traditionally been called "ego" or "sin" is the persistent tendency to feel and believe that we are simply separate selves in a dead, mechanical dog-eat-dog world. According to the consensus trance, this is just "the way things are," but this perspective is actually the result of an *activity*: the activity of contraction at the deepest level of our consciousness. It is something we are actively *doing*. It is going on at an extremely subtle level, far below the plane of our awareness. It takes accomplished practitioners decades to develop the mental focus and sensitivity necessary to notice it. But it is not simply "the way things are."

This contraction into separateness shows up on the surface as feelings—fear, sorrow, anger, laziness, dullness, greed, lust, anxiety, depression, and every other "negative" human emotion and limiting belief. Even when practice seems to have vanquished such gross-level expressions of contraction, at the very subtlest level of the being we are still very likely contracting into a subtle mental stance of separation.

Before we can perceive it, though, we can take responsibility for it—at least in principle. Through feedback and intention, we can increasingly live on the basis of the reality that precedes the self-contraction and transcends it. We can recognize that the self-contraction is *not* our bedrock reality. It is secondary to wholeness, which is inherently happy, graceful, and awake—genuinely free of problem and any sense of lack. *Living on the basis of that wholeness is practice.*

The recognition of wholeness reveals that, in spite of all the threats that we are faced with daily, there is an underlying context of goodness, of being sustained—of what Aldous Huxley referred to as the "fundamental all-rightness" of things. Sometimes an intuition of that goodness comes unbidden as a spiritual experience, and this epiphany draws individuals into a life of practice. But whether it comes early or late in the course of your life of practice, it can eventually produce a powerful emotional "conversion" in an intelligent practitioner.

In the moments when you remember to practice, you are acting based on your awareness that you have (at least at some point in the past) *seen through the illusion* of separation. You have penetrated the veil, and you can imagine and often feel the graceful reality of radical, nonseparate wholeness. This intuition guides your choices. Your heart has opened and you have known yourself to be not separate from all that is whole and holy. A seamless reality prior to self-contraction is the context. You have known yourself to be one with and in love with all existence, one with love itself. This becomes a guiding North Star, vitalizing your deepest emotional health, guiding you through hard times, resonating with your deepest experiences of love—the love you have felt in relation to your family, friends, pets, the whole of humanity, the natural world, and the pulse of life itself.

FROM SEEKER TO PRACTITIONER

People often discover a full spiritual practice after years of seeking. Seekers are looking for something they don't have. On the surface they may feel and act hopeful, but underneath that is a sense of separation and incompleteness. They are seeking to be more whole, healthy, and integrated. They want to be wiser, happier, less stressed, less confused, less inadequate.

The problem is that seeking actively prevents the happiness it imagines. The act of seeking itself presumes an underlying *lack*—or disconnection. There is an assumed problem and an assumed separation from the source of life, which seekers imagine is "elsewhere." When we act on our belief in that lack, we reinforce it. Paradoxically, in order for the objects of seeking to be found, seeking itself must come to an end.

To truly become a practitioner requires a shift in the ground of one's motivation—from a sense of lack to a solid grounding in the underlying reality that makes seeking unnecessary. How does that source condition reveal itself? It might be experienced as a tacit trust in life itself, or in God, or in one's own existence. It might be an intuition of miraculous grace that evokes a state of gratitude for life itself. It can be a very simple and modest "okayness"—a deep acceptance and trust of the way things are.

Once we become grounded in that deeper reality, our motivation is shifted beyond seeking—and practice is no longer about "getting something" or "getting somewhere." It is a matter of acting on the basis of that healthy wholeness or well-being or sacredness we recognize. The practitioner practices by *reenacting* that health and wholeness again and again. Not attempting to seek it, achieve it, or create it—but to *remember* it, to *experience* it, to *participate in* and *enact* it.

The distinction between seeking and practice is profound and essential. And this distinction is more important now than ever. Because the kind of practice I am speaking of—the life of practice that knows and trusts the reality of wholeness, sacredness, or fundamental goodness—expresses and transmits sanity, even amidst insanity. This is exactly what our revolutionary times require. The kind of "seeking" that many well-meaning people have considered to be spiritual practice will not suffice to bring us to the powerful new expressions of purpose, resilience, wisdom, courage, and self-transcending love we're called to.

Paradoxically, to engage in effective change requires a profound trust in what *is*—a deep surrender to a source we cannot name. Such trust is the essence of the true practitioner, and it is what is lacking in the seeker. Recognizing, trusting, and affirming wholeness, sacredness, and goodness tends to beget awakening into reality. It affirms what is so. And the solidity and unshakability of this stance, this practice "posture," tends to create an experience of resilience and self-trust that is also naturally generative.

And acting in service of something bigger than ourselves tends to generate a deeper and more durable "happiness"—more of an enduring, grounded joy than the fleeting happiness that is a response to circumstances. In a sense, it is "happiness for no reason," rather than the thin cheer that depends upon external causes.

Modern psychological research confirms the ancient lesson that trying to achieve happiness doesn't work. When it comes, happiness is most often caused *indirectly*; it is a byproduct of a life of compassionately caring for others and serving something greater than ourselves. Care for and service to others not only makes us happy; it also requires us to grow—and growth is something else that is self-validating. As we experience the joy of serving others, plus our own growth and development, we become interested in practicing more, in maturing and awakening and serving.

LIFE AS PRACTICE

Even those who devote their life to practice will oscillate in varying degrees between true practice and a falling-back into seeking. But once we are more firmly grounded in our prior state of wholeness, we can return to that state of deep trust and openness ever more frequently. Increasingly, it becomes the constant, deep wellspring of our lives—a continual "ground bass" beneath the ever-changing "melodies" that get played at the surface. That ground bass is our deeper intuition and recognition of what is obvious even if we cannot name it. It is the feeling-intuition of the Whole.

Our lapses thus become shorter in duration. If we "forget," we will remember again. And, however we feel at a given moment—even if we feel terrible; even if we feel nothing at all—our commitment to practice remains unabated. So, whether we have lapsed for a minute, an hour, a week, a month, or several years, we can always begin again now.

It takes more than changing our eating or sleeping or exercise habits for a month to change our bodies or physical health forever. We need to *continuously* eat well and exercise and get restorative sleep to maintain our physical health. Similarly, a glimpse of enlightenment can come in a flash, instantly, but it will not remain stable without a life of practice. Neither can we expect psychological insights, wholesome feelings, or energetic shifts, however profound, to permanently change our emotional patterns.

I remember Michael Murphy and George Leonard describing their tremendous excitement at the early weekend seminars at Esalen, which was a pioneering hub of the 1970s human potential movement. People were having mind-blowing insights. Their hearts opened. They connected with a higher power. Through tears and ecstasy and gratitude, they swore their lives would never be the same.

But then, just a week or so later, those same folks who had sworn their lives would never be the same would fall back pretty much to where they started. The transformations didn't stick. No matter how long the intensive, how seemingly radical the insights, how solid the changes felt, after a few days or weeks or months the effects "wore off." People eventually returned to their habitual patterns.

Murphy and Leonard reached the conclusion that the ancient paths were right: *A whole life of regular, ongoing practice is necessary. There is no "quick fix."* It takes an ongoing transformational *lifestyle* to sustain the fruits of practice.

Neuroscientist Donald Hebb has a famous maxim: "Neurons that fire together wire together."[30] We are always reinforcing the neural circuits associated with what we are doing right now. In other words, whatever way we are being, we're more likely to be that way in the future. *This means we are always practicing something*—whether it be relaxation or tension, acceptance or resistance, compassion or irritability, focus or distractibility.

In that same vein, we are either practicing a static, fragmented consciousness of separation or a dynamic, growing awareness that intuits wholeness and enacts it. We can always ask: Am I practicing separation and division, or wholeness and interdependence? Am I avoiding relationship with all that is, or moving toward it?

Murphy and Leonard—drawing on an ancient tradition that goes back to ancient Indian philosopher-mystic Patanjali—also noticed something else. *A transformational life of practice must include every dimension of the being.* To be most powerfully transformational, our life of practice cannot be *exclusively* focused on meditative awakening. Or merely on athletic skill, fitness, or somatic health and integration. Or only on our psychological growth and healing. Or exclusively on our relationship to the natural world, or our relationships to other people. Or only focused on our lives as citizen participants in our communities, nation, and world.

Practice catalyzes transformation, and transformation means, literally, a change in form. In individual inner transformation, the form of our self—the interface between our internal experience and our behavior in the world—is what changes. Often this is called "consciousness development," because the fundamental invisible structures of our inner experience and outer perception develop the ability to hold greater complexity and nuance—more wholeness. This "bigger picture" consciousness enables us to maintain awareness and calm in the midst of conflict and confusion, to be free of petty and defensive reactivity, to think creatively "outside the box," and to intuit higher syntheses of the polarities that are pulling us apart. The value of this kind of consciousness and these capacities at this moment in our predicament cannot be overstated. Transformation is a necessity, not a luxury—especially now.

CHOOSING TO PRACTICE IN EVERY MOMENT

We can begin exactly where we are—here, and only here. The beauty of this is that we can *always* begin, now, and again and again, to practice. This is true in every moment. It is a choice we can make in every moment. And to keep making those choices—to aspire and intend to do so, and to stay aware of this process of choosing again and again—is itself a practice. It is *life as practice.*

Through practices that cultivate equanimity, such as meditation, we might begin to find it possible to recognize that we are not a separate body-mind-self experiencing a world "out there." Instead, we might see that we are awareness itself, the still and unmoving witness of all experience. And awareness is witnessing the body, the mind, and the self just as surely as it is witnessing "others" and a world "out there." As awareness we have utter freedom from whatever is arising, and yet we are paradoxically inseparable from it all. Then it becomes possible to go even further and notice that awareness is shining back at us from everyone and everything we behold.

Then we can *rest as awareness*. In any moment in which awareness freely observes our contraction, there is at least a small measure of free uncontracted awareness—and that awareness is wholeness itself. This little bit of free awareness is key to our transformation. The grip of the tendency toward contraction and toward the false sense of separation loosens to some degree.

As practice deepens, attention opens up. We might notice a deep, soulful dimension of ourselves, amidst the animating subtle energetic fields that give rise to experience. We might eventually go so far as to be able to dispassionately observe the continual tendency to contract at all levels of our being. We can notice that we are contracting physically, in our breathing and in our muscular tension patterns. We can see that we are contracting mentally, perhaps becoming the slightest bit dull as if "going on automatic," and reacting to experience rather than proactively choosing how to relate to it. We can notice the momentum of our habits, and even notice that it is possible to choose to interrupt that momentum.

Each moment of life is a creative opportunity. We can choose how we relate to the moment. The practitioner leans into his or her highest possibilities, considering the full depth and breadth of life. How can I be present as love/awareness—how would love be, and what would love do? Where am I placing my attention? How am I compensating? Am I to any degree becoming unconscious or numb? What freedom and joy might I be closing off? How might I be subtly losing touch with my inherent well-being? How can I awaken from and transform reactive or unconscious patterns? How am I affecting others? How can I be of more benefit? In what ways am I avoiding conscious awareness of, and participation in, the infinitely deep mystery of existence? How can I show up more wholly in each moment of life—and specifically in this next moment?

The momentum of habit will inevitably prevail at times, but that is not best seen as failure; it is simply what we have to work with. The tendency toward contraction doesn't let go easily; it is a stubborn, pervasive habit. Your consciousness, like everyone's, will tend to go into trance, to contract from clarity, to lapse into thinking, to become lazy, to react to perceived slights and discouragements. Conditioned tendencies are strong. But there is no problem in that. It is what it is. We don't have to be held hostage by the self-alienating injunction that we should overcome such tendencies by using superhuman will power. That spiritual attitude (which we can characterize as "hypermasculine") can be replaced by a much more self-accepting (post-hypermasculine) and skillful disposition. It recognizes that it is never too late to notice *this very moment* as my next opportunity to show up fresh and open. I can always practice, always choose.

There is only the now-moment, which is always disappearing. I can either keep letting go and opening to it, or I can try to hold on. I can do my best to forgive and relax and trust and open up to the next new now-moment with an attitude of curiosity and willingness. I can recognize that it is an opportunity for creative engagement. I can realize that all this life is "improv." There is no "right" or "wrong" way to be, and no "right" or "wrong" thing to do. But I can always be "in the now"—or return to the now—by waking up from contracted patterns and opening into living contact with whatever arises in the *next* "now" moment.

Practice involves numerous complementary and synergistic elements. These elements—the inner and the outer, the contemplative and the activist, the practices engaged individually and in community, the physical and the spiritual—are not merely good in themselves; they reinforce one another. The whole spectrum of practices is far greater than the sum of its parts. The interplay of these elements is a virtuous cycle. Simply getting started allows for a certain degree of opening and relaxation, which makes more opening possible, which begets greater awareness, which allows more love, and on and on. Such positive reinforcement eventually creates an evolutionary momentum in the life of practice. Practice also means *choosing* not to believe the fragmented and separated "consensus trance" version of reality that tends to keep reasserting itself. It means we recognize it as a persistent illusion, and we live on the basis of the deeper wholeness that we know is the real nature of things. This means allowing wholeness, more and more, to inform our perceptions, thoughts, and feelings.

THE HEART OF THE MATTER

Wholeness is intuited at the heart. To live on the basis of wholeness, we must be able to recognize and trust that wholeness is our real condition. And this is not a merely cognitive decision; it is a deep knowing of the whole being, felt at the very center of the organism—at the heart.

Science is increasingly confirming that there is something akin to a brain within the human heart. Our heart's deeper intelligence is real— and very important in the context of life as practice, and all the practice that will bring us to our most evolved response to this moment. In the 1990s, I worked closely with researchers at the Institute of HeartMath, where our work measured and validated the fact that the heart is a vital center of intelligence in the human system.

We used to think that neurons were concentrated exclusively in our brain and spinal cord. Now we know that they are also concentrated in our heart and in our gut. The fields of neurocardiology and neurogastroenterology study the interactions of the brain and whole body, with the "second brain" in the heart and the "third brain" in the gut.

In both the heart and gut are extensive masses of neurons that behave similarly to the neurons in the brain. More than one hundred billion nerve cells can be found in the digestive tract (more than in the spinal cord). It may be that unconscious decisions are made by the stomach network, even if they are later claimed by the conscious brain in the head as conscious decisions.

The "brain in the heart" is complex and self-organized. It conducts a continuous two-way dialogue with the brain and the rest of the body, often registering changes *before* the brain in the head. People intuitively recognize its wisdom. As Antoine de Saint-Exupery wrote in *The Little Prince,* "And now here is my secret, a very simple secret: it is only with the heart that one can see rightly, what is essential is invisible to the eye."

At HeartMath, we observed that when people intentionally consult their heart's intelligence, it offers calm and unhurried perspectives, even when the thinking mind is agitated, anxious, worried, or defensive.

As I continued my own investigation I noticed something else. Heart intelligence has an *integrative* function. It is interconnected with the intelligences of the head and of the gut. And it is fully capable of intuitively mediating contradictions between them. It naturally integrates the total intelligence of the being. The intelligent integral heart is senior to and wiser than the disconnected brain, and much harder to fool.

Pierre Teilhard de Chardin famously wrote, "The day will come when, after harnessing the ether, the winds, the tides, gravitation, we shall harness for God the energies of love. And, on that day, for a second time in the history of the world, man will have discovered fire."[31] All this expresses the evolutionary necessity of a revolution of love, but not in the way that is commonly imagined.

Love expresses wholeness, felt and known from the heart. As we have seen, wholeness is the most primary, root quality of existence, and the heart is where wholeness is intuited—and love is its expression. To speak of love is, properly, to speak of this expression. This is a far cry from the love we speak of when we really mean either romantic attachment, enthusiastic liking, or even familial or tribal caring or loyalty.

Again and again, in the course of practice, it is important to recognize that wholeness is more deeply real—more primary—than the fragmentation, division, and separation that the mind tends to cognize. The heart is important because this recognition cannot be merely abstract and mental. Our mental intelligence, centered in the head, and our visceral intelligence, centered in the *hara,* below the navel, must be integrated via our heart intelligence in a recognition of the wholeness that is the source of sanity, strength, and health. And when we are actually doing that, we become love in action.

THE "HOW" AND "WHAT" OF PRACTICE

In the book *Integral Life Practice: A 21st-Century Blueprint for Physical Health, Emotional Balance, Mental Clarity, and Spiritual Awakening*,[32] I and my coauthors Ken Wilber, Adam Leonard, and Marco Morelli pointed to a key paradox.

It is not easy to make our life a practice of wholeness, so that our intuitions and intentions are sourced from that whole. Specific practice commitments are necessary. They are even more powerful if they are consciously held in a larger structure that explicitly intends to help the practitioner bridge from doing a series of discrete independent practices to living a whole life as practice.

Given (a) how diverse and unique human beings are, and (b) how rich the world of practice is, and (c) that everyone is a unique individual, there is no "one size fits all" recommendation for the best specific practices. But that doesn't just leave us with a jumbled chaos of disconnected individual choices. My colleagues and I observed some important principles, so we described a "modular" understanding of practice, and suggested four core modules that almost every life of practice should fruitfully include. They were:

Body practices, including diet, sleep, and many kinds of exercise, from qigong to yoga to strength training.

Mind practices, including reading, study, research, experimentation, calculation, critical analysis, discussion, mental exercises, and growing in our capacity to take more nuanced and self-aware perspectives.

Spiritual practices, especially meditation, and also including practices of loving devotion and prayer, communing with the natural world, and contemplation, including both mystical insight and natural philosophy.

Shadow practices, extending to other emotional work, and also including soul work and somatic work—ultimately embracing the full spectrum of psychotherapeutic healing and health.

At the beginning, when the intuition of wholeness is still growing, it is essential to ground one's life in the tangible specificity of particular practices. We don't want to get lost in the seemingly shapeless profundity of life-as-practice. You can build a life of specific practice commitments first. It is also valuable to do certain practices at certain times of the day and week and year. Such structures of commitment are foundational. Adding structures of accountability (like a checklist, practice partner, or a teacher) can take things even deeper, giving practitioners more transformational traction.

I have taught integral practice for more than a dozen years, and I have seen some interesting patterns:

- The first point was famously summarized by baseball Jedi Yogi Berra: "The most important thing about practice is … doing it." That's for sure. And that is why a focus on specific practice commitments is so essential at the beginning.

- Zen Master Richard Baker Roshi once said "Satori is a happy accident," but practicing diligently "makes us more accident prone." Specific disciplines can get us "in shape" and open up many opportunities for glimpses and insights into that unlimited wholeness.

- The life of practice described here must be lived from the "outside in" as well as "inside out." Our intention is only part of the picture; it's enacted by doing a whole suite of specific practices. And the practices aren't the point; they must become a whole life of practice.

THE FIVE M'S

In most cases, only after building a foundation of many healthy practices, small and large, does it become possible for the practice of love and wholeness to pervade one's life. Nonetheless, it is helpful from the beginning to have a *holistic context of understanding* that can integrate your relationship to your concrete, time-anchored, specific practice commitments.

As I continued to refine my way of teaching Integral Life Practice, I summarized it in new ways, to provide that context of understanding. I pointed not to the practices themselves, but to the key ways that people usually relate to practice as they gradually come to pervade our lives. I noticed five broad categories that, like tent stakes, can anchor the transition to an integrated life of practice. I used five words beginning with the letter "M" to name five general orienting principles: Mornings, Moments, Mission, Milestones, and Momentum—the "Five M's."

Mornings. Almost every serious practitioner begins by establishing a daily practice, and mornings are often the best time for this. Every day, I wake up and do some conscious physical movement, which helps me to integrate my gross, subtle, and causal bodies. I notice that I am a consciously embodied being, feelingly in touch with my nervous system, muscles, bones, and breath, which communes with the entire atmosphere. I perform a series of conscious movements that restore energetic balances and help me begin a healthy day. I take care of myself. I do that in a devotional mood, in relationship with the living God, the living Divine. As I experience and breathe in the blessing of being alive, I find myself lit up by gratitude and a desire to be of service.

If my day's obligations permit, I like spending ninety minutes or more each morning moving consciously, meditating, reading, and contemplating. This is what the greatest transformative saints, sages, and prophets have done. It is interesting to note that Mahatma Gandhi, the Dalai Lama, and Mother Teresa all spent between one and three hours in daily practice before doing anything else. How we begin our day has a great impact on how the whole day unfolds. Whether or not you take this amount of time, and even if your life dictates more of an evening practice, it is wise to do some conscious practice to reset your body-mind as you start your day.

Moments are all we have, since even the past and the future arise for us right *now*. So a primary way we can make all our lives a form of practice is to *bring intention to random moments throughout the day*. In this way, our intentions begin to pervade our whole lives. "Moments practice" means interrupting your unconscious, contracted, habitual way of being—just for a moment. It is good to build the habit of "pressing the refresh button" in small and large ways, for brief moments, many times every day. In just a moment, or perhaps over a few breaths, a quick practice can shift the state and orientation of your mind, emotions, energy, and behavior. Moments practices can be as mundane as adjusting your posture or as "spiritual" as speaking a mantra as a reminder of your intention to live as love. You can also simply take a deep breath, or a few deep breaths, and you can bring your attention to your heart, and remember the essential goodness of existence. You can take conscious breaks from the computer to stretch. You can remember and connect with your values or goals. You can bring your attention to the grace that supports your existence, feeling gratitude as an explicit intentional focus for a minute or so, until it begins to soften and open your emotions and shift their biochemistry. It is wise to frequently remind yourself of the living whole that is holding you.

You can commit to a certain frequency of a particular Moments practice—e.g., "at least three times a day"—but, as the practice becomes second nature, it is helpful to maximize its frequency, even while keeping these moments spontaneous and not rigidly programmed.

Our **Mission** is profound and fundamental to our whole existence: it is our life purpose, the intention that organizes everything. Clarifying one's life purpose and consciously committing to it is perhaps the most powerful of all practices. But purpose is not a static thing. It evolves across the life cycle. If we decide to put it into words, we may well periodically revise our purpose statement as our understanding and purpose evolve. Consciously inhabiting your purpose implies an ontological shift. "Ontological" means *relating to one's very way of being*. When we stand for something wholeheartedly, our whole way of being becomes congruent with it, and we actually do enact it. Our purpose begins to find ways to organize not just our own lives, but even our opportunities and communities. Eventually it can act in synergy with the purpose of others and the whole. Purpose, fully lived, is both dynamic and contagious. We naturally engage with others and enroll them in our purpose. This is a key way that practice brings awakening consciousness into the lives of others and affects the wider world.

Mission is powerfully bound to the fourth M—**Milestones.** One's mission is global. But one's actions must be concrete and time-specific.

That means that we enact our mission through a series of specific projects. We are always involved in projects, or Milestones—finding an intimate partner, raising a child, creating a home or garden, building a business, writing a book, preparing for a performance or competition, creating a website, seminar, podcast, product, publication—you get the idea. We actualize our purpose, or mission, through a series of specific projects. When we take on a project (1) for the sake of something bigger than ourselves, (2) in partnership with a higher power or source of grace, and (3) with a willingness for the process to teach and transform us, it becomes a very real and powerful practice. It can become a transformative passage, and when you complete the project you will have grown significantly beyond who you were when you began it. Much of the life of practice expresses itself in our Milestone projects. We all do this naturally. You are probably working on several milestones right now.

The fifth M is **Momentum**. By this, I am referring to the many other practices that we perform intentionally—all the practices we listed in the "modules" of Integral Life Practice. We have to keep sharpening the saw. So every day, in addition to our Mornings and our Moments, we practice in nature, at the gym, or in the yoga studio. We do additional specific physical, mental, psychological, spiritual, and social practices. We undertake specific practices across the whole spectrum of our lives, doing *integral cross-training*.

A life of diverse practices will engender healthy synergies. It can free up our energy and attention and break up stuck patterns in many areas of our lives and consciousness, creating transformational momentum. A whole life of integral practice allows our fixed identity and contracted sense of separation to be opened up and transformed by the open awareness we truly are.

INTEGRAL CROSS-TRAINING

"Integral Cross-Training" is the explicit cultivation of growth and development *synergies* among the practices we do in different spheres of our existence. In the book *Integral Life Practice*, my colleagues and I introduced this concept, noting the "cross-training" synergy that arises between the different modules of practice (physical, mental, psychological, and spiritual) described above. The spiritual practice of meditation can act in synergy with the mental practice of critical analysis, which can in turn synergize with the physical practice of cardio and strength training, just to cite a few examples. Because we are whole and the movement toward wholeness is a drive within nature itself, such cross-training has surprising benefits.

Ken Wilber has often described a beginners' class in mindfulness meditation, in which a subgroup took up weightlifting. Several months later, the meditation teachers were asked to evaluate their students. Interestingly enough, a disproportionate number of those whose meditation had matured most rapidly were students who had also taken up weightlifting. The teachers did not know who had been in that group. These people hadn't meditated any more than the other people. And we all know that most of the skills of weightlifting have nothing to do with mindfulness meditation! And yet they matured more quickly. Why? I suspect that when we liberate energy and attention by practicing excellence and breaking up the stuck patterns in one area of life, we catalyze a holistic state of growth, liberating available resources for transformation in all of our being, sometimes setting up virtuous cycles.

A 2016 research study formally confirmed that multiple transformative practices produce important global effects that are more than the sum of the parts of the isolated interventions.[33] In this study, one group of students did an hour a day of supervised stretching, resistance training, and balance exercises, followed by an hour of training in mindfulness and stress reduction, which included quiet walks and meditation. In the afternoon, they exercised for another ninety minutes. Twice a week they completed two interval-style endurance workouts. They attended lectures about nutrition and sleep and kept daily logs detailing their exercise, diets, sleep patterns, and moods.

Six weeks later, the students retook the original tests. Those in the control group showed no changes. But the ones who had engaged integral cross-training were substantially stronger, fitter, and more flexible;

scored much better on tests of thinking, focus, and working memory; and reported feeling happier and calmer, with higher self-esteem. Their brain scans showed patterns of activity believed to indicate an enhanced ability to stay focused.

The improvements generally exceeded by a large amount what had been seen in many past experiments whose subjects altered only one behavior. The study's authors believed that one kind of change, like starting an exercise regimen, amplifies the effects of another, like taking up meditation. These improvements persisted: another set of tests six weeks after the experiment's end showed that the change-everything students still scored much higher than they originally had on measures of fitness, mood, thinking skills, and well-being, even though none of them were still exercising or meditating as much as they did during the experiment.

This validates a "modular" integral approach to practice. Many traditions (like Patanjali's eight yogas, the emphasis placed on both athletics and study in ancient Greece, and the disciplines of the monks of the Shaolin Temple) suggest an integral approach to practice. An integral practice intentionally combines practices in the domains of body, mind, spirit, shadow, and soul.

Rather than "modular," I prefer the term "spheres" of our lives, because it directs our attention to the different realms of our existence (all of which are transforming) rather than to the "modules" we are working on. While integral practice may begin as a kind of self-improvement project and thus may be thought of in modular fashion, it ultimately becomes a simple, healthy, pleasurable way of life. When we are sustaining practices across the various spheres of our lives, remarkable synergies deepen growth.

Core Modules of Individual Practice

Let us more deeply explore those first four "core modules" of an Integral Life Practice as spheres of our lives, and then continue to a more comprehensive description of the key spheres of such a practice:

Body practices relate primarily to three domains—exercise, diet, and sleep. Physical exercises build muscular strength, cardiovascular aerobic fitness, and/or neuromuscular conditioning (athletic coordination). Subtle energy practices such as yoga, tai chi, and qigong enhance both physical conditioning and harmonious states of body-mind integration. Body practices are foundational. They powerfully synergize with all other practices, and are essential to enabling us to shine bright with healthy life force.

Mind practices can include reading, educating ourselves, building our mental focus, solving complex problems, taking courses, writing, conducting research, and engaging in critical analysis and intelligent discussions. There are specific mind practices in most skilled professions. Through them, we can sharpen our intellect and learn to take more complex and flexible perspectives that make more nuanced sense of our experience, enabling us to respond more effectively. We also get smart and stay sharp. This includes media literacy and insight into human affairs, which use critical thinking to separate truth from spin. By making good choices about how we direct our attention, absorbing and digesting useful new information, research, and cultural movements, we can also discern the hidden wholeness and meaningful patterns that are otherwise concealed in the information avalanche.

Spiritual practices such as meditation, prayerful communion, and contemplation are the foundation practices for awakening to the radical Unity that is prior to separation and fragmentation. That Unity is a deep Mystery, radically beyond any human perspectives. But human beings cannot help but engage perspectives, so there are three broad categories of spiritual practices, corresponding to the three personal pronouns. In 2006, when Ken Wilber first made this distinction, he called it "the 1-2-3 of God." During this time, I was working closely with him and suggested an alternative name, "the Three Faces of God," which has since been widely adopted. Briefly, the "three faces of God" are first-person ("I"), second-person ("You" or "Thou"), and third-person ("It" or "That").

- In third-person practices, we contemplate "It," the Mystery of existence, sometimes abstractly and philosophically, such as what we are doing now in noticing these distinctions; and sometimes in sensory terms, as we do when contemplating the sensuous beauty of the natural world.

- In first-person practices, awareness relaxes back to its ground or source, and we rest as the open intelligence that simply witnesses all experience, awakening as the Self or "I-Am-ness," free of our stories, released into every new now-moment.

- In second-person spirituality, we recognize that we are social creatures, whose neurology is structured to relate to others. Our spirituality would be impoverished if it didn't engage our relational wiring, so we turn toward the Mystery of existence as our primary Beloved, allowing wonder and gratitude to open our heart and breath to the grace that is our most intimate relation in every moment.

Through such practices, our habit of separation and fragmentation is helped to mature into an ongoing recognition of prior unity and interdependence. This gives rise not only to higher states and stages of consciousness, but also to surprising new levels of trust in life, freedom, courage, creativity, and innovation.

Shadow work involves just one dimension of the **psychosphere.** It is also the domain of emotional and psychological and much subtle energetic practice. Through shadow work, we become more conscious of, and free in relation to, the underlying repression, shame, fear, and compensation that otherwise tend to pattern and sabotage our responses to experience. The psychosphere also includes **soul work,** including the practices of depth psychology, ecopsychology, and earth-based spirituality—and it often integrates that work somatically, yogically, and energetically. Through such practices we deepen and integrate our psyche and deep feeling-life. We also come to know our calling, our unique gifts and contributions, and our life purpose.

We identified these four spheres—Body, Mind, Spiritual, and Shadow work—as the "core modules" of Integral Life Practice as it was presented in the book of that title. But they are all **individual practices,** focused on *my* body, *my* mind, *my* spiritual realization, and *my* psychological integration.

Equally important, and even more ultimately consequential, are *relational practices,* or "social praxes," to which we now turn our attention. We cannot address our increasingly urgent large-scale global and social needs alone, and our spiritual growth can no longer be truly healthy if it cannot help us dynamically participate in a world of relations beyond the boundaries of our personal psyches.

Relational Practices

Our inner transformation, which changes our personal subjective experience (or upper left quadrant in Wilber's matrix), can transform our behavior (or upper right quadrant) and our ways of relating to others, bridging into our *inter*subjective agreements and ethics and interpersonal dynamics, or culture (the lower left quadrant). And a transformation of culture can enact the sorely needed and consequential changes we want to make in our systems and institutions, governmental policies, and financial and economic structures (the lower right quadrant).

There are three obvious major spheres of social praxis: **intimate relationships, work and creative service,** and **civic participation**—the practice of being citizens of our communities and of the world. Each of these spheres differently expresses practice in the lower left quadrant, the "we-space," so that it can bring more love, efficacy/efficiency, and powerful wisdom into life.

Intimate relationships are central, wonderful, and infamously challenging. Nothing is more important to us than love and intimacy, and nothing is more difficult to keep fresh and conscious.

In past centuries, marriage was not expected to fulfill us. It was a legal contract and a necessary social convention, even coexistent with polygamy and prostitution. Today we expect so much more—we want our partner to be our romantic and sexual beloved, our best friend, our comfortable companion, someone who enjoys the same activities and interests and people, a responsible, contributing full partner in all the challenges of our shared life, and our soul mate—and someone who will *keep* sharing our interests and values even as we each change over time. For people to encounter and navigate all the twists and turns and disappointments of life and love as true allies who keep falling in love is a great adventure. And the growth of intimacy can be a profound and unending path of personal and relational growth. But it's not all upside.

None of us are immune to feelings of betrayal. They are present even in the most conscious and loving relationships, where new levels of creative opportunities and challenges emerge. None of us are immune to karma and disappointment. Whether on a physical, emotional, mental, or spiritual level, any measure of "perfection" is set up to fail. But there are pressures in that direction everywhere—on the internet, in advertising, in other media, and among peers. As a result, we become rabid seekers after conditional states of being that are largely unattainable, and we tend to want our chosen intimate "other" to fulfill (or help us fulfill) our impossible expectations. Since life delivers nothing but two-sidedness, it is no wonder that more than half of all marriages end in divorce.

If we are lucky enough to fall in love and commit our lives to another person, we have an amazing possibility. But we must become partners in earning its fruits. The initial surge of special magic, if there was one, will modulate over time, while we are learning to be friends, companions, and partners in life. If we commit to exclusive monogamy and possibly children, opting for "secure psychological attachment" (which is such a major factor for a child's thriving or failure to thrive), all our own childhood attachment wounds will be stimulated. Even secure attachment is touched by at least traces of the more common traumatic patterns—avoidant aloofness, clingy insecurity, inconsistent ambivalence, and often a touch of plain old nasty craziness. Not to mention addiction and depression. The only fruitful response to the challenges of intimacy is to *practice* with these challenges.

Intimate relationships are, for many of us, the primary arena for transformation. An individual can practice on their own in response to the challenges of their relationship, or both partners can agree to practice together. And there are many ways to practice—in fact, any ordinary context can be an arena for practice: compliments, listening, date nights, cheerful alone time, travel, seminars, retreats, social adventures at conferences, explicit couples' counseling, or other conversational and sexual practices. Mature marriages between committed practitioners sometimes find a way to regenerate the in-love spirit of the honeymoon. They can ultimately become a sacred experience of intimacy and common mission that can be a gift of love not only to each other but to all their relations, unfolding an ongoing revelation, wave after wave, for decades.

Intimate relationships also include our relationships with friends, our children, and our parents and other family members, a place where many of us are learning our deepest lessons. How can we express love and support, and still set some necessary boundaries in order to coexist with people who are sometimes intimate strangers, and at a whole different stage of life? We mature as we sustain and manage and ideally deepen our family ties, friendships, housemate relationships, and neighbor relationships. I won't describe them here in detail, because they take on a much larger range of patterns than intimate sexual relationships. But it is important to more liberally define the domain of "intimate relationships" to include the variety of forms of intimacy people are sharing.

Work and creative service is where we function at our best and earn our living. To do this we must practice everything from time management or electronic and online literacy, to all the specific skills and practices that enable us to foster functional excellence in our roles, and make us good team players and leaders. Organizational psychologists have helped many leading corporations to cultivate a culture of inquiry and growth that can scaffold new levels of excellence. This leads to another order of practice, where the evolutionary purpose, the "wholeness value" of the business itself, is examined and embraced, which allows more enlightened corporations to improve our society.

Civic participation in community is not just mandated by our predicament, but it naturally expresses some of the new capacities we are developing as we evolve spiritually. We are just barely beginning to be able to live our lives as a total field of practice. Our species is learning new, important lessons about our responsibility to come together to care for our human future, even as evolution presents us with new survival challenges. We want to do our part to heal our world and culture. We want to make a positive difference. We are willing to change our behavior to become more involved in politics. This impulse has been awakening for years. It has risen sharply while the severity of the ecological predicament has been becoming visible, and recently was magnified tremendously worldwide after the shock waves following the U.S. election of 2016. In order for our activism to be truly healthy, responsive, balanced, and stable, it must be undertaken in the holistic context of a whole life of practice. (Hence, this book!)

RELATIONAL "WE-SPACE" PRACTICES

Our lives are largely tested and fulfilled through our interactions with others. In a time of existential challenge and rapid change, this implies that we are called to new ways of relating. We each have a responsibility to discover and embody deeper and more dynamic interactions, relationships, friendships, families, organizations, communities, alliances, and collectives of all kinds. If our institutions and systems are going to change, it is only going to happen by countless individuals coming together to create a healthier human culture.

It is useful to practice these skills. A whole new category of workshops, seminars, courses, and gatherings specifically focuses on helping us learn to communicate more successfully. Innumerable misunderstandings blight human relationships on every scale, from intimate to global. It has been said that we can best heal (and function beyond) wounds that were inflicted in relationship in the context of relationship itself. Group psychotherapy and encounter groups accomplish something important, and distinct from what takes place in individual psychotherapy. The fields of dialogue, collective intelligence, family therapy, organizational development, group facilitation, and mediation reflect how richly we are learning about how to communicate and relate.

One particular body of interpersonal work pays attention to the quality of the relational field itself. When people make eye contact, they often experience something more than "me" and "you." There is a third presence—the "we"—which is located in the "between," midway between the two pairs of eyes. As people attend to the quality of this third presence, often through structured exercises, the "we-space" itself changes, deepens, and becomes more aware. It is profound and delightful to shift from a subjective to an intersubjective locus of awareness, awake to the shared field, as an experiential sense of awakened collective awareness becomes fuller and deeper and freer. Practice allows these qualities to come forward. It can even become a new form of spiritual authority (some think the "we" can be an alternative to a human teacher).

It can also become a novel setting for creative philosophical, cultural, organizational, and political conversations that can advance culture directly. Such a field can push the envelope of our capacity to imagine our future—a place to explore the implications of newly emergent perspectives and insights, and to apply them, to give us new ways to address current social, cultural, and political challenges. But what is most significant is that it can reveal what evolution feels like from the inside out.

Over the past twenty years, there has been a slow but surprising development in "we-space" practices. Unlike the group process and therapeutic work that emerged in the 1970s, these explorations are not particularly therapeutic. Instead, groups of human beings are coming together to explore mutual awakening, collective intelligence, and collective wisdom. They draw on what has been learned in the field of dialogue, but the shift from a subjective to an intersubjective orientation distinguishes we-space practices. Some of these experiments have been done in the context of intentional communities; others occur in workshops, courses, retreats, or virtual communities over a period of time.

This new we-space work shifts the foundational assumptions of human relationship and culture from separation ("We are each individuals who seek to find relatedness with one another") to connection ("We are participants in and expressions of a larger field of consciousness, which can uplift us, work through us, and itself evolve"). We-space practices are essentially transpersonal practices of wholeness.

Personal spiritual awakening doesn't have to be private. In fact, if it is exclusively private, it is missing something essential. In general, the less private it is, the more integral it is. The more it is understood as relating to all four quadrants of reality, which includes all other human beings, the more potential spirituality has to transform culture.

RELATIONAL PRACTICES AND ACTIVISM

Relational practices are a field in which we can bridge divisions, preparing the ground for wise collective action. But talk will not, ultimately, be enough. Our most substantial practices are tangible initiatives to support the health of, and help evolve, our social structures, systems, and institutions—the lower right quadrant systems in which we live. These include our ecosystems, political systems, governmental policies, energy and food production, transportation, and waste processing systems. System change, as we will soon see, requires *activist citizenship* of three kinds: *in-the-system activism, against-the-system* activism, and *around-the system* activism.

Even when we don't engage outer activities that look like "activism," we all have a contribution to make, and therefore a responsibility. We are each transmitting our inner states, communicating to the larger culture the attitudes and values we are living. Our ways of being are rippling out, influencing others and the world at large. Because the nature of reality is holographic, who I am, who you are, is a reflection of the whole. This is one of the most extraordinary mysteries that science has shown us and that we have yet to internalize and work with.

The consequential and revolutionary potentials of the we-space would begin to be realized if groups of people could learn to sustainably relate to one another on the basis of balanced self-care and altruism, without hemorrhaging energy, and in a way that confers significant selective advantages and mitigates any selective disadvantages. Game theory analysis challenges altruism with the deep riddle, "How can cooperation compete, especially within a larger competitive economic and social and political environment?" Perhaps a new post-conventional level of in-group altruism, combined with appropriately prudent (even wary) goodwill toward out-group members and strangers, provides us with the broad guidelines for a new and positive tribalism. Experiments in this direction reflect a crucial dimension of intersubjective practice.

How might we practice it? We have to discover. But we can see certain principles at work. Any serious experiment along these lines, I believe, must be powered and guided by the integral heart intelligence of the whole being. Merely mental "head" intelligence alone is inadequate. It has dominated and mediated decision making during the recent modern era. And now it is failing, as legal and communication strategies "game the system," thwarting the exercise of the wisdom of the whole in our collective decision making. The head is too easy to fool and cheat. The heart is a wiser poker player. And we need the street smarts of our hara, or gut intelligence. Our reference point must be an ability to make collective decisions and adjudicate differences governed by a shared perception of the intelligence of the "integral" heart, which integrates and mediates the intelligence of the head and gut.

These subjective changes imply changes in behavior. And it is changes in *actual behavior* that will be consequential for our total predicament. So let's look at a system for practicing the ways of being that enable us to behave in ways appropriate to a new human adulthood.

FOUR WAYS OF BEING A LEADER

In Werner Erhard's and Michael Jensen's recent seminal work on leadership, they identify four "ways of being"[34] as the foundations for successful leadership. These are four broad, subjective choices, commitments, or orientations to living that manifest as a whole range of discrete observable behaviors. These behaviors are necessary to the success of corporate leaders, and they also increase the success of any endeavor, including one's personal life. They are each capacities we can develop across a whole lifetime. I have been teaching several of them for years, using different language. But I think Erhard's and Jensen's synthesis provides us with an excellent framework for integral practice and effective evolutionary activism.

I will describe these four ways of being here, because they so directly and effectively cut away the self-deception that has undermined the health and wholeness of human society as a whole. As Harvard professor Chris Argyris wrote: "Put simply, people consistently act inconsistently, unaware of the contradiction between their espoused theory and their theory-in-use, between the way they think they are acting, and the way they really act."[35]

Hypocrisy is a nearly universal human failing. And it is at the root of how we have created our current crises. Penetrating hypocrisy on a social scale requires us to first face and transform it very personally. Erhard and Jensen trenchantly comment, "If you think this does not apply to you, you are fooling yourself about fooling yourself."

They crafted their descriptions of these four essential distinctions with great precision, so I paraphrase liberally from the abovementioned paper in the following descriptions of these four ways of being.

1. The first is **being authentic.** We commonly talk about this as "walking your talk"—behaving consistently with who you hold yourself to be. We all try to do this. But we can also hide from ourselves the fact that we don't—usually because we don't want to look bad, and we are afraid of losing the respect of others. But one cannot *pretend* to be authentic—by definition, that's inauthentic. Paradoxically, the only path to being authentic is to be authentic about your inauthenticities. You must be willing to discover, confront, and tell the truth about where you're falling short—even where you're hiding or pretending. You won't enjoy seeing this. But I have learned that showing my foibles and losing face is not as bad as it seems. It gives me a powerful opportunity to go beyond shame and deceit and realize that I am actually bigger than my weaknesses. It also gives me authentic contact with others. My heart intelligence recognizes that the trade-off is well worth its costs. But this is a continual, lifelong practice, because new inauthenticities crop up every day, new opportunities to choose to be authentic.

2. The second is **presuming to be "at cause" in regard to everything in one's life.** This means that you are willing to view and deal with life from the perspective that you are "at cause" or "fully responsible" for your experience. It is not true that you are the cause of everything in your life. You may even be, in some sense, or in certain respects, a victim. But even when you are responsible for only 1 percent of the causes of a situation,

it is powerful to focus on what you *can* be responsible for. It situates you in relationship to your power rather than your powerlessness. You no longer deal with life from the perspective of a victim, in which you assign cause to the circumstances or to others. This is a stern discipline, but it can produce a dramatic increase in your effectiveness and power. I continue to work with this discipline every day.

3. The third is **being committed to something bigger than oneself.** This is obviously a theme that pervades every chapter of this book. Without the passion that comes from being committed to something bigger than ourselves, we are unlikely to persevere when nothing goes right. This is where the "guts" of leadership come from. When no help is available, how can I find in myself the strength to persevere in the face of impossible, insurmountable hurdles and barriers? If I am truly committed to something bigger than myself, I can reach down inside and find the strength and passion and charisma that are required. I can continue; I can be courageous and creative.

4. The fourth is **being a person of integrity.** This was a huge theme in Erhard's influential work from the 1970s. In this model, integrity is a matter of *one's word* being whole and complete. If we work together, we must be able to rely on one another to do what we say we will do—and when we have said we would do it. As integrity declines, workability declines, and as workability declines, value and performance decline. So optimal performance requires integrity. "Without integrity nothing works."[36]

If you are not able to always keep your word, you can always honor it. Honoring your word, whenever you will not be keeping it in the time frame you agreed to, requires communication. As soon as you become aware that you will not be able to keep your word on time, you can tell everyone impacted that you will not be keeping your word, but that you will do so in the future, and by when—or that you won't be keeping your word at all, in which case you can say what you will do to deal with the impact on others of this failure.

Erhard and Jensen admit that no one, themselves included, is completely in a state of integrity. Integrity, they say, is a "mountain with no top," so in their paper they point out that we had better "get used to (and grow to enjoy) climbing." Nevertheless, all failures of integrity result in problems. We fail to perform, miss appointments and deadlines, and disappoint our partners, associates, and friends. And we are impacted by others whose functioning violates integrity. The effects are huge. It is a powerful practice to face and bridge these gaps responsibly.

Integrity is the necessary and sufficient condition for workability, which gives us the opportunity for performance. When you operate in integrity, there are no communication breakdowns. You have cleaned up any mess you have caused for others. Without such breakdowns people can accomplish remarkable things. We are called upon by our current crisis to accomplish great things, so we'll do well to embrace the practice of integrity.

These four ways of being, and the behaviors that flow from them, are an essential dimension of practice. If a new republic of the heart is to come into being, its citizens will need to rely on one another for more than goodwill. We will need to do a great number of things together—effectively. That is a very practical challenge. We will need to be able to rely on each other to stay oriented to higher commitments—not to blow them off when things get tough. We need others to hold us accountable for practicing at all times, even when we fall short. We will also need allies who can start and lead effective, high-functioning organizations.

Thus, these four ways of being represent powerful practical principles we can draw upon as we navigate the process of implementing the practice of wholeness in social terms. They are essential at work and in our projects and organizations—in fact, they are essential in everything we do as activists and as fellow practitioners.

OUR GREAT SHARED WORK—
TRANSFORMING HUMAN CULTURE

Our future will not be created only by the rich, famous, and power-ful. We each have a chance to make a contribution. The responsibility for our planet cannot lie exclusively with people like Barack Obama or Angela Merkel, or Bill Gates or Warren Buffet, or Bono or Angelina Jolie, or Larry Page or Elon Musk. It cannot accrue only to Pope Francis and the Dalai Lama and the saints of all religions. It must reside with every single one of us. We are each more powerful than we tend to imagine, far beyond the narratives that reduce us to being mere consumers or voters or opinion poll numbers.

And yet, it is not easy to work with other human beings. As difficult as our own transformation may be, transforming the ground of human relationship and how we are *with one another* is much more difficult. That is why it is important to embrace shared expectations for how our ideals are expressed in our behavior.

That's on the high end. But as we see all the time in virtual forums, even the best of us find that in virtual space it is remarkably easy to become arrogant, to dehumanize the "other," to flame, to troll, to demonize, to behave antisocially. It is easy for our ways of relating to one another to degrade due to the loss of human contact that is the result of urbaniza-tion, mobility, and the breakdown of the family and community. The loss of empathy that comes from this makes trust inappropriate. And mistrust becomes a self-fulfilling prophecy.

In many arenas, human culture has regressed to a level of ethical com-promise and noncommunication appropriate only for the least trustable of our fellow humans. We are inadvertently allowing the psychopaths among us to dictate the terms of our relationships to friends and neigh-bors we haven't met yet, in a mad race to the bottom, far away from our highest (or even our more ordinary) human potentials. And we wonder how we can avoid the hell that is our brutal "lowest common denomina-tor" ways of relating to one another.

It is hard to trust people we don't know, even if most of them have good intentions. And it is effectively impossible to trust people we cannot see—especially to trust them more than we feel able to trust those we *can* see. But mass communications now enable us to see people all over the world. Because our attention is drawn to the most bizarre, shocking, and horrific news, and because so many human beings are so different from us, and because we do sometimes encounter psychopaths and sociopaths, our bonds of appropriate mutual trust have been rapidly declining. We often feel that we lack a rational basis for trusting others— even the majority who *are* very trustable.

Such a profound cultural shift is a considerable undertaking that must overcome formidable obstacles. But we are hardly impotent. Our individual transformations can synergistically exert disproportionate power—through many avenues, including our at-first seemingly inconsequential efforts—to shift our whole civilizational system. It is true that they can often function in ways that defy what we perceive as logic.

The popularity of ideas like the "tipping point" or the hundredth-monkey stories are not simply tall tales. As already mentioned, Ken Wilber has pointed to the claim, rooted in the historical evidence of the late 1700s and the American Revolution, that when 10 percent of the population grows into a genuinely higher structure of consciousness, the nature of public agreements and power exchanges can be restructured according to a higher set of (postmonarchical, constitutional, democratic, meritocratic, free-enterprise) rules.

On a common-sense level anyone can recognize that there is a greater whole in which we are all participants, and our actions really do matter because they coincide with and affect that whole. A genuine practitioner with a clear, powerful commitment and strong relational capacities can generate synergy with others, especially by enrolling them in a series of shared agreements like the four ways of being described above. Indirectly, individuals can cogenerate enormous impact. A solid higher commitment stands firm and organizes the randomness of events in much the way that an unmoving obelisk (think of the Washington Monument) placed in the middle of a sandstorm would organize the chaotic patterns of the swirling sand. A few extraordinarily committed practitioners can have outsized impact ("the strength of ten thousand men").

History has been swayed more than once by "great awakenings," by spiritual renewals that have also become political movements. Authentic integral practice can thus be the basis for a transformational cultural and political movement. If it makes use of all the principles described here, it can accomplish great things, *while at the same time deeply nurturing the human heart.* This can transform the practice of political activism. If political activism only means going to boring public meetings and venting your anger after having waited a long time for your turn, most people aren't going to want to be involved.

However, if we can come together with one another in a spirit of celebration, care, and intimacy, in which we are energizing and uplifting one another, then political participation can become something of a celebration—of heartfelt fellowship, and a transformative opening into a new possibility. If we can also rely on one another to embrace authenticity, integrity, and responsibility, we can stand up to the tests of time. Thus, practice can enable us to be the beginning of something truly new. Spiritual fellowship can fortify us to do the hard, "thankless" work that may also be necessary (and we can thank each other for doing it too!).

THE POTENTIALS OF PRACTICE

While on the great archetypal journey, the hero usually gets lost—temporarily. And not just once. At those times, we might feel we've failed, even though we've been transformed and uplifted, and are growing. The journey is both empowering and humbling.

The path teaches us to cherish profound values worthy of lasting commitment, worth years and even decades of "delayed gratification." We act on those values and sustain them over time. (And sometimes we don't.) We find ways to practice every day. (And sometimes we lapse.) Slowly but surely, if we return to the work, it uplifts and transforms us, freeing us from unconscious habit patterns and awakening insight, wisdom, and compassion.

We gradually learn to have more fulfilling relationships, live more happily, or better manage our dysphoria, and be more productive and effective. We feel calmer, saner, healthier, more balanced—and often more inspired, alive, and passionate. If we achieve conventional successes, we see them simply as what they are. And at least for a while, some of us become self-actualized, free, and given over to creative expression of our gifts. We enjoy the wonderful yet temporary fulfillment that life can offer.

Some of us even become "enlightened" in a sense. No one seems to be getting perfected, but *something* keeps happening. We begin to notice that our true identity is consciousness, love, and bliss—an all-encompassing wholeness radiating out of the heart. And yet our friends are suffering, and we see and are part of an endangered world. And, paradoxically, once we have fallen into the wholeness of the heart, even though we are profoundly happy, the sufferings of humanity and nature not only continue to matter—they matter even more than before! Like the great bodhisattvas, today's activist practitioners respond in the fullest way to the suffering of others and of creation, even while being absorbed in and drawing their strength from the awe-inspiring Mystery that suffuses all things.

The path not only has no end—it begins with every new breath. And it is our human condition that the mind tends to drift, numb out, fall asleep. When we tense up into fear and separation, we begin living the small story of the ego.

In this next moment, are we awake enough and willing and courageous enough to become beginners again—and again? Can we open in wonder to the heart of the mystery of existence? Can we awaken from our *ideas* of the mystery to the reality—the living presence of the mystery of this very moment? Once we have opened in astonished wonder, it is all so obvious, and it can seem obvious for a while. At some point we will probably tend to start thinking we now "know" the secret; then, when we're least self-aware, the trance will invisibly creep back.

If we're lucky, we'll keep stirring from that sleep, vaguely noticing that we somehow subtly lost touch with the vivid, tender, glistening aliveness of real awakening. We will realize we've gone on automatic again, and then we'll choose to start anew. The only "final" realization is unconditional willingness to show up fresh and awake in each new moment and to begin the path again, and again, forever.

The New Stories of Our Souls

Please know this. You are not an encapsulated bag of skin dragging around a dreary little ego. You are an evolutionary wonder, a trillion cells singing together in a vast chorale, an organism-environment, a symbiosis of cell and soul.

—JEAN HOUSTON,
EGO DEATH AND PSYCHEDELICS

Our normal waking consciousness ... is but one special type of consciousness, whilst all about it, parted from it by the filmiest of screens, there lie potential forms of consciousness entirely different.

—WILLIAM JAMES, *THE VARIETIES OF RELIGIOUS EXPERIENCE* (1902)

Everything you see has roots in the unseen world.

—RUMI

The ultimate awakening, say the great wisdom traditions, is radical, nonseparate, "nondual" awareness—stable, conscious wholeness. Paradoxically, though, applying nondual orientations to the messiness of life often results in delusions. In practical terms, transcendental spiritual teachings are certainly an incomplete description of what it actually takes to engage in a total and integral life of practice. For most people, a second and simultaneous mystical adventure is also real and necessary. I call it "soul work."[37]

This kind of mystical growth is visible in the life journey through its tests, lessons, and adventures. Soul work contacts intuitive guidance, cultivates character, and discovers purpose. It draws upon the power of the foundational structures of the human psyche and human culture as they are revealed in archetypal stories. Every one of us is living out a unique story, even while we all share a collective story. Today, all those stories unfold in an unprecedentedly urgent context. We are living through a particular moment in our great collective story, and it confers an extra dimension of meaning and purpose on every individual life journey.

Whereas the ultimate spiritual awakening is to radical and transcendental consciousness, soul work intuits and participates primarily in the subtle animating energetics of our lives and their sources of guidance and inspiration.

PURPOSE AND SOUL

A great deal of dynamic personal growth work focuses on purpose. Purpose gives us meaning. Meaning confers value. Value is a basis for dignity. And dignity is essential to health. People who have a sense of positive purpose thrive more. Research documents that a sense of purpose or meaning correlates with dramatic benefits to mood, quality of relationships, success in careers, cognitive function, cardiovascular health, immune function, and longevity.[38] Egoic purpose is sufficient for basic health, but larger purposes beyond the apparent separate ego—for example, those centered around one's community, or nation, or the world, or the cosmos—have the potential to liberate progressively higher levels of happiness and thriving. As a result of these observations, the fields of coaching and psychotherapy have evolved a new specialty, in which people are guided into a full, healthy relationship to their life purpose.

As methodologies are charted for thriving at a new level, we learn the art and science of mastery as it emerges organically from meaning and motivation.

This is an important contemporary expression of the ancient tradition of soul adventure and maturation, which is celebrated in the esoteric traditions of all religions. In that ancient framing, the hero's purpose was his story. He or she seized a means by which to live a meaningful destiny. Today, we all must become the heroes of our own stories. None of us wants an insignificant, ignorant, impoverished, diminished destiny in a diminishing world. We feel called to be the heroes of our lives, and perhaps heroes of our collective life. So a focus on purpose is an ever more crucial dimension of personal transformation. It is an important dimension even of indigenous soul traditions. Ecopsychologists like Bill Plotkin have been exploring how people can incarnate their soul life and purpose by deriving virtue, vitality, and guidance from relationships with natural places, animals, trees, and plants. From both local and global foundations we can become heroically related to our whole more-than-human world.

Socrates, as related by Plato in *The Republic,* told "the myth of Er," which describes what happens between lifetimes. After death each soul drinks the water of Lethe and forgets everything of the life just ended and all past identities. But your character, shaped by the virtue you cultivated in your previous life and lives, remains. And on the basis of your character, you are assigned your *daemon,* your life's soul companion, the carrier of your deeper flavor, your soulful nature and guiding spirit. Then you go before the Fates: Clotho, Lachesis, and Atropos.

On the basis of your character and daemon, Clotho spins forth the unique circumstances of your birth—including everything we ordinarily associate with both heredity and environment—as your "spindle destiny." Next you go before Lachesis, who assigns your luck, the subtle magnetism that surrounds your daemon, attracting and repelling certain people, events, and qualities of experience. This too is responsive to your character, and like your character, this magnetism remains malleable as you continue to practice and cultivate virtue. The last fate, Atropos, assigns the moment of your death, which is determined before you are even born. She was "she who cannot be turned"—not malleable at all.

The deeper significance of this ancient Greek view is what it says about a soul's task, which is to cultivate virtue, to develop character, and to build a relationship with one's daemon—to learn to listen to the voice of the daemon with the "ear of the heart" and to realize one's soul's highest destiny. This resonates with James Hillman's "acorn theory" (1997), in which, like an acorn, which is potentiated to become an oak, the soul is potentiated to gradually express its unique character across the trajectory of a human life. Serious soul work is directed at discovering and realizing the soul's deepest purposes.

In this work, we ask to hear the voice of our soul, our daemon. And then we make ourselves a pleasing offering and wait in silence. After a time, it blesses us by awakening a channel of communication, eventually helping us discover that our own way of being, our own way of seeing things, our own way of going through the world, is, paradoxically, a kind of salvation. By this means we arrive in soul-level authenticity, where our purpose can naturally show itself to us, and show us how to grow to incarnate it more and more fully, and discover its far corners. As we each do this, traveling every step in our unique paths, we can discover that together we are all dancing a precise, beautiful holographic choreography, through which the soul of the world is working out its passionate logic, or entelechy.

FROM THE TRANSCENDENT TO THE SUBTLE

Soul work is very different from spiritual practice of transcendental wholeness. Ultimately these two dimensions of practice and growth are complementary and unitary. They engage different levels of our conscious experience—corresponding to the *causal* and *subtle* sheathes of our esoteric anatomy. It is useful to understand that even though the causal level is senior, radical, and fundamental, the subtle is equally necessary and central to awakening the kind of consciousness and culture that will be adequate to navigating our epochal developmental transition. So let's digress and clarify what that means.

The deepest organizing principle of practice is wholeness. Spiritual growth, both transcendental and embodied, begins with an intuition of wholeness. Transcendental spirituality is the "direct path." It proceeds by the release of all contracted patterns that can obscure wholeness; and it culminates in the transcendence of identification with separation, in which the diverse world of apparently individual parts and beings and forces becomes transparent to its underlying divine unity.[39]

A new, deeper motivation flows from this recognition, usually felt intuitively rather than conceived mentally, since it releases thinking. If verbalized it might be: "My highest destiny is to serve, or to be used by the larger wholeness that is my real nature. How can I keep awakening from contracted patterns of separation to consistently experience and enact wholeness and serve this same freedom in others?" This transpersonal love flows spontaneously from intuitive freedom.

Such awakening to the transcendent divine catalyzes deep humility—the recognition that we exist to serve the whole, in its goodness, truth, and beauty. We come to recognize and celebrate the fact that, while there are profound moments of fulfillment in this life, they are byproducts of a life that is more fundamentally all about *giving*. Our highest happiness comes from being of service, transparent to the Whole, a catalyst for the evolutionary emergence of unprecedented kinds of health and wholeness. The revelation of the undivided divinity of the Whole keeps inspiring and humbling us. It brings us into more authentic cooperative mutual relations with one another. It levels all arrogance. The being simply enjoys and rests in radiant wholeness, with no motives to seek anything. There is just kindness, and a free, caring impulse to be of help.

In a way, you could say that such awakening uplifts us into a transcendental relationship to life, and that it also brings us to our knees in humble service. But we cannot live all of life in the sky or on our knees. After flying we have to land, and after bending we have to get up. Either way, we have to engage the messy fray—creatively, and each in our own unique way. To live our lives along a meaningful trajectory that responds creatively to our current predicament, transcendence isn't sufficient. While the perception of unity leads us to respond to life in dramatically new ways—because the entire living cosmos is, as the Native Americans say, "all my relations"—it doesn't tell us exactly how.

Transcendental consciousness has nothing to say about our specific life choices. Shall I marry this one or that one? Move to a new city or stay put? Study medicine or philosophy? Should I go to the Amazon to support indigenous people fighting Big Oil? Should I write another book? Commit to starting a new business? Sell my house and live communally? Retire now or later? These are hugely consequential decisions. It is important that they be guided by our highest wisdom. But transcendental consciousness and radical realization do not engage them. They offer "no comment." The deepest source of specific guidance regarding the particulars of our ever-changing lives comes from the "subtle" field and the soul. Our access to subtle intuitive information can be powerfully enhanced (or, alternatively, bypassed entirely) by our orientation to transcendental awareness, because it is a distinct domain.

THE SUBTLE REALM OF PRACTICE

According to the universal mystical cosmology known to ancient India, Egypt, Greece, and China (and echoed by indigenous shamanism), there are three broad domains of existence: *gross, subtle,* and *causal.* Our familiar, concrete, *gross* physical reality corresponds to the waking state, and it has knowable laws. But the creative shape of its randomness arises from a spectrum of dancing *subtle* energies, which correspond to hypnogogic theta or dream states. Finally, there is the *causal* (also called *extremely subtle)* domain of consciousness itself, corresponding to deep sleep.

The vast range of the subtle realm has been codified in numerous ways. Perception of it is dependent on one's state of attention and consciousness, so it is often therefore regarded as "merely" subjective. It is far more significant than rational skeptics realize. But knowledge about it involves a very different kind of "science" than the physics and chemistry by which we measure and understand the gross physical universe. And the "art" of that "science" has many expressions. One's intuitive faculties are awakened, and one becomes interested in the beliefs and the metaphors, the archetypes, the stories that pattern the expression of the subtle energies.

Popular self-improvement projects often relate to the subtle domain indirectly, by recognizing the powerful connections between thought and reality. For the most part, the self-improvement phenomenon recognizes a correspondence between beliefs and experience and works to use it on behalf of our desires for love, fortune, status, and good luck. Although this is widely exploited with regard to the desires of the ego personality, it relates to the real dynamics by which subtle energies create concrete experiences.

Whole bodies of practice cultivate subtle awareness and intuition. With expanded awareness practitioners learn to tune in to the subtle field containing vast domains of intuitive knowledge, and even more deeply the voice of their *daemon* or soul and their deeper life purpose. They can learn to release subtle obstacles and participate in the subtle domain in a way that attracts freedom and blessings.

The human psyche's hypnogogic theta states and dreams are subtle experiences. But so are emotions; so is the energy of will, power, and commitment; so are acupuncture meridians. So also are the sublime spiritual states of *savikalpa samadhi* (a high meditative state in which sublime subject-object experience continues). There is a broad spectrum of subtle energies, from the edge of the causal to the edge of the gross physical. The seven chakras, including the three primary energy centers of the body—the hara below the navel, the heart, and the "third eye" in the center of the forehead—express three broad domains, layers of density with different dynamics. All of this lies within the totality of the subtle body.

Subtle-realm mysticism is associated with visions, nonordinary experience, and certain powers. In its purest forms, aligned to although not concentrated in the causal, and embodied concretely, we find a spectrum of individuals we often call "saints."

Indigenous spirituality does not view humans as separate from nature, and it is very much attuned to the animating energetics of the primal forces, places, and creatures of the natural world. Indigenous cultures are replete with stories of these encounters, especially as they confer some measure of influence over life events. Indigenous spirituality attempts to "see" how the subtle soul "dreams" gross physical life events. It knows (in a way that most "civilized" Westerners do not) that it is important to take care of Gaia. In taking care, it is sometimes guided in extraordinary ways.

In this context, the integral evolutionary scale needs to be understood correctly. "Higher" levels of culture and consciousness are of tremendous value and are valorized appropriately; they can scarcely be overemphasized. And it is also true that the "lowest" are most basic and fundamental, and the "higher" are utterly dependent upon them—and thus, in a sense, the hierarchy operates in both directions and sometimes must be stood on its head.

There are human beings who have gone out in the desert alone, taken care of themselves, and stayed safe—even, for example, running through a cactus-strewn desert on a moonless night without any missteps. This is a vivid illustration of how the subtle can exercise powers in the gross realm. Wild nature has been in conversation with us since our most archaic origins, so it's no wonder.

Indigenous spirituality draws on the universality of the human being and the human structure, so it has elements of all three centers. But it is especially strong at the root. It is rooted in the feet and the hara, the vital center and the bright vital force of creation that affirms life.

Radical integral ecology integrates transcendental and earth-based spirituality. It recognizes that nondual realization must be lived *in relationship* with conditional experience, where we are family with the whole more-than-human world. And we can do that most efficiently by inhabiting a role in a story that organizes our faculties. Thus, it is true to our heart impulse, but also *easiest and most productive* to worship our Mother Earth, to repent of our violence to her, and to discover a new, technologically advanced spiritual relationship with her. That is only healthy and sane. Indigenous people all over the world are imploring us to stop dynamiting the mountains, damming the rivers, and polluting the oceans and skies. They are right. An integral spirituality may start with the transcendent recognition of Oneness, yet it also must include the subtle dimensions, the soul, and our vital, living connection with the Earth and all our relations.

At this point in the journey of the human species, an integral revolution of the heart asks us to reclaim and reopen our connection not only to radical consciousness but also to the embodied heart and soul, and not only to ourselves but also to the vital energies and intelligence of the living earth. As an Australian aborigine elder of the Warlpiri people said, "It was the land that cultivated the people, before the people cultivated the land."

THE ROLE OF THE TRANSCENDENT
IN SUBTLE SOUL WORK

This middle, subtle position of soul is called "the transformation realm" or *Sambhogakaya* in Tibetan Buddhism. It stands between the gross realm (*Nirmanakaya*) and the *Dharmakaya*—the transcendental Reality. The subtle realm is a place of profound and necessary practice, although it can also be a slippery domain that easily gives rise to confusion. The highest spiritual realizations of the Dharmakaya are transcendental and radical, while the subtle (Sambhogakaya) is concerned with the characteristics that are unique to each of us.

Subtle soul work is necessary—and it cannot be fruitful unless it is informed by transcendental, nondual wholeness. As you develop in relation to the energies of the subtle, you get to a place where instead of passively feeling the effect of the subtle influences around you, they begin to organize around you. You become a more forceful presence. You begin to attract the energy of the universe. Instead of being on the receiving end of others' ego energy, they are at the receiving end of yours, and it feels almost like magic. But without being informed by the disposition of radical self-transcendence, these feelings can lead to a profoundly deluded "spirituality" based on ego-inflation—a spirituality with a big "me" at the center. You may believe you have a very special, unique purpose—or that you will achieve a life in which all your deepest desires are fulfilled. The subtle field can be an enormous trap for the ego—that part of one's self that only really cares about itself. This is why the subtle field that holds the soul needs to be understood in the context of the transcendence of ego.

Many high spiritual teachings agree that human beings don't really exist as separate entities. My first teacher, Adi Da Samraj, taught that what seems to be an "entity" is only a superficial arising pattern. The actual consciousness of each so-called person is identical to Being itself—and Being is what it is that is showing up as the dream of conditionally manifested existence. We presume ourselves to be such entities when we identify with experience, and at best we think the realm in which we are "one with God" is somewhere "else." But actual divinity is simply the shining, conscious being that is our nature at all times and under all circumstances. My teacher described his awakening as the literally felt realization that the body is arising in the psyche, rather than vice versa—in other words, the perception that the body is a psychic manifestation, not merely an elemental one. Then it is obvious that the true self is not hidden deep within us, attainable only through dramatic mystical experiences. Spiritual realization is simply awakening to the direct stable perception that all beings are already and only the one Beingness of all things.[40]

Informed by such an intuition of one's inherent nonseparate identity with the universal, you can engage all of life—including subtle soul work—in an ego-transcending fashion. You become moved to surrender at all times to a higher principle. Full enlightenment isn't required, but an intuition of this orientation is a necessary foundation for a healthy relationship to soul work.

Eventually the limitations of "me"-centered spirituality *must* be transcended. Nothing in the world exists in a vacuum, and no part of the world can achieve fulfillment apart from or at the expense of the whole. As we continue to push past so many "red lines" on global warming, and the social fabric that held us together is torn apart, does seeking one's personal glory, wealth, and fulfillment even make sense? Is the ego immune to a threatened life-support system?

Our interconnectedness makes an intuition of radical wholeness absolutely critical. It shifts our identity and our sensitivity so that we begin to allow the *animus mundi,* the soul of the whole natural world, to operate through us, from our deepest psyche to our most ordinary behavior. Then transcendental, causal, and nondual spirituality (most radically understood) can instill an intuition of a larger identity and an aspiration to be of benefit to the whole. This is the telos of wholeness. It "wants" more health and thriving and coherence and integrity, extending always wider.

A glimpse of the nondual undividedness of all being can function as an initiation. It can make a lasting imprint on the soul. Transcendental spiritual practice helps us to develop the spiritual strength to continually open to the transparent aliveness that is the essence of all experience. It is called "Luminous Emptiness" in Tibetan teachings. It can confer a self-transcending intuition, liberating the ability to see through the fears and resentments and pride and greed and insecurities of the separate self. Again and again one sees that this life is not for the "separate me." We awaken to love as a fundamental attitude and life commitment. We want to serve and glorify life itself. We discover that our deepest, truest soul purpose is the hero's journey of being used by, shaped by, and transparent to that greater life.

THE HIDDEN NARRATIVES OF OUR LIVES

When we orient toward the transcendent, we sometimes use practices that realize "the emptiness of self" and "the emptiness of time." We wake up from the story of our lives. It can seem as if it all was just illusion. In a way that's true. We expand beyond the conditional boundaries of the self in a process that "expands" our consciousness, which is an apt metaphor, because transcendental spirituality is analogous to space.

But when we open to our deep interior life, carried through time through the soul-lineage of our ancestors, something shifts. We feel the whole living Earth, the universal, free, primitive spirituality of every tribe on Earth, and suddenly we are selves—bands of individuals—moving in *time* through our life journey. This is known to everyone in any sincere soul-based or earth-based spiritual practice. For this purpose, we accept a perspective in which our self and soul are real, and time and space are real too. Instead of transcending it, we meet the soul directly, discover its story, and enact its journey—even though, from the radical transcendental perspective, it is ultimately nothing but the playfulness of luminous emptiness.

From this perspective, even radical, nondual enlightenment and the dissolution of the separate self sense—even the ultimate realization—would still be an event in the story of the soul's journey. Everything can be viewed in terms of that journey. The "final" truths of nonduality are true too. But every perspective is both true and partial, including the very "highest." So our life story is another valid and very useful perspective. Much can be understood and accomplished using this perspective; a strictly transcendental perspective does not provide this information. Both perspectives are profoundly true, but when alienated from one another, they are each also critically *partial*.

What a journey we are on—all of us. Describing it in the poetic language of the soul, we could say, "We all chose to take birth at this moment in evolutionary time, right when we are beginning to blast off into amazing technological advances, right when we are beginning to imperil the health (to human-friendly conditions, at least) of our Mother Earth with our population and pollution. We have stepped onto the stage of life at precisely the moment that an almost mythic heroism seems to be called for—and from as many awakened people as possible."

STORIES OF TRANSITION

The modern narrative has failed us. We are not just separate egos competing in a meaningless materialistic world for dominance, in societies that must grow or die. The postmodern narrative too has failed. If we embrace our feelings and all creatures and other victims of the system, rejecting all "grand metanarratives," we find ourselves lost in the aperspectival madness of a posttruth world. The integral narrative of evolution opens up a space in which many stories can reveal new levels of meaning and purpose.

A single coherent narrative can return, one that engages our imagination far more than the mere ascent of a staircase. The story of the unfolding and complexification and awakening of spirit in matter is beautiful, inspiring, and capacious; there is room in it for many stories. And we are each living out a particular *story*. We show up most fully in our lives by inhabiting an identity on a journey, so that our way of being is organized by metaphors, archetypes, and stories. When we fall in love, a sense of joy pervades the being and our attention and interest are magnetized to our beloved. Although we could do practices to cultivate love and hope and positive expectations, it is simpler and more intuitive to simply arrive in an actual love story, inhabiting the powerful archetype of the lover. We can fall in love with all existence, with Mary, with Shiva, with our own Buddha nature, or with another embodied human being, but it is a real love story, regardless. Metaphors are an empowering shorthand that organizes our attention and neurology and intention.

Joseph Campbell and other neo-Jungians have mapped many great archetypal stories that human beings have tended to enact: the hero's journey, the divine romance, the death and rebirth cycle, the coming-of-age ritual—and on and on. Meanwhile we are all waking up to the fact that we are on a journey together—and that it is time for the human species to undergo rapid transformation. So our soul's archetypal story involves participation in the archetypal metacrisis we are collectively encountering—which calls for our humility, maturity, and heroism.

How can we make sense of this crisis? What is our real story? Certainly, the entire cosmos is one unfolding evolutionary story. But its drama contains plot twists—moments of extinction, birth, and transformation. Stars and dinosaurs have gone extinct, as have 99 percent of the species in our planetary history, as have whole ecosystems millions of years in the making. Meanwhile, there have been extraordinary times in which many new creatures have developed. So, how would we describe our present moment, taking into account all levels of physiology, purpose, and commitment?

Futurist Duane Elgin has observed that social and cultural transformation will depend on the stories that we believe and inhabit—stories that can either keep us paralyzed, or catalyze new responses to our predicament. Elgin reports that when he asks people how they perceive the future, the answers are telling. "Many people say: 'We are going to hit the wall,'" he says. "People have a very diminished, impoverished, and frightening view of our common future. As a consequence many people pull back in denial, living in the present and ignoring the future. And if they are not in denial, they are often in despair."[41]

Two stories come from these responses. One is "It is not happening," which allows us to go on living as we are. The other is, "It is happening and there is nothing we can do about it," which ends up leading to the same thing—inaction—as well as depression. Although the collapsing and rebuilding of civilizations has happened throughout human history, the world is now one integrated system (geologically and sociologically)—so we will rise or fall together, depending on how we respond. "We need a story that will take all of us to a more promising future together," says Elgin. "But what kind of story is that?"

Elgin argues that the climate crisis is *not* such a story. The crisis itself needs to be contextualized and placed within a story to give us human beings a way to coordinate and cohere our imagination and energy. "The climate crisis is fundamentally a communications crisis," he says. "We are not going to handle climate change and the crises that it represents unless we begin to communicate it more effectively. I think for this reason a story is helpful." Elgin offers several overarching narratives that can hold the reality of climate change and the other, interlocking tensions and crises I have been speaking about:

- *Humanity is growing up.* We are in our adolescence as a human family. We are rebellious and reckless, our thinking is short-term, our appetites large, and our behavior impulsive. All of us adults remember how difficult this passage was in our own lives—it is an initiation that most of us end up figuring out ourselves because our culture doesn't provide us with any guidance as we make this passage from child to adult. Imagine, then, our entire species of 7.5 billion people trying to make this rite of passage with no guidance.

- *The global brain is waking up.* More than three billion people have internet access today, and within the next few years five billion will have access. This gives us an extraordinary capacity to communicate. It is a remarkable coincidence that, just as we are in this transition, we are developing new ways to communicate, to develop collective understanding, and to share human consciousness. This is new in human history. The entire world is being woven together into this communicative web. What can happen if this "global brain" becomes more conscious and even self-aware?

- *This is a time of planetary birth.* Like a woman's labor pains, this process is painful, frightening, difficult, and unpredictable. Amazingly, on the other side of that pain and contraction is new life! What we are seeing now is the labor pains of a new species civilization getting born. How can we help this birth process along? How can we hold the intention and "live into" the new life world that is coming?

The Great Transition Story project[42] has imagined more than a dozen other positive narratives, which can be freely "woven together." This may be a great hero's journey, whereby humanity learns to trust the power of love and chooses to evolve consciously. Perhaps it is a great reconciliation, in which the hypermasculine modern world learns to appreciate the divine feminine and integrate indigenous wisdom. Maybe we are awakening from a false dream of a dead world and reconnecting with the living universe. Maybe our travails express a great healing crisis. Maybe humanity is coming together as an emergent superorganism with a new kind of wisdom and intelligence. (And perhaps our story is that we are "waking up from all stories" into unmediated wisdom that can even begin to organize our life.) Clear and resonant stories enable us to understand who and where we are and what we are doing, so we can respond effectively to our current challenges. We can contemplate them and be inspired. They are not mutually exclusive—in a way, each is a metaphor for the others. Imagine how remarkably different our experience would be if these great transition stories became the working metaphors for global culture—and we followed up by enacting them.

Sinking deep into yourself, do you see a trajectory for your life in any of these stories of transition? What powers and capacities are called into being? In what ways do these roles require you to practice and evolve? Maybe your heart says, "The world is in trouble and I feel called to rise heroically to defend Gaia." How can that guide and shape your choices and behavior and capacities to enact that heroic archetype?

By inhabiting a narrative, our beliefs, behaviors, and speech become coherent. The fragmented parts are made coherent by the story, and we also invoke subtle energies and graceful synchronicities. The laws of the subtle realm are implicit in the structure of mythic and archetypal narratives. If you are at first uncomfortable with the "irrational" nature of this principle, think of living a narrative that is congruent with your being and the reality around you, one that can empower your participation in life.

THE POWER OF ARCHETYPES

A single metaphor or archetypal story can much more efficiently and powerfully uplift our state and our effectiveness than a series of disconnected daily practices can. All practices, however powerful, have new meaning and coherence when enacted as expressions of an archetypal story. Realizing, for example, that this whole world is my Beloved transforms how I move through my day. Whatever is before me is God! In these times of challenge, that metaphor can take us deep, through layers of defense, doubt, and compensation into a fundamental trust in life that can withstand an environment of confusion and chaos. Metaphor is how we are structured. Story is how we are built. Archetypal stories make sense to us neurologically.

At this point in time, it is critical that we discern archetypal stories that can be *true for us individually and also culturally.* Luckily, the great transition stories we've mentioned above weave together organically. On one level, we seem to be asked to grow into our true identities as sovereign protectors of our Mother Earth. On another, as I said earlier in this book, we are also addicts, called now to finally break our collective addiction to our comfortable but degraded lives of bourgeois consumption. We can support each other as brothers and sisters in the good work of addiction recovery—like a twelve-step program run by the whole living planet. But we also perhaps feel like peaceful revolutionaries. That archetype resonates in me—after all, I was raised in an intentional community,[43] and mentored by my co-op aunts and uncles to be a nonviolent revolutionary. And some of us feel called to serve as a doula, supporting Mother Earth in her difficult birth of a new civilization. All of us are awakening, perhaps going through a process of dissolution in the chrysalis, and subsequent metamorphosis into a human butterfly.

To quote Michael Meade's *The Genius Myth:*

The answers to the overwhelming problems and daunting global issues we all face cannot simply come from the limited consciousness of abstract reasoning and scientific attitudes that currently dominate the world. The problems run deeper than the simple facts of the matter. The answers must be found in deeper places as well. The loss of a felt connection to the divine spark hidden within each person may be the greatest curse of modern mass societies. When the dark times come around and great changes are afoot, it becomes more important that awake people remain awake and that more individuals awake into the nature of the spark they carry within. And the great drama of life, the human soul becomes the extra quantity and distinct living quality needed to tip the balance of the world toward creation.[44]

When we begin to participate in the subtle field, an enormous range of potential opens up. We discover that we are conducting a whole symphony of animating poetic energies through our bodies and psyches. We can become lightning rods to the greater energies of the anima mundi or World Soul. This is the domain of practices that teach our gross life to honor the subtle, opening a new dimension of creativity. We can learn to let in the bigger forces that want to enact a particular archetypal story through us—the warrior, the magician, the tragic hero, the lover, the mother, the king, or the queen.

Human beings are structured to experience all of this bodily. We *feel* it. Like an actor inhabiting a character, we feel our way into our role in the archetypal story we are actually living. This resonates within us at multiple levels. It draws on a wide range of hidden abilities by reverse-engineering the neurological cues that trigger higher capacities of the brain, the nervous system, and our biochemistry. Without naively believing in the objective ontological truth of these archetypes, as someone with a prerational magical or mythic perspective would, we can still "believe" and inhabit them in powerful ways. Taking up the archetype organizes and liberates our gross, subtle, and causal capacities—particularly the subtle—which in turn affects our bodies.

Living a new story is unavoidable, in any case, now that we have entered an era when our world drama has flashed its apocalyptic teeth and stopped making sense. The absurdity and existential danger of the world crisis that is gaining momentum gives us leave to take risks, to take theatrical poses, to assume the mantles of our archetypes, and to lovingly and playfully unleash their power through a kind of ceremony of transformation, a magical dance, whose intent is to conjure forth a better story for all of us. To the degree that our larger human world is in crisis, facing new challenges that require new responses, this is expressed not just in gross physical ways but also in subtle energetic and psychic ways.

There are larger subtle dynamics, even an impulse in the soul of the world that is trying to express a new level of intelligence through each of us. Recognizing this, soul work opens up a political practice, a form of subtle activism that complements the gross. We are each artists, showing up face-to-face with the soul of a world that has summoned each of our souls to its unique destiny. We are all in play with other souls, tasked with becoming new human beings in a new kind of human culture, one that naturally cocreates a healthy future for one another and for our children, our species, and all our other relations on this planet.

It is clear to climate activists that our governments and industry are responding far too slowly to the reality of global warming. But the physical trends leading to disaster don't tell the whole story. Subtle and other nonlinear dynamics are also at play, and they open space for additional hope. Too often, we forget that collective ceremonies and rituals and other communal psychophysical enactments of archetypal metaphors and narratives can be valid dimensions of activism—ones that perform the vital function of restoring gross, subtle, and causal harmony and wholeness to both individual activists and their whole community.

MY OWN SOUL WORK

To give you an example of how one can engage in what I call Integral Soul Work, I will share my own reckoning with the hero archetype. The hero is a primary archetype, particularly for men. The original magic and mythic heroes were male, and their journey from the safe harbor of home and mom out into a worldly quest, battle, victory, and subsequent return has been a subtle blueprint for men's lives for millennia. This myth has always resonated in me. But in light of our current global predicament, my understanding of it has gone through dramatic changes.

I come from a line of people who go back to the Pilgrims, intrepid, righteous pioneers who came to the New World in a quest for religious freedom. A generation later, as settlers, our forebears pioneered a life on a new continent, trying to live a new pious, hardworking way of life in a wild new place. In the process at least one of my ancestors became a perpetrator of the genocide of the native people, but not before his wife and children had been victims of native slaughter.

Although it was invisible to me for many years, I have been shaped by the character of my lineage. They held and transmitted the idealistic values that drove the whole Western civilization project, I now see, with a nearly overwhelming tendency to subordinate all other values to their own. This same hubris enabled other members of our WASP tribe to believe wholeheartedly that they were "doing good" when they introduced "savages" to Jesus and his gospel of love, and did the work of spreading their "civilized" way of life.

I remember my grandparents teaching me reading and math and history and the great Western literary canon and the value of hard work. They nurtured in me the classic values and capacities of white

Anglo-Saxon Protestant culture. These values are in my blood, and were in my mother's milk. I contain in me the dignities and disasters of the modern spirit, and also its growth into pluralistic postmodern values.

But now that project is colliding with planetary limits, and our overshoot of our planet's carrying capacity is doing untold violence. Seeing this, I want to respond heroically. To do so, I must question my heroic instincts, since they are rooted in the very worldview that has created the predicament I feel called to address.

Ironically, the lifestyle of the great global educated middle class *is* the very unsustainability I want to transform. Conscious practitioners are all now asked to question and transform the nature of the striving by which we perpetuate our well-being. We are in many respects the very hope of the world, and yet the fact that there are so many of us, consuming so much, means that we are also the greatest threat to the world—the very thing that is most overheating our biosphere and noosphere, diminishing our descendants' prospects and our own well-being, and threatening our planet. We can say again, "We have met the enemy and he is us."

After periods of renewed hope and despairing recognition, I struggled to absorb the implications of this for months. Even though I understand the futility of moral self-flagellation, I also recognized the allure of too-quick self-justification. Heroically, I had taken it upon myself to face and comprehend the crisis of our moment. And in confronting the complicity of my own lineage and lifestyle, I realized I must question my very way of being. The heroism of progress and idealism embodies the very arrogance that has brought us to the brink of destabilizing the balances of the whole biosphere.

Ironically, the climax of my hero's journey wasn't a heroic battle and victory; instead, it took me into uncomfortable new territory. It did not look or feel or taste like any heroism I could have imagined when I began. In the hero's journey, at the apex of the drama, the hero does battle with his nemesis in the underworld and is nearly killed, but then realizes who he is and uses his magical powers to slay his adversary and emerge victorious.

But it seems now that this story needs to be turned inside-out. Instead of slaying an outer nemesis or enemy "other," I am asked to slay the monster within, subtle arrogance that tends constantly to creep through the aperture of idealism into our life quests. I must act, but first I must watch and listen.

Out of this emerges a new hero archetype, that of the *yin hero*. Instead of winning a conventional victory by slaying a discrete, incarnate "other" adversary, a very different "inner heroism" is called for. I can perhaps meet and slay the residues of the whole legacy of arrogance within me. I can repent of it. I can be converted. There can be authentic renunciation. There can be service and kindness and generosity. Instead of a heroism predicated upon a presumption of separation from the world, this might be the heroic spirit that sees through that separation and enacts wholeness in its place.

Not only is this humbler than the classic heroism of the ancient myths, it is nobler than the story of the ironic antihero of so many films and stories. It is a new story, of humble spiritual heroism. It is perhaps a *feminine* heroism—not just balancing the previously masculine heroism and its excesses, but expressing an important developmental advance.

I didn't commit the sins of my lineage but I did inherit its privileges. I can own some responsibility and face the reality of my tribe's role in the human predicament. The white man's tribes conquered the globe. I am part of that. I can seek relationships of depth: within my ancestral tribe, and across tribal boundaries, with other tribes, and also with new tribal brothers and sisters—people who are now "my tribe" by virtue of our shared commitment to the wisdom of the heart. I can perhaps "declare peace" and approach others humbly, genuinely intending to be of benefit.

The model, then, is not the warrior hero, but the humility of the saint. Not Achilles, but St. Francis. Maybe now is the time to wash the feet of the leper. So my first intention in transforming this archetype in myself has been to be honest enough to face what I would rather not see, and customarily avoid. By my example, I can perhaps thereby elicit others' courageous honesty.

This is not a *yang* (masculine, active, agentic) matter of *doing* or *asserting* insight or strength, like an ancient mythic hero. The heroism that is needed now is *not* for me to assertively act upon my existing level of understanding of the big impossible questions posed by the human predicament. The answers I already have at hand are an insufficient basis for effective action.

The new challenging truths of our predicament must be *opened to and received*. It is a *yin* (feminine, receptive, communal) matter of allowing a much bigger view of reality to register in awareness, and to surrender into full apprehension of its totality. This yin yoga requires building new attentional and attitudinal "muscles," new capacities human beings have not until now often exercised and developed. This requires a deep, sustained capacity for *receptivity*. But it's not that simple; at the heart of yin heroism there's a call for a new level of yang action.

WILD OLD STORIES

It's important to appreciate that these great archetypal stories are not the only tales to which we can turn. We are busily writing new stories of many kinds, large and small, and discovering old ones. The great integral evolutionary metanarrative is perhaps the simplest, biggest, and newest of all these stories. Contemporary storytelling is groping for new terms—using everything from comics to sci-fi to myth—to startle us awake and into contact with a deeper relationship to life. And some are reviving our oldest stories, which can work a different magic, informing the psyche of aspects of their depth.

The primary great archetypal stories are seemingly very neat when compared to our most numerous ancient stories—the richly textured and often macabre folk stories, fairy tales, and myths whose origins are lost in the shroud of prehistory. There are thousands of such stories. We know just a few, such as the stories of Hansel and Gretel, Iron John, and Rumpelstiltskin. Each of them expresses in some way a great archetypal story—but with indelible dark images and special plot twists, each one unique and resonant. These stories, perhaps five thousand years old, are replete with vivid details and terrifying ugliness. But in them we can sometimes catch a glimpse of something more than human speaking to us in a strange but familiar symbolic language. Perhaps that is in part because they have no particular author—they have been passed along by countless oral storytellers. They originated in a domain the aboriginal Australians called the "dreamtime," a place where humans encountered something powerful, fierce, sacred, and deeply humbling. Something in that "other side" was dreaming the human story in terms that might offer us keys to understanding our humanity now. These dark old folktales may help us unlock the doors through which each of us must pass in order to find our way through and to the other side of the great Genjo Koan we are facing now.

As our culture is broken open by the consequences of our careless destruction, these dark, complicated stories may prove more resonant and revealing than ever. They express a sensual, reflective, troubled psyche, quite like our own inaccessible depths. Maybe the ancients knew something that we have forgotten and now need to remember, something that underlies our anxiety, something that opens up a vital, exciting new way of being human together. I've discovered the importance of discovering and invoking the stories that resonate with me—insights that go back to a time before I knew too much to be wonderstruck.

In my own journey into "yin heroism," I find meaningful instruction in the story of the lindwurm and his bride, as told by mythologist and storyteller Martin Shaw. In this Norwegian fairy tale, the future of the kingdom is held hostage by a royal dragon (the "lindwurm") who demands a bride before the only prince will be allowed to marry. But each maid he weds disappears and is never heard from again, until there are no more takers. A shepherd girl from the edge of the kingdom agrees to wed him—in a year and a day. She makes this offer on impulse, without knowing why. Then, wandering in the woods, she encounters a wise old woman and asks for her guidance.

Marry the lindwurm, she is told, but here is her price: She must spend this year making herself ten white nightgowns. She is to richly embroider the bosom and heart of every layer, so that each gown is fitted to wear over the last. She must procure a tub of lye, a tub of milk, and many whips. Come the wedding night, she will offer to disrobe, but must order the groom to first shed his skin too—then another, and another, layer after layer, until all the skins are shed. She will then scourge him soundly with lye-soaked lashes and then bathe him in milk—and embrace him.

All goes according to plan. When the monster has shed his last layers of protection, the bride embraces her handsome prince. In the morning, the apprehensive court opens the door of the bedchamber to find the pair sleeping in each other's arms. There is great rejoicing, another wedding is held, and the two live happily ever after.

This kingdom was saved by a poor unknown young girl, one who stepped forward without knowing why, who spent months stitching, caring for the heart, layer after layer. She was willing to give herself completely to the unknown, but learned to require a reciprocal submission, layer upon layer.

In this story I catch sight of rich, mysterious instruction. Some monsters need to be transformed and loved, rather than only fought and slain. I identify with the lindwurm's bride. Each stitch to the bosom of the wedding shirt prepares me. I need to wander into the forest to find higher guidance. My guidance and heart intelligence allow me to negotiate from strength; after all, even my "adversary" wants and responds to wisdom and love.

Like me, my fellow citizens of this new republic of the heart will discover themselves stepping forward before they have a plan. They too will need to find their unique guidance. It may be our willingness to love what on the surface looks unlovable that will make a crucial difference to the kingdom. We may need "a year and a day" of active preparation.

And we are advised not to expect our love to be reciprocated until we have applied the balm of milk, and after requiring the stripping off of many layers of mutual defenses and being strong enough to apply the most painful kind of healing medicine.

There is much darkness to transform, and the single lindwurm of the story has in our time multiplied into a thousand serpents and a few vile dragons, all of whom must be married and transformed into princes. But fierce love, defying fear, is a potent secret weapon.

FROM YIN TO YANG

Practicing wholeness draws me to the yin posture of deep receptivity. Typically we tend to opt quickly for action, rather than a prolonged engagement with the big questions. We live in a maze of culturally constructed narratives and mental structures that are always limiting what we can perceive. The big questions of our time require us to open our minds and hearts via a whole series of profound shifts and an ongoing process of resting in profound inquiry, questioning our assumptions.

This is hard. Our nervous systems did not evolve to remain in deep receptivity for too long. And we are afraid of what we'll see. It is hard for me, but I seem willing (perhaps to an unusual degree) to tolerate the discomfort that prolonged questioning provokes. It stretches the range of the nervous system, which hasn't adapted fully to doing such a task on such a scale. Most people become impatient when a decision requires more than a few hours of deliberation. It can be torture to press into urgent questions for days at a time, let alone months or years or decades. And yet the nature of humanity's great Genjo Koan seems to ask us to build this capacity, individually and culturally.

The human nervous system rebalances the stresses of sustained receptivity with the flow of the experience that unfolds once we go into action. It is a relief to go from the abstract to the concrete particulars of direct life experience. We gather a different kind of data that way, grounding our interior lives with real-world feedback. But for us to be effective agents of change requires alternating cycles of receptivity and enactment. We gather data, but then we design a strategy. We may question that strategy, but then we revise it and execute. We take in information, but then we analyze it and draw conclusions. Action is never far away, always an essential part of the process.

Our desire to short-circuit the yin process results in our almost universal tendency to jump to premature conclusions. Our unprecedented encounter with planetary limits and the exponential complexification it involves places us in a radically new situation requiring profound receptivity to a new kind of logic. But we are structurally biased to interpret our situation using our familiar, inadequate cognitive and intuitive structures.

To respond to this new and changing reality, our action must be grounded in a greater wholeness, which calls us to an entirely new mode. We must become capable of taking perspectives and metaperspectives (perspectives *on* our perspectives) that we cannot yet fully comprehend. That requires surrender—the yin mode of being.

Surrendering means relaxing the compulsion to act based on the overconfidence of the analytic, separative mind. The yin mode of being allows us to drop into a sense of undividedness, so that we are informed by the whole of which we are a part. This creates the ground for transformation. You have to let go before you can come together in a new way. Through the most profound yin receptivity, I allow myself to be reorganized by contact with that which I have not previously been able to see and know. It is a profound process, one that leaves me with little to hold on to, which is why it requires humility and spiritual courage—to trust the unknown.

From this yin receptivity, new action unfolds. In the classic yin-yang symbol, a spot of yin (white) lies at the center of the yang (black) field, and yang (black) within the yin (white).

This points to the fact that, paradoxically, the most powerful, quintessentially yang essence comes from yin, and vice versa. Our predicament calls for action, but truly effective yang action must arise from the receptivity of yin. In cultivating this deep receptivity, we "slow down to speed up." Although the transformations dictated by our predicament are certainly urgent, an anxious, uptight sense of urgency arising from the already-known yang agency will only trip us up. What *will* help is curiosity, humility, openness, a sense of humor, and compassion for ourselves and one another. These are the qualities of a yin approach.

Yin receptivity brings us in touch with our soul. This deep receptivity drops us into *being* (with which you might sometimes feel like you are very much in touch, or barely in touch at all). You are always already utterly inseparable from your soul. You've always been in touch with the voice of your soul. You must simply sink deep enough to recognize it.

Nietzsche evokes this in the third of his Untimely Meditations, "Schopenhauer as Educator":

> *How can man know himself? It is a dark, mysterious business: if a hare has seven skins, a man may skin himself seventy times seven times without being able to say, "Now that is truly you; that is no longer your outside." It is also an agonizing, hazardous undertaking thus to dig into oneself, to climb down toughly and directly into the tunnels of one's being. How easy it is thereby to give oneself such injuries as no doctor can heal. Moreover, why should it even be necessary given that everything bears witness to our being—our friendships and animosities, our glances and handshakes, our memories and all that we forget, our books as well as our pens. For the most important inquiry, however, there is a method. Let the young soul survey its own life with a view of the following question: What have you truly loved thus far? What has ever uplifted your soul, what has dominated and delighted it at the same time? Assemble these revered objects in a row before you and perhaps they will reveal a law by their nature and their order: the fundamental law of your very self. Compare these objects, see how they complement, enlarge, outdo, transfigure one another; how they form a ladder on whose steps you have been climbing up to yourself so far; for your true self does not lie buried deep within you, but rather rises immeasurably high above you, or at least above what you commonly take to be your I.*[45]

What is surging forth here is existential, passionate, and assertive, which is profoundly yang. Each of us has a vital need to discover the *real* shape of our being, to live our life's real purpose, to bring to life and action our soul's reason for bringing us into our mother's womb.

We must say "Yes!" to this—we must *choose* it. It is what makes it possible for our busy minds to get out of the way so that we can fall silent and take the dictation of the voice of our soul. Something profoundly passionate and active is the basis for our most profound openness.

This is the yang at the heart of the yin. At this point in the journey we must dive deeper into the depths and discover a hidden treasure that shines in the darkness. We tune in to this deepest yin essence and discover not an escape, but the soul's passion to show up in *life*. Our yin listening has earned us a depth that makes something new possible. We can act and choose in yang mode without just going back to the superficial, compensatory, reactive level of our being. Something whole and new becomes possible.

In this, I discover that a deeper level of yang heroism is possible. I imagine that it might naturally emerge as the redemption of my pilgrim ancestors. This heroism is not rugged individualism, but instead is likely to cocreatively dance in *mutuality* into a collective nobility.

This discussion of soul in the context of culture requires an acknowledgement of something else: tribe. Souls make tribes. And tribes have souls. Nations' and tribes' souls are the source of the positive evolutionary purpose and meaning of nationalism. This is how we can all coexist. Now tribes of national and ethnic identities are asked to go beyond the "us versus them" mode of behavior and cooperate peacefully and discover new synergies, not just with one another. Globalism and nationalism are an enduring dynamic polarity; neither can vanquish the other. These tribes can thrive by cocreating an enduring relationship to a new species of globalist tribes.

Most human beings participate in many tribes—local, virtual, biological, noetic. Many of our tribes are globalist in their flavor and disposition. But most of us have dual (or more!) citizenship in tribes of overlapping and nonoverlapping domains. And it is the archetypal stories by which our tribes make peace—and make a shared future—that will matter for the time ahead.

DISCOVERING AND TRANSFORMING YOUR ARCHETYPE

How can you come to know the narrative thrust and arc of your own life? You begin by awakening beyond your narrow preoccupation with petty egoic concerns. But that is just the first step. What follows is a visioning process in which you allow your soul, or daemon, to assert its dominion over your destiny, and to connect you with your collective soul destiny.

You begin this process by dropping down into whatever it is that glows in your bone marrow, and asking from the heart, and from the very depth of your being, for help with aligning you to your soul, to help you learn to hear its voice. Knowing that you cannot come to know its unique contours simply via awakening as wholeness or the aliveness of pure awareness (as absolutely essential as that is), you begin to feel into the pulse of the sap that rises through your body and soul. You wait to hear a new, deeper, previously hidden voice. You ask, and then you fall silent and faithfully keep a vigil of listening, until you are able to discern the still-small voice of your soul.

You open your feeling further, to learn what is being said to you by the DNA of the protoplasmic informational energy that surges, nurtures, and replenishes your very consciousness, the actual nerve spark in your cerebrospinal fluid. Your soul or daemon is recognizable because it speaks in chorus with your heart and blood. Life wants to live. That which has always animated evolutionary emergence is still alive in you and wants to keep evolving. And it has a particular way it wants to more fully express this right now through your body, your emotions, your mind, your imagination, your relationships, and your creativity.

Metaphors that make vivid the journey from your "current way of being" to your "new way of being" are part of the transformational process as it is taught by New Ventures West and by Integral Coaching Canada.[46] The new metaphor provides the vibrational signature through which we can attune to, resonate with, and embody our next higher possibilities. In coaching, new "capacities" are methodically cultivated. But the work derives a great deal of its efficacy from the ease with which the body and imagination can feel and inhabit a clear role in a story. This is why inhabiting a metaphor or an archetype is a skillful way to elicit our best capacities.

Such profound transformation ripens over time, and deeply. As Carl Jung wrote, "I ask myself what is the myth that you are living and I found that I did not know. So I took it upon myself to get to know my myth and I regarded this as the task of tasks. I simply had to know what unconscious or preconscious myth was forming me." Likewise, in Integral Soul Work we ask: What is really going on? What archetypal stories am I enacting in my life? Generally, we come to realize that we have been living out some pretty unproductive stories, stories that limit us, based on limiting beliefs we hold about ourselves and the world we are in. And we make new choices. As Rumi said, "Don't be satisfied with stories of how things have gone with others. Unfold your own myth." So, at this stage, we tune in to the metaphors and archetypes, these deeply familiar story lines that we have been living, in order to enable our particular transitional stories to come alive. As we practice accessing an archetype for a new way of being, we access something clear and fresh and full of possibility—a clean, blessed energy of grace that washes us and opens us.

What might this look like? While there are common themes within our common history, each individual's particular metaphors are unique.

Some lives are heroic in their experience of discomfort, pain, and distress. In such cases, the heroic task is for the heart to rise and willingly hold this pain, so as to transmute it, rather than just contracting or withdrawing and pulling away in the face of the pain. The hero's work is to find a way to use the pain, working with opposites, holding tensions and paradox, recognizing that life in a violent, mortal world in crisis is not black and white. Radical compassion and great empathic capacities are necessary to any truly mature consciousness or society.

Perhaps you (the hero) are accosted by an enemy who is going to slay you, and you have to discover a new power, a new magic quality, to become invisible and to change form. Something new is necessary in order not to be blocked on your path. Or you may be at a moment where an old way of being is getting in your way. Suddenly, you notice, what was impossible becomes possible. It needs to be released, and then something new can come into being. Maybe your story is about tenderly holding a key wounded part of your own being that has not previously been loved, opening your heart to the disowned part, bringing this aspect of yourself into the family, and giving it a place. The work is wide-spectrum—largely aspirational (eros), but also charitable (agape).

In soul work we tap into the archetypal energies that are driving us apart on this planet, and we begin to work with those energies to care and to heal division.

At this momentous time in the human planetary journey, your unique way of being heroic—your way of being a lover, a warrior, a king, a queen, a sage, a leader, or a citizen—matters. Even your unique way of entering into the process of your own death will allow the fullness of life to course through you. Something original and unique happens at an energetic level when you do this authentically.

Blocked energies want to flow. When we let go into a new story, these energies begin to flow through us with new power. When a myth begins to show itself, it often signals us somatically. You can *feel* an archetype taking you over and imbuing you with new capacities. You discover that something in you is ready to take over, an intelligence that already knows how to be the sovereign—the lover, the tantric, the tragic hero, or the magician. This is a fractal pattern that is enacted again and again, in micro and macro scales, during the process of authentic soul work. It can take place in an hour even while it is unfolding in larger terms over a period of months.

Consider the following pairs of metaphorical terms. In each case, the first metaphor might describe a way of being toward which you might be tending, as your *current way of being,* and the second metaphor might describe a *new way of being* toward which you might be growing when you practice. Perhaps this evokes a sense of how metaphors can catalyze growth.

Warrior → Sage

Seeker → Practitioner

Secret Prince → King

Orphan → Loving Parent

Martyr → Beneficent Elder

Hungry Hunter → Wise Gardener

Anxious Planner → Faithful, Confident, Powerful Listener

These evocative inner journeys name only a very few of your ultimately infinite metaphorical options. There are dozens of powerful
archetypes and mythic stories that you may be unconsciously acting out
of or moving toward. Allow yourself the time to contemplate your life
narrative, in relationship to the larger context of the story of our great
transition that resonates for you. If you are able to consciously identify
"current way of being" and "new way of being" metaphors, a transformational narrative can begin to inform your life, intuitively, every day, in
random moments. You might notice opportunities to shift from one way
of being to another in any moment, perhaps many times a day. And over
the course of years of practice, a powerful transition will begin, mature,
and even stabilize.

COLLECTIVE TRAUMA AND SUBTLE ACTIVISM

We don't only enact our archetypal stories individually of course,
but also together, each of us playing a unique role in a larger drama
through which the soul of the world, the anima mundi, is living out its
own great story. The great evolutionary journey of life and our human
cultural and civilizational experiments are expressing their character
through our collective behavior. The subtle fields of human collectives
are multidimensional, including a full spectrum of soul qualities and
feeling intelligence, but also collective traumas that tend to reenact
themselves. Every family, clan, tribe, and nation has its own soul qualities, its own shadows and karmas, its own archetypes, angels, demons,
and heroic qualities.

Working with the subtle fields and shadow dynamics of students
in German-speaking countries, Thomas Hübl discovered a shared deep
trauma in the collective subtle field, related to the holocaust and the
Second World War. After exploring it for some years, he arranged large
events in which thousands of Germans met together, with a video link to
a group in Israel. These events resulted in the surfacing of the trauma in
everyone's subtle field, thus allowing this collective shadow to heal. He
noticed that underneath the numbness people had layers of fear, grief,

shame, and anger. He saw that trauma creates "frozen ground" in the subtle fields of both individuals and collectives, which diminishes the flow of life energy, intelligence, and functionality. By developing additional subtle competencies, one can hold a space in which these layers can be felt more fully and precisely. When that is done consciously in the present moment in a relational field, the "frozen ground" can begin to melt, and life energy can start to move down into the field and the somatic being, restoring intelligence and functionality. Hübl brought this collective trauma work from Europe to America and Israel. Now he has been joined by other healers[47] in attempting to restore coherence to a fragmented world by deepening understanding of the nature of collective and intergenerational trauma and its integration. This work focuses on both universal principles and local particularities: raising awareness of collective and intergenerational trauma, and building cultures of prevention that can reduce the effects of PTSD and cycles of abuse. An intended goal of this project is to create "pockets" of healthy, integrated coherence in individuals, groups, and cultures where shared trauma is otherwise dominant.

This is perhaps a new transrational expression of an ancient intuition. Mystics and shamans from all cultures have long enacted ceremonies on behalf of their community, intending to elicit grace and win blessings. In his book *Subtle Activism*, David Nicol describes the emerging cultural response to our collective emergency—the thousands of people and organizations who are exploring the power of collective meditation and prayer to support a positive shift in society as a whole, seeing it as a potentially crucial component of a more integrated approach to social change. This work is not a substitute for practical activism, but rather a dimension of integral transformation.

Collective trauma, shadow, soul, and healing are deep patterns in the subtle dimensions of our lives. Every one of us is participating in them and shaped in part by them. Thus, our lives of practice are an arena in which we can express and magnify the healthy motive toward healing and wholeness that is so crucial to our collective future. A more conscious relationship to the science of our interior and subtle lives—individual and collective—together with the emergence of more and more vivid and compelling stories, may enable us to more rapidly reweave the fabric of our psyches and society, and thus restore our inherent wholeness.

DEATH AND REBIRTH

All of this has intensely personal implications for each of us. Some part of us must die to our old ways of being in order for a new level of capacity, courage, love, presence, and consciousness to be possible. This implies an ordeal—but every archetypal transition contains within it a process of death and rebirth. It is a metamorphosis, like a caterpillar becoming a butterfly.

The caterpillar weaves a cocoon, goes inside of it, and lets go. It turns into mush. It becomes completely disorganized. After a while what scientists call "imaginal cells" begin to appear. At first, they seem alien to the immune system of the caterpillar, and it tries to kill them off, but then more and more appear. After a while, some of them clump together bit by bit and become "imaginal disks." Then they overwhelm the immune system and a new principle reorganizes it. The imaginal discs gradually become the wings, the antennae, and the body of the butterfly. Everything that is ready to be reborn out of the process of dying into disorganized mush takes shape. Its own new quality comes into form. A similar process of death and rebirth occurs in each of us as we let go of our old, limiting stories and open up into a new, healthier way of being.

It is often shocking to recognize the archetype that you have been living. A role, story, and identity have been patterning your life outside your awareness—which has deep roots in your psyche and even in your somatic patterns of tension and compensation. And this must take place on a cultural scale too. In facing the unfathomable enormity of our ecological predicament, we recognize our own lives and projects as part of the collective cluelessness, collusion, and denial that has produced the mess. While this is not our "fault," it does require reckoning, repentance, and reframing our larger story and our roles within it. If we go deeply into this we must wonder whether our "higher purposes" are ways to control our basic anxiety, to deny our terror of our own inevitable death, or to keep the crisis and our collective mortality out of our awareness.

That is what Ernest Becker described in his classic book *The Denial of Death*. Sam Keen, in his introduction to that book, summarized it well: "We achieve ersatz immortality by sacrificing ourselves to conquer an empire, to build a temple, to write a book, to establish a family, to accumulate a fortune, to further progress and prosperity, to create an information-society and global free market."[48]

Becker coined a term for all the things we do to give our lives meaning: "immortality projects." Paradoxically, human immortality projects inevitably come into conflict with each other, becoming engaged in life-and-death struggles: "my gods against your gods." Because nothing could possibly be more important than *my* immortality project, I am willing to sacrifice all other values that seem to conflict with it. And thus, in a grand tragic irony, we have brought the greatest evils into the world by pursuing the "higher good" of our heroic immortality projects.

This recognition can deepen and profoundly humble us, but we must not let it negate our life's higher purposes. They are crucial if we are to create a sustainable, thriving world instead of destroying ourselves. Becker's observation, however, reminds us that at least some of the motivations behind our best intentions are often self-serving. In engaging our archetypal transformation, opening to some measure of responsibility for the future of human and ecological life on this planet, you will probably eventually face what I described in my own journey—the ways that our desires and inner myths express the forces in our world that have been causing so much destruction. Our old ways of being have developed an inertia that we will need to skillfully parry, like the aikido move that flips an opponent using the force of their own momentum. Then our new way of being can reveal and confer a new kind of power and motivation that transcends our personal pleasure, comfort, fame, wealth, or fulfillment. This doesn't mean becoming hostile to our human needs and embracing self-abnegating asceticism. But we can contact a source of joy and passion rooted in a much larger and higher purpose on behalf of life.

Our life can be grounded by our care and commitment to serving the embodied wholeness of life, even while everything seems to be coming apart. When our practice enacts wholeness via our unique role and story in a stupendous collective journey, it helps develop our soul strength—what Gandhi called *satyagraha*.

The journey of each soul is cyclical. It inevitably requires repeated expeditions into the underworld, times when we must face terrible truths we had previously avoided. These self-discoveries shock us, break our hearts, humble us, and ground us. Each time, we are shaken. Like the hero who narrowly avoids defeat, we are driven to the brink of despair. It takes great soul strength to find the inner resources we need to bounce back, despite everything. It takes the reclaiming of our naive, intense vitality, our "will to power," our "third intelligence" (centered in the hara, or gut), and the genius of will—which powers all success, for good or ill. We must not only find a way to embrace this powerful vitality; we must find a way to live it with yang excellence. These yang powers operate at a whole new level once we make the yin journey to the underworld, and plant the seed of yin that is the heart of a new level of yang dynamism.

As we turn this evolutionary corner, it is our moral responsibility to affirm life. We must contact and conduct the irrepressible, unreasonable happiness that is willing and ready to go on even in the face of what seems unendurable. We must become the bold, daring, creative, loving, wise heroes that create a new human story. This is an evolutionary challenge toward which all of us can aspire, but humbly. It is a new emergent opportunity. It requires a deeper strength, something that comes from the very depths of the being, rising up like the sap of a great tree. That strength expresses itself as innocent willingness, commitment, leadership, love, and courage. It is the raw power that is the true fruit of our soul's journey. And it is the "X factor," the primal love of life that is the engine of survival for every individual, every family, every city, every nation, and our whole species. In the words of a famous Rumi poem,

> *Out beyond ideas of wrongdoing and rightdoing,*
> *there is a field. I'll meet you there.*

Awakening into Evolutionary Activism

A spirituality that is only private and self-absorbed, one devoid of an authentic political and social consciousness, does little to halt the suicidal juggernaut of history. On the other hand, an activism that is not purified by profound spiritual and psychological self-awareness and rooted in divine truth, wisdom, and compassion will only perpetuate the problem it is trying to solve, however righteous its intentions. When, however, the deepest and most grounded spiritual vision is married to a practical and pragmatic drive to transform all existing political, economic, and social institutions, a holy force—the power of wisdom and love in action—is born.

—ANDREW HARVEY

I am writing these words in the surreal ambiance of mid-2017 America. Day after day, we hear news about the subversion of the U.S. 2016 election, suppression of checks and balances, unprecedented ethical violations, censorship, planned dismantling of governmental agencies that provide services essential to our—and Earth's—well-being and even survival, acts of disrespect to America's long-term democratic allies, exploitations of divisions of race and culture, and countless actions that threaten not only liberal values but the fundamental conservative values of stability and respect for tradition. More important, we are seeing a great political consciousness-raising—the beginnings of a coming wave of political activism and engagement. There is every reason to expect this will become an enormous historical force. But what is *most* significant, I believe, is that this mobilization will carry far beyond popular resistance to the Trump administration, to the broader predicament that must be addressed. This new activism is an expression of our very health, sanity, and character. It is slower moving, but deep and inexorable. What is most fundamental is wholeness reasserting itself.

When we think of the creative activities that are required to preserve our collective life and future, perhaps no metaphor is more appropriate than one relating to the soil—and to the living processes that literally create soil. There has even been a recognition in some quarters that—at a certain level—"soil is the critical solution to climate change."[49] Huge amounts of soil are generated from mycelium, which is something like the root system of a fungal or bacterial colony, made up of a mass of branching, threadlike structures. Through photosynthesis, soil, with its plant partners, "takes CO_2 from the atmosphere and releases oxygen, driving the carbon down to its roots where it is exchanged for nutrients the plants and trees need, sequestering the carbon underground where it belongs."[50] Mycelium is able to sense water and nutrient availability and need, and it redistributes those resources, making its area of the forest (which can extend for many miles) more healthy. This healing function in nature helps restore balance and counters the effects of climate change.

In a very similar way, life-generating processes are countering the common life-destroying thoughts, habits, and behaviors endemic in the world today. What is healthy and wholesome and loving and generous in human connections is already present, under the surface. Our innate goodness, like the mycelium, is often relatively hidden and out of sight—though it is present, and it grows always, "going underground" in suppressive cultural environments. But it is what keeps us going, so it never dies completely. Often, it grows massively but silently and invisibly.

And yet when the time is right, the mycelium suddenly sends out shoots and blossoms. Baby mushrooms suddenly glisten in colonies scattered across the forest floor. In the same way—even when hidden—all that is good and healthy in us and between us is already present and real. Although we cannot predict the multitude of ways and times it might fully manifest in our world, we can trust that our life-generating nature will be free to show itself when the time is right, like an overnight mushroom bloom.

Biological metaphors relating to development and growth are appropriate to activism. We are a living process, like the mycelium, like Earth itself. Shelley Sacks (an Oxford Brookes University professor of social sculpture and activist)[51] and others have eloquently invoked this metaphor, pointing to our "social mycelium."

There is, today, a new culture growing roots that are spreading across the planet. Right now, much communication and innovation is occurring "underground," not fully visible to the larger culture or popular media. But we know that new shoots are forming, and a forest is in the making. Our mechanical models of reality do not account for this deeper dimension of things, and yet the biological metaphor points to amazing potentials. Like the mycelium, we are not isolated lonely cogs in a machine, but creative participants in a larger natural process, richly capable of self-transformation.

We are invited, and drafted, to participate in this extraordinary process—truly a bifurcation point in the progress of human civilization. Circumstances seem to require impossible, unprecedented levels of creative ingenuity, but we are not required to do all this by ourselves. Our ingenuity is just part of something vast that is pervading everything—the ingenuity of the evolutionary process itself. What is best in us expresses the entelechy of the great, mysterious wholeness that animates and envelops us all.

INNER AND OUTER WORK ARE INSEPARABLE

We have already described a kind of inner work that brings us into alignment with wholeness. It leads to new behavior, individually and collectively. Our relationships change. We develop new values, interests, and concerns. We find new ways to make a positive difference. We draw on what has been learned from the activism of the past, but it is an entirely original and contemporary phenomenon.

Our outer behavior can't help but express our consciousness. That is why practice is critical to activism, especially if we are to respond adequately to the evolutionary pressures of our global crisis. Now, as we turn to that outer work, we start with this understanding: Only through our own growth and development, arising from our humble surrender to questions whose answers we do not yet know, can we be catalysts for the evolutionary revolution that is needed. Like the mycelium, our life-enhancing service makes a contribution immediately, but in the future it will yield exponential returns.

In the short term, we won't always know exactly where we are going. We are all charged with manifesting solutions that cannot be prefigured. That means we are obliged to participate in a whole series of cultural experiments that will yield varying degrees of success. The results of this open-ended process will only be knowable after repeated iterations. Although challenges will beget new and unexpected challenges, the process will keep advancing.

This asks for profound growth and practice. *First, it requires awake, free, open, and self-transcending awareness.* This ongoing process must profoundly redefine our identities, worldviews, motivations, and relationships. Ultimately it must allow us to dream a new dream and live out a new story. Thus, our personal practice is one of the key front lines of this new cultural and social revolution.

Second, as soon as—and to whatever degree—this new consciousness appears, *it has to find powerful, effective outer expression in all of the domains of our lives.* Action begets consequences, and we learn from them, refining our consciousness and our behavior, including our initiatives. We cannot wait for perfect solutions, or for our own perfection. Whatever the deficiencies in our skills or understanding, we must start from where we are, immediately. That is how we will learn. "If you create a time lag between the whisper of intelligence and understanding in you

and your action, then you are preventing the cerebral organ from growing into a new dimension," said the rational spiritual teacher Vimala
Thakar.[52] "The voice of understanding, the voice of intelligence has an
insecurity about it. How do you know that it is the right thing?" We
must act, doing our very best even while knowing that the messy conditional world is not a place where perfect action is possible. "Unless you
commit mistakes," Thakar continues, "how do you learn to discriminate
between the false and the true? In learning there is bound to be a little
insecurity, a possibility of committing mistakes. Why should one be terribly afraid of committing mistakes?"

The whispers of this new intelligence are tasked to find expression
in creative work that betters the world in whatever ways it can, certainly
including politics. But it is by no means an activism that is restricted to,
or even focused on, political power and influence. There are many "front
lines" in the struggle of cultural evolution. As conscious practitioners, we
find ourselves leaning out into a wild new frontier where many, many
experiments are necessary. This is the context for a new kind of activism.

THE INTEGRAL HEART IN ACTION

This is a time of intensifying complexification, acceleration, fragmentation, and incoherence. Thus, it is a time of stress and corruption. What
is most radical and subversive now are the most timeless virtues—integrity, wholeness, health, coherence. Finding our way to health and to
our hearts, finding our way beyond the fragmented common mind that
is endlessly broadcast to us—that's truly revolutionary. It doesn't seem
revolutionary, because we tend to recognize revolution in its familiar
costumes—marching in the street in opposition to systemic injustice,
organizing, designing a "hostile takeover" of the levers of power. And,
indeed, revolution sometimes wears those costumes as well.

But the original meaning of the word "revolution" is "turning"—to
revolve is to turn. We turn by awakening from unconscious patterns
and enacting *wholeness*—healthy consciousness, behavior, relationships,
ecology, and truly integrative initiatives. We will be a positive social and

political force to the degree that we are able to enact a new level of maturity guided by our highest intelligence. Since that is an inherent drive, it is already happening in myriad ways. We do well to observe this and to trust that the process is natural and unstoppable. And yet this is only so because countless individuals are choosing it. So this great matter really does depend on *us*.

Our challenges call us to a *politics of human maturity.* This is the revolutionary "turning" in which wholeness reasserts its primacy over fragmentation and regression. Our most essential political priority is cultivating, eliciting, and exercising more maturity and wisdom—so it can shape our lives and relationships, and then our public decision making. Another way of stating this is that our whole lives must be guided by *heart intelligence.* Ultimately, human maturity expresses itself as effective, wise, caring action for the benefit of the whole, putting no one and nothing out of our heart. Wholeness, maturity, and love, then, are at the core of effective evolutionary activism (which in our time is also, in a real sense, revolutionary).

To enact love in the domain of politics is profoundly tricky. It is, after all, the very embodiment of "the simplicity on the other side of complexity" that I repeatedly invoke. We have only a few models for it, but it lives in our best instincts. Charles Eisenstein states the problem very well: "As we enter a period of intensifying disorder," he says, "it is important to introduce a different kind of force to animate the structures that might appear after the old ones crumble. I would call it love if it weren't for the risk of triggering your New Age bullshit detector, and besides, how does one practically bring love into the world in the realm of politics? So let's start with empathy. Politically, empathy is akin to solidarity, born of the understanding that we are all in this together…. I see its lineaments in those marginal structures and practices that we call holistic, alternative, regenerative, and restorative. All of them source from empathy, the result of the compassionate inquiry: What is it like to be you?"[53]

This is entirely different from the kind of activism that intensifies polarization, scorning those it opposes. It counters progressive activist tendencies to demonize political enemies—tendencies that inevitably mobilize resentment. It doesn't sacrifice wholeness for short-term political advantage. Therefore, "love" is really our best word for what is able to defy the dysfunctional gravity of hyper-partisan gridlock.

However, this politics of love includes and cooperates with almost all established forms of activism, even those that may temporarily create or exacerbate divisions. It participates in an integral revolution of the being, in which love and wholeness are magnified—in every moment, in every individual, and in every relationship, organization, and group.

A politics of love arises naturally when there is profound recognition of nonseparation. Adi Da argues for a revolutionary enlightened politics based on the intuition of radical "prior unity."[54] Such a revolution by its nature takes place in each heart-mind through ego-transcending practice (which he calls "the way of the heart"). It doesn't focus on political "issues" but on the self-regulating integrity and authority of "everybody-all-at-once." Such love is not a mere feeling; it is a radical recognition of our actual condition and situation.

After stating that we are "in this together," Eisenstein asked rhetorically, "In *what* together? For starters, we are in the uncertainty together." *Exactly.* If we eschew all idealism, what might be our actual opportunity? Perhaps it is simply to abide intelligently together in the impossible questions of our situation and our opportunities. We can allow ourselves to be deepened and changed by the Genjo Koan, our existential challenge, even as we also learn by acting decisively (since the world is always giving us feedback). How to effectively engage the sociopolitical domain *as love* is a major facet of the great koan. Thus, it has no answer. Instead, it is an art form, an ongoing inquiry, a crucial exploration—one that can only be engaged imperfectly, as a passionate process, inevitably replete with mistakes.

This is utterly incomprehensible to a fragmented intelligence. It takes integral intelligence to recognize politics as an ongoing process of learning that is inseparable from personal growth. This means we must draw upon all three of the primary seats of our intelligence—head, heart, and hara. Much public discourse is at the level of merely mental intelligence, driven by the gut and clothed in sentiment. Acting alone, the mind is easily fooled, and is incapable of the inquiry described above. But the intelligence of all three centers, integrated at the center—by the intelligence of the heart—is uncommonly smart, wise, and effective.

Every moment is a learning opportunity. We are not only learning as individuals, we are learning collectively. As we learn to bring integral heart intelligence into our relationships, our collective learning will accelerate profoundly. That is another reason the future of community is bubbling with exciting possibilities. Activist sanghas or "communities of practice" will increasingly begin to function as social and spiritual resources for their members, uplifting and integrating their intelligence and care even as they cooperate to magnify their social impact.

Heart intelligence calms us by reminding us that everything (however at risk) is, in a very real sense, totally okay. After all, the Whole *includes* everything. Holistic activism is hugely generous, but it is not only directed selflessly toward greater goals. It is also entirely self-compassionate, friendly to our own needs as members of an alienated society. The heart can recognize that it is entirely appropriate and necessary for us to serve the whole *while* serving ourselves—sharing life, enjoying friendship and community, growing and learning, and enjoying a richer existence because of and through our relationships with one another.

THREE DOMAINS OF EVOLUTIONARY ACTIVISM

As we have said, the true integral revolution isn't along the left/right spectrum. Rather, it is the revolution of wholeness against fragmentation. A revolution of wholeness is inclusive; it does not leave people, or good ideas, behind. In many ways, the integral revolution is uncharted territory, yet its basic principles are clear.

It is useful to examine the three domains of activism: working *within the system, against the system,* and *around the system.* Sometimes these are presented as competing alternatives or options. But evolutionary activists work in all three of these domains—although as individuals, based on our skills and opportunities, we may choose to focus our efforts on just one or two.

In-the-System ⤝

Every nation's system is different. I'll comment here on working in the system in the United States, but analogies can be drawn to working within the system in any democracy.

Like most Americans, I've assumed all my life that I lived in a relatively free and open liberal Western democracy, and that I always would. Elections might matter in terms of policies and progress, but the fundamentals were solid. I didn't have to get involved in politics in order to defend the basic foundations of my society's way of life. That assumption suddenly no longer holds. We actually might fall prey to authoritarianism. We could lose our ability to defend the planet in these fraught times, and we could even lose important civil liberties. And the only thing standing in the way is the political engagement of sufficient numbers of citizens. That makes in-the-system activism a moral obligation.

The continued evolution of consciousness and culture is utterly dependent upon civil order, education, and the free exchange of ideas. And those survive only if they are held by a network of civil institutions—all levels of government, including local police and firefighters, and extending to the justice system and regulatory agencies. Equally, we need a free press, a network of influential NGOs, and our financial institutions. We chafe under the bureaucracies of such organizations, but our freedom is contingent upon their presence. Activists are often first inspired during adolescence, so it's no wonder that the spirit of activism is influenced by a youthful idealistic rejection of intransigent institutions. Storming the barricades can seem heroic and romantic. But it is rarely wise. It is often said that when civil order breaks down, "the intellectuals are the first to go."

For that reason, as we will explore in more depth a bit later, many who appreciate that revolutionary whole-system change is necessary are focusing on affecting the structural dynamics that undermine the health of political systems. They are working in the system by getting buy-in from influential political players for *transpartisan* approaches to public policy and political reform. Transpartisanship is distinct from bipartisanship, which is oriented toward finding agreement between two factions (like Democrats and Republicans in the U.S.), and it differs from non-partisanship, which avoids all political affiliation. It advocates for inclusive solutions that transcend and include all polarized political positions and promote collaboration across the spectrum for the benefit of the whole.

Although government and politics do not supply a solution to every problem, they are the arena in which we encounter our fellow citizens, adjudicate disagreements, and exercise collective decision making. They are how we allocate power and influence. After the bank bailouts of 2008–2009, two popular political revolts emerged—the Tea Party on the right and Occupy Wall Street on the left. The Tea Party had far more impact precisely because it worked pragmatically *within the system* rather than standing outside it as the Occupy movement did.

That is why it is an absolute moral and practical necessity for citizens of any imperfect democracy to participate directly in the political process. That means that **voting is a moral obligation.** This is especially true in the United States, where only about half of eligible voters cast their ballots, and elections are often decided on the basis of the different degrees of voter participation among different constituencies. But it is also true in all the world's democracies. The only way to address inequities in the electoral process itself is to participate in it in every way that is available. The most basic is casting your vote.

And much more vigorous involvement in the system is necessary too. But here, it is appropriate to celebrate the absolutely necessary public service of people who are attempting to make our political systems serve the common good. We need public servants willing to take responsibility for our democratic institutions, including getting their hands dirty by engaging in partisan politics on behalf of specific candidates and parties. Among them are many exemplary leaders—sincere, dedicated, and competent. The fact that they are serving at a time when those institutions are breaking down under stress doesn't diminish their contributions. In fact, it only heightens their significance. Being a competent politician is a high-performance athletic art form, often run in a sincere attempt to bring good governance. If the game gets nasty, playing to win won't always be pretty. But the effort to wisely steer the ship of state is a noble and necessary function, one we all depend upon. Politicians, dirty hands and all, are sometimes very practically attempting to accomplish some of the exact things we're discussing in this book.

Any individual, however, can influence the system in practical ways—by participating in get-out-the-vote drives; getting involved in a party organization; running for office oneself; signing (or creating) petitions; working on local or state or national campaigns; working within a major or minor political party; donating money or volunteering for causes; showing up at meetings to voice one's concerns; and calling and writing one's local congresspeople, senators, and state and local elected officials. One can also have impact by participating in influential civic organizations and institutions, or by blogging, writing op-ed pieces or letters to the editor, or writing or researching an article or book.

An engaged citizen, even one working full-time, can exert significant influence. After the U.S. elections of November 2016, the *Indivisible Guide* (www.indivisibleguide.com/guide/) clarified practical step-by-step guidelines and advice on using the very practical tactics successfully used by the Tea Party to shift American politics in a more progressive direction. Elizabeth Warren advocates that citizens "do one thing every day" to effect political change. What might that be? You can call or write your representatives, show up at their office or town hall, write a letter to your local newspaper, phone a few likely voters, donate money, attempt to persuade others by posting something online, or, if you are really busy that day, sign an online petition.

But many modern and postmodern citizens either sigh in frustration or roll their eyes in cynicism at this kind of activity. In fact, political participation in America has been declining for decades. Politics has become a specialized field, dominated by the small subset of "political" people who are attracted to the cause and the battle—which is not the case for most people. To most citizens, direct political engagement seems like an unpleasant, extraneous, burdensome duty—and one they can easily shirk, invisibly, with no consequences. That is why progressive politicians so often exhort their supporters to get more engaged in the political process—and it is also why so few respond. Working in the system isn't always lots of fun. But it is nonetheless a foundational practice of civic responsibility. It is a very necessary practice, if you have understood and taken to heart the realities we are considering here.

Journalists are a special category of in-the-system activists. They are a culture's very eyesight into the processes by which power blocs contend for influence over their government and resources. It is investigative journalists who, at crucial historical moments, have kept our country free. They are an indispensable central institution of democracy. And some among them are influential storytellers, public intellectuals, commentators, and historians, all of whom participate in the cultural processes by which our best intelligence tries to translate itself into collective choices.

Unfortunately, internet journalism was suddenly overtaken during the 2016 election campaign by a microtargeted swarm of bots (technological simulations of real people) designed to boost fake news that reverse-engineered existing prejudices and predictable neurological responses. It exploited voter credulity and subverted the healthy social role of a free press. That is not journalism. And it does not deserve the constitutional protections granted to journalists. With that enormous exception, however, the great body of journalists are crucial in-the-system activists. They are saying the things that capture our attention, and they are educating us. But the business of legitimate journalism is under threat. Creative journalistic activism has become even more crucial in this cataclysmic climate.

Those of us with modern and postmodern cognition think systemically. To us, the perversions and inefficiencies of our current system loom large. Special interests have "gamed the system," and the outsized influence of money upon politics has subverted the intent of our nation's founders. What we really want are radical changes—things like effective campaign finance reform, the elimination of the electoral college, the abolition of the two-party monopoly, the revocation of corporate personhood, the recognition of the rights of nonhumans, restoration of press standards, exposure of fake news, and more. But all realistic paths to achieving such major and fundamental changes begin with incremental changes that are far less sexy and inspiring. We're nonplussed.

This brings to the surface additional key facets of our critical big questions. We must ponder: How can in-the-system political activism be approached so that larger numbers of people come to enjoy and value and get involved in it? How can the practice of activism be self-sustaining, feeding activists rather than draining us? In the meantime, how can citizens understand and embrace and engage our civic responsibilities (even if they still seem burdensome) and actually *change* our national and international politics? These are questions we will be exploring.

Bringing it back to earth, I suggest that we regard in-the-system political activism as analogous to brushing one's teeth. You can skip it today and tomorrow, but eventually you'll be sorry. It is an unavoidable dimension of holistic hygiene. It is essential to vote, of course, but also to accept responsibility to engage more creatively. What can you do? Everything described above, and more. Americans do well to think of our friends in other countries. They cannot vote or contribute money in American elections. Aren't we connected to them in a brother/sisterhood? Don't we owe it to them to oppose or prevent irresponsible actions by the world's preeminent superpower at a time when the whole planet is in crisis?

Against-the-System

Sustainable systemic change must be embodied in institutions, laws, policies, and procedures. In-the-system activism is therefore the primary means for creating lasting change. But the system as it exists also needs to be changed. It sometimes needs popular pressure that operates *outside* the existing institutions, exerting pressure indirectly.

Demonstrations and protests build such pressure by displaying the size of a constituency that cares passionately about issues the system is not able to address. This has changed the world on occasion. But it can be more smoke than fire, as we learned from the Arab Spring. Many demonstrations have produced little tangible results, and it pays to learn from those experiences.

In recent years we have seen the Occupy Wall Street movement, climate marches, demonstrations in support of the Standing Rock tribe and opposing the Dakota Access pipeline, and the widespread world-wide women's marches following inauguration day of 2017. These are all expressions of grassroots energy whose effects reverberate. Some have immediate effects. I believe that, after President Trump's first "travel ban" executive order, fewer Muslims were radicalized than would have been the case if Americans had not rushed to our airports to aid those whom the ban had affected. In some cases, demonstrations have been inspiring examples of building spontaneous connections and speaking truth to power. Even when truth "loses," it is at least spoken and heard. In our critical generational challenge, it is crucial that the climate movement have political power. And millions of us have stepped forward, adding our voices to those of Al Gore, Paul Hawken, Bill McKibben, Joanna Macy, Vandana Shiva, and so many others.

Against-the-system activism also gives people who are functioning as a kind of cultural "immune system" an opportunity to coalesce as a subculture, to begin to become a new global tribe. A new political movement seems likely to emerge from the excesses of the Trump presidency. Protest is not always the highest-leverage form of activism, but sometimes it pressures the system to generate transformative results and it always at least exerts a little influence.

Even so, it is not itself a sufficient strategy. One problem with demonstrations and marches is that they may attract individuals with different agendas. It is impractical to vet participants in marches and demonstrations, so they don't all bring the same conscious intention to the event. Violent anarchists have derailed many otherwise peaceful protests. Demonstrations and other public gatherings usually involve people at many stages of growth and maturity and sincerity.

There are also many ways that people put pressure on the system through local actions—sometimes just the waving of placards, or chanting, or arriving at meetings to present grievances against governmental representatives. Activism on local issues can be very effective—opposing the building of a dam or a big box store, or demanding affordable housing. And if one initiative fails, other approaches to the problem (often more savvy and more widely supported) are likely to follow. Activists have brought attention to local issues like access to healthy food in minority communities, police brutality, racial profiling, and environmental justice issues. Politicians usually act, if at all, only after activists have laid the groundwork and changed perceptions.

Integrity is a core evolutionary value. Corruption is rising as perhaps a globally unifying theme. It is an issue that needs to be addressed "in the system" *and* "against the system." It will perhaps be the central political issue internationally in the years to come—not just in the developing world, but now in Western democracies. It is becoming central in the U.S., and visible in response to President Trump's consistent flouting of multiple ethical norms. Exposing corruption has become a major issue of the opposition party. But nonpartisan initiatives like Represent.Us and its proposal for an Anti-Corruption Act are crucial to truly enduring reform.

Polarization makes it harder to address corruption. Both the collusion of those who benefit from corruption and the uncompromising idealism of those it exploits tend to be a roadblock to effective rational legislation. It is not a partisan issue. Some against-the-system activists (largely immature postmoderns on the left) refuse to work within the system at all. For some individuals, *any* level of corruption—including any form of participation in a corrupt system—is rejected. Thus, to work within the system (even to make it more responsive) is automatically equated with empowering its flaws. They claim that even voting for a flawed candidate over a disastrous one is wrong.

The reality is quite different. Many corporations and governments have been transformed by activists working within the system. *To refuse to work within the system at all is to deny the possibility that individuals and institutions can be transformed.* And yet immature radicals sometimes tend to imagine that only they are "true" activists. A much more capacious view of activism is necessary in this time.

Around-the-System ✤

Integral evolutionary activism has most effectively worked by going *around the system.* If you help educate girls in the Third World, you are not directly changing political or environmental policies, but you *are* chang-ing their future. If you get involved with a new technology that has the potential to make fossil fuels noncompetitive, you are not doing anything that appears to be within the system or against the system. If you build out a new worldview and educate people, helping them grow into higher states and structures of consciousness, you are not at first addressing politics directly, but over time your work has the potential to impact the system profoundly. You are going *around* the system, but you may well be doing things that could remake our future. You are no less an activist doing this than protesting or visiting your congresswoman.

Around-the-system activities include microfinancing enterprises, many varieties of social entrepreneurship, activities that improve the lives of poor people, creating new healthy currencies, and developing new models to help organizations function more efficiently and humanely—to name but a handful of many possibilities. Paul Hawken famously described the proliferation of more than two million NGOs all over the world as "the largest social movement in all of human history."[55]

Our planetary crises are calling forth countless spontaneous expres-sions of social care. This is an organic, leaderless process, moving from the bottom up instead of the top down. To the degree that it is a movement, it is self-organized and leaderless. Hawken saw it as linking three broad movements: social justice initiatives, environmental activism, and indig-enous resistance to globalization. But these overtly activist movements are interconnected with a broad network of other social-entrepreneurial and philanthropic initiatives that aim to facilitate sustainability, care for nature, evolve culture, and uplift the human condition. Thus it is even bigger and broader than he described.

A cultural sea change is gathering force; our social ideals are being transformed. What has become even "cooler" than wealth and celebrity is using wealth and celebrity to benefit society. Our idea of ultimate success has evolved from images of the mansions and cigars of gilded-age tycoons to images of Bill and Melinda Gates, Bono, Angelina Jolie, and George Clooney using their wealth and celebrity to help the global poor. A number of years ago my nine-year-old neighbor, Vivienne Harr, opened a lemonade stand to buy freedom for human slaves, and with the support of her parents and social media, birthed a movement (that included lemonade and software companies) and became famous. She expresses a whole new zeitgeist. This notion that it is cool to be of benefit is transforming our ideals, our definition of success, and our aspirations.

We see these same principles in evidence-based and venture philanthropy. The Gates Foundation is just the largest of a whole new generation of nonprofits that attract talent from the business world and use the power of data and measurement to maximize results. It has been criticized as a high-level enterprise led by members of an elite that is out of touch with the suffering it intends to alleviate; and certainly the new philanthropy has more learning and evolving ahead. But these initiatives are already bringing creativity and rigor to the effort to make a difference. They are improving efficiency, achieving measurable results in numerous areas, aiming at scalability, and uplifting the disenfranchised. It may not yet be changing the fundamental rules of how power operates, but it is already a significant source of important, systemic beneficial impacts.

Countless creative initiatives are pioneering genuinely novel approaches to engineering social change. Many small nonprofits are collaborating with one another and creating diverse new social entrepreneurial projects. "B" (benefit) corporations are proliferating, and professionals are working pro bono to realize social-change goals. Some of them are working together in the service of profoundly creative approaches based on genuinely new thinking—high-leverage systemic and metasystemic interventions in culture and society.

These initiatives are working to create affordable sources of clean water and electricity for people who lack them. They are educating children in the developing world. They are organizing neighborhood commitments to reduce carbon consumption, block by block, in U.S. cities. They are financing and empowering poor people in the Third World to become entrepreneurs. They are supporting sustainable businesses in the developing world that reduce carbon consumption while empowering participants with entrepreneurial skills. They are designing creative educational programs aiming at transforming worldviews and eventually changing the paradigm out of which human culture makes the choices that shape its future. They are building public-private partnerships aiming to jump-start research, shortening the development cycle of a new generation of truly sustainable new energy sources and technologies.

Meanwhile, organizational change-agents have begun enabling "next stage organizations," nonprofit and for-profit organizations whose social purpose transforms the very way the organizations function day to day. People are realizing that human organizations are living systems, and that people function optimally when their agency, creativity, and need for meaning are engaged. So they are exploring new principles, structures, practices, and processes. Traditional top-down hierarchies are giving way to employees managing themselves based on peer relationships. These organizations see themselves as having their own purpose and sense of direction, which is constantly evolving.

THE HOLISTIC SYNERGIES OF EVOLUTIONARY ACTIVISM

What is most exciting about working around the system is that it not only employs but requires higher structures of mind—a holistic systemic way of thinking that notices potential synergies, coherence and incoherence, and potentials for emergence.

Already, change agents have been coordinating and synergizing their efforts more and more effectively. Much cooperation is spontaneous and emergent. Some is brilliantly deliberate and strategic. With sufficient formal agreements, people are able to address multiple causes of social challenges with remarkable results.

Social innovation researchers John Kania and Mark Kramer defined five general principles for optimizing "collective impact."

1. All participants have a common agenda for change including a shared understanding of the problem and a joint approach to solving it through agreed upon actions.

2. Collecting data and measuring results consistently across all the participants ensures shared measurement for alignment and accountability.

3. A plan of action that outlines and coordinates mutually reinforcing activities for each participant.

4. Open and continuous communication is needed across the many players to build trust, assure mutual objectives, and create common motivation.

5. A backbone organization(s) with staff and specific set of skills to serve the entire initiative and coordinate participating organizations and agencies.[56]

Collective impact initiatives have addressed a wide variety of issues, including rainforest conservation, education, health, animal welfare, homelessness, poverty reduction, and youth and community development. They were formally recognized by the White House Council for Community Solutions in 2012. Of course, in the context of the questions we are asking here, what is obviously necessary is deep, fundamental transformation of our whole civilizational system to one that supports human and nonhuman flourishing. To address our holistic predicament, the concept of collective impact must be further expanded. And it must encounter new challenges. Top-down social impact strategies will converge with the bottom-up intelligence of communities of practice. Individual projects can collaborate for collective impact only insofar as they can each remain coherent and focused, even while interconnecting and expanding—to include, ultimately, everything.

Collective impact can bring together distinct initiatives that work around, in, and against the system, all on behalf of key shared outcomes. Advocates for collective impact believe it is absolutely necessary in this time because "there is no other way society will achieve large-scale progress against the urgent and complex problems of our time, unless a collective impact approach becomes the accepted way of doing business."[57]

All these new forms of activism express an awakening into a new level of thinking. They reflect systemic, and sometimes even metasystemic, holistic and intuitive reasoning. They express awareness of the fact that we live in a profoundly interconnected world. They are aimed to benefit everyone—or the whole biosphere—rather than just our own group or species. They usually sidestep confrontation, finessing cultural resistance to social change. They often help poor people by ameliorating many of the underlying causes of their own misery and poverty. They often transcend the paradigm of benefactor and recipient, partnering with those they help, requiring and assisting everyone involved to grow and develop, individually and collectively.

This evolving consciousness is already making its way into activist culture and transforming the whole world of activism. It expresses a rising current of innovation and synthesis that is rapidly gathering steam. And yet it is not separate from anything. It is transforming the internal culture of mainstream businesses as well as charities and activist organizations. The whole nonprofit world is rapidly changing, integrating insights from innovations in the private sector. Private corporations are discovering their "evolutionary purpose." The culture of activism is not only diversifying, it is cross-pollinating, coevolving, and transforming rapidly. It is becoming more integral and evolutionary.

Evolutionary activism is integral. On one hand, it expresses a serious commitment to whole-system change, and the emergence of a life-sustaining global culture. On the other hand, it expresses a serious commitment to becoming the kind of people who can create and enjoy a life-sustaining global culture. That means simultaneous care for and engagement with individual human beings and local initiatives *even while keeping the metasystemic big picture in mind*. Evolutionary activists view all their initiatives as collectively impacting a whole-system transition. We keep our hearts on the prize of a life-sustaining global culture. We stay human, humble, and real, and we keep growing. Then we can also notice the synergies and commonalities among our projects, and we can harmonize apparent conflicts and cultivate a greater coherence.

FOUR EXAMPLES OF INNOVATIVE INTEGRAL INITIATIVES

I have been inspired for years by a wide range of enlightened integral projects that work around the system to create social and cultural change. The ones I know best arose within the integral evolutionary cultural ecosystem, where such initiatives are incubating intensely. Sean Esbjörn-Hargens and MetaIntegral have expanded on Ken Wilber's pioneering work to establish interdisciplinary integral scholarship and to fund and empower a wide range of other initiatives. Gail Hochachka and Integral Without Borders have brought integral theory into international development projects across Latin America and in Africa. Barrett Brown has brought integral leadership development to organizations on five continents. And countless additional projects and project networks are making their unique creative contributions. To understand this creativity requires a deeper look, so let's consider a few examples with which I am familiar. Here I recount the outlines of four inspiring initiatives founded by four of my personal friends.

The Slocan Integral Forestry Cooperative

My friend Stephan Martineau moved in 1992 to the Slocan Valley, a beautiful Canadian mountain valley with a diverse community of about six thousand people. The social landscape included First Nations voices; a conservative faction made up of loggers, miners, and farmers; a highly concentrated and vocal green community; a multifaith landscape; two internationally recognized environmental organizations; a strong artist community; and the multinational forest products company that held rights to cut timber and was the valley's main employer.

The forested watershed around the pristine Slocan river and lake (northwest of the town of Nelson in the West Kootenay region of Southeastern British Columbia) was 95 percent government-owned, and the residents had polarized into distrust through decades of controversy and conflict over forestry practices and water quality. An increasing number of forestry workers were losing their jobs, while clear-cut logging continued at the same pace due to mechanization. By the early 2000s, more than 120 locals had been arrested at protests. The provincial government had sponsored nine initiatives to resolve these conflicts across thirty-five years at a cost of hundreds of thousands of dollars—all without success.

In the fall of 2003, the provincial government announced its intention to offer forest rights to local communities. Martineau recognized that after thirty years of failed processes this was an opportunity to start over with an integral approach. If the Slocan Valley were to make a successful bid for a community forest tenure, all sides of the ongoing conflict would have to come together to agree on a single vision. They would have to change the historical pattern and replace mistrust with a new direction that would benefit all members of the community.

Martineau was inspired to make use of the many lessons that could be learned from the past and to take all the players into consideration. Would it be possible for the union, the logging company, recreation enthusiasts, First Nations, environmental organizations, and the residents to come together under one vision? Through his many conversations with the various factions of the community, the following guiding principles of an integral approach to community mediation were articulated:

1. Residents hold perspectives and value systems in relation to the forest that surrounds them.

2. These perspectives and value systems are guided and influenced by a mix of social, economic, scientific, spiritual, psychological, cultural, political, historical and institutional lenses.

3. Each of these perspectives is valuable and pertinent and must therefore be considered in solutions that will work for all.

4. By including and building upon these perspectives, solutions found will be more complete and viable in considering how the community and the forest can interface.

Martineau found many allies who came to hold this vision with him and began reaching out to the various stakeholder communities, two or three individuals at a time. The intention was that by the end of each meeting, everyone would see value in the project, would not feel threatened by it, and would feel appreciated for what they had contributed and could contribute in the future.

In particular, Martineau contacted people who had key qualities, such as integrity, a capacity to listen, flexibility, a willingness to learn, and a sincere care for the greater community. These individuals were open to multiple perspectives, able to empathize and to practice impartiality. They were genuinely interested in understanding others' insights, values, worldviews, and knowledge. They were respected by their constituency and could offer them a voice of reason and encouragement. Through their participation, elements from each subculture that needed to be included in any single overarching direction were clarified.

Gradually a diverse core group formed that would co-own the implementation of this initiative from the start. A series of public community meetings solicited more input, further clarified the path forward, and gathered broader community support.

Eventually, loggers, city councils, environmental activists, the Ministry of Forest and Range, a variety of local residents, and three resident associations came to agreement on guiding principles, management guidelines, organizational structure, and a plan for profit distribution. This groundbreaking project received more than seventy letters of support from local governments, businesses, community organizations, and individuals across the full spectrum of values and perspectives. Through numerous negotiations the acreage they had originally been offered was doubled, and a complex multiyear process resulted in an agreement that the Slocan Valley Integral Forestry Cooperative (SIFCo) would manage 35,000 acres. After their preliminary and final community agreements and forest stewardship plan were approved, SIFCo finally signed a twenty-five-year Community Forest Agreement (CFA) with the province of British Columbia in 2011.

Today SIFCo has twelve to fifteen employees and more than a million dollars in revenue each year. It defines integral forestry as forest practices that, first, determine the ecological limits to human uses of a specified land area, and then, given these limits, apply management strategies that will maintain a fully functioning ecosystem over time. Second, integral management strategies consider humans as part of the ecosystem and aim to improve social conditions such as local employment levels, community stability, local economic opportunities, community safety, fire preparedness, and respect and understanding among residents. In addition, the board officially embraces the principles of integral community mediation listed above.

SIFCo's purpose statement explicitly prioritizes all the "triple bottom lines" of ecology, economy, and social benefit. "Our overall purpose is to serve as a model of integral forestry by owning and managing forest lands in a manner that is ecologically and socially responsible, economically sustainable, and that provides the community with all the amenities of a fully functioning ecosystem," explains Martineau.

Ecological factors include soil protection, biological diversity, ecosystem restoration, wildlife enhancement, proactive wildfire management in the face of climate change, water quality and flow, and the effects of climate change on species distribution. Last year, SIFCo released a multifaceted wildfire protection plan for the Slocan Valley, based on an innovative landscape-level approach—the first of its kind province-wide—to mitigate the increasing intensity of forest fires due to climate change. Economic factors include a diverse range of forest products, specialty woods, long-term sustainable yields, enhancing the community's economic diversity, local employment and retraining, nontimber forest products, and retaining profits in the community. Social factors include inclusive, ongoing transparent public involvement, youth training programs, minimizing the visual impacts of harvesting and road building for the benefit of the growing tourism industry, and protection of First Nations cultural heritage.

Martineau has noted that one of the most important lessons he's learned from this process is that truly integral solutions must relax abstract idealism in order to meet the people involved where they are currently. Then one step forward at a time can be taken, not achieving idealistic purity, but with mechanisms in place that enable the systems to keep evolving over time. If, for example, the aim is to reduce wood consumption in construction by 70 percent, it is better to achieve 20 percent reduction than to hold out for 70 percent and get nothing, especially if there are means for 20 percent to become 30 percent and then 40 percent. He is convinced that integral mediation and ecology offer crucial insights and tools for implementing solutions that respond to our planetary crisis, locally and globally.

Taxi Excel

In the mid-2000s, Grant Hunter was inspired by the transformational potential of social enterprise to lift people out of poverty in the developing world. In 2007 he traveled to Lima, Peru, to do research, having defined two criteria for success: The individual small businesses had to be profitable enough to pay back the loan required to launch them within five years. And they had to be able to lift the entrepreneur into at least the lower rungs of the middle class. Hunter was excited about what could be done using the franchise model, with its developed world standards and ongoing support.

After about a year, Hunter founded Taxi Excel, a fleet of taxis in Lima with various competitive advantages. He identified a higher mission, company identity, branding, and positioning. The company's mission was "green" in that it made use of the opportunity to replace gas- and diesel-powered vehicles with eco-friendlier ones powered by compressed natural gas. Taxi Excel identified affordable "better" vehicles, uniforms, standards of vehicle cleanliness, quality of service, and driver conduct. Then it systematized these best practices and standard means for teaching and enforcing them.

The company designed the franchise system for the individual franchisees with the distinctions of integral philosophy consciously in mind—both the "exteriors" and "interiors" of the franchisees and the culture that permeates low-income developing world markets. Taxi Excel provided a path out of the informal economy of Lima's taxi driver culture (which reflected a cutthroat, survival-of-the-fittest, Wild West mentality), through which they could transition into the formal economy (with rules, regulations, standards, laws, and property rights).

With the higher standards of the brand and better customer service, they could serve higher-paying corporate clients. Taxi drivers were trained in basic English, customer service, and basic automobile maintenance. They also offered drivers the financing to purchase their own eco-friendly vehicles. Thereby, they could increase their standard of living, accumulate capital as they paid off their own taxis, and begin to internalize the modern values and standards of hard work, individual responsibility, excellence, and economic self-reliance through small-business ownership.

At the same time, Hunter went to socially minded investors in the United States and Europe, people with politics across the left/right spectrum. They all found things they liked in microfranchising. Those on the left appreciated that it could uplift disadvantaged people out of poverty and that it was eco-friendly. Those on the right liked the focus on individual responsibility, hard work, and free enterprise. He was able to offer market rate returns in line with thirty-year stock market averages (~10 percent), secured against an insured asset (the taxi). And all of this was accomplished while helping a man lift his family out of poverty in a sustainable fashion.

Taxi Excel ultimately fulfilled all of its key criteria. It reached breakeven and paid its investors competitive returns as the cars were paid off. Many of its drivers emerged from poverty and developed personally. However, the enterprise was unable to obtain sufficient expansion capital to scale up, and at its small scale it wasn't profitable enough to be sustainable for the franchisor. So, after four years of operation it closed down, but not before successfully demonstrating a multidimensional integration of purpose and profit. Concerns for social justice and environmental benefits were achieved while also generating a financial return—successes in all three of the "triple bottom lines" accounted for among socially conscious investors.

This example is remarkable because, by pushing ownership down to the level of impoverished individuals, its social benefit is interwoven with its business model. Becoming a business owner requires and produces increased self-efficacy, responsibility, and personal empowerment. The franchisees learn to control their own financial destiny (usually for the first time). This is integrated directly into the financial success of the franchisee and the franchisor. This kind of "micro" franchising is truly integral and holistic because its social benefit *is* the entrepreneurial success.

Keystone at Xochimilco

My friend Juan Pablo Rico and his partner, Arturo Farias, formed Keystone, a private investment firm in Mexico City, in order to apply holistic and metasystemic principles to complex ecosystem problems. They see business opportunities in the diverse values that can flow from better solutions to challenges like traffic, water, air pollution, agriculture, and urban development.

In 2016, they were hired by the government of Mexico City to design a process to regenerate Xochimilco, the remnants of the original wetland lake on which Mexico City was founded by the Aztecs almost seven hundred years ago. Xochimilco is at the source of the symbols and myths of Mexican culture: a UNESCO World Heritage Site, a 14,000-acre *chinampa* (wetlands agriculture) area on the south end of the city. The Xochimilco wetlands have been farmed for almost two millennia, even while they supported enormous biodiversity. Chinampa agriculture systems like Xochimilco are perhaps the most productive and sustainable of all human forms of agriculture.

However, in recent years Xochimilco has been dying. Its water has been diverted to urban use and replenished with treated sewage, so it no longer supports the ecosystem and agriculture as it once did. Four percent of its area has been converted to housing every year, a rate that would cause it to disappear in a decade. It was once a tourist destination, but only a dwindling stream of tourists retain a vague memory of the place that was once known as Mexico's "floating gardens."

In their work for the Mexico City government, Rico and Farias analyzed the situation holistically and identified key intervention points where small interventions could achieve big results. They validated their analysis with top experts and government officials—in itself a major achievement. This was the first time so many experts had been so much in agreement in half a century of efforts to rescue Xochimilco.

They identified four key leverage points: water quality, agriculture and related businesses, sustainable tourism, and housing. Surprisingly, they found that even though it had talented people and good intentions, the city government was not in a position to solve the problem. Governments, by their very nature, solve problems by adding layers of control. But adding layers of control to a complex system reduces creativity and efficiency. Such approaches make matters worse, quickly becoming unmanageable. And that is where Xochimilco is today.

Rico and Farias approached the problem differently because they recognized that Xochimilco, like most ecological phenomena, is a complex system. Complex systems cannot be controlled or managed, even using sophisticated, complicated approaches. They can, however, be guided by incentives.

Thus, they suggested two broad approaches, both public and private. The government can institute regulations, generate public support, and foster continuous learning. A private initiative, supported by governmental action, can channel capital to projects that are aligned with the regeneration of Xochimilco. By writing new rules for a set of new companies, they have been able to attract significant investment for agriculture. With an investment fund for agriculture, they have helped bring about a consortium to operate large-scale sustainable tourism, which they expect to take over the concession for the 250-acre park. There they hope to regenerate the local ecosystem, and host the agriculture pilot projects, the value-adding operations, and the tourism business.

Even though this project is in its early stages, their progress validates their method and principles. Three crucial major achievements coincided: experts reaching an agreement about the path forward for Xochimilco; the city government, local people, and investors all aligned around a single plan; and large-scale private funding for the agricultural and tourism development.

Their business name, "Keystone," refers to "keystone species"—animals that increase the abundance and ecological diversity of the ecosystem in which they live. Examples include wolves, bees, sea otters, and elephants. They developed an original methodology to address complex ecosystem problems using a novel map of systemic root problems and root solutions. They expect Xochimilco to regenerate, and to be a visible example of humans functioning as a keystone species over the coming decade.

Cosmos Co-op

My longtime friend and collaborator Marco Morelli recently conceived and joined with others to launch a project designed to foster the *scenius* (the collective genius that emerges from highly creative scenes) that naturally gives rise to new kinds of thinking and artistic creativity, cultural experiments, communities, and projects.

It's a community, he says, of "writers, artists, programmers, designers, philosophers, and otherwise ordinary people who feel passionately about exploring the depths and potentials of our shared reality, joining forces to produce works of collective genius." Working online, they intend to incubate a rich ferment of innovation in art, literature, and culture that they have dubbed the Cosmos Co-op.

Appreciating our cataclysmic moment, and the nature of exponential change, this project is acting on the necessity for the revolution in consciousness and culture I am calling for in this book. It intends to cocreate it in innumerable ways that reclaim authentic relationships and communication from the commercialization, commodification, and cheapening of the "fire that burns within each of us"—encouraging original thinking, creative collaboration, honest dialogue, and other "deeply satisfying experiences." They want to engage one another in a way that will bring forth a whole family of new stories "about who we are, what's possible, and what we're here to do."

Cosmos Co-op has already launched a networked series of websites: an online journal, *Metapsychosis*; a social network, Infinite Conversations, and a podcast network of the same name; a publishing imprint, Untimely Books; and a network of book clubs, study circles, and community events called Readers Underground. It envisions more: a marketplace, an internal currency to support member livelihoods, and even a system for collective governance.

It has started humbly, without much funding, but with a bold vision. Morelli and the other participants in this experiment are engaging with one another vulnerably, boldly, tenderly, and poetically—and of course sometimes clumsily. They are sharing art, literature, and ideas, and their naked responses to art, literature, and ideas. They are finding their way directly, not in the familiar terms of discourse of intellectual elites (like in the pages of the *New Yorker*). They've created a space in which they can speak to what moves them and think thoughts that defy familiar patterns. It's a place to touch and to be touched, a space where they can try new things, unafraid of experiments that might fail.

In several ways this initiative stands apart from the others I've mentioned here. Its intent is intimate and cultural, while the others are directed at social and ecological impacts. The Dark Mountain Project, mentioned later, is another example of this progression from a social to a cultural focus—a theme worth contemplating.

Although its business model is still unproven, the Cosmos Co-op is pioneering a quality of contact between participants that has already demonstrated something disarmingly beautiful. It epitomizes the holistic, metasystemic creativity that characterizes all the initiatives I've highlighted here. It addresses questions about the future of culture directly—*by being culture, doing culture, and taking action in human terms.*

But it doesn't presume to arrive at final answers to the questions it is asking: How can we meet the challenge of our wild time except by talking with one another? How can we color outside the lines of our familiar media and discourse so something beautiful, true, and genuinely new can happen? How can we foster a whole wave of authentic creative encounters and experiments in how we talk and listen and relate? Instead, it enacts an ecosystem of spaces in which many people, ideas, and experiments can interact, in which better and better answers to these questions can evolve.

I point to this fledgling project because I have so much respect for Marco's brilliance, talent, and courage, and because I'm excited that he has been attracting and is interacting more widely with other original thinkers, artists, and brave, ordinary souls. I also trust that the lessons learned in this process will bear unpredictable fruit. A passionate, holistic, metasystemic creativity is embedded in the very structures of the Cosmos Co-op. Morelli and his colleagues are attempting to work together with "candor, ethics, and compassion as essential to our creativity." In so doing, they are simultaneously experimenting on the evolving edge of collaboration, art, and culture.

EVOLUTIONARY ACTIVISM AND LEADERSHIP

At whatever level we are forging solutions—local or global, even with metasystemic approaches like those above—we interact with governments and politics. For that reason, activism that goes around the system cannot be a replacement for in-the-system political solutions. Our global predicament must be addressed politically; and it clearly calls for solutions that express a higher order of intelligence than that of our current public discourse. If we could raise the level of our discourse with our so-called "enemies" to where we could find common ground to address our shared challenges, it would seem like a miraculous advance over our current situation (in which, in the U.S., the two main political parties have devolved into an almost completely adversarial relationship). In imagining new approaches, we can derive inspiration from heroes of the past. In acknowledging the interests of all sides and demonizing no one, Gandhi was able to initiate dialogue where none had existed—and extend it all the way to creating agreements where they had not been thought possible.

This does *not* mean taking the position that all sides have equal legitimacy. Sometimes it is necessary to strip away pretenses and expose disingenuous thought, speech, and actions, revealing that the emperor wears no clothes. In fact, to a much greater degree than ever before, we should not tolerate doublespeak, evasion, denial of provable facts, or out-and-out lies by anyone, especially politicians. But that is not the same thing as demonization. To demonize is to create an insurmountable good-versus-evil polarity—and to attack others in ad hominem fashion rather than dealing with the content of the disagreements. Instead, like Gandhi and Martin Luther King, we need to place equal demands on everyone to adhere to standards of integrity, excellence, maturity, civility, tolerance, and compassion. To take our own medicine is ultimately a winning strategy.

Humanity is being asked to grow up into a new species of adulthood, as in "Humanity Is Growing Up," one of Duane Elgin's primary "Great Transition Stories." We are asked to grow into a *new* human adulthood. That means our familiar forms of maturity will not be enough. Our wicked problems call for solutions that can emerge only from a whole new structure of consciousness, from the "simplicity on the other side of complexity."

Important clues to the nature of such an intelligence can be found in the discourse among integral and evolutionary thinkers. An idea central to both evolutionary and integral thought is that *consciousness and culture are always evolving through distinct stages of development.* Each stage of development is a coherent, multigenerational body of agreements and attitudes and capacities and exchanges that cohere harmoniously. Each of these "worldviews" is dynamic, responding to challenges in both healthy and unhealthy ways. Healthy responses to challenges develop new awareness and new capacities. Those new capacities eventually cohere in a whole new higher structure—a new "stage" of consciousness and culture. It is valuable in going to the next level, because it is better able to account for the current challenges. It has selective advantages; it can respond to situations with more and more nuanced complexity, consciousness, and cooperation.

INTEGRAL POLITICS

Integral sensibilities are emerging throughout culture and politics. And significant initiatives are taking shape on both the right and (especially) the left. In the following pages, however, I will confine my exploration to explicitly "integral" political activists and theorists who conceive of themselves as "agents of cultural evolution." They—or, shall I say, *we*—have been involved in public education and community building and original scholarship, building an integral evolutionary worldview, and creating the basis for integral politics, recognizing how crucial it is to achieve maturity in collective decision making. It is a many-faceted initiative that addresses all the key cultural challenges we face, including partisanship, nationalism, globalism, and our relationship to our ecological and climate predicament.

Even while the negative effects of polarization are all too visible, integral consciousness notices an important category of polarities that may seem to be opposites, but are not really "good-bad" polarities. They are, in fact, "good-good" polarities, in which each pole expresses an enduring value, and they function together in a mutually complementary fashion, at least when the system is optimized. Each needs moments of emphasis—and moments when its position is released—like inhaling and exhaling. But to reach this constructive result requires that we hold each polarity in a very mature, nonattached, nonreactive way.

Integral politics also looks beyond the single axis that characterizes policies as liberal and conservative. James Turner and Lawrence Chickering, for example, expand the analysis to two axes—between freedom and order and between left and right.[58] More recently, integral philosopher Steve McIntosh has identified another axis of polarity that integral analyses should include: the tension between nationalism and globalism.[59] Most fundamentally, any integral politics is aware that *cultural evolution unfolds dialectically, through conflicting principles and ideas,* by the synthetic reintegration of the partial truths of apparently opposing points of view (thesis and antithesis). Thus, integral politics naturally takes a long view, even while caring about what may be at stake in the political battles of the current moment. It knows that progress happens by carrying forward the enduring strengths—while simultaneously pruning away the pathologies—of conflicting worldviews and political positions. The values of left and right, of order and freedom, of globalism and nationalism will continue to endure, but their creative conflicts must power the progress of cultural evolution.

In the United States integral political analysts mostly take an optimistic view of human affairs.[60] At the sunny side of the spectrum, the integral political commentator Jeff Salzman introduces his Daily Evolver Facebook page by calling himself "heartened by the state and future of things" and affirming his belief that "life is animated by the power of evolution," which is taking us toward a better world. Even at the more somber end of the spectrum, where there is profound concern about our planetary metacrises, there is skepticism about predictions of imminent collapse, and keen awareness of the human psyche's temptation to succumb to apocalyptic narratives.

The central theme common to all of integral politics is a recognition of the centrality of human maturity on multiple levels and an emphasis on serving its emergence. This implies a shift in personal values, and the expansion of our definitions of education—for children, adolescents, and adults. It understands the importance of developing all the capacities necessary for informed, engaged, and effective citizenship. Integral researcher and writer John T. Kesler has made an important recent contribution to integral political theory by focusing it squarely on this integral agenda—human maturation—and translating the stages and characteristics of leadership maturity into terms that apply to contemporary politics in America.[61] Kesler even takes it further, as we will see, hoping to see a more explicit and mainstream integral political movement contribute to the broader transpartisan movement, promoting personal and cultural maturation through education, collaboration, advocacy, and public outreach.

A series of explicitly integral reports, or "white papers," containing political analysis have been issued by the first avowedly integral think tank in the United States, the Institute for Cultural Evolution (cofounded by integral philosophers Steve McIntosh and Carter Phipps). In its published white papers, the institute advocates that postmodernists transcend the limitations of traditional progressive politics and become more effective at working for sustainability and social justice, by outgrowing the ways they have inadvertently contributed to the tensions underlying our culture wars. The institute has identified progressive distrust of globalization and of blind economic expansionism as a culturally important source of polarization. (The institute's work, especially envisioning a Future Left and Right, is discussed in the section on the transpartisan movement below.)

In a series of ebooks and blog posts, social entrepreneur Robb Smith has interpreted contemporary and historical economic and demographic data to discern the structural dynamics of societies at different phases of their existence.[62] He views the dysfunctional Trump era as a symptom of what he, following Sean Esbjörn-Hargens, calls our "meta-crisis," and he uses another term, "the transformational era," to describe one of its most important dimensions, the economic transformation wrought by the automation of most forms of human work. All this, in cyclical terms, is prelude to a collapse and regeneration of our economic and financial systems. The collapse will result in a period of chaos and finally a complex reorganization of the economic and financial order. His economic and financial analysis can easily be reconciled with the predicament and tipping point described in this book. And he points to "a thorough politics of resilience" as essential to surviving it. His approach focuses on fostering the key factors that correlate with social resilience: social trust, communal resources, shared prosperity, the prioritization of higher purposes over lower ones, individual autonomy, innovation, and resource diversity.

In service of resilience Robb defines key positions of more sophisticated versions of both conservativism and progressivism—his vision of a "Future Right" and "Future Left." We should all be able, he says, to acknowledge the value of entrepreneurship even as we acknowledge the limits of markets and capitalism. We should also acknowledge the potentially stifling inefficiency of government mandates and regulation, even while recognizing the necessity of some market regulation. His total analysis provides a spectrum of implications in terms of specific integral economic and political policies, animated by a creative dialectic between new sophisticated conservative and liberal understandings that admit the failures of current orthodoxies. Specifically, he calls for campaign finance reform, the pricing of negative environmental impacts (including carbon and methane taxes), the reduction of regulations that produce waste and inefficiency and handicap the market by obscuring price signals, evidence-based approaches to education and health care, and what he calls a more forceful "Constitutional Tribalism." Resilience requires us to let go of rigid ideologies—anything that diminishes societal resilience.

Despite the troubled and turbulent nature of our historical moment, Robb is optimistic, based on the scale of likely technological and scientific innovation, the power of integral understandings of mind and society, and the intelligence, flexibility, sophistication, and spirit of millennial leaders and entrepreneurs.

THE USA'S RED/BLUE DIVIDE

Let us look at the defining cultural polarity of twenty-first-century American culture—the divide between the so-called "red" (Republican) and "blue" (Democratic) cultural and political factions. "Conservative" (Republican) policies traditionally reflect a mindset that construes problems and solutions in terms of internal qualities such as personal virtue, morality, and intelligence, which can be proportionally rewarded or punished, producing a preference for market solutions, economic freedom, moral constraints, and small government. The "liberal" (Democratic) pole has characteristically prioritized policies that address and mitigate external causes of social problems—for example, advocating institutional solutions that provide guidance, resources, and structural protections for people who are not thriving.

From an integral perspective it is important to account for the dynamics of both internal and external causes and effects of policies, and to lead and respond creatively, with all the factors that bear on the whole system. Every situation has unique requirements, so both conservative and liberal policy ideas have a place in an integral approach. A core integral principle is that it cannot work to permanently privilege one pole of any true polarity at the expense of the other.

But there is more to our current polarization than the divisions between left-wing and right-wing attitudes. In addition to freedom and order, and nationalism and globalism, there are deeply ingrained moral dynamics. According to the moral foundations theory proposed and popularized by Jonathan Haidt,[63] certain moral intuitions have a primitive neurological basis. Liberals and conservatives are preoccupied with different moral intuitions. Liberals generally feel it is self-evident that care for others and the minimizing of harm and suffering are the highest moral considerations. They also care about fairness and justice and concerns about equality of opportunity. Conservatives, on the other hand, pay attention to loyalty to one's family, town, or clan, obeying authority figures, and an ingrained revulsion to perceived impurity. And they think of fairness less in terms of equality than in terms of proportionality (you should reap what you sow). In today's America, conservatives dominate in rural areas (even in "blue" states), and liberals in the cities (even in "red" states).

The left-versus-right polarity has been overlaid on America's racial divides. African Americans and some Hispanic Americans have long voted Democratic. White working-class Americans have increasingly voted Republican, especially since immigration has turned America into a nation where minorities are becoming the majority. The economic pressures of globalization and radical postmodern cultural changes have evoked powerful "us-versus-them" sentiments, especially among less-educated whites. Political contests have gradually become a great proxy war between nationalism and globalism, individual responsibility and social welfare, entrepreneurial capitalism and democratic socialism, whites and people of color, educated knowledge workers and hard-working, enterprising "real" Americans. Adding to the polarization are competing narratives, debates over factual truth versus disinformation, and the corrupting influence of corporate capitalism on our political and media institutions.

The contest over American identity and our ideological culture wars between left and right have intensified and degenerated. They are no longer working out the legitimate dialectic between right and left—an emphasis on individual responsibility challenging and evolving care for those the system tends to leave behind—so that the systemic causes for personal and social problems can be effectively addressed and corrected. When the polarity functions in a healthy way, contending conservative and liberal perspectives evolve culture. Now, gridlock paralyzes intelligent collective governance and decision making. It is a critical global problem when this happens in the world's superpower, which has often been called "the indispensable nation."

The real contest being fought now is against our own unconscious demons, or psychological shadows. Since this is a battle within the psyche, and what cannot be acknowledged cannot be faced and integrated, partisans just keep questing to vanquish one another, reenacting the same old identities and agendas, spinning their wheels. The most mature participants thus are held hostage by the self-destructive impulses of the least mature, but everyone is caught together in the self-fulfilling prophetic dynamics of partisan bitterness and self-destruction. That is how this zero-sum political polarity has been able to ratchet tighter and tighter, reaching a critically pathological state of paralysis. This bondage—the underlying psychological logic of our culture wars, media bubbles, and two-party monopoly and gridlock—has made the system almost structurally incapable of allowing cooperative solutions.

The Republican Party has long been rooted in traditional values, but until recently it has been committed to a hybrid in which American traditionalism thrived in a modern, competitive marketplace. A majority of Republicans have more mature values and action-logic, but most have proved susceptible to supporting less-mature leadership, via appeals to the impassioned opinions of their supporters' cultural identities and their cherished political objectives. This has led to a critical pathology and today's insurrectionary mood among Republican voters, who carried the party into its high-risk experiment with the Trump presidency. At least at the time of this writing, the party has been captured by a malignant, opportunistic, and ethnocentric leader and faction.

The directness of impulsive, opportunistic leadership has its attractions. It at least has the appearance of decisiveness and strength, although it can be seriously compromised by corruption, opportunism, and lack of discipline. It also tends to erode the rule of law, the separation of powers, civil rights, modern pluralistic values, and democratic institutions, and—as we have seen more and more in every election cycle—it has opened the gates for money to influence politics more than ever, allowing for widespread corruption. American democratic institutions are a system of checks and balances, but the Republican Party has become reluctant to accept responsibility for applying those constraints.

In contrast, the Democratic Party is worldcentric. It spans modern, postmodern, and integral sensibilities and values, so it is the place where the healthy immune response to the malignancies of the right are most often concentrated. But the brand has big problems. To some traditionalists it seems infected with the "stink" of postmodernism that so many traditional and rural people have instinctively rejected and to which they recoil. As Ken Wilber has trenchantly observed,[64] postmodernism is exactly what Trump campaigned against. The modernist and postmodernist wings of the Democratic Party have an opportunity and a responsibility to evolve and come together for the good of the country and the world, but it will not be easy to achieve sufficient coherence. The reconciliation of modern and postmodern factions is so culturally significant, it may be a crucial opportunity for integral interventions.

The nation has been losing its ability to come together, even when the values and collective interests they share are threatened. And selfish special interests have acquired disproportionate political and communicative power via populist appeals to emotions, bypassing any genuine contest over ideas. As a result, both parties are in crisis—each party in itself, and both together as a dialectical system. The two-party system has always had problems, but it now seems close to critical breakdown.

The current stuckness will need to yield to healthier, more flexible politics. Major change is structurally inevitable. The status quo is unsustainable. Evolutionary pressures will require more intelligent collective decision making, as the consequences of stupidity underline the seriousness of this responsibility. We can trust that, even amidst no small amount of chaos, circumstances will find a way to bring forward previously latent capacities for leadership and wisdom. This transition may be worked out underground and emerge unnoticed, or it may evolve under emergency conditions, but it is inevitable, from a structural perspective. The question is not whether but when and how.

The questions have to do with the nature of the transition. Transition is uncomfortable, disorienting, and, when it goes on too long, exhausting and traumatizing. To what degree will worldcentric culture be able to bring the kind of consciousness and conversations described here into today's chaotic environment? How healthy and influential will this movement prove to be?

What other forces will be unleashed, and how will everything interact? How soon will a new political order emerge? How benign will the transition be? How much disruption, destruction, and violence will accompany it? How quickly and by what path will we find our way back to sustainability? Can we soon achieve a more sustainable, healthy, and fulfilling relationship with each other, our planet, and our universe?

Each of us, at best, holds only a few strands in the great tangle of efforts and historical currents that will codetermine these results. Let's appreciate the gravity of our responsibility to foster a "soft landing," a benign transition from our overheated pattern of living to a sustainable human future.

THE TRANSPARTISAN MOVEMENT AND INTEGRAL POLITICAL INITIATIVES

People of good faith on both the right and left have recognized the pathology of hyperpartisanship, and they have been joining together to depolarize American politics. Several dozen transpartisan initiatives have been founded in recent decades—and these efforts have been multiplying and intensifying. One of the most visible is NoLabels.org, led by cochairs Jon Huntsman Jr. (a Republican) and Joe Lieberman (a Democrat-turned-Independent). No Labels has been working on committing members of Congress to a more mature approach to leadership by getting congresspeople from both parties to pledge to put the country first—to move *forward* rather than right or left.

Several others, such as Village Square, Living Room Conversations, and Better Angels, convene groups of people from different cultural identity groups for dialogue and mutual understanding. Other initiatives promote civility in public discourse, citizen conversations across the red/blue divide, greater civic involvement, community meetings, student dialogues, congressional training sessions, civics education, relationship building, and much more. Van Jones endeavored to bring red–blue dialogue into national view after the 2016 election in a cable TV series *The Messy Truth.*

All of these initiatives are making a positive contribution, even though the problem of intensifying polarization is historical, structural, and stubborn. The transpartisan movement has tackled a very big project. As we pointed out earlier, transpartisanship does not require transcending all partisanship. That is entirely unrealistic, in any case. It means, in the context of partisan interactions, working to get things done by identifying common interests and values and complementary benefits. There is room for political horse-trading, but not for hostage-taking. Transpartisanship does not try to homogenize competing philosophies via a mediocre "splitting of the difference," but, rather, attempts to manage enduring tensions between competing interests and philosophies. It begins with human contact, which makes it apparent that more things unite us than divide us. Other efforts intend to rebuild diverse connections in local communities. This is exactly the point. It is no wonder that many activists in the transpartisan movement bring explicitly integral evolutionary sensibilities to bear—emphasizing developing greater human maturity as the common cause among diverse transpartisans.

James Turner and Lawrence Chickering have been elaborating an integral transpartisan political philosophy for two decades[65] and are now the publishers of the transpartisan movement journal *The Transpartisan Review.*[66] Longtime transpartisan activist Mark Gerzon has become an eloquent advocate for the crucial importance of this movement in his recent mainstream book, *The Reunited States of America,* which appeared early in the 2016 election campaign cycle. With John Steiner, Gerzon founded a transpartisan umbrella organization called The Bridge Alliance,[67] which connects seventy-five groups nationwide that attempt to bridge partisan differences and model mature political dialogue, focusing on civic engagement, governance, and policymaking, and campaign and election processes.

Many other organizations, such as Undivide Us, are teaching people to apply best practices to generate productive dialogue. Gerzon and Steiner have called for local citizen summits in towns and cities that bring together people across political boundaries to discover mature collaborative approaches to complex issues in the face of hyperpolarized dysfunction. One of the first of these was organized by John Kesler in Salt Lake City. It built on two months of dialogue throughout Utah that modeled constructive dialogue across differences, and culminated right after the 2016 election in a productive meeting cochaired by Salt Lake City's Democratic mayor and Utah's Republican lieutenant governor. In the trenches, projects such as these are developing the insights and best practices from which polarization can evolve beyond its gridlock. Such transpartisan activism does the basic hard work of reknitting the social fabric, regenerating wholeness in the midst of fragmentation.

New York Times columnist David Brooks articulated a healthy integral communitarian insight when he suggested that, if he had half a billion dollars to spend to improve American politics, he would focus on fostering unlikely friendships rather than working conventionally to boost the political center. He imagined a network of adult "camps" where people would spend two weeks with a small, manageable group of people from outside their cultural bubbles, living together, making and cleaning up their meals, studying big ideas, but also playing sports and building things and having casual social celebrations, with a bar and music—all while temporarily isolated from outside input.[68] Brooks imagined unlikely friendships eventually forming through these conjunctions, reknitting our social fabric. This is precisely congruent with the spirit of transpartisan integral politics.

The Institute for Cultural Evolution, mentioned in the Integral Politics section above, has envisioned and convened a sophisticated initiative that gathers political leaders for a more long-term project—to conceive a healthy "Future Right" and "Future Left" that can function beyond the dead-ends of our current political gridlock. Such a left and right might take years to become influential. But in a future moment they will be able to naturally converse and compete with each other in productive ways—such as enacting a dialectic through which our political culture can evolve capacities to bring the necessary creativity to our collective challenges and predicaments. Interestingly, the "Future Right" project immediately began to get traction.

The Institute's integral political analysis largely resonates with and yet also expands on Ken Wilber's critique of postmodernism. According to one of the think tank's position papers, a key strategy and tactic of an integral politics is "reducing postmodern contempt for both traditionalism and modernism," and it adds that "helping postmodernism to evolve—helping 'uncork the bottle'—is a key to producing cultural evolution overall."[69] One front in cultural progress asks postmodernists to recognize their responsibilities as the most advanced political constituency in the popular world. That means transcending the limitations of traditional progressive politics. It argues that we can become more effective at working for sustainability and social justice by outgrowing the ways we have tended to inadvertently cocreate the tensions underlying our culture wars. At the same time, it also points out to traditionalists that if they become less ethnocentric and imperialistic, they will protect their nation more effectively. It regards the political polarity between left and right as "relatively permanent and existential, continuing to reappear in new forms as society changes and evolves."[70] Although this approach does not seem to adequately include the urgency of our ecological predicament, I respect and appreciate that it is ultimately an orthogonal politics, neither left nor right—one that seeks to further cultural evolution by joining with actual political players across the spectrum, thus helping to restart the evolutionary engine of their dialectical interaction.

The division and polarization of the American electorate is widely seen as the most consequential cultural dysfunction holding back effective responses to our ecological predicament. Integral observers like Jeff Salzman trust that the process has its own intelligence, despite all appearances. Ken Wilber advocates for education and uplift, to help more people mature and catalyze the critical 10 percent tipping point we described earlier. Transpartisan activists are directly crossing cultural boundaries to build human bridges. And, as mentioned above, there is work being done to plant seeds for a "Future Right" and "Future Left." These diverse approaches to this stubborn divide are each potentially complementary, and they're perhaps among the most potentially consequential forms of integral activism.

There are also other explicitly integral political initiatives appearing all over the world, in diverse expressions—in the form of fledgling political parties, factions within larger parties, and movements outside them. A new integral political party has appeared in Switzerland, and integral thinking is surfacing more generally in western Europe, reflected in part by the policies of a number of political parties in many nations. They don't have to win majorities, because parliamentary democracies allow minority parties to influence policy in small and large ways.

A surprising recent development has been the election in 2017 of French president Emmanuel Macron. The year before, he had created a new French political party, En Marche, which sought to transcend traditional political boundaries. Although it wasn't explicitly integral or evolutionary, it did have a transpartisan aspiration—and a stated effort to unify left and right—from the beginning. Angela Merkel of Germany embodies a different but complementary integration of conservative and progressive values and policy. Individuals such as these give many hope for a European leadership that can take the place of missing American leadership in the Trump era—although Europe too faces complex ongoing challenges, and the future of such leadership is far from secure.

Another creative international—and explicitly integral—political initiative is also worth mentioning: Simpol. It originated in the UK and has begun to get traction in Europe. Simpol promotes a commonsense mechanism for coordinating responses to international problems by passing reforms (such as financial and environmental regulations and taxes) *that will not go into effect* until they can be simultaneously implemented in a critical mass of other nations ("Simultaneous Policy" or "SimPol"). This is significant because it enables individual nations to commit themselves to making sacrifices in order to address global problems without subjecting themselves to problematic competitive disadvantages. This way, individual nations can show global leadership. And their example can be the inspiration for local activists in other nations.

Thus, new policies have the potential to gather momentum for enlightened global policies as other countries follow suit.

It's important to recognize that the necessity for transpartisan engagement doesn't diminish the necessity for partisan engagement "in the system" itself—particularly insofar as our ecological emergency is concerned. My own approach to integral politics points in the same directions as those of my transpartisan colleagues, but it expresses radical integral ecology, explicitly recognizing the necessity of ongoing partisan engagement on behalf of the health of the living Earth. And it joins with partisan advocacy for indigenous and marginalized people all over the world. It also joins with the partisan defense of universal rights and values, of reason and science, and of democratic institutions. My sensibilities have evolved beyond the leftist values of my upbringing, but those roots express essential values that cannot be abandoned. The healthy left, present and future, is grounded in reason and *care*—for the whole human family, all living things, and the health of the whole. And care is one of the deepest and most broadly significant of political values.

WHAT SHOULD YOU DO? FOLLOW YOUR HEARTBREAK—AND YOUR GENIUS— WITH YOUR FRIENDS

An integral sensibility directly perceives the profound interconnections that weave together our world, our problems, our individual lives, and our great predicament. That confers many advantages, but it also presents the challenge of understanding where and how to focus your own creative efforts as an activist. If I try to help orphaned children, I discover the problems of money corrupting politics. If I try to address global warming, I may first need to break partisan gridlock in America. If I try to engage politics directly, I may come to the conclusion that radical change won't be possible until large numbers of people mature into higher orders of mind. How can I best engage? What exactly should I do?

Andrew Harvey answers this question directly: "When my friends and pupils who want to help ask me what they should do, I always say the same thing: follow your heartbreak. Determine which one of all the causes in the world really breaks your heart. When you identify this, you have found the cause you will always have the energy and passion to work for."[71]

Harvey is responding to Joseph Campbell's injunction to "follow your bliss." Since he sees, like I do, that the human predicament requires our engagement, he is interested (as I am) in flatly arguing against the ivory-tower solipsism of a private bliss indifferent to our collective plight.[72] Since our care is the source of our heartbreak, our heartbreak puts us directly in touch with the healthy care, the wholeness, that motivates our best work. So he is right—if you locate a way to address what you care about, your activism will be directly connected to your heart's intuitive and creative impulses.

But love and gratitude and generosity are powerful motivators too— sometimes far more empowering than grief and outrage. For all of us, they represent an enormous reservoir of power, and they are inherently attractive. And there's something deeper there too: our unique character and its impulse toward self-actualization. We all yearn to give our unique gifts to life. In his book *The Genius Myth*, Michael Meade proposes that a unique expression of the genius of life itself appears in each human being. He argues that the world's impossible problems *require* that our genius express itself. In a way, the soul of the world is crying out for what is best in our character—for our fullest creativity, generosity, and leadership.

In both in-the-system and against-the-system politics we encounter people from outside our social circles. We have opportunities for mean-ingful conversations, friendships, and new ways of being. All human relationships can be thought of as a kind of politics—politics on the most intimate scale. Healthy politics is the uplift of human relationships. Contemporary televised political power struggles have degraded public discourse, whereas healthy politics restores civility, mutual listening, and social trust. We reknit the social fabric by restoring our ability to have meaningful conversations about things that matter. The uplift of what we call "politics" rests on the uplift of the intimate politics of human relationships, in which friends join and take action for the common good—and in the process, new friendships are formed. We don't have to do this work alone—indeed, we *can't* do it alone.

So I propose a refinement of Harvey's elegant summary. **Follow your heartbreak *and* your genius with your friends.** Your genius will show you the unique way that you can most powerfully act on your deepest care, and your genius and your heartbreak will guide you to others with whom you can take action.

It is important to understand the word "genius" as it is used here. It doesn't refer only to your special talents. It points to the *daemon*, the unique animating spirit of your character. This is a quality that shows up in both your highest abilities and your unique flavor of being. It is especially evident in your self-transcending goodness, your capacity to respond to life generously and appropriately—doing many things that are *not* your special talents. In our narcissistic culture, we easily become preoccupied with a precious version of genius, and the world has found itself burdened by "too many leaders and not enough followers."

Your genius is your special way of seeing things. It fills a gap that would have existed if you had not shown up. Most of the time it manifests as generosity and service. Far more than your heartbreak, it directly guides you in how to bring forward your special light and flavor, and the communities and creative channels through which all the energy of your being can find its way into your contributions.

THE ACTIVE JOY OF INTERBEING

Our ways of being activists will have to keep growing for the rest of our lives. The familiar qualities of grievance and resentment are insufficient (even though many individuals have more than just cause for feeling aggrieved). Likewise, one can get carried away with the entrepreneurial enthusiasm discussed above. Like technology, entrepreneurship is simply a means to an end. Just as personal practice and public engagement are inseparable and must occur together, entrepreneurialism (or the discovery and implementation of new fixes and technologies) is just an unsustainable distraction unless entrepreneurs are grounded in a deep ecological awareness, a whole life of practice, and an appreciation for their responsibilities as members of many human and more-than-human communities.

The Vietnamese Buddhist teacher Thich Nhat Hanh coined the beautiful word "interbeing" to penetrate our modern trance of presumed illusory independence, and to point to our inextricable connection with each other and with all of life. "Interbeing" recognizes that we are all fundamentally interconnected, inseparable from one another. Awakening from this trance, and discovering that inner and outer are one, are what will sustain us and make our efforts together as activists, and as human beings, joyful and rewarding.

Above all, as activists and as human beings, we must increase or restore wholesome health—to ourselves and our relationships and organizations—magnifying all that is life-generating. Our activism is an expression of our practice in a way that is analogous to the mycelium that generates life in the soil and suddenly blooms when conditions are right as ten thousand mushroom "flowers." We must have faith in a process that, while unknown in many ways, is inherently trustable—for we are no different from that process. We are not separated from the Whole, and we are one with the miraculous transformations of evolution. Happiness and joy are inherent to us. We already have the paradoxical ability to relax into the demands we feel, realizing that if we knock, the door will be opened to us. Dead formulas are not what we need. We already are part of a living biological process—and, beyond that, a great, overarching reality.

Yes, we will feel vulnerable. There will be setbacks. Our hearts will probably be broken, and not just once. We will suffer losses and weep for the suffering world around us. But we will not disengage. Genius permeates the biological and spiritual world, and we are all one with that genius. We are each unique, and in some ways very limited, but not isolated. We are all capable of accessing that genius in one way or another, at one level or another. We live in interesting times, during which much around us is dying. But the fruits of our consciousness and labors will sprout, and at some undetermined point we will feel awed by our accomplishments.

At some point, the Whole, or God, or Source, decided to differentiate into all the wild, diverse manifestations of existence and exist in space-time. We are all one, yet we are multiple. Together we complement one another synergistically. We reawaken in this "we-space," and as we move forward we will increasingly experience our inner and outer lives—and "we" and "others"—as a single great magnificence.

We will now further explore the nature of this we-space that we are beginning to consciously engage, and look at how we might transform our capacity for friendship, cooperation, and collaboration.

A New Tribalism and a
New Republic of the Heart

The next Buddha may very well be a sangha.
—THICH NHAT HANH

*I have a profound responsibility to support your transformation,
to make sure you are living the most honored, respected, whole life
possible. Because if you aren't I cannot. If you aren't it is simply not
possible for me to do so. Because we are interconnected. We are One.*
—ANGEL KYODO WILLIAMS

What will catalyze our best realistic future? I believe it will in part emerge from self-transforming *communities* of practice. These communities understand practice as not only personal, but interpersonal as well. Our ways of communicating and responding and learning together can become more conscious, generative, and powerful.

I previously introduced the newly emerging field of mutual "we-space" practice. If we attend to the quality of our conscious contact with one another, we begin to talk about *how* we talk, and how we listen—not just between you and me, of course, but in our families, our communities, and throughout our culture. In my work with groups, I have been exploring new ways of being in conversation that are structured to cultivate depth, intimacy, and tenderness on the one hand, and authenticity, freedom, and ragged truth-telling on the other.

We can draw on a growing body of wisdom emerging from many creative experiments: in generative dialogue, the dynamic facilitation of conversations, cultivating collective states of higher consciousness, and accessing collective wisdom. The arts of dialogue and communication are ancient, but new dynamic experiments have exploded over the last five decades. The "we" is now a whole field, and a hotbed of creativity.

This is a broad cultural phenomenon. All kinds of organizations are experimenting with ways to have more creative and meaningful discussions and productive, enjoyable meetings. Intelligent, vital conversations exercise, challenge, and advance our fullest intelligence, courage, and creativity. They can be tender and bracing, ecstatic and poetic, penetrating and brilliant, powerful and generative. Conversations among mature people presuming responsibility for their own experience are integral to our best futures.

Our intensifying global predicament is making a whole series of collective emergencies highly likely. They will force us into unprecedented levels of cooperation—and communication. I often point out that *interventions* are called for, analogous to an addict's family sitting him or her down for a life-changing conversation. As a human collective, we are getting a signal that asks us to a "new sobriety" as we rapidly change our lifestyles, our economy, our very ways of being "civilized" human beings. We are beginning to have this intervention conversation among ourselves. Our impulse to deny, avoid, or hide from our predicament is becoming untenable. Some of us are beginning to get real, to speak with one another about the elephant in the room. Out of such conversations will come our process of recovery.

There is no simple formula for entering into consequential conversations about our most pressing shared concerns. But we will have to come to terms with the full complexity of our situation and all its unique contours, as they appear in ourselves and one another. That's a tall order. And the way we do this will express our character. But it's not like we can choose a "position" for which we might "vote," like a plank in a political platform. We are being drawn into a cultural process—a whole ongoing *conversation.*

The practice of constructive dialogue requires a great deal from each participant. And that takes practice, which is how we develop our capacity. Higher levels of discourse, then, constitute an art worth cultivating—by individuals, and also by groups. It is an emergent but crucial art form, still in its infancy.

Something important is organically emerging now, a discovery of emergent intersubjective possibilities of many kinds. That field is still young, but this practice of conversation that is attentive to the quality of the "we" is a powerful opportunity, pregnant with possibilities. It is especially compelling for practitioners and activists who take their civic responsibilities seriously.

"WE" IS THE ONE WE ARE WAITING FOR

In our lifetimes, evolution is becoming conscious of itself. We—together—are coming to a dawning realization that we are coresponsible, in part, for the future of human and biological evolution. The collective behavior of human beings will determine the future of the entire planetary ecosystem. Meanwhile, new insights into human development and communication are opening up means to design interactions that spur individual and collective growth and transformation. A healthier, wiser human culture is the one thing that would most powerfully impact all life on Earth—from the coral reefs off the Australian coast to the giraffes on the African plains to the icefish in Antarctica. This moral responsibility for life is calling us to talk with one another and work together in ways that we never have before.

Almost all of our old ways of being will be inadequate to these new, complex, paradoxical challenges. They will fail and we will try out new ways of being. Some of these efforts will buy us enough time to change further. That's how evolution has always taken place. But from our perspective we're talking about a life and death struggle and revolutionary changes in our whole way of life. In the process, the nature of friendship will evolve. So will morality, and trust. They will all have to become something more than they've been in the past.

How will that emerge? It is unlikely to come through a top-down grand strategy, and more likely to bubble up organically. Here and there, and in increasingly more and more places, deep friendships, powerful alliances, fuller cooperation, and new levels of community will break new ground, building know-how and new capacities. These pilot projects and cultural experiments might at first seem like exceptional fringe phenomena on the edges of culture. But when the capacities they cultivate become crucial to collective well-being, they will be understood as having been far more central than they appeared.

The survival necessities of human civilization will rule the day. Even though it will thrive temporarily because of its short-term political advantages, autocratic, opportunistic, combative leadership cannot address the actual human challenges of the twenty-first century. This kind of leadership is incapable of the mature, nuanced action-logic that is necessary to wisely navigate these stormy seas. In fact, our challenges will not easily be overcome, even by our best deliberative evidence-based and outcome-oriented rational leadership. Next-level leadership and cooperation will be necessary. Leading-edge organizational development professionals are already experimenting with exciting new practices and processes. Leadership that will actually be adequate to our new life conditions will only emerge from a rich cultural process of multiple experiments in conversation with one another.

Business organizations are pressing the leading edges of such experimentation. But other lessons are being learned in small groups, tribes, and fledgling communities who aspire to work or live cooperatively. They're experimenting with mutuality, coresponsibility, and practice in relationship, functioning as living laboratories for new possibilities in human relating. Some of them transcend and include the "I" to create a self-aware "we" with new potentials for creativity and intelligent action.

Because they are spontaneously emerging "through the cracks," there is no single focal point where all these diverse communities, practices, theories, and schools for social synergy can all recognize each other and connect. And any of these experiments in culture and conversation might stumble upon important breakthrough discoveries, so no one can claim to understand this whole field. Even so, I will share what I can. I have participated in and led a number of experiments in the integral evolutionary ecosystem where many are in conversation with one another, developing theoretical principles and best practices.

"We-space," as I mentioned, is a relatively new term, used in the integral evolutionary community to describe an emerging set of practices to catalyze an intersubjective awakening of a higher order intelligence, in which "we is smarter than me." "Intersubjectivity" refers to our shared interiors, including shared meanings and understandings, but also a shared felt sense of the fields between people when there is any degree of mutual understanding—the "agreement space." This is an inherent dimension of our being, as old as evolution, and vast in size and scope. It includes all of human culture, especially what is implicit rather than explicit—in other words, everything that "we all just know." Culture is always dynamic—and lately it has been evolving faster than ever.

Historians still debate whether history is really about impersonal cultural evolution or the leadership of great individuals whose choices shape our collective destiny. It is obvious that during times of rapid change, great men and women sometimes become the focal points for social transformation (even when that transformation is the inevitable product of larger forces). When it was time for colonialism to end in India, Gandhi functioned as an inspiring example of wise moral and political leadership. When it was time for legal institutional racism to end in America, Martin Luther King functioned similarly. When it was time for apartheid to end in South Africa, Nelson Mandela did his great work.

Our current ecological predicament and crisis is much more complex and multidimensional than any of these earlier great cultural transitions. It will require a series of much more fundamental and challenging transformations of human behavior. Those historical examples remain a source of great lessons and inspiration, but I don't believe our next transformations will hinge on any single individual. Instead, along the lines of Thich Nhat Hanh's dictum that "the next Buddha may very well be a sangha," it seems to me that the cultural renaissance our global crisis requires will probably constellate around some kind of human *collective*.

That points to a profound level of potential significance in our experiments in community. Even our relationships with our families and friends can be among the key "front lines" in the (r)evolutionary transformation our predicament requires. We are perhaps making a bigger difference than we thought when we experiment with listening and hearing one another better, speaking more essentially and effectively, or asking, deepening, and refining questions together and letting them change us.

A NEW GLOBAL TRIBALISM

The family, the band, the clan, the village, the region, the church or temple, the ethnic group, the nation—our groups have always defined us. In-group/out-group dynamics are tattooed onto the neurophysiology underlying human psychology. Nonetheless, we are arriving in a planetary era, facing global challenges we can only solve together, across all boundaries. The nationalist backlash to globalization has demonstrated beyond doubt that our tribes are too central to human identity to be ignored. Tribal identities and boundaries are not rigid; they erode and regenerate and evolve and change over time, but they are intrinsic to us, they are powerful, and they must be honored. We earlier noted that nations and tribes have souls. They also have shadows, karma, archetypes, angels, demons, and heroic qualities. Our tribal souls will only get us through this new crisis if they learn to relate to other tribes in new ways. And the relations of our various tribes (including our new global tribes) will in part write the story of our planetary future.

New dialogic conversational practices may help a new kind of tribal practice to emerge. Community experiments like eco-villages, conscious businesses, and activist collectives require new levels of cooperation— and new levels of friendship. Some of these communities of practice are profoundly intense and intimate. Some are grounded in a sense of responsibility for addressing our global challenges. Some directly aspire to build a sangha that can help manifest the next Buddha. They have a long way to go before they'll be seen as anything but fringe phenomena in the tribal politics of the larger world, but long before that, their discoveries might have transformative influence on those intra- and inter-tribal dynamics.

Even though these experiments have a world-centric disposition, they can meet ethnic or other local tribes with respect and learn from them. Many will appreciate that most human beings (including themselves) participate in more than one tribe—local and virtual, biological and cultural. And they will learn to recognize and navigate the paradoxes that attend a new age of global tribalism. Instead of a simplistic polarity between globalism and tribalism, they can acknowledge that most current social tensions are between the differing values and interests of particular competing tribes, all across that spectrum.

As we are using the term here, tribes are diverse. On one end of the spectrum are traditional, culturally homogeneous villages, neighborhoods, and townships that hold people's entire lives. Its members belong to only one tribe and one religion. At the other end of the spectrum are post-postmodern communities of practice whose members live all over the world and come together only occasionally, sometimes by voice or video link rather than meeting in person. Its members belong to many tribes. Each extreme, in a very different way, exemplifies wholeness.

The totality of our world can be more fully comprehended by people connected to a multiplicity of communities, engaging multiple languages and practices of discourse and communion. But the simple instinctive forms of ordinary, healthy humanness are more fully and integrally expressed in the life of a *village* sustainably related to the larger web of life. The "archaic revival" and the idealization of indigenous wisdom is resurgent because, in undeniable ways, it relates to humans' only "proven model" of sustainable culture. It seemingly represents the Occam's-razor (simplest and most obvious) solution to all sustainability challenges. A whole new logic is taking people back to the land, away from stores and commodities and plastic bags and packaging, and into the project of devising and opting for ecologically integrated technologies, and against ecologically harmful choices. But a mass transition to such simplicity seems unlikely. So we look in a different direction, especially because progress into our newly emerging potentials seems so exciting. Maybe our *most* refined capacities, the high flowers and fruits of centuries of exuberant expansion, contain potentials that might seed a new kind of human culture and a new kind of relationship among human tribes.

Let's consider some of these new potentials. Tribe-to-tribe communications are a crucial frontier, as we will explore. These new tribes form and develop and evolve by talking with one another, communicating *internally*. But at some point they will discover how valuable it will be to learn to dialogue with *other* tribes, including some of our many ethnic tribes. Other frontiers involve our racial and ethnic tribal divides, and we will continue to learn to engage ethnic identity issues more frankly and fruitfully. It is crucial to learn to conduct generative conversations that cross boundaries of race and tribe, conversations in which not only are all participants heard, but all learn and change and hear one another.

There are equally significant frontiers *within* tribes. What will happen when white evolutionaries start showing up at white identitarian gatherings, sincerely acknowledging their tribal connection and even brotherhood with their racial cousins? Instead of rejecting and refusing to participate with "racists," they might begin to reknit some deep divisions in the fabric of their broken extended families. That would be a new world.

Another frontier comes from recognizing that most of our "traditional" ethnic tribes are paradoxical, postmodern phenomena; most of their members belong not just to their original ethnic tribe or clan, but also to other social, religious, philosophical, or spiritual tribes, maintaining a kind of multiple citizenship. We will never again be held by a ubiquitous, ancient cultural container that should not be questioned. But we are in the same lifeboat with people who are drawing on their traditions to cope with life's challenges. We must find ways to cooperate and tolerate *and* communicate meaningfully with one another. And so we must listen, and actually connect.

We must also learn how our tribes can engage their struggles safely, fairly, and productively. This conversation is primarily directed to people with "evolutionary" sensibilities, or at least a mind that can engage with integral insights and can see and appreciate and honor the necessity, validity, and unique wisdom and beauty of all our fellow tribes across the spectrum. Together we can observe that the fortunes of all tribes have always risen and fallen, as some grow and some decline, in a process that is natural and evolutionary. We can ask how the relations among our competing tribes and special interests (including what we call "political factions") might change enough for us to effectively cooperate for our mutual survival and sustainability. But how? So many destructive weapons and powers seem destined to find their way into the hands of irresponsible people, in an open society in which knowledge is free and expanding exponentially. So a key task of evolutionary tribes is to develop ways of being and living together that provide every tribe *most* (or at least enough) of what it needs, even while frustrating some (perhaps much) of what it wants, such that tribes can compete fiercely but nondestructively. This seems almost impossibly idealistic, but it is not optional. A politics that can adjudicate conflicts between groups in ways that strengthen their capacities for ongoing cooperation and tolerance is a critical requisite dimension of ecological sustainability.

Conversations *between* tribes adjudicating the relative power of competing factions are potential flashpoints. That means that our rules of discourse will ultimately have to discourage or disincentivize whatever ulterior motives degrade honest communication. Experiments in intertribal discourse have been evolving, informed by traditional praxes and the fields of mediation and negotiation. They will increasingly be informed by experiments in generative dialogue, we-space, and collective wisdom. Breakthroughs hold the potential, ultimately, to prototype a new kind of human politics. After all, conversations among tribes, in a sense, *are* politics.

People are already spontaneously evolving a new global tribal practice by meeting in camps, seminars, group outings, and online conversations, as well as classes, conferences, and celebrations with international participants. There is an inherent systemic necessity at work: the urgent need for human maturity to guide our collective decision making. How will these global conversations evolve? One thing is clear: we will need two kinds of conversations. We need open forums that welcome new participants, and draw new people into this practice of conversation. But we will refine our praxis and be personally transformed by deeper, more personal and intimate conversations in closed groups of people we can get to know. These can become communities of practice where we and our tribes can actually evolve.

This teaches many lessons that can be transferred to conversations across tribal boundaries, and especially to our important public conversations. The movement for civil discourse is making a necessary point: Mutual respect and civility are crucial to the synergies that enable us to productively explore serious questions together. It is becoming obvious that important public conversations cannot be fruitfully conducted as "debates." Their function is to produce good collective choices, which require the capacity to listen, reflect, and be affected by what we hear. But it has to go further. We need conversation partners and facilitators who help keep us oriented to our shared values, so that we can venture together into challenging creative territory. Our conversations are often already educational, and we are learning how to teach one another better and better. But beyond debate and persuasion and instruction is *inquiry.* Among our most crucial conversations will be serious, open-ended inquiries. Productive inquiry rests on knowledge, intelligence, and expertise—*in the context of sincere and explicit care.*

In the next phase of our cultural evolution we will counter the common unconscious human tendency to meet only at the surfaces of our being. It is from the depths that we meet and bond, showing and exercising our values and wisdom, and it is from there that we mature. Depth and seriousness, however, must be balanced by humor—which my first teacher, Adi Da Samraj, usefully defined as "intuitive freedom from the implications of experience" and the basis for "unreasonable happiness" independent of circumstances. Healthy seriousness is not "heavy." But without a capacity for *humorous* seriousness, the weight of consequence bears down on us. So let us experiment with conversations that are, at the same time, extremely serious and genuinely humorous—not a mediocre splitting of the difference, but a simultaneously free and responsible intimacy with one another and with the creative potential of the next moment of life and existence.

WHAT IS "WE-SPACE"?

Quality conversations have always been central to what it is to be human, from earliest tribal councils to Socrates's dialectics as recounted by Plato. Profound discourse has long inspired action, and community, and deep consideration of who we are. We've seen it among Jewish rabbinical students, among Sufis, from St. Ignatius to the studios and salons of the Renaissance and the Enlightenment, and since then in our academies, at Quaker meetings and in the transcendentalist and New Thought movements. Communication, inquiry, and group dynamics have been explored in psychology, sociology, philosophy, education, business, and many other fields.

Advances in conversational practice have accelerated ever since physicist David Bohm's creative experiments in dialogue during the 1960s.[73] Tremendous passion, experimentation, and creative innovation have been fermenting in the fields of dialogue, team building, group therapy, organizational development, group processes, the arts of hosting and convening, and other practices that consciously cultivate the quality of communication processes. The social potential of generative dialogue and collective intelligence and wisdom have been recognized and championed by Juanita Brown, Meg Wheatley, Tom Atlee, Alan Briskin, Alexander Flor, Jim Rough, and many others. At the leading edges of culture, many experiments are breaking new ground.

Here, I'll share with you the stories of those experiments with which I am most familiar. Every possible human interaction involves a "we," a collective interior dimension that holds shared language, values, beliefs, and energies. But the specific term "we-space" has been used in the integral evolutionary community for the past decade to describe an emerging phenomenon in which intersubjective possibilities are evoked and explored using practices that cultivate higher shared states.[74] The aims of these experiments vary. An awakened, enlivened, and perhaps even enlightened quality can emerge not just in the subjective experience of practitioners, but in the "between," in whatever it is that arises when two or more people meet—the indefinable third presence that is neither my subjective experience nor yours, but is the "we." The individuals may have strong experiences of nonseparation or deep communion, but what is unique to we-space is a sensed presence of a source of interpersonal intelligence, usually sensed to be wiser than any individual.

Because we live in societies of alienation, people are hungry for the experience of deeper connection, which responds to a whole variety of social needs. So we-space grew rapidly in the integral community and has found a variety of expressions, not all of which have engaged the depth of transpersonal consciousness or the personal and communal transformation that I will be pointing to here. Nor should they—it is not necessary to tackle the problems of the world before we begin healing our disconnection and learning to relate with others in more fulfilling ways.

Current we-space work has two general emphases: (1) practices focused on creating shared experiences of intimacy or other higher intersubjective states and capacities, including direct experience of group fields of intelligence and energy; and (2) practices that are focused on creating innovative, meaningful conversations in which the content of the discourse is the focus, because it advances important insights and new understanding, creative innovation, group cohesion, and/or problem solving.

We can abbreviate this to a primary emphasis on (1) higher states or (2) meaningful content. But in both cases, this work is pioneering new frontiers of intimacy and cocreativity. Both function in important ways to establish a group container for collective transformation.

Shared depth and real meeting in community give participants a collective experience that extends beyond the self's boundaries, opening up a sense of a mutual participatory arc of growth. It is also easier in groups to relax attachments, to explore and access a variety of new perspectives, and to discover generative ways of thinking, learning, and being together.

The shift "from me to we" makes a move into a level of experience in which we are not radically separate. This collective phenomenon mirrors the integral shift *from thinking "from the parts to the whole" to thinking "from the whole to the parts and back again."* This is a new social orientation, particularly for postmodern Westerners who take great pride in their individuality.

Integral we-space intends to create conditions where the most conscious and creative intersubjective experiences and learning are possible. The goal is to establish conditions where they can be continually cogenerated and coevolved by a whole community of participants. Then wisdom and awakening can be coemergent, arising from a higher we, shared by everyone ("many-to-many") rather than being transmitted only by one single authority ("one-to-many").

The highest and most powerful intersubjective states and the most remarkable creative thinking require a great collective investment of time and energy by a whole community. And many things can sabotage the effort. For that reason, some we-space experiments establish ground rules, standards of conduct and participation, shared agreements, and systems of accountability.

It is rare for we-space to achieve its fullest promise, but I believe these practices have the potential to transform spiritual culture. This is especially true because the "we" is wise, free, and postpersonal, and has for many groups offered a new basis for spiritual authority that is not associated with a specific teacher or person.

Social evolution from separation to greater and deeper wholeness is essential to the broader future of civilization. It is already underway, showing itself in small but successful cultural experiments like those I am describing here. Those are most common and most likely in communities of practice, places where subcultural pockets of practice and awakening and intimacy and generosity are naturally appearing. These experiments can serve a critical evolutionary function. Dynamism at the leading edge creates an attractive force that draws others toward new emergent possibilities. When we are making real strides into collective awakening, it will energize even those who are indirectly associated with us.

If something really electric and fantastic is happening, it magnetizes creativity, and a "scene" can breed a whole wave of creativity, as in the "scenius" mentioned in chapter 8. Brian Eno defined it as "the intelligence and the intuition of a whole cultural scene ... the communal form of the concept of the genius."[75] Kevin Kelley has pointed out that "scenius can erupt anywhere, and at different scales," ranging from a corner of a company to an entire region. He cites examples including the Bloomsbury Group, 1920s Paris, Silicon Valley, and even NYC lofts and Burning Man.[76] I experienced the "scenius" phenomenon directly in the 2000s, when the integral evolutionary movement had come on the scene and the excitement and electricity were birthing dozens of creative projects.

Mathematicians, structural anthropologists, evolutionary psychologists, and other social observers sometimes apply principles of mathematical game theory to social relations. Thinking in these terms, it is obvious that important efficiencies and competitive advantages will likely arrive for members of more highly cooperative groups. If they can sustain a higher level of (in-group) mutual trust and altruism, and they can cooperate for their common good, they often thrive. As a cooperative group they should be able to out-compete isolated individuals, or other organizations less able to trust one another. Game theory also predicts that they will probably need to continue to be wary of out-group adversaries and free-riders. That would imply "in-group altruism" and (as a necessary practical strategy) at least a measure of "out-group wariness."

This principle is visible in biological and cultural evolution. For example, it was cooperation between early bacteria that created the first nucleated cell structures and made photosynthesis possible. Evolution proceeds by a process of differentiation and reintegration. Human individuals have differentiated to a degree that has become pathological. We are ripe for a new level of reintegration, for arriving together as a cooperative "superorganism." Evolutionary theory predicts that our next level of cultural evolution will come about through the convergence of what is just emerging in individual practice and the current leading edge of culture. That is a human superorganism. This is often the subjective experience that arises in we-space practice—the shared field becomes a presence in itself, bigger than any individual and yet including them all. If highly developed individuals with a self-transcending capacity can become friends in new ways—truly coherent and profoundly trustable—their new tribes can be a powerful force for social change. This is one of the ways I currently understand the organic telos of this spontaneous cultural experiment. This is part of what I mean by a new republic of the heart.

By "tribes," I mean "communities of practice" or sanghas that share key values and practice them moment to moment. These nascent "we tribes" are a new octave of an inherent human experiment, yet in another sense they are nothing new. Communities of inquiry have always powered cultural evolutionary advance. The Rochdale weavers didn't join the Luddites in machine-breaking; they formed the first Western business cooperative and determined the principles of the whole co-op movement. In every generation, new community experiments break new ground. Experiments in the integral or evolutionary cultural niche, with which I am especially familiar, have mushroomed from a larger social mycelium that has many other expressions, and this larger network is also growing, connecting, and developing a new potential for human culture.[77]

PARADISE MEANS "WALLED GARDEN"

Paradoxically, in order for a community to forge extraordinary bonds of trust and practice, some structural separation from the outer society is needed. Without such walls around the garden, the whole effort will be diluted and will likely fail. Of course, the ultimate objective is to extend connectedness in every manner possible, but first it has to be incubated within the boundaries of a safe intentional community.

While these new, experimental we tribes are breaking genuinely new ground in important ways, they are still tribes, who must still at times be tribal (in the best, most necessary sense). This new and rare intersubjective development simply cannot survive without a discipline that requires a degree of insulation from disruptive influences, which reflect the current norm of mistrust and alienation in the larger culture. The most delicate living explorations of human potential are only possible when their membership is restricted to sincere practitioners who can sustain certain intentions and/or commitments. Only in this way can these evolutionary experiments hope to succeed.

So, at first, these experiments in deeper relatedness often begin with enclaves of serious practitioners who come together based on their shared understandings, intentions, responsibilities, and commitments. While they may share an existing practice that the members are already adept in, they also practice opening up beyond the known into something new and emergent. Their success will depend upon one another's presence, openness, awareness, skill, and capacity. Then the "we" can come forward and all participants can experience an exciting, alive territory in which something can begin to happen that has never happened before.

But the we tribes, as they are emerging, are not a new monastic order. They are not interacting inside the walls of a monastery and never seeing anybody outside of it. As serious we-space practitioners, they are going to have allies and collaborators in all the different projects in which they are engaged, so their values and practices will disseminate into culture more broadly. They will want their new ways of being to be increasingly available to others and to ultimately extend to and, hopefully, permeate human culture more generally.

Certain qualities of the collective, and of the members of a we tribe, enable their relationships to be qualitatively different from conventional relationships. First, both individually and collectively, they must have a creative relationship with the unknown (and often unknowable), so that what is presently emerging in the "we" can be a potentially limitless source of awakened energy, intelligence, and guidance. This is what can lift everyone out of the powerful, unthinking automaticity of familiar habit patterns. It takes tremendous energy for a group to become coherent enough to break that momentum. The source of the energy and intelligence for such positive social change can be neither the willpower of separate individuals, which is simply too weak, nor the "group-think" of a cult or mob, which lacks the intelligence to self-correct and evolve.

The energy and wisdom is transmitted by the intersubjective field itself, which then can become a source of spiritual authority.

Actively exercising heart-based feeling-intelligence can enable we tribe members to rediscover and connect with the mystery of existence as a moment-to-moment practice. This can mature to the point where practitioners are able to navigate through life by constantly opening and giving to the source of everything they receive. This is a self-regenerating process that taps into a reservoir of almost limitless inspiration and energy. Importantly, it is both self-renewing and intelligently self-correcting and -evolving. In the past, religious and spiritual groups have sometimes accessed this tremendous energy and inspiration, but it has usually been belief-based, or teacher-based, or ritual-based, or otherwise incapable of ongoing self-correcting evolution and creative emergence. In contrast, we-space practitioners draw strength from conducting heart intelligence and energy, to create an extraordinary, coherent field.

Deepening trust is a key to group coherence. As I have said, commitment to practice makes us individually trustable. This is also true for groups. Exploring and cultivating trust in life (in all its mystery), in oneself, in one another, and in the ineffable intersubjective intelligence at the center of practice can generate the group's resilience. And this also requires the personal virtues of integrity, responsibility, authenticity, and stable commitment, which are the necessary basis for the practical day-to-day trust essential to the work. Such integrity, and the authenticity through which we can be accountable—even when we are not perfect—enable a community to sustain trust over time. But this great project of inner and outer work is always a work in progress, so we must always be willing—individually and together—to embrace practice in the next moment, and the next.

Whereas individual and group competition has always determined evolutionary success, now a new level of collective cooperation (one that doesn't jettison the benefits of competition) will determine our survival. In that effort, individual trustability becomes a powerful advantage. In this space we continually strive for honorable, trusting, mature, heart-based relationships—and when we fall short of that mark (as surely we will), we immediately and sincerely do our best to restore things. The transformation of culture largely depends upon groups of people becoming trustable and trusting one another and thus becoming coherent and dynamic in ways we have not seen before.

Shifting one's identity from a primary focus on self to a focus that includes the whole—extending to the group, then to the whole inner and outer world—inevitably reveals defensive patterns and protective layers of self-image that get in the way of deep authenticity, openness, and intimacy. Shadow work is key to the healthy development of individuals in a close-knit collective.

All we tribes, to use developmental psychologist Robert Kegan's term, are "deliberately developmental organizations." While perhaps not an organization in the same sense as a business or institution, a we tribe is a collective with an identity, norms, and a purpose that is directed not just toward the good of the whole, but also toward developmental advances in the individuals and the collective itself. Such a we tribe explicitly intends to help cocreate a next stage of culture—a truly integral stage. That includes a practice of noticing how their consciousness and behavior tend to be subject to limiting habits and patterns. What might previously have been resisted, because it is unflattering, is allowed, because it is revelatory and therefore opens up new options. Seeing this, people intentionally and naturally drop these limiting patterns over time. "Making subject object" is Kegan's compact phrase for the maturation involved when one's own previous way of seeing reality is understood and gone beyond—a process similar to the shifts that Piaget mapped in children as they mature into higher orders of mind. Within this we-space there is also an emphasis on liberating the patterns of relating that are the invisible structures of the status quo.

One powerful shared we tribe agreement is that something genuinely novel, vital, and important can happen at any time. This generates a crucial attitude for the most powerful we-space work—an attitude of positive expectancy, curiosity, spontaneity, and attentiveness. Much can happen when this attitude is coupled with a paradoxical combination of (a) deep well-being, rooted in personal maturity and spiritual practice, and (b) a profound sense of life mission, engendering self-transcending willingness to be of benefit to others, in service to a greater principle.

What will this look like from the outside? It will look like a tacit acknowledgment of our connectedness, as fellow members of the human family. It will take the form of making more-frequent meaningful connections, involving, for example, inviting unintrusive eye contact with strangers in public, and with friends in private. (That simple gesture of eye contact is, in a way, the most basic revolutionary act—to pierce the veil of anonymity that isolates every member of an alienated society.)

Within the tribe, it will be about coming alive in connection, about deepening evolutionary friendships as well as deepening trust, mutual generosity, and altruism. These are all aspects of awakening together in a new we-space, becoming a new kind of tribe.

FORMING YOUR WE TRIBE

Conscious collectives are appearing here and there around the world, because conditions make this a natural emergent possibility. The first metaphorical "living cells" are appearing in the body of a new polity. Since I have participated actively in integral we-spaces in my cultural ecosystem, I have used the examples I know to flesh out this discussion. But we are by no means the only such cells. This "new republic of the heart" is emerging naturally and spontaneously in many people and places. One of the most tangible expressions of it is the "new tribe" movement. Some years back, community leaders Bill Kauth and Zoe Alowan invited a group of friends in Ashland, Oregon, to become a tribe, making an enduring lifelong commitment, almost like a marriage—that they will not move and that they will be tribe to each other. Drawing on Charles Eisenstein's inspiring writings on relationships and a gift economy, they infuse that work with a powerful spirit. They have embodied it in seminars and a book, *We Need Each Other*,[78] that can function like a manual for new tribes.

Bill Kauth was one of the founding fathers of the mythopoetic men's movement (which has raised masculine consciousness in America since the 1980s) and innumerable men's groups. Their work is already spawning a number of fledgling communities and seems poised to grow. So this is a movement with many "centers."

I mention this example here because it is rooted in successful community-building experiences, and it stands outside the common integral tendency toward elite self-specialness. The next generation of the integral movement is extending itself freely and creatively beyond its former boundaries, surrendering its sense of superiority and defying constraints to express its integrative impulse. In the spirit of radical integral ecology, I see a rich opportunity for cultural renewal in our recombination with communities expressing ecological and ecopsychological depth and health. This stream of original inquiry is producing many flowers and seeds that can cross-pollinate widely.

I expect many experiments will network and knit together, interpenetrating with other communities, physical and virtual, serving the emergence of a heart-based, transformative global human culture. But just as it is easy to speak of wholeness and quite a bit more difficult to *live* from wholeness, it is easy to speak of the "we" but difficult to get beyond the habits of the "me" in our thinking and reflexes. Adding to the difficulty is the fact that this fledgling cultural space is so new that there is no coherent vocabulary or set list of best practices and common understandings that clearly define it. But here I can offer some preliminary suggestions for the practice I know best—starting one's own experiment in integral we-space. The ultimate guide to this is your own deepest knowing: the soft voice that urges us toward truth-telling for the sake of life itself and all we love that seems at risk.

In my own early exploration of the edge and potential of communication, which for me meant a kind of speech that goes beyond "rhetoric,"[79] I began breaking through the walls of convention by speaking about the wicked problems we are facing and our shared existential "Genjo Koan." Amazingly, simply describing our situation charged the atmosphere, even though at that point I was giving a rather objective, or third-person, presentation of the information, facts, and research that frame my sense of our raw existential predicament.

Then I switched to the first-person subjective mode, in real time, authentically exposing my grief, my cognitive dissonance and insights, and my ongoing relationship to that confrontation and koan—and doing all of this unguardedly and boldly (as per ancient Greek *parrhesia,* or "ragged truth-telling"), but also intimately and tenderly (as per Sufi *sohbet,* or "speaking with the tongue and ear of the heart"). On that basis, with the third step I spoke directly to my conversation partners, in second-person mode, asking how it felt for us to be in this here-and-now together. I made contact with them as deeply and authentically as possible, opening up a space for us to sit together, realizing that our very way of being related to one another might possibly shift in a way that might enable us all to more effectively and holistically respond to our shared existential koan.

I encourage you too: Dare to have a conversation with your smart, sincere, deep friend, in which you say, "I realize that it is possible for our relationship to become even more alive and fruitful, and for us to edge into something new. I greatly value our connection, and I wonder what else might be possible. Where can we go where we haven't gone before? Where are the limits here?" It can be useful to try the 3-1-2 sequence I observed: first, invoke the third-person objective reality; then speak your first-person experience, including your heartbreak and hope; and, finally, address your conversation partners directly in the second person, to invite them into deeper felt contact and a shared inquiry—and dare to lead by example. When we risk losing the comfort of the familiar to venture into something new with our spouse or with our fellow practitioner, we are right now daring to be the impulse of evolution in relationship.

Beyond that, you can approach a dear friend, partner, or fellow practitioner. Consider the groups and people you know who might be interested in change from the bottom up, starting with liberating their relationships. You can organize a tribe. Even before you are ready to commit to such a project, you can create circumstances in which you experiment more and more deeply. I have experimented and continue to do so—and I know creating a real tribe is not at all easy in our fluid, busy, hyper-mobile culture. This book describes such experiments objectively, in third-person mode. The work of living it and community-building is appropriately more passionate (first person) and practical (second person). It is how we all can learn to grow in authenticity and integrity.

Bear in mind that the best possible preparation is to apprentice with someone who has been successfully experimenting with integral we-spaces or other forms of healthy community. You are going to have to go to the edge of your own practice, with the help of people further along the path who can help you go beyond it. You need the best companions and guides you can find. To that end, you want to seek out exceptional company, in order to be drawn forward into genuinely new territories of sociocultural synergy. In order to engage the best experiment you can, you are going to need people who understand the practice in the same terms you do, so you can practice together, expand your capacities, and stretch into your highest mutual possibilities, exercising your evolutionary impulse, the eros that drives development.

This is a companion practice to other conversations that embody the spirit of service and agape and care, which sincerely and reverently honor everyone and recognize that we are all equally precious and magnificent manifestations of the Whole. And it is this spirit of humble, selfless service that gives us the moral ground necessary to bless our attempts to sustainably defy cultural gravity.

Each individual is characterized both by unique beauty and peculiar limitations. Everybody is flawed, and also a portal to the conscious mystery of existence. This divine dimension of another person is rarely witnessed, addressed, savored, or empowered. But the practice of doing so opens everyone to the sacredness of the mystery that is living us, and the indefinable "we" that arises between and among us. It offers a powerful metaphor for opening self-focused minds up beyond themselves, to omnidirectional wonder, gratitude, service, and transparency. To see the divine in another person is to catalyze their own recognition and discovery of their own divinity.

This can be an enormously powerful transformational move; actually practiced, it's both transmissive and invocatory. When we notice this aspect of another being, contempt becomes impossible, however imperfectly or inconsistently they may embody their sacredness. Then we can actually feel another's divine humanity, not just as some abstract principle—which we could casually grant even to vicious criminals—but as a unique living reality.

Most people view others in ways that reify their limitations as central features of who they are. To behold and participate in the radiance of human connection is a very new cultural mode, still quite rare. For you to see my divine humanity, and thus bring it forth in me—and for me then also equally to be doing that in relation to you—is blissful. When our shared divinity is present as a tacit understanding and an ineffable third presence, the "we" also comes forward, even more sacred and trustable. This is heaven on Earth. All souls thirst for such communion. Even the tentative first expressions of it naturally create amazing fluidity and dynamism.

Such practice evokes our very best. When we join with the divinity of another person, a portal opens to another mysterious, intersubjective intelligence and wisdom that is actually *more* than the sum of the best of each of us. A third, even higher state of being, the "we," is given space to arrive. When it does, it expresses its own unique flavor and intelligence. The back and forth of listening and sharing becomes like breathing. What is alive, awake, intelligent, and beautiful in us is taken in and appreciated in a moment, but in the next moment it comes forth in the other and is naturally received reciprocally. And in our play, the greater we that holds your "me" and mine keeps blossoming, becoming even more gloriously sacred. It is liberated and empowered to function at a whole new octave. This seems like a valuable way of describing the frontiers of human relating right now. Starting with one, or two, or a few dear friends, you can begin to open up a space of sacredness that, as you develop, can become the foundation for a radically new *we.*

SELF-RESPONSIBILITY AND ADEQUACY

Only when every individual is entirely self-responsible can we relate to one another without being burdened by one another. While this may sound harsh, we can't cocreate conscious community with people whose motivation to "join" is based on a felt need for a parental authority to help them cope with their lives. If I don't stand in my own autonomy and self-responsibility, then I am useless, because I will just drain you—and the community will in turn become impotent to transform itself and be an effective agent of change.

On the other hand, the requirements of personal responsibility can easily leave us *too* separate, even though we're all in this together. It's not as simple as "I have to be responsible for my life and you have to be responsible for yours—and never the twain shall meet." That is the basis for our common, alienated society. That disposition tends to make it impossible for us to arrive together in a sustainable "we" at all. It doesn't acknowledge our shared destiny and shared responsibility for our common life.

We are vulnerable and need friends and community. If we go "all in" to explore our responsibility for our world, we do not leave behind our humanity. So, while the higher "we" rests on personal responsibility, it also requires openhearted embrace of one another, including embodied friendship, which includes generous care for one another in our mutual vulnerability.

It is true that, to have any meaningful conversation, we need common ground—a "community of the adequate." Theoretical physicists can't discuss their latest discoveries except with people who understand sufficient theoretical physics, rendering them "adequate" to the conversation. But there are many kinds of adequacy—relating not just to mental knowledge and acuity but also to lived experience, existential depth and maturity, psychological balance, spiritual awakening, moral agreement, and wise judgment. What defines adequacy for participation in a higher we-space? What kinds of skills and capacities are necessary?

Generally, participation in a higher "we" requires psychologically healthy individuals who inhabit modern, postmodern, or preferably integral cognition and worldviews. They need to be able to relax and observe the activities and patterns of thought and emotion, and to begin to sense the subtle and transpersonal space between them and another person. There is also the ability to focus and to direct attention. There must be some insight into one's psychological shadow, and ongoing, sincere inquiry into shadow dynamics. Participants must have some capacity to endure discomfort and delay gratification. They also need enough integrity and courage to let go of the nearly universal need to "look good."

All in all, one has to have enough emotional intelligence, health, and compassion for self and others to be able to hold high levels of cognitive and emotional dissonance while remaining present with and open to others, holding a sense that all is fundamentally good and non-problematic. Over time, one develops the capacity to stably rest one's attention on others and the we field so that one begins to identify more with the emerging process than with one's own mind and feelings. When one develops competence with this, then one can begin to engage with others *from* the whole, the we. From there, one gains access to a new realm of intuition and intelligence fueled by the transparent sacredness alive in "the in-between space" of the we.

SHARED AGREEMENTS

Shared agreements are critical for a we tribe to develop coherence and become a real "community of practice," a microculture. All cultures reflect agreements about the nature of being human, about relationships, and about reality itself, even if they are often unconscious and unwritten. *The first agreement that defines a we tribe is commitment—to one another and to the work itself. The second, equally critical agreement is to a clear shared intention.*

Commitment is essential. The level and nature of participants' commitment is what creates the we-space and also what limits its potential. Commitment affects the field in two primary ways. The first is *coherence*—when there is commitment there is regular attendance, and participants get to know one another. And, like a sports team, they get good at what they are practicing together. A much greater degree of intimacy and coherence follows. This facilitates greater intersubjective depth.

The second is *accountability.* When all participants know they can count on one another—to show up, to practice, to be authentic, to care about the work, and to do their best to awaken from unconscious patterns—the telos of their shared exploration can gain traction and build momentum. It is good if there is clear visibility, and perhaps consequences when people fail to meet their commitments. However, accountability should be designed to eliminate or at least minimize complications arising from either resistance or attraction to authorities. Both coherence and depth are powerfully magnified by commitment—especially when participants commit to work over a longer time frame of trainings or study, or even to open-ended or lifelong community involvement.

The second domain of agreement aligns participants' intentions. The most powerful and influential single factor that generates and shapes we-space is the stated shared intention with which the work originates. Even that shared intention is only effective to the degree that it is lived and expressed in the intentions and behavior of each individual participant—which is why accountability is so necessary. Most we-space practices begin with explicit or implicit statements of intention, such as "to awaken together" or "to serve the evolution of consciousness and culture." These largely determine the character and quality of what emerges.

Skeptics might dismiss this as mere suggestibility—a "placebo" effect. And placebo dynamics certainly may apply. Of course, we are talking about subjective and intersubjective experiences, which are not measurable and quantifiable, except indirectly. In the domain of subjective experiences, the most powerful factors are intentions, beliefs, shared agreements, and the subjective states and structures of participants—the context of "set and setting." It is no wonder that the factors most essential to subjective experiences apply equally, and perhaps even more powerfully, to *inter*subjective we-space experiences and practices.

We tribes sometimes set their intentions on very different values, either explicitly or implicitly. Interestingly, they usually achieve what they most value. Below is a list of some of the primary intended values that integral evolutionary we tribes have embraced:

- Interpersonal intimacy
- Transpersonal soul-level intimacy with Source and one another

- Awakening together in higher states of consciousness—subtle, causal, or nondual
- Opening up higher intuitive faculties, and accessing and sharing new information
- Becoming transparent to and voicing the intelligence of awareness itself, the ground of being
- Becoming transparent to and expressing the emergent aliveness of shared field, moment to moment
- Becoming transparent to and articulating the intelligence of the impulse of evolution itself
- Animating and advancing the evolutionary intention to evolve culture amidst the global crisis
- Becoming a happy, sustainable, and always-growing we tribe with a lasting commitment to one another

Each of these values and potentials can be exciting and inspiring. Each can open vistas and develop capacities of relationship that feel fresh and new, and that resonate with sacredness or wholeness in ways that evoke nothing less than awe. But they do not all have the same destination. The list above reflects a spectrum of intentions that are increasingly ambitious. What is most important to the success of each experiment is not the scale of its ambition but how well we fulfill it. Ideally it is appropriate to our capacities, even while it stretches them.

Each we-space experiment will lead to a unique and unknowable destiny. This is both the challenge and the thrill of this adventure in consciously creating a community of practice, a new microculture.

WE-SPACE PRACTICES

We-space is created through present-moment, conscious intersubjective practice, which means paying attention to the quality of the awareness shared among all participants in an intersubjective field. As we've pointed out, when "I" and "you" make contact, there is a third presence in addition to the two of us, a "something more" that is called into being—"us" or "we"—and it can possess its own intelligence. We-space practices aim first to awaken a conscious "higher we," and then to be guided by its wisdom. As practice becomes strong, and an awakened we emerges reliably, the group builds upon it and develops further capacities.

As was also noted earlier, some we tribes focus simply on creating powerful, expanded intersubjective *states* and do not focus or depend at all on the content of what is actually spoken. Others focus on cocreative inquiry and intelligent problem solving, and the meaning and content of what is said is of primary importance. But the nearly universal injunction, across all these differences, is to keep redirecting attention to the present moment, and to relate directly, here and now. Participants stay in the present moment while opening and resting as awareness, more and more deeply and spaciously. This injunction applies across the whole spectrum of intentions.

At the most personal and practical level, honestly relating present-moment experience and feelings immediately gives your conversation partners access to your experience. That is the first building block of interpersonal intimacy. Among the simplest of we-space practices is narrating "what I'm feeling [or noticing or experiencing] right now."

Every we tribe is unique. They can have a spectrum of intentions, which express a variety of higher purposes. Some have been stated as leaning into the future of healthy relationships; the evolution of consciousness and culture; awakening together; emerging from collective trauma; opening to the soul of the world; and evolving consciousness to meet our human challenges. These different purposes frame different qualities of group practice.

What exactly are participants practicing and intending? It varies. In some contexts, participants sense into the felt qualities of the subtle, shared intersubjective field, while in other contexts they will orient toward expressing the intelligence emerging from expanded, shared awareness, or toward very immediate, personal emotional or interpersonal content. Some practices orient away from all content, toward awareness itself, a shared field of spaciousness, consciousness, love, or joy. There can be a progression, in which participants focus on one orienting principle, and then on another, and another.

Attention almost always shifts from the gross level of sensory experience. It may go directly to the intersubjective field, but often it is first redirected to subtle or causal levels of experience, in ways that are informed by practices of meditation and contemplation. Sometimes the injunction is to relax back into witnessing awareness, becoming attentive to—and as—awareness itself. When this is practiced authentically by a group, consciousness itself can seem to intensify palpably.

Other practices involve opening awareness into subtle information fields containing intuitive information and wisdom that is normally unavailable to mental consciousness. Another widely embraced purpose is to tune in to the universal creative evolutionary impulse as it expresses itself through the subjective experience of the participants. All these higher principles can be directly experienced subjectively when practiced alone by each individual, but when individuals come together and practice them effectively in a group, they show up more powerfully in the collective field, deepen, and self-actualize.

PRINCIPLES OF EVOLUTIONARY DIALOGUE

The we-space work of Thomas Steininger and Elizabeth Debold focuses on meaningful conversations that intend to advance human understanding. Although this work does produce changes in participants' intersubjective states, those state changes are not the focus. Steininger and Debold offer five very practical and effective grounding statements for engaging in what they call "emergent dialogue practice." I have used them with groups myself, and have found them to be extremely powerful.

By emphasizing the dialogic nature of the we-space, they draw attention to the cocreative process between practitioners, which can liberate them from the self-concern and self-consciousness that can inhibit the shift from "I" to "we." They caution that these grounding statements are not meant as rules that group members must follow, but express the qualities of engagement that emerge through an awakened "we."

Steininger and Debold call this work the Emerge Dialogue Process.[80] They recommend that groups that are experimenting with "we" practice explore these statements one at a time. Each one tends to reveal and hold within it the seeds of the others. Together, they form a holistic perspective that enlivens the space between people.

These five points are quoted here:

1. *Real dialogue arises when we are more interested in what we do not yet know rather than in what we already know.* The position of not knowing and wanting to know creates a space that helps undercut the fixed positions that individuals hold, particularly when the dialogue is about matters that are emotionally significant or have critical implications for the participants. Moreover, listening for what isn't known places the attention of the group on the living moment and the creative potential within it.

2. *It is easy to be too intellectual or too personal. Dialogue comes alive through our shared interest in what emerges, between us, in our developing understanding and in the field of consciousness.* Being too intellectual means speaking in a way that is disconnected from one's own human experience. We can engage in highly philosophical matters when each statement arises from a reckoning with what is real or true. Being too personal means being caught in one's story, which pulls the attention of the group away from creating a shared we-space. Authenticity in this context means that a broader truth shines through the specificity of individual experience. Engaging from such an authenticity creates a currency of aliveness from which develops deeper comprehension and an increasingly palpable field.

3. *Really listening to each other enables us to develop a conversation that builds on each other's contributions. Really listening allows us to come together in an ever-opening comprehension.* "Really listening" means attending to the field from which the contribution is coming, while suspending one's usual habits of reaction and judgment. Really listening means not slotting another's contributions

into one's own preconceived ideas or frameworks. From really listening, responses come into shared consciousness that are unexpected and alive....

4. *Every conversation lives through our active participation. Even when you are not speaking at the moment, stay with the others and be with the conversation. Bring yourself fully in.* This is the most directive of the foundations: dialogue demands engagement. This doesn't mean that every participant must speak; however, each needs to pay attention and give oneself energetically to the whole. Otherwise, the circle can have "dark" spots that affect the creative momentum itself and prevent valuable information and perspectives from entering the dialogue.

5. *Each dialogue finds its true meaning in recognizing itself as part of a larger dialogue.* When a group begins to access the Higher We consciousness field reliably, there is often an exhilaration that can very quickly turn into a group narcissism—the hubris of specialness. The desire to engage in dialogue, the movement toward integration, is an evolutionary movement that is happening across the globe. Searching for new possibilities in the face of the increasingly complex problems we face is simply the work we have to do.[81]

These grounding statements for catalyzing emergence in group dialogue are not exclusively applicable to the development of we-space, but are useful for almost any deep conversation. They can also energize meetings, brainstorming, community gatherings, and any other group situation where creativity is called for. The results can be surprising. You begin to see that, whether all participants can see this or not, this we-space work and intersubjective orientation catalyze an intelligence and dynamism that is universal to our humanity.

A special kind of connection becomes possible among serious integral evolutionary we-space practitioners, and it can spread into the whole spectrum of conversations we have with our family and friends and colleagues and churches and organizations—with anyone. Practicing with a we tribe, and then crossing over into other conversations, we naturally bring the fruit of our practice—more openness, spontaneity, wholeness, receptivity, and emergent intelligence. We become freer in relation to whatever questions are troubling our culture, such as race, religion, the political divide, and our collective predicament and crisis. As we each become more adept at operating from a deeper field of awareness, in contact with our universal humanity, we can engage more readily in the boundary-breaking conversations that are so urgently needed right now.

A NEW REPUBLIC OF THE HEART

Because its center is everywhere and its circumference is nowhere, wholeness cannot be pointed to. It has no particular location, because it is not "other" than anything. But if is anywhere, it is *here*, at the very center of each "when" and each "where." The wisdom of the center of the being reflects the character of the whole. And we intuit its intelligence at the heart.

A new tribalism implies not just productive intertribal communications and negotiations, but a web of agreements that can hold tribal life. A republic is a representative democracy, in which constituencies choose representatives who meet together to make governmental decisions. If we are at once global and tribal, then we must learn to make global decisions that account for our tribal natures and needs. This, at least metaphorically, parallels the structure of a republic.

It is important that our best integral intelligence, centered in the heart, is never overpowered by the sophistry of clever debate. The universal impulse of evolution is expressing itself in each of us, in our desires to serve wholeness, health, and well-being. We come to care not just about benefiting ourselves and our families and friends, but about the well-being of the whole human and more-than-human collective. When we understand our whole lives as a field for the practice of wholeness, we awaken to a powerful opportunity for in-the-moment presence, reverence, and learning. In the process we find ourselves belonging to an inherent brother-sisterhood that extends to everyone else, especially those who share these understandings.

But even most people who share none of these transpersonal values still express a baseline of basic goodness in their relations to others. They show courtesy for pedestrians when they drive, and they give directions to strangers. They are kind to animals and avoid stepping on flowers. They want to laugh at a joke. The vast majority of human beings bring generalized goodwill to others and the whole world (allowing for the 0.5 to 3 percent of human beings, including psychopaths, who lack the capacity to feel empathy). That is why so many people believe that "people are basically good."

Thus, there is a great hidden body of all that is healthy and whole about our connectedness with one another—the "social mycelium" we have described. Let's not underestimate the potentials of the great underground reservoir of all that is good and healthy in our connectedness to one another.

Our inherent desire to serve wholeness and health in part expresses something deep and transpersonal, our social mycelium. This becomes more fully conscious in practitioners of integral heart intelligence. Thus, although we certainly continue to be citizens of communities, cities, and nations, we also become citizens of something broader and deeper.

This is already occurring. It will be increasingly important for us to recognize ourselves as "citizens" of that deeper connectedness, wholeness, and goodness. When we arrive in a commitment to act in accordance with all in us that is healthy and connected, practicing wholeness as our way of life, we become trustable citizens of what I call a "new republic of the heart."

That new republic already exists, as our social mycelium, and as our intuition and intuitive attraction toward a still-unmanifest possibility. It is already fully present, but mainly as a potential. It is where we are heading, our telos or omega point. It is like the "strange attractor" that conjures order out of a chaotic open system as it transitions through a bifurcation point into a higher-order state. Even though it is still out of reach, it functions to orient and organize all our values, actions, projects, and plans. Moreover, as an attractor of *the* heart, not just *my* or *your* heart, it reveals a new potential in human relatedness rooted in the deepest truth of our nonseparation. I am also "we," for real.

We are being attracted to a new *stage* of development—a level of consciousness resonant with the intelligence of the heart. In 1974, when I was living at the ashram of my teacher, Adi Da Samraj, he first described "seven stages of life." The "fourth stage of life" is said to begin when practice matures in the awakening of what he calls "the psychic heart." That is the stage when people begin to practice heartfelt awareness of the ultimate Reality and Source-condition and become aware of and able to magnify the current of conscious life-energy. It represents the true beginnings of a spiritual as well as more fully human life—a life of love, humor, spontaneity, and service. People we think of as saints often exude these qualities.

Long before that realization is full, its qualities come into the noosphere and begin to manifest widely. People everywhere are becoming inspired to practice living as love, simply on the basis of an intuition of higher consciousness. To the degree that they do, they reinforce a higher, more coherent "agreement space" at the level of heart intelligence. Analogous to the 10 percent tipping-point principle, a small group of people coherently living as love can hope to affect many people, and ultimately transform society. Many people in all walks of life—individually and in communities of practice—are already beginning to attempt to "live as love." We are increasingly realizing that trying to live in "the better world our hearts know is possible" makes us brothers and sisters in a new nation—a new republic of the heart.

This new republic is being powered from below, sprouting from the social mycelium, and called from above, by an evolutionary impulse toward conscious wholeness. It is both humble and ambitious, both organic and revolutionary. Insofar as it is revolutionary, it expresses the "radical sobriety" that comes from taking to heart the "intervention" that asks us to turn the corner from addictions to our high-consumption lifestyles. But this seriousness is also profoundly happy, humorous, and loving. It is an action-inquiry that weaponizes love in service of an integral revolution into a new stage of our social life.

We do well to relate to this new republic or "nation" with the humility of a novice approaching a monastery. It is a whole new stage of consciousness, which we have to actually grow into. We rightly understand that the "nation" to which we owe our highest allegiance is at first subtle, but nonetheless real. We do well to be careful not to dishonor this sacred brother-sisterhood by taking it for granted, disregarding its mystery, losing touch with our reverence, or acting like we can know it or own it. It is only appropriate to modestly and sincerely aspire to become worthy of such citizenship, and to be faithful to that aspiration. We approach the door anticipating a period of preparation and training. And the new republic comes into being invisibly to the degree that we are practicing in this moment. When we are exercising the total intelligence of our being, integrated at the heart, in service of something greater than ourselves, we are opening the door. When we are opening to the wholeness of this moment, in a spirit of humble mutuality and courageous leadership, we are tentatively stepping inside this new republic of the heart. To the extent that we are able to do this with others who are also daring to engage wholeheartedly, we can even begin to sense the fragrance of this new fellowship, this new polity. Through our open-ended commitment to growth, and our authenticity and transparency, the new republic becomes ever more real and tangible, and this tacit reality inspires others.

Our current predicament will, in time, inevitably evoke an entirely new ethos of citizenship and leadership. There is much about human relations we would do well to change. When people cannot trust one another, we waste tremendous resources in protecting ourselves from each other, even those we can trust. Our homes are locked, police patrol our streets, and our computers are equipped with spam filters, security systems, and passwords. Our energy for other, larger challenges and opportunities is handicapped. And meanwhile, living in a society with low levels of mutual trust further taxes us and diminishes our well-being. To recover trust and efficiency seems impossible.

But it can be accomplished, by a multigenerational project of global, whole-system social change, cultural renewal, and individual transformation. Imagine what it will require to upend the psychological and social dynamics that give rise to fraud, corruption, cheating, stealing, and lying.

We are already longing for it. Our hearts yearn for a whole new level of simplicity, trust, and care in our communal relations. Those longings are threaded underground, part of the social mycelium of a new republic of the heart.

Conversations That Matter

Never doubt that a small group of thoughtful, committed citizens can change the world; indeed, it's the only thing that ever has.

—MARGARET MEAD

Nothing has given me more hope recently than to observe how simple conversations give birth to actions that can change lives and restore our faith in the future. There is no more powerful way to initiate significant social change than to start a conversation. When a group of people discover that they share a common concern, that's when the process of change begins.

—MARGARET WHEATLEY

Some of our most important leverage for addressing our predicament is a new species of *conversations*. Talk is not enough, of course (as in "all talk, no action"), and yet whole system change must begin with human society and culture—and we enact such change, in part, through conversation. So certain kinds of conversation are among the most important actions we can take. But there are many hardwired structural obstacles to the kinds of communication breakthroughs that are now necessary.

Profound intelligence and creativity can emerge from real meetings of awakened hearts and minds. Powerful conversations can catalyze not just new understanding and insights, but new friendships, communities, projects, and even movements.

In this chapter, we will look closely at the nature of conversations—what is keeping them from happening and their benefits and implications. Consequential communications are critical to change, but we are still learning to realize their fullest possibilities. We will also look at the different kinds of conversations that are necessary for whole-system change. Then we will go on to explore in depth a few very specific, potentially consequential conversations.

We might usefully think of the most urgently needed conversations as encompassing three broad categories:

1. **Conversations among practitioners,** like experiments in integral we-space. In committed communities of practice, conversations deepen our consciousness, understanding, and capacities for friendship and mutual understanding. They create the basis for inter-group altruism and new levels of cooperation.

2. **Intertribal dialogue** across the boundaries between the many different cultural and ethnic tribal identities in the global human family.[82] An important sub-category in America now focuses on transpartisan conversations across the boundaries of our red/blue culture war, in order to reknit our torn social fabric.

3. **Serious conversations across the boundaries between three specific communities of discourse, whom I call the innovators, the ecologists, and the evolutionaries**—each of which is passionately and intelligently imagining, creating, and preparing for the future. (Unfortunately, today people in each of these groups are mostly talking only among themselves.)

Although I hope this discussion will be useful to activists and peacemakers bridging the boundaries that divide the whole human family and America, I feel best prepared to serve the conversations described in the first and third points above. We just explored integral we-space, in the first category. In this chapter we will turn our attention to the conversations taking place among innovators, ecologists, and evolutionaries, and how bridging them can open new pathways to a heathy human future. These are enormously critical conversations. Let's begin by taking a look at their revolutionary context and the structural obstacles that they must overcome.

THE CONTEXT OF OUR CONVERSATIONS

In this critical time, our ecological and sociopolitical systems are beginning to experience breakdowns. At the same time we are also seeing the beginnings of a wave of break*throughs* into advanced transformative potentials in human knowledge, power, wisdom, and communication. Interestingly, while our breakdowns relate to the functions that are "low," or basic and fundamental to our well-being, we are approaching breakthroughs in our "highest" potentials. At the leading edges of human development we see a flowering of creative innovations across multiple fields, but they can only be sustained if our roots hold.

We haven't yet grounded and integrated our cognitive and imaginative triumphs. In fact, we are wasting tremendous energy straining against one another—energy we may now need in order to join together to defend everything we all share and depend on. Reconciling and cohering after our divisions have become so extreme would be truly revolutionary. But is it even possible?

In fact, achieving a unified voice is not only possible, it has already begun—although one may have to look beyond the usual places to find it. It is expressing itself in countless ways—in the simple goodness of people helping neighbors, treating strangers with courtesy and respect, taking care of people in need, and deferring their narrow self-interest in service of larger purposes. It is in the social mycelium that is always underfoot, unnoticed but pregnant with power. We can also see it among activists and among practitioners, among the most "elite" (in industrialized societies) and among the most ordinary, rooted people living simple lifestyles. It has expressions in the integral, evolutionary, and ecological worlds I have inhabited and in many others I have only read or heard about. We see it in the rise of transpartisan movements to "undivide" America and the world, and in the many programs that sponsor dialogue between individuals and groups that usually don't speak with each other. Some of these movements seemingly exist on the margins, but they are setting in motion what could become a conversational revolution.

What might such a revolution look like? Perhaps we will see a nearly overwhelming wave of moral and spiritual awakening the likes of which we've never seen (not in tension with rationality this time around). This is significant, since "great awakenings" have taken place periodically through history, in America and around the world, when the time was ripe for new inspiration and ideas. Even though historical utopian movements have never realized their ideals, they have sometimes unleashed waves of dynamism, awareness, and energy that have washed through cultures with long-lasting consequences.

Wholesome, wholehearted participants in a fragmenting culture are nonviolent agents of our deeper wholeness. We can appropriately call them revolutionaries, because amidst fragmentation wholeness is what is *most* revolutionary. Revolutionary change marks a turning, perhaps a radical turnabout, a transformation of the order of things. The great wheel revolves, and the world is turned upside-down—or seems to be, from our former point of view. It sets up a whole new stage of cultural evolution.

As we move forward into this revolution (or are carried into it), let's skillfully hold its paradoxes, balancing our excitement about that which has never existed before with healthy caution against stressing our foundational social order and institutions, appreciating the pervasive human propensity for delusion. We are tasked with wisely incubating a new and wholesome cultural possibility. Poised as we are on the edge of something new, none of us knows yet quite how to enact it. We are feeling our way. Our capacities and consciousness are the growing edges of something to come. We do well to become quiet, observant, willing participants, listening for the current of a greater intelligence—humble practitioners of what Korean Zen master Seung Sahn called "don't-know mind."

OBSTACLES TO ESSENTIAL CONVERSATION

If your village were very slowly sliding into the sea, and your fellow townspeople were arguing over whether it was really happening, and fistfights were breaking out among them over whether it was real, with no clear plans emerging about what to do, and if this persisted for decades—what would you do? One of the things you would do is to find someone you could really talk to, to have a real conversation that could lead to effective action. You would look for people awake and grounded enough to help you cut through the fog and confusion.

Today many of us are noticing the unsustainability of our global village and starting these kinds of conversations about what is really happening now in our world. Many more people are participating in these conversations, often vigorously. And some of us are being changed by them—becoming practitioners, innovators, and activists, and even changing aspects of our lifestyles. Vital discussions are appearing here and there throughout culture, subversively breaking the taboo against questioning the popular social consensus that keeps most conversation superficial and pleasant. This is no minor thing—those taboos are entrenched, dominating even many of those who could otherwise be valuable participants in the conversation.

These conversations must overcome other obstacles too, as does every conversation. It is still very hard for us not to talk *past* one another—if not in blatant terms, then subtly, taking turns with our soliloquies. Rather than cocreating mutual understanding, we most often simply present our views, sharpening them as we bounce them off one another.

Consider your own experience. Haven't you found yourself, time and again, feeling frustrated, waiting for your conversation partner to finish elaborating on a point, as he says something you could have predicted or repeats ideas you've heard many times before? Too often, our experience of conversation is one of accommodating other people's needs to be listened to. Worse, conversations often are set up as competitions, in which one person is allowed to be the "winner" based on their assertiveness or persuasive skills (convincing everyone that they are right and the other side is wrong), or adherence to formal rules of debate or presentation, or other forms of one-upsmanship. We have all been imprinted by popular cultural habits that implicitly validate these strategies. Today's form of "debate," with its point-scoring, is widely considered a way to get at the truth—although we have certainly seen otherwise in the non-communication of our wearying political debates.

This is regrettable but understandable. Our habits, shaped by our ecological and economic adaption, have us tensed up, biased toward relating as competitors. It's no wonder our modes of discourse have tended to be defensive and assertive, more interested in outsmarting or taking advantage of one another than we are in learning from, appreciating, and helping others advance a shared understanding. It's hard for us to listen well and then add meaningfully to our understanding of what is happening to our village and what we can do about it. All too seldom do we deeply hear and metabolize what others say, and learn from it and be affected, and then respond intelligently and creatively. Rarer still are the occasions when our responses are truly heard, so that there is not only shared understanding, but a conversation that moves forward. Rarest of all is the revolutionary act of inquiring together, listening for new emerging possibilities, experimenting with them, and advancing into genuinely new territory.

As a human family, very few among us have learned to trust ourselves or one another enough to engender such a breakthrough of discourse. We don't know how to be undefended, authentic, and curious in each other's presence. We don't know how to ask and listen to the big questions we are facing, let alone how to do that together, with all the vulnerability that implies. And if we do, it is with a special few, and only with people with whom we share many values, understandings, capacities, and perceptions.

Realizing that none of us has a handle on the whole truth helps us to maintain what philosophers call "epistemic humility." It is the opposite of "epistemic closure," the closing of the mind to perspectives we have an aversion to. Epistemic humility requires us to really know, deeply and consistently, that however much we know, what we *don't* know is just as important, and probably more significant.

The common current conversational praxis, even when it seeks mutual understanding, usually tends to value the speaker's own perspective above others, rather than prioritizing conversational synergy and the emergence of something new. It's understandable, though, for many of the reasons examined in this book—data smog, the consensus trance, the shadow of fear, and numerous other factors. It's no wonder that truly creative conversations are not terribly common—even among people who are motivated, serious, and who largely see the world in similar terms.

But many of us don't share the same worldview, or even the same ideas about what constitutes a good conversation. As pointed out in the previous chapter, any worthwhile conversation depends on the participants sharing a common ground—of knowledge, attitudes, values as to what contributes to meaning, and even modes of conversation. The "community of the adequate" for worthwhile scientific discussions must have enough specialized knowledge to understand and participate. Every worthwhile conversation needs some shared agreements, even if they are usually unstated. We must agree about what is interesting and relevant and what isn't, about what constitutes a valuable contribution to the conversation and what is a distraction, about listening to one another and noticing the implications of what is said. Generally, we need to share a worldview, or at least some of its critical elements. Every discussion must have what we can call "terms of discourse" in order to be coherent and focused—and in order to keep us from getting sidetracked, ambushed, or bogged down in irrelevancies. It is the implicit context of every serious conversation—so pervasive we usually don't even notice it.

OUR MOST SERIOUS CONVERSATIONS AND THE WALLS AROUND THEM

Within the boundaries of these agreements, some of humanity's most consequential conversations are taking place now—and here. I am using the word "conversation" expansively, to include bodies of cultural discourse that contain books and articles and scientific research and conferences as well as countless conversations. Brilliant intellectuals—scientists, philosophers, scholars, futurists, and sages—are making use of our best knowledge and wisdom to imagine (and even to reimagine how to imagine) the future. They are offering hypotheses, refining them, inquiring into their implications. They are challenging themselves to anticipate and respond to coming challenges and opportunities. Sometimes they engage public conversations about politics and policies. But they are also participating in conversations that make no concessions to public opinion or political realities. They unleash their best intelligence to take in the implications of our civilizational and planetary tipping point—and then go (in conversation) to where almost no one has gone before in imagining possible futures and alternative ways of being.

These conversations about what is happening, and what it all means, have found their way into distinct cultural neighborhoods. In each of them, one or another of humanity's many forms of genius is in conversation with itself, working out its best understandings, channeled through the minds and hearts of brilliant individuals all over the world. In each of these separate cultural neighborhoods, we are considering how our predicament affects our village and the ways to halt its metaphorical slide into the sea. In some of these conversations people are considering how we can invent our way out of our troubles, or how we can adapt. In others, we are considering how to return to a right relationship to the living earth, and how to be authentic and healthy versions of our selves under the changed conditions of our probable futures. In still others, we are considering the nature of how the future will unfold, in and through ecology and technology and culture, as they interact, and how we can practice being the best versions of ourselves.

These conversations—and the boundaries that define and protect them—are precious to everyone involved. We are implicitly aware that our worthwhile conversations are already overcoming formidable obstacles. In the process we naturally gravitate toward people who share our worldview, our values, our cognitive biases, our cultural sensibilities, and our ways of validating truth. We have unstated agreements with them, through which we coalesce a community of coherent discourse. With that in place, we get traction and the conversations move forward, and we refine our understanding.

Each of our conversations, whether consciously or not, has established terms of discourse. These rules filter out perceived irrelevancies and stupidities—anything too frightening, alien, or that otherwise threatens the foundations of our worldview. They violate our terms—meriting what Paul Kingsnorth has named "terms of dismissal"—so we decisively close our ears. Certain conversations are too discordant, depressing, or potentially destabilizing. They are a preposterous waste of time—irrational, deluded, ridiculous, beneath contempt. They are pernicious, oppressive, dangerous, or potentially destructive and/or evil. They are utopian or nihilistic or fascist or soulless or irrelevant. So we don't hear them at all. We shut them out.

This serves the necessary function of shielding us from cognitive dissonance that we instinctively sense might confuse or distract or otherwise undermine our conversation. Excluding alien discourse allows us to tune in and focus on a delimited community, a smaller conversation that we can make sense of. The human organism functions well only within a certain range of stress. If we could not in effect tune out big chunks of the human conversation, we fear we would be overwhelmed—like trying to use the internet without a good search engine. We would at least lose our ability to gather with a smaller circle of congenial conversation partners, and advance human understanding. Without some agreements, we wouldn't be able to have any real conversations at all.

So our discourse tends not to question certain foundational assumptions. And, in the process, even our best conversations self-select their way into isolation from one another. We inevitably tune out more than just the ill-informed, paranoid, delusional, or otherwise irrelevant discourse. We also write off whole bodies of serious, original, vital conversation about our shared and personal futures. We shut out the communities whose contributions are most significantly different from our own areas of greatest competence. We are unable to listen to and learn from them, at least not right now. We are too busy with our own important work!

CONVERSING ACROSS OUR BUBBLES: WHO AREN'T YOU LISTENING TO?

In a hypercomplex world, the future will be shaped by myriad factors, so no single perspective or worldview can account for it all. It is inevitable that we all see the world through a particular lens. The integral evolutionary cultural ecosystem came into being in a great attempt to integrate all truths into a fully adequate metatheoretical narrative. Wilber's achievement in that regard should never be undervalued.

But every perspective, no matter how inclusive, is both true and partial. Structural limitations constrain our efforts. However complete our perspective, it will be subject to limitations. So the attempt to achieve "a theory of everything" is a contradiction. By standing somewhere, anywhere at all, there's much we will *not* be able to see. We can account for the limitations of our perspectives, though. Simply by "being in conversation with" differing perspectives, being informed by their insights and concerns, we can emerge from the universal myopia that otherwise pertains. However, as we have just seen, that is not an easy or quick task. We tend to automatically shut out perspectives that deeply clash with our own worldview. If we are truly serious about this necessary conversation, in which we live into the question of our time, we do well to enter into conversation with perspectives we otherwise would dismiss and ignore.

Who are you refusing to listen to? It depends on who you are.

If you are fundamentally optimistic, you probably don't want to listen to those who are deeply pessimistic about our human future, whose attitudes sound only like a self-fulfilling prophecy. And if you have faced the "terrible truth" about our situation, you don't have much patience with the delusion-reinforcing narratives of the various species of "hope addicts"!

If your primary value is reason and scientific progress, you probably don't take very seriously the voices of mystics, yogis, or sages. But if your worldview is informed by spiritual awakening, or even psychological and philosophical introspection, you may have a hard time respecting what can be achieved exclusively by science, technology, objective measurements, and rational logic.

If you are a "person of action"—an entrepreneur, politician, activist, or journalist—you are probably impatient with scholars, philosophers, mystics, and poets. If your interest is in human psychology, you are probably dismayed by the rampant superficiality that is so often justified in the name of pragmatism or action.

If you have achieved social or cultural or professional prominence, you may feel superior to those who have not, and reluctant to waste your time listening to them. If you are participating in marginalized subcultures, you may well critique and reject the "arrogant" systematic cultural biases by which our cultural gatekeepers define the bounds of legitimate mainstream culture.

If you are a global citizen, you probably feel superior to "provincial" people who haven't seen the world. But if you are a farmer, deeply rooted in your knowledge of your particular place and its weather and cycles and creatures, you probably think urban dwellers and world-travelers are blind about something essential.

If you are a person of color, an immigrant, or a gender nonconforming individual, you probably are tending to judge others who are not sensitive to your experience—especially white people—as privileged and ignorant and morally deficient. And if you're white, you probably feel subtly superior to marginalized people, without even realizing it, since much of your privilege, understandably, tends to be invisible to your own eyes.

If you inhabit a worldview that is committed to positive action, constantly investing yourself in engaging the resurgent creativity of innate human goodness, you probably have trouble hearing the views of those who posit a darker human nature. And if you are actively confronting and seeing the darkness in the human soul, you probably don't have much patience to listen to those who avoid facing it as you have.

These are only a very few of the many divisions among our ways of being human and ways of conversing. But, as we have seen, these many divisions naturally organize themselves according to certain broad worldviews—traditional, modern, postmodern, and integral. In each of these cultural neighborhoods we see vital conversations about the human future—conversations in which human intelligence has been unleashed to make genuinely new discoveries that can push the envelope of human possibilities.

Because we can converse only with a limited number of other people and perspectives, we need to exercise "terms of dismissal," to protect our conversations from irrelevant digressions. But in the process we reinforce our worldviews and prejudices.

Humanity's best intelligence is grappling with our predicament in specialized conversations that don't interact. Each fails to benefit from edifying challenges to its implicit assumptions. The terms of discourse that defend our most consequential conversations are preventing their integration and advance. Human civilization as a whole is held back from the catalytic, healing integral discourse out of which we could bring our best intelligence to our collective decision making.

INNOVATORS, ECOLOGISTS, AND EVOLUTIONARIES

Let's consider three ongoing bodies of discourse about our human future. Each of these is immensely important, but each takes place more or less in its own bubble, separate from the other two ongoing conversational threads. I am calling these three groups the *innovators,* the *ecologists,* and the *evolutionaries.*

Each of these groups is engaged in a serious conversation in which an aspect of humanity's best current intelligence is asking the most central questions it can about the human and more-than-human future. Each is making real discoveries, and each is facing, preparing for, accounting for, and creating our future in unique ways. Although each of these conversations embodies perspectives that are partial in some respects, they each are accounting for aspects of reality better than either of the others. Each of these conversations is going on separately among three distinct expressions of humankind's intellectual leading edges. The *innovators* reflect the brilliance and limitations of modern worldviews, capacities, and values. The *ecologists* reflect the vision-logic, deep empathy, and limitations of the postmodern worldviews, capacities, and values. And the *evolutionaries* express the metasystemic holism and limitations of spiritual awakenings and integral capacities and values.

Each of these conversations has diverse participants; each contains much nuanced thinking and many controversies. But each of these conversations is acknowledging and addressing essential dimensions of reality that will shape our shared future. When it's happening, each conversation may seem to be *the* most important conversation of all—and participants often tend to talk more than listen—which can lead to "epistemic closure." So the participants are not really in active conversation with one another.

Our predicament and critical moment of truth requires this to change. Each of these conversations is vital. Each represents a crucial dimension of humanity's best intelligence and wisdom. They each are engaging important perspectives that have vital contributions to any adequate consideration of our future.

These perspectives often tend to be distinct and it is fine for them to stay that way. It is not even appropriate for them to try to arrive in full agreement with each other. They each have a different genius and a distinct function, intellectually and culturally. But by interacting they can each evolve in important ways. If each is more fully "in conversation with" the others, that dialectic can begin to "true up" all three bodies of discourse, and all participants, and thus it can evolve culture.

Let's introduce them in turn, painting a brief (and necessarily over-simplified) picture of each.

Innovators

I use the word "innovators" to describe people committed to creating an intelligent human future by means of creative scientific and technological innovations. They include entrepreneurs like Bill Gates, Larry Page, Elon Musk, and John Mackey, as well as writers and thinkers like Sam Harris, Nick Bostrom, and Ray Kurzweil. (It's not an exclusively masculine crowd, but the current stars are mostly men.) For the most part (but with significant variations), they largely subscribe to a powerful, internally consistent story about the nature of reality and of our future that goes something like this:

Positive advances driven by human reason, science, technology, and cultural innovations are even more central to our probable future than is our ecological predicament. Climate science and climate change are real and sobering; clearly many disasters are inevitable. But we can innovate rapidly and wisely, respond to new problems, and a benign future can result. Our biggest problems can be addressed by identifying their essential discrete categories and devising effective solutions. Important innovations might include some that are environmentally significant, like carbon-neutral energy and transportation systems, capturing and sequestering atmospheric carbon, restoring the health of the oceans, reducing and recycling waste, and more. They also include advances in artificial intelligence, nanotechnology, robotics, and bioscience.

When we harness the miraculous powers of technological innovation to those of the free market, nearly magical progress results. We are most focused on imagining positive futures on Earth. At the same time, it is wise to hedge our bets by exploring geoengineering and learning to travel through space and colonize other planets. It was inevitable that an intelligent species would make some mistakes and learn some hard lessons on our home planet. But we will resolve these problems and/ or adapt to them. In the meantime, it is critically important that we innovate wisely and that we not turn back. Progress is directional, urgent, and potentially miraculous. It is our job to create a future in which human intelligence enables us to overcome our constraints. The human future has unlimited potential.

Their conversations range widely. They are curious to explore issues surrounding life extension, the replacement of human labor by that of robots, the emergence of artificial "superintelligence," and the exploration and colonization of outer space. They debate the timing of social changes such as the adoption curve for driverless cars, cheaper and higher-efficiency batteries, electric vehicles, and a guaranteed annual income. They are highly individualistic, but resonate with both conservative (usually libertarian) and liberal (at least socially and culturally liberal) attitudes. Innovators are trying to accurately imagine, design, and execute the radically transformative advances that will uplift the human future. They have the knowledge, data, intelligence, and resources to capitalize on the best information and predictions, and they are highly entrepreneurial—moving ahead at a remarkable pace. As a group, they possess tremendous knowledge, power, and money, which they sometimes devote to laudable humanitarian efforts.

To innovators, the achievements of modernity loom very large— the fact that science, industry, free markets, and liberal democracy have delivered millions from a brutal, exposed existence to lives of unprecedented safety, comfort, knowledge, mobility, and creativity. It is not clear to most of them that anything important can be gained, even psychologically, spiritually, or existentially, from deeply contemplating the collapse of industrial civilization or its catastrophic destructive impacts. They are suspicious of doomsayers and Luddites. Their curiosity tends not to extend very deeply into realms where reason cannot translate inquiry into concrete responses. In general, they have not learned to "abide in" profound unanswerable questions, or to appreciate what can be gained by doing so. In general, it is hard for them to fully take in the likely cataclysmic impacts of our ecological and cultural crises; they are cognized only abstractly.

Innovators respect the biological, climate, and ecological sciences, but most of them resist synthesizing them into a holistic ecological or integral worldview, especially if they suspect it might be hostile to continuing economic and technological progress. They are, in general, skeptical of nonmaterialistic models of reality. Although they may appreciate scientifically validated mindfulness meditation, they usually dismiss even intelligent transrational spirituality as "New Age" silliness. They tend to interpret the tangible fruits of scientific and technological advances, including their own success, wealth, and influence, as evidence of their own relevance and rightness.

But they are only seeing part of the picture. They are at the leading edge of a vector of thinking and creativity that will have far-reaching impacts on our human future, so their insights are tremendously consequential. But what they are able to see is by no means complete or conclusive. And what they are able to accomplish, however impressive, is not necessarily wise and benign. Even though they are able to imagine exponential technological progress with granular insight, they do not and cannot know exactly how the future will unfold.

Society and culture are hyper-complex, as are the ecological dynamics of the living world. Innovative achievements will bear their fruits in a dynamic future that will be significantly shaped by biological system dynamics that include elements that this group does not understand as fully as do the ecologists. The future will also be shaped by cultural and spiritual dynamics about which they can learn much from the evolutionaries.

A series of technological breakthroughs and fixes are an insufficient response to our predicament. The biosphere is not analogous to a machine; it is a dynamic living system. Is it possible that it has interiority, sacredness, and inherent, intrinsic value? It is important not to dismiss this possibility, especially not without investigating it thoroughly.

As powerful as the innovators may be, they will not be alone in creating our shared future. It will be cocreated by the whole biosphere, including all its other human beings and nonhuman creatures, including many that don't see the world the way they do. Innovators would do well to find other serious and intelligent ecologists—conversation partners who can open their eyes to vistas they tend to exclude and challenge their assumptions.

However, certain innovators are the masters of contemporary society; they are wealthy, powerful, and very influential. Their power confers upon them special responsibility. What do they have to gain by listening to ecologists or evolutionaries? Their best reasons are rooted in intellectual and moral integrity. They are in the process of creating the future, so what they do is consequential. For them, epistemic closure exposes them to the risks of myopia, recklessness, and a poisonous legacy. They would benefit from becoming curious about, learning from, and entering into conversation with both ecologists and evolutionaries.

Ecologists

Those most willing to contemplate the full implications of climate science and the implications of the problems with the cornucopian myth can be called "ecologists." They have internalized the persuasive but terrifying pessimistic narrative expressed in the next two paragraphs:

> *Scientific modeling and measurements tell us that we have already overshot our natural planetary carrying capacity. In fact, we have now begun to degrade it significantly. We have inadvertently caused a massive series of species extinctions (the sixth Great Extinction event in our planetary history) and many interpenetrating ecological crises. It may be too late to avert horrific destruction, but it is certainly not too late to radically change the ways we live. We civilized humans have become dangerously destructive to our fellow creatures, indigenous cousins, and all the cycles of our Mother Earth.*

> *The most important issue of our time is the future of the more-than-human living world. Alas, it may already be too late to restore health to the biosphere in time to prevent the breakdown of social order in civilized societies. People have so many psychological barriers to facing this reality that we generally fail to face the existential issues of our time. What is worthwhile, satisfying, and meaningful amidst this reality? How can we best relate to and learn from our fear and grief and anger? What remains wonderful amidst these terrible truths? How shall we live and relate to one another? Can we live in a more authentic way? How can we honor and defend and care for and be sustained by the living earth now?*

I have raised many of these questions here in this book, because they are fundamental and necessary questions. If the "terrible truth" of our predicament is the primary issue of our time, ecologists are the ones who have had the strength of mind and character to first face it squarely. As we earlier observed, denial is the first stage of grief. We humans are reluctant to accept our losses, especially the inconvenient truths of global warming and ecological destabilization. People have powerful psychic barriers to accepting pessimistic narratives, so our consensus trance defaults to denial of our predicament. Since we sense that pessimism might be a self-fulfilling prophecy, we recoil from any worldview or narrative that suggests we will be unable to rise to meet our crises. Ecologists are those who have the intellectual integrity and moral courage to go beyond our commonplace denial and face reality.

The Dark Mountain Project in England came into being when Paul Kingsnorth and Dougald Hine, facing the likelihood that humans were not going to address global warming in time to prevent civilizational collapse, wrote a manifesto, founded a literary magazine, and organized a festival. They connected with others willing to face what they were facing, pondering the stories worth telling, the songs worth singing, the conversations that are meaningful under these circumstances. They join with the mythopoetic movement in contemporary culture, as expressed in the work of Martin Shaw, Robert Bly, and Michael Meade, who are recovering and sharing wisdom and inspiration from our most ancient stories. They are also "in conversation with" some wisdom from indigenous teachers. And indigenous wisdom is crucial to the time ahead. They are the only people alive who know how to live happily under zero impact conditions. The Pachamama Alliance was founded when the Achuar people of the Ecuadorian Amazon asked Lynne and Bill Twist to help them "change the dream of the north" to a happier future earth. Ecologists also bring the intelligence of the living earth into the conversation, so they are holding some of the most crucial of human intuitive wisdom.

Joanna Macy, Carolyn Baker, Derrick Jensen, Andrew Harvey, Michael Dowd, John Michael Greer, Peter Russell, and David Abrams have done something at an analogous level (but each in very different ways) in the U.S. Philosophers and activists are enlarging this human confrontation with reality in Europe, Australia, Asia, and Africa. James Hansen, Michael Mann, Vandana Shiva, Paul Hawken, Nicolas Hulot, and Bill McKibben have become influential, internationally recognized leaders in the practical activism that our climate predicament requires.

All these people have allowed themselves to depart from our consoling social consensus in order to inhabit a worldview that requires a new level of character and grit. Such voices must be at the table for our conversations to be complete. Some of these perspectives are grounded in science and data predicting ecological disruption. Some also offer the well-founded, rational arguments for respecting the complexity and nonlinearity of the biosphere, regarding it as a living system that is in some ways robust, but in other ways fragile, with finite adaptive capacities that impose limits to the growth of human economies. And some help the conversation land in the soul, and proceed with its guidance.

Ecologists, as I am defining them here, recognize that the world monetary economy is not our ultimate context; it is a subset of Earth's ecology. They extrapolate from our present experience that continued human population growth will result in more pollution and more mining and drilling and consumption of natural resources, with intensifying impacts on the quality of our air, water, and soil. They recognize that we will probably be crossing critical thresholds that could carry us past certain tipping points, unleashing positive feedback loops that exaggerate the imbalances even further. Although some of them find grounds for significant hope, they do not hide from the implications of the coherent Malthusian narrative that connects the overshooting of carrying capacity and the drawdown of nonrenewable resources to the probability of the severe degradation and eventual collapse of human civilization. The grim data on recent, rapid global temperature increase provides powerful evidence for this view, and suggests that a cascade of additional difficult, irreversible effects is already (at least in part) unavoidable.

Further, ecologists also think metasystemically. They appreciate the enormously complex nature of our global ecological community. They have opened into a profound and soulful recognition of our relationships with our larger biotic planetary community. They recognize that humans are only a part of a greater whole, the living Earth, Gaia—and that our well-being depends upon Gaia's health. They are curious about an eco-psychological shift, not only into stewardship and regard, but also into deep learning and communion with the larger natural world. Similarly, many ecologists (such as Bill and Lynn Twist and John Perkins) are taking the lead in opening to the wisdom of indigenous elders, arguing that their long success in living in harmony with nature is a key source of guidance in relation to our current predicament.

They respect reason and science, but are highly skeptical of the confidence (they would say arrogance) of technological optimism and scientific materialism. To them innovators seem blinded by an egoic psychological self-centeredness that denies reality. Some of them are also dismissive of spiritual responses to material challenges (such as those of evolutionaries). Evolutionaries, to them, seem good-hearted, but naive, ineffectual, self-indulgent, and irrelevant. To them, neither innovators nor evolutionaries seem able to have a reality-based conversation about the human future, and this only deepens their sobriety.

However, as a group the ecologists too are seeing only part of the picture. They are willing to face and process realities that others will not, and for this they deserve great respect. But, like other perspectives, theirs tends toward epistemic closure. Like all of us, they tend not to be able to recognize that their understanding of reality, however much it does account for, is still incomplete. Reality is alive and dynamic. So are the potentials of technological and social innovations. If ecologists really see the emergency they've described, and if they are fully committed to co-creating the future, then they need to find conversation partners among the innovators and evolutionaries.

Ecologists need to remind themselves that they do not and cannot entirely know how the future will unfold. Humans for millennia have shown a built-in propensity to be attracted to apocalyptic thinking, so that must be factored in to ecological epistemic humility. This is especially important because beliefs can function as self-fulfilling prophecies.

Another potential pitfall is righteous contempt for differing perspectives. It risks exerting a dangerous, potentially regressive, destructive influence on culture. Optimists are more likely to thrive than pessimists, even when their expectations are less factually accurate. Therefore, it may be a moral failing to propagate a dark vision of our ecological future that leaves no space for possibility and hope.

Ecologists recognize the sacredness of the living earth. That can be extended to the human experiment. Human culture and civilization reflect something beautiful and transcendent, despite their destructive impacts. The same evolutionary impulse that has driven biological evolution can be seen in human culture. Even if it unleashes destructive powers, it is an expression of something good, true, and beautiful. It deserves to be honored. In their revulsion to human delusion and their reverence for the nonhuman world, some ecologists risk veering into unproductive and even pathological misanthropy.

Doubting technological optimism is legitimate, as long as that doubt is tempered with epistemic humility. Technological changes will likely be a central factor in shaping our planetary future. Ecologists might need to understand and partner and converse with innovators. They also would do well to enter into deep conversation with evolutionaries. They need not suspend all their doubts about whether there really can be dramatic changes in culture, consciousness, and human behavior, but they would do well to acknowledge that these are hypercomplex, unpredictable domains, which means that they cannot rule out their potential for emergent transformation. Changes in consciousness and culture may be as essential to our shared future as reducing our dependence on fossil fuels.

Ecologists may need to partner with evolutionaries to deepen into epistemic humility and a more expansive, multifaceted dialogue. Ecological initiatives will bear their fruits in a dynamic future shaped not only by ecological factors, but also by social, cultural, and technological changes. Ecologists' own discourse risks irrelevance if it refuses to listen to, be informed by, and evolve through conversations with innovators and evolutionaries.

Evolutionaries

"Evolutionaries," as I define the term here, includes everyone whose worldview has been reshaped by wholeness—through awakening as well as integral and evolutionary worldviews. Evolutionaries make a unique contribution to this conversation. When we are at our best, we are quite aware that even our own perspectives are "true but partial," so we're willing to turn the mirror on ourselves, and to humbly learn even from people whose perspectives seem to us obviously incomplete.

I have previously described the nature of integral evolutionary consciousness and culture—including its awareness of wholeness and its impulse to enact it, its humble optimism, and its willingness to engage life as a never-ending practice. It is clear to us evolutionaries that our actual human future will be shaped by the chaotic interplay of many factors—*both* interior *and* exterior. Changing patterns and habits and practices of consciousness and culture will interact with changes in ecology, biology, behavior, and systems—often in startlingly unpredictable ways. It is obvious to us that every perspective (including those of innovators and ecologists) contains important truths, even as it may inevitably leave out other important aspects of reality. When we are actually walking our talk, we relate to everyone and everything as a teacher.

My colleagues in evolutionary culture are refining and clarifying a new integral evolutionary worldview, articulating it, educating people about it, raising awareness, and actually empowering people to develop their spiritual, mental, emotional, physical, and civic lives. We have spawned dozens of diverse initiatives that are catalyzing real positive changes in people's lives. Our project is profoundly gratifying. We naturally gravitate toward this transformative work, inviting others to join us in a kind of elegant, evolutionary spiral. We can identify and praise many remarkable evolutionary accomplishments.

And we are capable of critical self-examination. The integral evolutionary perspective is often compared to an eagle's-eye view of the territory. The eagle has a sweepingly inclusive point of view. It sees the ocean, the river, the mountain, the meadows, and the creatures. As evolutionaries, our panorama extends into the past and future of our developmental processes. It feels to us like we have an all-encompassing perspective. But we can see that there are limits to that achievement. The eagle can also see that there is much it cannot see—beneath the trees and bushes, hidden in crevices, burrowing under the earth, there are territories and creatures it doesn't notice. Those creatures can smell and taste and touch and know local realities that lie outside the panoramic perception of the eagle. Every perspective, even the most comprehensive, is in its own way partial. The integral evolutionary worldview—even with its active interest in science and philosophy and activism and self-transformation, even with its panoramic awareness of how states change even as world-views constellate and self-reinforce—tends not to notice its own limits. That tendency toward arrogance is inherent to *any* perspective.

So we realize that a single perspective will always be limited. A truly integral awareness must be informed by, or "in conversation with," a wide range of viewpoints different from our own. The practice of being "in conversation with" other perspectives is crucial to participating in a reality that is shaped not just by everything that does loom out to our notice, but also by narratives of people seeing things in ways very unlike we are, so we are curious to recognize every partial truth that is being held by the people we disagree with. We must keep valuing and practicing *epistemic humility,* "knowing that we don't know" so clearly that we never stop learning. As a result, even though we might think we can clearly see the characteristic limitations of innovators and ecologists, they are deeply engaged in a conversation that might have something crucial to teach us. We can recognize that we must be in conversation with and learn from these other serious people.

An integral consciousness can hold paradox. It can advocate for its perspective without denying the legitimacy of conflicting ones. It can model and teach listening and receptivity without imagining that receptivity equates to agreement. Truly evolutionary dialogue refuses to get bogged down in oppositional sophistry. Its conversations are never win-lose or zero-sum. This allows those conversations to go deeper.

Mature evolutionaries can even mobilize passion and emotional intensity without becoming aggressive. This makes for dynamic, playful, creative conversations. If all participants are willing to be challenged, they are then freed up to challenge one another. That means we can take more risks. We don't have to be right. We can even point out our differences and explore them. Consequently, evolutionary conversations can lead to much greater intimacy. They also can move through a much bigger territory of thought and imagination.

Therefore, I think evolutionaries have a sacred responsibility to convene catalytic conversations. And we can recognize that if we do so with any degree of arrogance—any degree of blindness to our own limitations—this will present a critical obstacle. And yet, as we've pointed out, everyone tends toward subtle arrogance—evolutionaries most definitely included. In fact, historically this has been our biggest liability. So we proceed humbly, with caution, curious to learn whatever this task will teach us. We think we are capable of epistemic humility. But we are also entirely capable of arrogance and delusion. Let's aspire to humbly get beyond that hubris or tragic pride, and self-critically find our courage to offer our bold contributions.

That means we are obliged to practice, to keep becoming our very best selves, and to be of service. Some of us can help convene a whole series of necessary conversations. Some of us have been working to serve the emergence of integral we-space and the practices of evolutionary dialogue as described here. Some of us are helping convene or facilitate transpartisan conversations like those just mentioned. And others will focus on another body of crucial global conversations, ones that will draw upon lessons learned in all these domains, to invigorate productive conversations among different tribes, ethnic groups, classes, nations, religions, and political factions. And some of us will focus on an emerging discourse with innovators and ecologists about faithfully cocreating an auspicious future.

WHO REALLY OWNS THE FUTURE?

All of us—ecologists, innovators, and evolutionaries—are holding a different necessary "bottom-line" perspective on our predicament and our future. There is something to be deeply revered and respected about the foundational sacredness and sensitivity of the living earth. There is something to be revered about the dynamic creativity of reason and science, and the potential good it can do.

There is also something to be appreciated and honored about a multidimensional, holistic, process-oriented evolutionary understanding of reality. This evolutionary view, advocated here, is awake to (and as) consciousness, wholeness, and sacredness, and yet able to converse meaningfully with innovational and ecological insights, priorities, and realities. It is the participant in these conversations that should be most keenly aware of the provisional and nonultimate nature of all perspectives, and therefore able to be the most open and catalytic participant in such conversations.

It is difficult enough for us to achieve profound, meaningful, groundbreaking conversations, even *within* our chosen communities and shared worldviews. It is wonderful but, alas, rare to be listened to intelligently and thoroughly, and to be heard deeply. For a conversation to genuinely advance understanding, the participants must take in what is said, letting it penetrate their preconceptions and actually affect them. We must listen and open up and allow ourselves to be changed. This usually requires moments of shared silence. Then we must be able to articulate what we have understood and the questions it brings forth in a way that is observant, insightful, and grounded. And we must then be heard by our conversation partners, who must receive what we have said.

This iterative process can build a momentum of intelligence and care that propels it through familiar turf into new territory. This sometimes happens, but not nearly frequently and deeply enough. It is dramatically more rare, almost unheard-of, for *communities* of conversation to enter into productive dialogue *with one another*. To do that they must surmount even deeper challenges. They must bridge diverging vocabularies, competencies, stories, values, worldviews, identities, and styles of interaction. But this is what will be necessary for us to bring our fullest capacities to address our megacrisis. Yet at present, even wise human beings are only very occasionally honoring voices from other communities of discourse as real conversation partners, and then usually only on their own terms.

Each of these three conversations is now mostly independent of the others. Each is rooted in a worldview and perspective that sees a whole dimension of reality crucial to the future—one they've earned the hard way over time. Each brings an expertise or capacity that is absolutely necessary for a conscious relationship to the future of our species and planet. But it would be a mistake to think that we can learn each of these and synthesize them into a new, radical holism that would adequately include them all.

Rather, each of these perspectives is analogous to a lens. We must look through a lens to see what it reveals. And we cannot gaze through multiple lenses at once without losing sight of what each uniquely reveals.

Each of these different truths is far-reaching. They are not something anyone can quickly consume, understand, and summarize. The communities of innovators and ecologists are specialists in a meaningful and holistic sense—both intellectually and experientially. We evolutionaries should listen to them, learn from them, and become related to the world they see. And they would do well to reciprocate.

It is unrealistic to expect that we will soon witness the iconic leading lights among the innovators or the ecologists coming forward to reach some sort of grand agreement that spirits the whole culture into a higher synthesis. Rather, the early stages of these conversations will probably involve a few thoughtful participants from each of these conversational worlds choosing to talk with each other. If they do so with openness and curiosity, and if the conversation is well facilitated, a catalytic synergy will slowly, tentatively develop. That conversation will hopefully pique broader interest and participation, over time coming to inform the primary discourse of both the innovators and the ecologists.

No matter how successful the project is, tensions between the ecologically minded and the progress-minded will continue. This is one of our culture's "enduring polarities." Even if we succeed in reaching agreement on broad principles, the devil will inevitably emerge in the details and a host of new questions will arise. For example:

We may come to agree that we should constrain our own human presence on the planet in order to minimize damage and to care for Earth's recovery, but by how much?

We may come to agree that some emergent kinds of technological progress could *possibly* provide solutions for our human future, enabling us to restore a more sustainable human presence on the planet, but how far down such roads can we go, knowing that these decisions may directly or indirectly cause additional ecological damage?

We may come to agree that cultural uplift is crucial, but what kinds of education and cultural initiatives will really work? Can we cooperate to generate larger-scale cultural change?

Evolutionaries will immediately recognize the value of such conversations. Gradually, more and more individuals in both the ecologist and innovator camps will realize the importance of "out of the box" conversations like the ones I'm proposing here. More and more people will be humbled by events and insights. And these conversations, when they are successful, will attract more participants. The possibilities opened up by epistemological humility will be visible. More and more individuals will be willing to step outside the boundaries of their faction's chauvinistic attitudes and tacit codes. If the right kinds of invitations, conversations, and facilitation appear, a new wave of crucial conversations will change not just *what* we think and do but *how*—with far-reaching effects.

This dialogue will probably start slowly. The innovators' conversation especially tends to be hermetically sealed, made confident by its superior cultural status and power, and defended by "skeptics" committed to attacking perspectives and evidence that challenges their reductive mindset. A great moral certainty arises among ecologists that makes epistemic humility profoundly challenging for them as well. Evolutionaries too will need to give up a subtle sense of epistemic, moral, or evolutionary superiority. But courageous, creative conversations will take place, and they will show some measure of progress. These conversations will, in time, uncover compelling commonalities, subversive points of agreement and insight, potential for innovative synergies, and much more. Experiments in dialogue and we-space will inform some of these boundary-spanning conversations.

Because the innovators effectively own the cultural mainstream, cultural progress will require overcoming resistance to the insights of ecologists and evolutionaries. These are the conversations that must be advanced, and to gain additional influence they will need evolution and refinement. This is where radical integral ecology can play a key role in the evolution of our central conversation. It is a step in the direction of that integration, a move among integral evolutionaries to open into deeper conversation with radical ecologists. Integrated, their perspectives may evolve to represent the needed corrective medicine that can inform the innovators' conversation about the future it is so busy creating.

But we must start where we are. In our subcultures of discourse we tend to gather only with those with whom we can most readily resonate, grouped around a limited range of conversation topics, always in ways that share various tacit assumptions. When we are most lucky, courageous, creative, and smart, we actually break into new ground with our conversation partners and our conversation moves forward and evolves. Changing this is an art. Like the divisions and frictions across lines of race, ethnicity, gender, and religion, differences in worldview will have to be honored and engaged in ways that acknowledge those differences without intensifying divisions, and that elicit mutual understanding and encourage courageous shared inquiry.

It is important to bring together all the leading-edge conversations about our human future. How else can the best of their diverse knowledge and wisdom synergize on behalf of our collective human and more-than-human future? It will begin with a few courageous ideological apostates, defecting from the insular superiority of their camp. That trickle, if their conversations are fruitful, might become a stream and then a river, the vanguard of something extremely consequential. These conversations can matter. Convening and facilitating them will be a privilege and a precious opportunity.

WHERE IS AN INTEGRAL REVOLUTION?

These conversations will arise in a world that will be rapidly changing. We are already living through a greater and more primal revolution than we tend to realize. It is a commonplace observation that we are living in revolutionary times. But we are slower to recognize the multidimensional and radical (or "integral") nature of our current transformation. It defies our categories even as it is reshaping them.

This epochal "intervention" demands that each of us steps across a threshold into a new reality. As we've said, that means whole-system change—an integral transformation, implying new consciousness, behavior, culture, and systems. We must find our way into the newness organically, rather than conforming to our ideas of what things should be. But we can catch a vision of what this revolution requires by noticing that it has multiple bottom lines:

Interior: This revolution's essential nature can be viewed as *subjective*. It is a transformation of our way of experiencing life and reality and sharing it all with one another. It is a multifaceted revolution of consciousness and culture.

Exterior: Simultaneously, this revolution's essential nature can equally be viewed as *objective*. Whatever is not lived and acted upon is only partially real; *to be*, fully and altogether, is also *to do*. We are ultimately asked to enact a revolution in the way we work, eat, relate, reproduce, raise our children, and create the new. And it is a revolution in the way we feed, house, clothe, transport, warm, and cool ourselves. It is a revolution in the agreements, rules, policies, and institutional structures and systems through which we cooperate and adjudicate our conflicts, and through which we regulate and power our relations with one another, with other living things, and with Earth itself. It is even a revolution in the way such agreements and structures can continually change and renew.

Individual: You can only truly understand this revolution when you choose to live it. If it is not happening within you personally, now, and again in each new moment, it disappears, concealed from your view, and becomes unknowable, abstract, and unreal.

Collective: And yet you cannot recognize and choose it without enacting it with others. The revolution inside you needs to integrate with the revolution taking place inside others; otherwise even this process of self-recognition is incomplete. And once mutually recognized, the integral revolution implies mutual enactment. It is pondered abstractly only until it is lived, and lived *now*. And yet it is also an organic, lifelong, ongoing multigenerational process.

It is a revolution of paradox—already, in a real sense, a fait accompli. And yet it is also nascent, barely beginning, an insurgent underdog, in need of our personal, heroic participation. It is also in its prime, in mid-stride, and on the verge of emerging victorious. And failures will be inevitable, because the more things change, the more they stay the same—there's a real sense that nothing ever changes.

The revolution is also an ancient process, stretching back at least ten thousand years. From a future perspective, historians may look back at the entire period from the emergence of tribal societies to the singularity as a single evolutionary event, a single revolution in consciousness, becoming self-aware and self-actualized as a trans-planetary phenomenon—the coalescence of the planet as a single, unified conscious being, what Teilhard de Chardin called the "noosphere."

Yet even from where we stand, as sentient motes in the light of awesome cosmic processes, there are textures and qualities to this revolution that we can call out:

The radical turnabout that is upon us is *holistic* and *integral.*

It cannot be reduced to a revolution of sustainability, even though that certainly looms urgently.

It is not merely a political revolution, although it will inevitably eventually reshape our politics and institutions.

It is not *essentially* a technological or scientific revolution, although it certainly includes all of that in a profound way.

Nor is it merely a cultural and psychological and spiritual revolution, even though it is transforming our interior lives in ways more profound than we commonly realize.

It marks a revolutionary transformation in the whole trajectory of human evolution, especially our relationship to our planet and our whole human and nonhuman family, and yet it is not merely ecological.

It is already happening in individuals and in relationships, in families and communities, in businesses and schools and organizations of all kinds.

And it is almost invisible to us—even as the process accelerates.

So let's talk.

It's Not Too Late, and It Never Will Be

Throughout history there have been many cultural shifts, but what is looming before us now is a collective shift—faster and more complex than any the world has known. Other times thought they were it. They were wrong. This is it!

In this time of extraordinary transition, we can no longer afford to live as remedial members of the human race. A new set of values—holistic, syncretic, relationship- and process-oriented, organic, spiritual— is rising within us and around us.

—JEAN HOUSTON

Activism begins with you, Democracy begins with you, get out there, get active! Tag, you're it.

—THOM HARTMANN

If you don't like the news, go make some of your own.

—WES "SCOOP" NISKER

The bottom line is starkly simple: We *are* it.

Our evolutionary predicament calls us each *to be the change we wish to see.* That implies an open-ended commitment. In terms of our own growth, it means intending to develop all the best human qualities and virtues, with no end in sight, and a commitment to bring them into every moment of our lives. This is no conventional commitment; it is an existential commitment to all we hold dear, all *you* hold dear. You see it in others—the heroes and saints of history, and the ordinary heroes and saints you may know personally. And others must and will see it in you. The commitment never ends, because life itself needs and will always need our very best, and because consciousness and feeling do not want to become unconscious and unfeeling. We are the lifeblood of the universe, and once we see that, we cannot help but embrace life—and we would not want it any other way.

If you have any understanding of what is at stake, you are qualified for this mission. No other "qualifications" in the usual sense are necessary. We have to be keenly aware that every last one of us tends to fall far short of either heroism or sainthood. But many of the greatest heroes and saints of all time were keenly aware of how inadequate they were for their world-changing roles. In fact, *just being aware* of how far one falls short can be said to be a qualification in itself.

There is no superior race of human beings that is going to show up and do what our further evolution requires. You and I, exactly as we are—with all our fear, laziness, self-indulgence, irritability, pettiness (you can fill in the blanks)—are the ones who have been chosen (by virtue of time, place, and circumstance) for this important mission.

There is no way out but through.

If we were to zoom way back and look at the big picture, seeing our planet as if through the wrong end of a telescope, we could see it holistically as a dynamic system—and right now, although astonishingly beautiful in one sense, it is, in another sense, not a pretty picture. All aspects of human civilization appear mired in varying degrees of dysfunction: our economic systems, our political systems, our energy systems, our transportation and food systems—and our cultural, social, psychological, and spiritual lives. It is like a disease that affects every organ system in the body, and also affects the mind and the spirit. Seeing this whole picture, one can't help but wonder where and how anyone can begin to make a positive difference. Where the heck is the energy to dislodge all these logjams going to come from? We seem to have arrived at an incredible multidimensional dead end. What kind of awesome power will be necessary to break through this impasse, and open up a path forward?

But if we then look deeply and closely into the heart and soul and spirit of every single individual, we discover a huge untapped reservoir of latent heroism. We can find it in our capacity for love, our open intelligence, our impulse to be of benefit, to extend care beyond ourselves, to embody excellence and courage, to become true friends, and to forge new kinds of communities. This is a huge power source. It is largely untapped, but it is present as potential nonetheless. We clearly have the power to create a new "we," expressing higher cocreative synergies. All the energy and intelligence that is needed to effect a complete transformation of our dysfunctional world is latent in the human spirit. If we can find a way to come together in a way that unleashes that suppressed potential, it will be like channeling nuclear fusion. In explaining the nature of heart intelligence in chapter 5, we quoted Pierre Teilhard de Chardin's famous statement that when humans finally harness "the energies of love … for a second time in the history of the world, man will have discovered fire." It is, quite literally and realistically, that significant.

That spiritual power and boundary-breaking love have been unleashed throughout history by rare individuals—people like Buddha, Socrates, Jesus, Gandhi, and undoubtedly countless other saints, sages, and activists—and even at times by ordinary people. Whether from stories surrounding great figures, or from personal encounters with them, our hopes and energies and spirit become transformed, even to the point where, at least in given instances, we may become embodiments of love, compassion, and courage. Those who most consistently embody that disposition have been able to effect miraculous changes in human individuals and in the societies in which they lived. You and I may not consistently have the extraordinary attributes of such people—but we can be indispensable participants in a larger consciousness that *does* function that way.

At this point in the human saga, as we have said, the next Buddha will have to be a sangha—a collective practicing and developing an ever more responsive, creative "we." Individually, we each are in effect asked by circumstances to grow and evolve, and if possible to become participants in the "body-mind" of an emerging saintly and heroic collective. Together we are the unwashed raw ingredients of a sorely needed new human adulthood.

It is not too late. Disasters, calamities, and transformative breakthroughs can open critical windows of opportunity for more fundamental systems redesign. The idea that it may take disasters to do this at first seems depressing, but it actually creates a huge opening for realistic hope even in the midst of disasters. It is also a road map to a new, more grounded form of long-view activism. It may seem that we face challenges so urgent that there is no way they will be adequately addressed by the slow process of cultural, social, and political reform. (Notice that this is the unstated subtext of many anxious "progressive" political communications.) But in fact, some of the most powerful change is likely to come *after* it is "too late."

IT IS NEVER TOO LATE

The wholeness of our more-than-human living earth utterly defies analysis. It cannot be accounted for by linear chains of cause and effect. Systemic complexity accounts for some of this unpredictability, but it also has to do with something about wholeness itself—its radical potential for aliveness and creative simultaneity. Thus, accurate predictions are impossible. Even the subatomic world appears to reveal signs of this creative simultaneity. Physicists speculate that the not entirely random pathways of atomic particles might best be thought of as their "play."

Tracing our evolutionary history, we can infer that life wants to live, to thrive. Evolution wants to keep evolving. Gaia is powerfully resilient. Our efforts to respond, which may seem too little, too late, will create changes throughout the biosphere in ways that we also cannot know. On the negative side, these efforts may initiate disruptions, even what we call "cataclysms"—but they will also be triggering the self-regulating resilience of the living planetary system. We are not separate from the intentionality that will naturally surface under these systemic conditions. Times of catastrophe are moments when the system is breaking down and breaking open. Surprisingly, they can present remarkable opportunities to create larger systemic change.

Most of us tend to think of change in very limited ways. When we think of change, we tend to think only about the projects that we can imagine human beings actively accomplishing. We hope that those will prove to be therapeutic pricks of a "social acupuncture" needle that will catalyze virtuous nonlinear dynamics. We hope for positive feedback loops, the crossing of "tipping points," and subtle field dynamics that will help our best-laid plans succeed. And yet events are never so consistently benign, so the story is not so tidy. Change often comes amidst disruption, after a crisis creates a window of opportunity. It will be the "black swans," the unforeseeable game-changers—like another financial meltdown—that will open the opportunity for something radically new.

Consider the Fukushima nuclear disaster of 2011. On March 11 of that year, a megaearthquake (measuring 9.0 on the moment magnitude scale) unleashed a fifteen-foot tsunami across Honshu Island, the main island of Japan. Some 19,000 people died. Then the nuclear power plant at Fukushima Daiichi lost its generators, and within three days several of the radioactive cores melted. The world watched as one of the largest nuclear disasters of all time unfolded in slow motion, and everyone seemed helpless to stop it.

Meanwhile, in Europe, a group of Swiss advocates for sustainability moved into action. They had anticipated another Chernobyl-type disaster, and they had prepared for it. Over the years leading up to Fukushima, they had built relationships of respect and influence with people at the highest levels of Swiss politics. They had also quantified the cost of the premiums for a private insurance company to insure Switzerland's nuclear industry against public liability. (Like the U.S. and most nuclear-armed nations, Switzerland had passed laws indemnifying the owners and operators of nuclear power plants from public liability. Their research had carefully quantified and documented the size of this enormous public subsidy.) Moreover, they had done the work to compute the (lower) costs of subsidizing other clean energy technologies in preference to nuclear power. Thus, when the Fukushima accident happened, they were ready. And they then reached out to the decision makers and supplied them with white papers that built a carefully reasoned argument for dramatic policy decisions. All of this happened while the inertia of the status quo was interrupted and a window of opportunity for more fundamental reform was open.

Two months later, Germany made the same decision, and for similar reasons. In May 2017, Germany hit an all-time worldwide record for a nation its size, using 85 percent renewable energy.

The key is to liberate our thinking and our activism without triggering our paranoia. We can prepare well, to take advantage of the *windows of opportunity* that disasters will bring for initiating *more fundamental systems redesign.* And this can and absolutely should be done in tandem with preemptive kinds of activism. Let's minimize destruction, regression, and suffering, human and nonhuman. Let's preserve our mother planet and our brother/sister creatures. *And* let's *expand* our thinking and creative action.

We need to do what we can, where we are, even while disasters are on their way. Entangled, hypercomplex system dynamics link human activity with our diverse, living planetary ecosystem. We can't realistically "figure it out" in full detail. And yet we need a vision of how we can move forward despite our current political and cultural gridlock.

Against this resistance, we must initiate a discussion, at the level of politics and the media, about what should be one of the most significant political issues of our time: how to create pathways to sustainability with minimal catastrophic disruptions. We can call this a "soft landing." We can focus on optimizing global human culture's passage through an epochal adaptive transition. Since our current social patterns and habits are overheated and unsustainable, the goal is to transition as quickly as possible to more sustainable modes of living, while minimizing traumatic disruptions. It is especially important not to trigger cultural regression ("dark ages" or dystopias, on any scale).

Preparation is everything. Realistically, most well-informed observers believe that big disruptions are probably inevitable—huge shocks, disasters, and crises seem not only likely, but maybe even necessary to catalyze the political will for us to change our collective choices and behavior. The "silver lining" is that these crises will disrupt our current deadlock. They can "unstick" our stuckness. Each will present windows of opportunity for more fundamental systems redesign. We can anticipate and prepare for them. This is an enormously important aspect of evolutionary activism.

GETTING OVER OUR POSTMODERN SELVES

Meanwhile, we are continuing to cause massive damage and destruction to the planet. At the same time that Switzerland and Germany have chosen alternatives to nuclear power, radiation from the Fukushima reactors is leaking into ground and ocean water, and has spread across the Pacific Ocean. Meanwhile, two-thirds of the Great Barrier Reef off the coast of Australia has died in the last few years of rising sea temperatures. In 2017, polar sea ice cover retreated to record lows. I could go on and on—the litany of horrors is long and stark.

We don't know what next calamity might knock our society or Mother Earth off her metaphorical axis (or her literal axis, as some are predicting), causing unforeseeable upheaval. We haven't mobilized the political will necessary for the massive rapid changes that are necessary—certainly not in key countries such as the United States.

We have been outfoxed by the speed of our own inventions and the acceleration of the pace of change in every area of our lives. Our nervous systems are overwhelmed by stimuli to which Homo sapiens is unaccustomed; all of us are suspended in a virtual world laid onto our 3D experience. We are just beginning to discover how to navigate its challenges to our well-being. Our mediated virtual selves are powerfully influenced by postmodern attitudes of passivity, reflexive reactivity (when things really go wrong), and resignation. But what can we do proactively to alter the balance of power, and "do good"?

If we are to fulfill our greater destiny—as well as simply survive—we have to recover from the disempowering, outsider, cynical, defeatist orientation of postmodernity, in which we falsely believe ourselves to be under the effect of systemic forces beyond our control. Such a disposition is the essence of pathology and the refusal of the attitude of practice. Remember the addiction analogy. We are all addicts—to fossil fuels, to consumerist culture, to our consensus trance, to ineffectual consolations. We can admit that we're addicts, and affirm our process of recovery, one day at a time. That means saying "yes" to life, forgiving ourselves, and taking seriously our responsibility for the future, today.

Let's permanently cast aside the option that it is enough to take a "position" and feel that we're "right." Identifying with opinions or interpretive structures, even stories—whether political, social, or spiritual—is not a substitute for actual participation. That emperor has no clothes. Simply holding an opinion—especially one colored by cynical attitudes—is a total cop-out. But such modes of engagement are pervasive, and are in fact what most of us are tending to do, myself included. We are all falling short when measured by the standard of taking responsibility for the full scale of our civilizational predicament. But the attitude of positive responsibility is essential.

It is particularly important to renounce and to counter cynicism. Alas, cynicism is becoming more common among millennials. Boomers have certainly driven into an evolutionary ditch and left the next generation a mess. But that was humanity's collective doing, over many generations. It is understandably overwhelming to come of age in a world in crisis. But cynical and relativistic responses have suicidal implications. Millennials are sometimes called "the whatever generation," because so many questions are answered with an eye roll and a single word, *"Whatever."* Can millennials (and all who came before and after them) recover sincerity and hope, and a willingness to go beyond irony? Can we help them to do so? We are all called to a *postironic* relationship to our experience.

Self-aware millennial postirony might sound something like this: "I can see all the different perspectives in play, and the pervasive hypocrisy. I am self-aware, and expect others to be too. In a way, yes, everybody is a little ridiculous. Our only popular cultural heroes are antiheroes, because that's what is most believable to us. I can't believe in any of the old gods, that's true. And yet, despite all of this, I am not, at the core of my being, cynical. I do care. I love. I choose to stand for life. I value beauty, goodness, and truth. I want to grow clear and strong enough to actually be the change I'd like to see in the world." Can this new generation step over the bloodless corpse of irony to embrace the messiness, immediacy, ecstasy, and heat of this test of our species' ultimate character?

That was my generation's idealistic hope, and in a new way it is the quest of all living generations—Generation X, my parents' "greatest generation," the millennials, and the "postmillennials" who are just now arriving. The opportunity of all future generations is going to depend on everyone's ability to renounce cynicism and hang in, continually and creatively engaging all the turbulent challenges of a world in critical transition. We are all challenged to outgrow the universal tendency to give up, or to blame others, and also to recognize the broad, hypercomplex systems dynamics that have given rise to our collective mess. We are asked to take responsibility. Irrespective of "who created the mess"—or, put another way, "who is responsible"—we (meaning all of us, whatever our generation) have inherited it. And everyone who has ever lived has inherited someone else's mess. The act of blaming—or of resignation—is the act of absolving oneself of responsibility. And that leads to the greatest "sins" of all—cynicism and passivity.

A POSTIRONIC RELATIONSHIP TO POWER

Perhaps Stephen Levine's work with cancer patients provides a useful analogy for taking responsibility. In his work with the dying, Levine addressed the dilemma of people who have come to believe that their inner states and thoughts can profoundly affect their physiological health. They would then begin to imagine *they* were responsible for their diagnosis, such as cancer. He would teach people, "No, no, no, you're not responsible *for* your cancer. That's simply not true. However, you *are* responsible *to* your cancer. It is what is actually happening, and therefore it is your teacher." In the same way, while none of us are uniquely responsible for our generational predicament, we are responsible *to* it. This is and will be the defining test of the character of every generation. The failures of other generations are irrelevant. The attitude of complaint and grievance is a way of giving ourselves carte blanche to perpetuate our crisis by our passivity.

It is up to us—*all* of us—to pervade the fabric of culture and society and politics and power and business and finance with a new human adulthood. This involves our taking responsibility, individually, for becoming quiet heroes of an integral revolution, citizens of a new republic of the heart, true friends of *all* our fellow earthlings. In this work it is especially consequential to consort with the powerful. We want wisdom to gain access and influence, through which it can reassert itself in human affairs. Then, when these "nonlinear windows of opportunity for more fundamental systems redesign" (which most of us think of simply as disasters) present themselves, we will already be there and ready to act.

What if wise advisers to Hank Paulson and Ben Bernanke and George W. Bush had already thought through the implications of a liquidity crisis? What if they could have acted in time to influence the critical decisions that were being made? Remember that the 2008 financial crisis created an environment so open to radical solutions that the nation's large banks could all have been nationalized. What if the powerful and influential people of that moment had thought through the kinds of solutions that would have eased a transition toward sustainability rather than just delaying the inevitable moment of reckoning?

Right now, like the underground threads of the mycelium, an extraordinary generation of enlightened beneficial projects is appearing, and these innovations are extending their reach throughout world culture. Solutions to diverse aspects of our critical challenges are emerging in every community. Human goodness and creativity are evergreen and irrepressible. Many innovative approaches are weaving their way into our social, artistic, and cultural life, reweaving a new pattern for our social fabric. They are already beginning to pervade the periphery of our collective institutional life.

Social enterprises are orchestrating synergistic value exchanges among public, private, and philanthropic actors. Impact investors are working with venture philanthropists to generate outside-the-box creative initiatives. The alternate currency movement, from local currencies to blockchain, is an enormously important band in a spectrum that also includes people working on reducing the influence of money over politics and others experimenting with a "gift economy." The Rocky Mountain Institute, among others, has been developing projects of net-zero energy and net-zero water, as well as highly efficient designs for vehicles and homes. There are any number of other technological advances that are being prototyped in someone's garage. Consider all the innovative organizational practices allowing distributed decision making, as well as the practices we have described for entering integral we-space, bridging cultural divides, and accessing collective intelligence and wisdom.

There is a grand spectrum of objective technical and technological fixes, as well as practices for engendering a more conscious culture. Together they represent a vast array of "spare parts" that can be drawn on during a transition to a life-sustaining society. Each may be a crucial element of a whole process that we cannot yet fully apprehend.

To transform these possibilities into a new reality calls for what I call the "Ancient Strategy." Ancient sages like Confucius, Lao Tzu, Chuang Tzu, and Bodhidharma transformed China by gaining the ear of the emperor, and when he would listen, helping him wisely create harmony in the kingdom.

THE ANCIENT STRATEGY

What is the Ancient Strategy?

Become a sage.

Gain the ear of the emperor.

To meet today's unprecedented challenges, we are required to mature into a more conscious and whole life. That means waking up individually, and coming together in more enlightened collectives. It means "going where no one has gone before." We will be drawn into a series of transformational shifts that will take us into new, uncharted territory. It is both humbling and profoundly empowering to embrace this intention.

Part of our practice is living from what in Zen practice is referred to as "don't-know mind" or "beginner's mind." Knowing that there is so much that we don't and can't know opens us up to wonder and curiosity. It puts us in touch with the creative potential of the present moment. We can then engage wholeheartedly with the aliveness and potential, along with the insecurity, that actually describe our situation.

Existence is a wondrous mystery. We really *don't* know what will happen. But we will be able to improvise, and make important discoveries in the process. Logical predictions are inherently impossible because of the nonlinear dynamics of complex systems and the inherent, interpenetrating wholeness of the living biosphere, human culture, and the total cosmos. The health of the system will depend in part on the health of human individuals and communities, led in part by communities of practice.

If the next Buddha is to be a sangha, some of our communities of practice are precursors, out of which it will emerge. This is what we point to when we say "Become a sage." The key ingredients that make possible our effective participation in that emergence are faith in the goodness of existence; trust in the power of wholeness, the human spirit, and evolution; and confidence in our own capacity to creatively respond. The sun will keep rising in the morning, always bringing a new dawn. We can be the presence of wisdom itself, and we will need to be.

Next, the wisdom of the sage has to find its way to the ear of the emperor. In ancient times, the emperors of the Far East governed in part by consulting wise men. In our time, wisdom must find a way to exercise power and influence over human affairs. It goes beyond the problematic relationship to power that characterizes postmodern sensibilities that can only "speak truth to power." An enlightened sangha or collective inspires and supports each member to make a difference. Through the challenging support of others, we take the necessary risks. We develop relationships and influence with those who hold power, not based on personal ambition but as an expression of our connections with our communities of practice and our care for the whole.

What would that have looked like during the subprime mortgage meltdown in 2008? What can it look like now?

A sea change is already attracting many more practitioner-activists to public service. While most public servants genuinely want to make a positive contribution, they are operating in a corrupt system—and cynical, self-promotional motives contend with altruistic intentions in every heart. Culturally, darkness is all the rage. Craven selfishness and corruption are normalized on the public stage and are played out in exaggerated terms on TV and in movies. This is cultural decay.

It is time for radical cultural renewal. To stretch our metaphor, we can think of ourselves as conscious cells in the emerging body-mind of "the sage," each growing into our greatest qualities. In our practice, we are growing in the postironic courage to care for the health of the whole, and to act on it. We discover ourselves to be members of an invisible brother-sisterhood with other sincere practitioner-activists and public servants. We choose integrity over cynicism, knowing how easily cynicism can undermine the wholesomeness to which we have all been conscripted.

Some of us will actually acquire power so we can make a greater difference. We will then necessarily contend with its corrupting potential. To the degree that we genuinely practice, we will succeed to an extent that leaders have only incompletely succeeded until now. That will be possible only because we will be supported by friends and a burgeoning, invisible brother-sisterhood of holistic practice, a new republic of the heart. And because of that, we will never be alone. We will always be grounded, guided, and accountable to the higher purposes that originally inspired us.

We can draw immeasurable strength from our fellowship with other flawed human beings who embrace their potential to manifest saintliness and heroism (even if they only succeed in brief moments). People who have taken to heart their best and their worst potentials, if they are intending to choose to practice in each new moment, can be trustable friends at a new level.

And that is the magic ingredient. Where our individual and collective imperfections meet our highest individual and group aspirations, a true alchemy is achieved. You come into the presence of something sacred. You never again need to feel alone. You no longer have to hide your own weakness. You need not bury your flaws and dark potentials OR your idealism. And each of us, together, can honestly acknowledge the gap between what we aspire to and what we can now embody. And yet, together, we are all still growing without limit, embracing our heroic and saintly potentials.

If a new republic of the heart is coming into being, it is taking the form of an insistent impulse to choose integrity, to be honest with ourselves and each other, to serve the health of the whole. We are invited to support one another in recognizing the universal temptation to turn anger or passivity into cynicism, to cheat and to lie, to do whatever we have to do to "get by." Together, we are drawn toward the recognition that all of these are hardwired impulses that deserve to be seen with self-compassion, even as they are overwritten by a resolute new intention. As hardwired impulses, they don't have to completely dissipate, even while other neurons are "wiring together" as a higher set of motivations repatterns us.

This deep inner work of self-honesty, combined with the aspiration to have influence in meaningful ways, creates the body and mind of this great sage we are becoming—one who will inevitably gain the ear of the emperor.

Our first frontier is our relationships with one another. Circumstances call for the coming together of a growing body of integral (r)evolutionaries. These are people who are integrally engaged with creating the future; who are tacitly, through a whole series of powerful, healthy personal choices, becoming practitioners, activists, change agents, and global citizens; and who are, in a wide variety of ways, stepping into a new relationship with our collective future. At first it is a private matter, in individual hearts; but we can engage collective practices. And eventually, countless personal and interpersonal acts can cocreate a social act, the knitting together of more and more personal virtue, strengthening the social mycelium, creating a new republic of the heart.

This new republic has innumerable growing edges. It comes into being through all of this—the consciousness breakthroughs, the embrace of life as practice, the adventurous conversations, the technological innovations, the scenario-planning, the renewal of activism, the creative evolutionary initiatives, the exploration of human possibility and of the future. Each is a different angle through which a life-sustaining human culture can come into being. Each is a tendril in a vast network of healthy filaments in the social mycelium of this new stage of human being. From this network, fields of dewy-fresh mushroom flowers will someday bloom, seemingly out of nowhere, almost overnight.

OPPORTUNITIES FOR SYNERGY

Since this book is written at a tumultuous political moment, events will move fast. Although I cannot see exactly how things will play out, it seems inevitable that a popular political movement is arising. Tens of millions of Americans, supported by their friends around the world, are mobilizing in response to Trump's overreach and will continue to mobilize as activists of many kinds—in-the-system and beyond. Among the people and communities who are and will be uniting in this work, there will be increasing opportunities for communication, practice, and community. New conversations and friendships are already reknitting the social fabric, and they will progress and intensify in the time ahead. We may even encounter opportunities to revise and improve our social and political agreements. But right now it looks chaotic—as if everything is falling apart.

I have found it instructive to contemplate the question "What is beautiful about the ugly Mr. Trump?" Something profoundly beautiful might emerge among those who come together to defend themselves and their nation from his malignant narcissistic machinations—something so consequential that we might one day remember Trump almost fondly, seeing him as the divisive toxin that vaccinated our social immune system, helping America emerge into a higher, healthier wholeness. Clearly, in-the-system activism will be a meeting place for a rainbow coalition, including those who will use it as a practice ground for citizenship in a new republic of the heart. But it will take us far beyond our fixation with politics-as-spectator-sport, drawing us from the stands onto the field. And in the game itself, as we learn to practice together, there's a kind of salvation that comes from playing with all our hearts.

Life-changing conditions, even (or *especially*) when they reflect intensifying pathology and chaos, require us to grow further. In time, our conversations must welcome such challenges and even be energized (rather than enervated) by them. Challenges of even a malignant kind can force evolutionary growth. Our experiments will teach us best practices for resilient we-tribes and cultural conversations. Different practices are appropriate depending on whom one is conversing with: people who share a worldview, or across divisions of worldviews. What we learn from these experiments can inform the progressive redesign of our communities and communications so they *keep evolving*. But we have not yet found ways for our gatherings to be simultaneously safe and open and dynamic—and to get stronger as they rise to meet challenges. These are important collective questions. They are worth living with, and abiding in ("living the questions"). We need to ask, "How can our communities become *more* coherent when they are tested by disruptive change, extreme weather, and psychopaths and sociopaths?"

As time passes, events will surprise us, bringing us to new moments of reckoning. Perhaps these words will in retrospect seem prophetic, or naively hopeful, or overly grim or paranoid. We may be seeing robust signs of the emergence of a new republic of the heart showing itself in countless diverse ways. Love may find innumerable new ways to effectively express itself as a new kind of activism. We already see images of community spirit, songs of unity, strangers holding hands and coming together in candlelight vigils, even while (as I am writing this) we see images of neo-Nazi or white nationalist intimidation and violence. Simple human goodness and friendship and community are the most meaningful kind of activism.

And practice also means facing reality. If you are reading this book in 2028 and a combination of technological and social breakthroughs are making the positive scenarios described in this book seem entirely prophetic, that will be very good. If by then you are already giving up on reknitting the larger social fabric, pursuing instead a "monastery" strategy, creating armed ecovillages and institutions that can be built to withstand periods of systemic breakdown and social disorder, then another potential described in this book will be at the forefront. But whatever our situation, it will be healthy to face reality directly, and affirm life—and facing reality is entirely compatible with either of the scenarios just described.

Whatever our situation, we simply need to wake up and do our best to help, to be of real benefit to others and the whole. We can practice and build our capacity to listen to others, to build healthier and happier and more conscious friendships and communities. We can keep waking up, growing up, and learning to be more resilient, happier, and more whole. We can learn to accept the total cycle of life and death and celebration and grieving. We can help others do the same, and cohere more and more conscious communities of practice. And we can look for genuine opportunities to bring that wholesome sincerity into our public life. In the meantime, there is much work to be done, on many fronts, engaging our political systems and sometimes protesting against them, and also going around the system, through the cracks "where the light gets in."

LET'S GET ON WITH IT!

Evolution is more alive and dynamic than we tend to imagine. In this time of punctuated evolutionary emergence, we each have a rare opportunity and responsibility. We can and will participate in cultural evolution, whether consciously or unconsciously. We can choose to evolve "on purpose." This situation will tend to awaken in many of us a sense of moral calling or an existential survival imperative. This ultimately will express itself in the urgent "whole system change" project we described—changing our whole way of being human.

We will be touched especially by certain motivations. Some of us may be inspired to reform and ameliorate the horrific destructiveness and cruelties of our economic and political systems. Some of us may be motivated to address our environmental and ecological predicament, limiting its destructive impact on the human and more-than-human future. Some of us may be inspired to pioneer a new, immediate, and socially relevant way to live a profound spiritual life. Some of us may be inspired by the joy and meaning that will flow from a new level of human friendship and community. Some will be motivated to cultivate a more wholesome and conscious relationship to food, education, sexuality, child-rearing, or race relations and justice. All of these are the evolutionary impulse awakening in us, calling us each in our own way to go beyond who we have been, and arriving at something radically new.

We earlier addressed the special challenges and opportunities of the millennial generation. Boomers have a special role now too. Many of us who came of age in the 1960s and 1970s believed—for a time—that we were going to remake the world. That did not happen exactly as planned, but it seems the real revolution is finally showing up. Boomers like myself are the ones who have lived long enough to have the experience, capacities, wealth, and other resources to make a certain kind of difference. If we devote them to a purpose greater than ourselves, we will redeem our generational journey. Those of my generation have been incredibly lucky, and now we are lucky in another respect. The revolution has regenerated, and we have another chance. If we want to live our ideals, this is our cue. It is rarely appropriate to sacrifice one's life for one's country or world. But people who have already enjoyed a full life have an additional basis for rising above self-protective fear to a new level of courage, commitment, and power.

People of all ages have an opportunity to cultivate capacities for more flexible and multidimensional perspective-taking. We can expand into and be energized by the innate wholeness that is the condition and nature of everything—a wholeness that is never threatened. However challenging or threatening the future may appear, in our most profound depths we are one with, and always sustained by, the Source of all existence. We need effective ways to remind ourselves and others of this truth, and to increase our engagement in a world that has forgotten its own deepest nature. By cultivating ongoing integral practice in both its inner and outer aspects, we are able to be sustained by the deep Source of our existence, and at the same time bring its radically healing and transformational energies out into relationship with our communities and nation. But in our very openness, we also see and feel the world's sorrows, and all the destructiveness and dysfunctionality around us, more acutely. Although that evokes grief in us, being grounded in wholeness allows this sorrow to become clear-eyed observation—which in turn makes us more effective in the world.

We need to cultivate the radical generalization of Carol Dweck's "growth mindset." Each of us can always learn and grow and practice, and so can all of our relationships, groups, and institutions. This attitude can enable us to concretely engage and transform government, business, and all our other institutions, such that our collective decisions are guided by wisdom and humility. We need to tap into the energies and talent of our friends and fellow-practitioners—but we must also form strong connections with a much larger network of individuals, organizations, and communities of good will who can join in an unstoppable network of change. Our efficacy will not result merely from confident agendas or good planning, but will express a natural evolutionary process that far exceeds what we can imagine, and that includes an invisible fellowship that extends far beyond those we know.

Our inner work is the healthy foundation for more effective outward action. Powered by our broken hearts and guided by our particular genius, our stubborn affirmation—combined with receptivity—will make us effective beyond anything we can now imagine. Our unique evolutionary circumstance will have opened us beyond our habitual comfort zone, into a profound willingness to learn, to change, to work, to cooperate, and to practice.

What, then, is at the very heart of this great revolution? The *inner work* is the healthy foundation for more effective outward action. It involves cultivating love, virtue, and fellowship. And the *outer work* involves cultivating functional excellence in work that will bring about a life-sustaining culture. The integral nature of this revolution of love creates an inclusiveness and flexible responsiveness that make it impossible—even ridiculous—to advocate for it directly and whole-heartedly. It involves listening as well as speaking. Integral activists are receptive, not exclusionary. Love cannot be true or effective without gratitude and appreciation. And both the inner and outer work are powered by our broken hearts and guided by our particular genius. We will be stubborn in our affirmation and, in equal measure, receptive listeners. Our unique evolutionary circumstance will open us beyond our habitual comfort zone into a profound willingness to learn, to change, to work, to cooperate, and to practice.

What is asked of us is the same no matter what—whether or not we "make it," and whether or not human civilization is given yet another cycle of innovation and prosperity (and evolution and learning and wisdom). We are seeing signs of this realization in people everywhere: we are an invisible brother-sisterhood, and we have already begun at least trying to relate to these circumstances in moral and spiritual terms, as a test and an opportunity. Five generations of saints-in-training, of every human type and texture, is asked to recognize its destiny and mobilize effective actions.

Perhaps we will be able to help a new cycle of human innovation and evolution to be guided by love and wisdom.

Perhaps, at the other extreme, we will bring wisdom and care to a planet and society in need of a great "hospice" project, under difficult circumstances requiring our practice and courage.

Either way, there will be dark moments, and very bright ones. And it will matter tremendously how much beauty and goodness rise to meet the karmic reactivity of separative selfishness and violence.

Either way, humanity's heart-intelligence is what will make the crucial difference. Luckily, our ancestors have been doing this work since the beginning, so in a sense we are already "naturals." The work is already well underway, called by many names, doing its work in many domains. And, as always, learning as we go.

ख़ ✿ ख़

Every moment of life is an opportunity for growth and practice. To grow into the light, we must dare to gaze into the abyss. Only by facing our fears and Earth's vulnerability with open eyes can we get to the other side of this great chasm. In any case, it is truth, not denial or escapism, that sets us free—and that allows us to make a difference.

Whatever we think we know is not the whole truth. Every perspective is both true and partial, and it is from partial perspectives that fear arises. None of us can know what the future holds. But, beyond our partial perspectives, we *can* know that life is infinitely trustable, that our true state is never threatened, that we are forever one with the vast Whole that is none other than love itself and joy itself.

And once we realize that we are That, we are free to love and to mourn, to grieve and to celebrate, to enact compassion to all beings and things, and to do battle on behalf of life itself.

To do all of this, you need not be a "better" or more knowledgeable person than you are right now. You can be both compassionate and challenging to yourself, just as you can be to others. You can live and act from your own heart's intelligence, from the root of your own joys and sorrows, from your heartbreak and your genius, from your deepest passion.

There is no better time than now to "get right with reality"—to be the change you want to see in the world.

The "consensus trance" isn't a happy place to hang out anymore. Those drawn into it (and that includes all of us to some degree) are watching themselves slide into an incoherent nightmare scenario—if they're not summarily refusing to cognize it out of terror. But we can awaken within the trance, and within the dream—and we can create magnificent realities out of them. We can choose to dream powerful, empowering dreams, and join forces with other awakening dreamers.

When you notice anxiety welling up in you, or around you, driving you and others to confusion and panic, notice also that you can make a different choice. Yes, of course, do whatever needs to be done practically, and do it as well as you can—that's key. But also keep remembering— every day, every morning, every hour, every moment—that you can *trust the process of your life*. To do so is joy; not to do so is madness.

When you notice irritability or resentment welling up, driving you to anger and separation, notice that it can easily take a wrong turn. Channel that energy creatively, and use it to change what needs to be changed. Don't let it make you an agent of the fragmentation you wish to counter. But if it does temporarily, recognize it, find self-compassion, release self-hatred, and move forward. Burn an even hotter fuel than hatred—love. Love is the best strategy for getting things done.

We can also trust the process of our collective lives. Regardless of the future—however "good" or "bad" things will get—we were built for the whole trip.

And it will be a wild ride—there is no question. Multiple disruptions threaten wondrous and awful changes simultaneously, so our tipping point presents us with extreme unpredictability, and calls for our expansive imagination. Although "New Age" has in the last few decades become a term of dismissal—and sometimes deservedly so—by traditionalists, modernists, and integralists alike, the central hypothesis underpinning the idea of New Age culture survives inspection: This *is* a time for a shift to higher states and structures of consciousness, expressed in new levels of leadership and citizenship and fellowship. A different kind of action *can* flow from wholeness, and from the recognition of prior unity. A fresh cultural utopian spirit *is* really necessary today as never before.

Revolutionary changes are in the air on every front. But, more than any revolution that preceded it, the integral revolution of our time is not so much political (although the political implications are important) as it is a change in our way of being with ourselves, each other, and with all of life.

We have seen many of the ways that revolutionary change can be enacted—through telling stories, through learning all the ways we can reprogram our nervous systems, through celebration of every kind, through the marketplace of ideas and technology, through communications—and through the creation of common ground through conversations and even eye contact with strangers.

There are enormous numbers of people on our life raft who are at each other's throats. Those who are psychopathic and functionally evil must not prevail. But most of our fellow human beings are good people who just want to meet their own needs while being a source of benefit to others and the whole. Our challenging assignment—or wicked problem—is to prevail against the forces of fragmentation and evil without becoming agents of escalating and dangerous conflict. It will take many "hostage negotiators" to talk people off the ledge and bring them back into relationship here on Spaceship Earth.

Recognize that your life really does have a higher purpose, one that converges with the purposes of many other lives. In a time when everything is accelerating toward a frenzied "end of days" moment, you and I and our friends can be a presence of calm sanity—of wholeness and trust.

Although the revolution is fought on many fronts, the center of battle is a nonviolent revolution in every heart. Patience and surrender and love are our most potent weapons. They express the intelligence of the heart, which integrates our best rational and instinctive intelligence. They also tend to attract a higher order of coherence and wholeness, allowing order and life to emerge from chaos and destruction. Thus, radically choosing and "weaponizing" wholeness and love may be the most subversive thing you can do, and the most important opportunity of our time.

Let these be the most inspiring, exciting, meaningful, and deeply happy years of our lives, all the disaster and destruction and grief (including our own) notwithstanding. Let's show up as the greatness of the human spirit, in all the ways our predicament is calling for.

It's time.

RESOURCES

This book would not be complete without listing some of the organizations, websites, publications, and other resources to which you can turn as you consider how you can connect more fully with the inner transformational work and the outer activist work through which you will make your most powerful contributions to wholeness.

As you are probably aware, there are countless such resources. None of them reflects the *entire* vision of *A New Republic of the Heart*, but they each enact one or more important dimensions of it. Like every perspective, every initiative is inevitably "true and partial." A new stage and structure of consciousness and culture is partially expressing itself wherever it can, responding to new challenges, and always finding new forms of expression. So, inevitably, this list is partial as well, and undoubtedly I have failed to include *many* important initiatives even while including some less significant. This list also reflects my personal experience in America, mostly in California. And, like every list, over time it will become dated. Despite these caveats, many useful and valuable resources can be found here, often ones I know first- or second-hand, that I think might be valuable to you. And some resources link to many others. Each is finding a way to co-create some aspect of this new republic of the heart.

I have limited this list to initiatives that are consciously attempting to enact cultural transformation in one way or another. Equally valuable dimensions of a new republic of the heart, however, are the much larger number of efforts that embody the health and wholeness and caring character of human culture—not only the international relief workers, as important as they are, but also the many churches and charities and other good works; the local nurses and doctors and teachers and social workers and firefighters and emergency medical technicians and other first-responders; the farmers and technicians; the workers and entrepreneurs;

and the countless community builders and leaders who keep re-weaving the social fabric. When the body (or body politic) is under siege, what restores well-being is not just the immune system, but also the vastly larger number of cells that just keep pumping the blood and lymph and nerve impulses, sustaining life and health. Although they are not listed here, these resources are identified in a spirit of appreciation for many, many others—the widest possible spectrum of forms of service and care and activism that are expressing the broad and ultimately universal emergence of a new republic of the heart.

An online, updatable version of this Resource Section can be found at anewrepublicoftheheart.org/resources.

Terry Patten

- **My own work,** enacting a new republic of the heart as I have described it in this book—including events, courses, community networking opportunities, blog posts, and video and audio recordings—can be found at **terrypatten.com** and a site dedicated to this book, **newrepublicoftheheart.org**. This is the primary way to stay in touch with the work that I will do following the release of this book.

- Also, for over seven years I have periodically conducted public conversations in the **Beyond Awakening series** (beyondawakeningseries.com) in response to the question, "How can practice and higher consciousness help humanity rise to meet our current challenges?" I expect to convene public "conversations that matter" in the time ahead. You can stay informed about them by giving us your email address at that site.

- Ten years ago I founded **Bay Area Integral** (bayareaintegral.org). This nonprofit, all-volunteer organization convenes speaker events, conversations, and celebrations in the San Francisco Bay area. Those on its mailing list are kept abreast of its public events.

Heart Intelligence

The **HeartMath Institute** (heartmath.org) has pioneered research validating and legitimizing **the intelligence of the heart,** which is so crucial to the present work. For almost thirty years, the people at HeartMath have been conducting biomedical research into the heart as a center of higher intelligence in human beings and creating tools and trainings that help people to activate it. Their ultimate mission is "to activate the heart of humanity" in its role as caretaker for future generations and the planet. (I worked closely with the HeartMath team in the 1990s and led the team that developed their first heart rate variability monitor.) Through organizational consulting, trainings, products, and the *Global Coherence Initiative,* HeartMath's work has expanded tremendously, reaching people from all walks of life all over the US and the world.

The **Pachamama Alliance** (pachamama.org), led by Bill and Lynne Twist, is a dynamic partnership between indigenous Amazonian Achuar people and North Americans dedicated to bringing forth an environmentally sustainable, spiritually fulfilling, socially just human presence on our planet. Its superb educational programs help inspire and galvanize a healthy transformation of the consensus trance shaping global culture and industrial civilization. Among the most important are "*Awakening the Dreamer,*" a powerful transformational educational training program, and "*The Gamechanger Intensive,*" an online leadership training aiming to shift concern over the state of the world into meaningful effective activism.

Charles Eisenstein (charleseisenstein.net) has produced books, blogs, audio recordings, and videos that have inspired thousands of people to attempt to create "the more beautiful world our hearts know is possible." With his heart's higher intelligence guiding his clear mind, he has also dared to imagine a sacred economics based on a gift economy. His website contains a wealth of resources to help people understand how to embrace and practice empathy and interconnectedness and become more effective agents of social transformation.

ServiceSpace (servicespace.org), founded by Nippun Mehta, leverages technology for altruism. Run entirely by volunteers, it has become an umbrella for many generosity-driven projects and provides tools for individuals to organize their own local service events. It thus helps ignite fundamental generosity for inner and outer transformation.

The Goi Peace Foundation (goipeace.or.jp/en), organized by Masami and Hiroo Saionji, sponsors many far-reaching initiatives, including the Fuji Declaration, the Goi Peace Award, numerous youth education and leadership programs, research studies, and symposia—all to nurture the necessary transformation of global society. It has official status at several U.N. agencies.

Integral Evolutionary Resources

The community of integral evolutionary thought and practice has been the primary context for my teaching work since 2004. Hundreds of books, conferences, seminars, meet-up groups, salons, articles, and blogs contribute to the integral evolutionary conversation. Here I only mention a handful of the most prominent and influential organizations.

- **Integral Life** (integrallife.com) is a membership organization that is also the primary web portal (alongside kenwilber.com) for the public work of the integral community associated with Ken Wilber. It offers a wealth of integral resources and educational and personal development programs online. It periodically offers major in-person gatherings for members of the international integral community. It publishes or produces most of the US-based projects formerly organized by the **Integral Institute**.

- **MetaIntegral** (metaintegral.org), founded by Sean Esbjörn-Hargens, is an alliance of three organizations—a training academy, a consulting firm, and a philanthropic think tank. It has sponsored four Integral Theory Conferences, publishes the *Journal of Integral Theory and Practice,* and offers rigorous educational and personal development programs.

- Since 2014, the **Integral European Conferences** (integraleuropeanconference.com) have become the main gatherings in Europe for the global integral community. But centers for integral thought, culture, and practice exist in many European countries, particularly Germany, where the **Integrales Forum** (integralesforum.org) has been active for well over a decade.

- The **Institute for Cultural Evolution (ICE)** (culturalevolution.org) is discussed under Transpartisan Initiatives.

- The **Center for Human Emergence** (humanemergence.org) founded by Don Beck, coauthor of *Spiral Dynamics,* is a global facilitator for conscious evolution with centers in the US, the

Netherlands, Denmark, and Germany and has also worked actively in the Middle East, Mexico, and South Africa.

- On **The Daily Evolver** (dailyevolver.com and on Facebook), Jeff Salzman regularly shines an integral light on current events in politics and culture through the lens of Wilber's integral theory.

- **Integral Evolutionary Educational Programs** are offered quite widely. I list just a few here:

  - Integral degree programs have been offered by **John F. Kennedy University** (jfku.org) and the **Fielding Institute** (fielding.edu). **The California Institute of Integral Studies** (ciis.edu) offers a wide range of holistic higher educational programs. **Meridian University** (meridianuniversity.edu) offers integral education in its graduate programs, and a leadership and social transformation program led by its chancellor, Jean Houston. **Ubiquity University** (ubiquity.university) offers undergraduate and graduate programs in liberal arts, psychology, and the pursuit of wisdom.

  - **Integral Coaching Canada** (integralcoachingcanada.com) has developed a rigorous coaching method built around the core distinctions of integral theory.

  - **Pacific Integral** (pacificintegral.com), founded in 2004 by Geoff Fitch, Terri O'Fallon, and others, offers integral evolutionary programs and consulting services focused on generating transformative change in human systems.

  - **Next Step Integral** (nextstepintegral.com), a partnership between SIFCO's Stephan Martineau and his wife Miriam Mason Martineau, offers online courses on Integral Parenting and Integral Education.

  - **Ten Directions** (tendirections.com) offers certification programs in integral facilitation with Sensei Diane Musho Hamilton and online trainings in personal development, coaching, and influence taught by her and Rob McNamara.

  - **Integral Academy Hungary** (integralacademy.eu), founded by Integral European Conference organizer Bence Ganti, trains and certifies psychotherapists, counselors, and coaches.

- **ID Academy Denmark** (idacademy.dk), founded by Ole Vadum Dahl, trains and certifies psychotherapists and coaches and teaches Essential Life Practice.

- **Integral Publications**
  - **Academic journals:**
    - *The Journal of Integral Theory and Practice*, published by MetaIntegral (https://foundation.metaintegral.org/JITP)
    - *Integral Leadership Review* (integralleadershipreview.com)
    - *Integral Review* (integral-review.org).
  - **General interest publications:**
    - *Emerge-Bewusstseinkulture Magazin [Emerge: A Magazine of Consciousness and Culture]* (emerge-bewusstseinkulture.de) contributes important original leading-edge thought and dialogue to the big questions asked in this book.
    - *Kosmos: Journal for Social Transformation* (kosmosjournal. org), founded by Nancy Roof, probably contains the most dynamic popular integral evolutionary articles in printed form in English.
    - *The Cosmos Co-op* (cosmos.coop) is described in chapter 8, and is both a publication and a community. It continues to express and further develop the dynamic intellectual inquiry that can still be found on **Beams and Struts** (beamsandstruts.com).

Explicitly Spiritual Activism

Many books and organizations are working to catalyze **spiritually inspired social change**. Each works in its own unique way, but many initiatives have important commonalities with the unique synthesis you see in this book. Here are a few:

- **The Work That Reconnects Network** (workthatreconnects.org). Eco-philosopher and Buddhist scholar Joanna Macy has shown how to connect with our grief over the state of the world. It is also an elegant process for connecting with gratitude and transformational insight, and this combination empowers effective activism. The network trains facilitators and offers support, guidance, and inspiration to people working for the Great Turning worldwide.

- **Engaged Buddhism** is beautifully expressed in the work of **Zen Peacemakers** (zenpeacemakers.org) founded by Roshi Bernie Glassman. For thirty-five years it has served the poor in the Bronx and Yonkers, especially through Greyston Bakery (greyston.org). More recently, it has also helped mobilize a worldwide movement of humanitarian, peace-building, social and civic action based on its three tenets (Not Knowing, Bearing Witness, and Taking Action), and it includes projects focusing on Auschwitz/ Birkenau. **The International Network of Engaged Buddhists** (inebnetwork.org), headquartered in Thailand; the national US organization **The Buddhist Peace Fellowship** (buddhistpeacefellowship.org); and **Green Sangha** (greensangha.org) in the SF Bay Area, are also conscious communities of practitioners passionate about the living, breathing intersections between Buddhadharma, social justice, and environmental action. All these (and many more) engaged Buddhist initiatives bring individuals together to meditate, educate, support one another, and to advocate for compassion, peace, justice, and the living planet.

- **Sister Giant** (sistergiant.com), founded by Marianne Williamson, combines a sacred, authentic, deeply humane "politics of love" with practical activism and endorsements in US political races to help achieve that vision. It is "dedicated to forging a deeper conversation about what is happening in America today—and what we can do to change it."

- **The Network of Spiritual Progressives** (spiritualprogressives.org) was cofounded by Rabbi Michael Lerner to "help transform the world from one based on power and control to one based on love and justice."

- **The Jean Houston Foundation** (jeanhoustonfoundation.org) extends Jean Houston's life work in 110 countries, training leaders and trainers in Social Artistry, a new model for leadership that applies at all levels, across cultures and continents, in developed and least developed countries. It inspires and empowers people to deepen their individual capacities to create a world that works for everyone.

- **The Institute for Sacred Activism** (andrewharvey.net/sacred-activism) was founded by Andrew Harvey, who defines sacred activism as "the fusion of the deepest spiritual knowledge and passion with clear, wise, radical action in all the arenas of the world, inner and outer." The institute trains activists, educates the public, and advocates for activism as a spiritual obligation in this time.

- **The Center for Transformative Change** (transformativechange.org) was founded by author and activist Rev. angel Kyodo williams. From its center in Oakland, CA, it provides meditation and yoga classes, spiritual guidance, and community for activists and marginalized communities. Its goal is to raise awareness of social justice and racial issues among activists worldwide.

- **Humanity Healing** (humanityhealing.org) is a nonpolitical and nondenominational spiritual organization trying to foster healing for communities around the world with humanitarian projects. Its initiatives are designed "to restore hope in the lives of children and communities that have lost it." Its participants commit to general guidelines involving practice, service, integrity, respecting others, direct communication, nonviolence, and cooperation.

- I am a member of a group of over one hundred **Evolutionary Leaders** (evolutionaryleaders.net) organized by Deepak Chopra and served by the **Source of Synergy Foundation** (sourceofsynergyfoundation.org). It is a network of dynamic dedicated evolutionary activists and educators who come together annually to catalyze and contribute to the evolution of one another and everyone whose lives they touch, and to magnify their ability to be of benefit. Each member champions worthy creative initiatives that express this new republic of the heart. They are not all listed here, but they can be found via the website.

- **The Association for Global New Thought** (agnt.org) provides its member churches (Unity and Religious Science) with resources and trainings in "spiritually guided activism," including community leadership, as central elements of inspired Christian living.

- **YES!** magazine (yesmagazine.org) investigates the biggest problems of our time in terms of their solutions. Online and in print, they outline a path forward with in-depth analysis, tools for citizen engagement, and stories about real people working for a better world.

- **Utne Reader** (utne.com) presents "the best of the alternative press," with emphasis on politics, culture, economy, and the environment. It speaks in many voices, presenting empowering, provocative, and sometimes debated viewpoints. It also holds an annual Independent Press Awards competition for the best alternative magazines.

- **Orion Magazine** (orionmagazine.org) publishes articles on nature, culture, environment, and sense of place, and administers annual Orion Book Awards for "books that deepen the reader's connection to the natural world."

- **The Sun** magazine (thesunmagazine.org) includes content (essays, memoirs, personal stories, fiction, and interviews) that, in the words of its founder Sy Safransky, "honors the mystery at the heart of existence." Reader-supported since 1990, its articles are steeped in the context of both local and global issues.

- **The Club of Budapest** (clubofbudapest.org), founded by Ervin Laszlo, works in over fifteen countries to facilitate a worldwide movement in service of the future of human evolution by catalyzing evolution consciousness through diverse coordinated autonomous projects.

- **Humanity's Team** (humanitysteam.org) communicates and demonstrates the oneness of all people and all life through online and in-person gatherings. Its conscious business initiative promotes awareness of unity among business leaders.

- **Greenheart International** (greenheart.org) provides student exchange programs, travel opportunities, camps, and conferences for young people and adults that enhance intercultural understanding and develop tomorrow's leaders.

- **The Global Purpose Movement** (globalpurposemovement.com) brings together individuals and organizations to express their unique purpose and to synergize for the overarching purpose of social transformation and sustainable flourishing.

- **The True Purpose Institute** (truepurposeinstitute.com) was founded by Tim Kelley to give messengers, change agents, and mission-driven organizations the training and support they need to create the impact they are meant to have in the world.

- **Purpose Guides Institute** (purposeguides.org) was founded by Jonathan Gustin to train coaches and therapists to guide individuals in knowing and realizing their purpose, unitizing all cutting-edge, purpose-guiding modalities, supported by top-level faculty.

- **The Pocket Project** (pocketproject.org) was founded by Austrian mystic Thomas Hübl in order to train people to heal the vicious cycle of recurring collective and intergenerational trauma, and ultimately to catalyze collective wisdom about integrating and reducing its impacts upon global culture.

Convening Transformational Conversations and Communities

Long before anyone heard of "we-space," conscious people were pushing the envelope of what could happen among them in groups. Whole fields of deep conversation have been a part of human culture as long as we have existed. Indigenous people sat in council. Socrates dialogued with his students in ancient Greece. The Chatauqua movement invigorated the civic life of America in its first century or more.

In the early 1960s, Rogerian and Gestalt psychotherapy informed a wave of "encounter groups" which tapped the power of group settings to catalyze personal breakthroughs. Around the same time, **Bohmian Dialogue** gave new life and focus to the art and practice of using intelligent dialogue to address cognitive errors and press the frontiers of human understanding, demonstrating it in a series of public conversations with Jiddu Krishnamurti. From both of these streams of intersubjective praxis a new wave of practices and insights and a whole field emerged, with many nodes. It is significantly supported by the **National Coalition** for **Dialogue and Deliberation** (ncdd.org) and the application of these techniques to furthering peace and understanding by the **Institute for Multi-Track Diplomacy** (imtd.org). A completely independent, but very important communications movement, including many local practice communities in sixty-five countries, has emerged from Marshall Rosenberg's worldwide teachings of Nonviolent Communication (NVC) (cnvc.org).

Facilitating Collective Intelligence

The Co-Intelligence Institute (co-intelligence.org) was founded by Tom Atlee to engage collective inquiry and facilitate collective wisdom. These experiments seemed to indicate that with skillful facilitation deep divisions can be consistently and authentically bridged, resulting in new learning and development and solutions. Jim Rough conducted similar experiments in his method of **Dynamic Facilitation** and **Wisdom Councils** (tobe.net) and in the book *Society's Breakthrough! Releasing Essential Wisdom and Virtue in All the People*. Atlee's experience was similar, so the Collective Intelligence Institute gave birth to the **Wise Democracy Project** (wd-pl.com) to which another significant dialogue practitioner, **Rosa Zubizaretta** (diapraxis.com), has made important contributions. This work is closely related to experiments in collective wisdom documented in the book *The Power of Collective Wisdom* by Alan Briskin, et al., (Berrett-Koehler, 2009) (alanbriskin.com), and well embodied in *The Art of Convening* by my friends Craig and Patricia Neal (Berrett-Koehler, 2011) and their work at the **Center for Purposeful Leadership** (centerforpurposefulleadership.com).

The **Art of Hosting** (artofhosting.org) is a community of practitioners who use state-of-the-art approaches to conversation, dialogue, facilitation, and personal practice to harness collective wisdom to address complex challenges on many scales. It draws from **The Circle Way** (thecircleway .net), **The World Café** (theworldcafe.com), **Open Space Technology** (openspaceworld.org and openspaceworld.com), **Appreciative Inquiry** (appreciativeinquiry.champlain.edu), **Action Learning**, **Collective Mind-Mapping**, **Collective Story Harvest**, and **Graphic Facilitation**. (Many of these leading-edge practices have been refined further by organizational development consultants and coaches such as Otto Scharmer's U-Process, and some of them are documented below under **Conscious Business.**)

Integral We-Space

Integral We-Space is most fully described in the book *Cohering the Integral We Space: Engaging Collective Emergence, Wisdom and Healing in Groups,* edited by Olen Gunnlaugson and Michael Brabant (Integral Publishing House, 2016); it is a peer-reviewed anthology of we-space practice approaches across the global integral world.

- **The We-Space Summit** (thewespacesummit.com) convened 150 practitioners, including Terry Patten, Olen Gunnlaugson, Bill Torbert, Terri O'Fallon, Thomas Hübl, Craig Hamilton, and many others, over five days in 2017 to create a rich and wide-ranging professional development resource for deepening skills and capacities of practitioners. If you're interested in experiencing its wide range of practices and expressions, this is perhaps the most comprehensive communication of the world of integral we-space currently available.

- **One World in Dialogue** (oneworldindialogue.com) was founded in Germany by Thomas Steininger and Elizabeth Debold, authors of the five principles of evolutionary dialogue described in chapter 10. It holds virtual Global Dialogue Labs that build integral we-space for intercultural conversations. It also sponsors an annual global subtle activism meditation marathon, One World Bearing Witness, usually in December.

- **The Authentic Relating Movement** was birthed in San Francisco and Boulder and how has centers in Europe, Austin, Mexico, and beyond. It advances the field of authentic, spontaneous, vulnerable, contactful communication. See authenticworld.com, integralcenter.com, circlingeurope.com, www.authrev.com, and circlinginstitute.com.

- The Austrian-born modern "mystic in the marketplace," **Thomas Hübl** (thomashueblonline.com), offers teachings and courses and programs in the mystical principles of spontaneous, intuitive "Transparent Communication." His students Stephen Busby (stephenbusby.com) and Nicholas Janni (corepresence.org) also write and teach on these topics.

- **The Evolutionary Collective** (evolutionarycollective.com) is a vehicle for Patricia Albere's work on evolutionary relating and mutual awakening, particularly her yearlong in-person programs. Her teachings can be found in her book, *Evolutionary Relationships* (Oracle Institute Press, 2017).

- **The Cosmos Co-op** (cosmos.coop), described in chapter 8, is both a publication and an online community of practice.

Additional Resources for Tribe, Community and Re-localization

- **Time for Tribe** (timefortribe.com) is the public work of a "tribe" of committed friends founded by men's group pioneer Bill Kauth and Zoe Alowan in Ashland, Oregon. They share their vision and practice for new non-residential but local (bikeable) tribal living in the book *We Need Each Other: Building Gift Community* (Silver Light Publications, 2011).

- **Global Ecovillage Network** (ecovillage.org) is a growing network of regenerative communities that cultivate ecological, social, cultural, and economic stability. Its website can link you to ecovillages all over the world and the partner organizations who are supporting these experiments in community. I can recommend the book *Ecovillages: Lessons for Sustainable Community* (Polity Press, 2013) by my friend Karen Litfin for a glimpse of the lived reality. **Auroville** (auroville.org), in Tamil Nadu, India, was founded as a place where Sri Aurobindo's teachings about human unity could be actually lived. It is one of the oldest and largest spiritually-inspired ecovillages in the world and has attracted about 2,500 residents and spawned a number of eco-friendly projects and enterprises. Another ecovillage, the intentionally integral Awakened Life Project, was founded by my friends Peter and Cynthia Bampton at La Quinta in Portugal (a community now working to recover from recent wildfire damage).

- **Local Futures,** or **Economics of Happiness** (localfutures.org), is a nexus for connection and information exchange for the worldwide localization and new economy movements, dedicated to the renewal of community, ecological health, and local economies.

It has co-sponsored the International Alliance for Localization as well as many local conferences.

- The **Transition Towns** movement consists of hundreds of autonomous grassroots community projects for practical cooperation to increase local self-sufficiency in the face of extreme weather events, ecological breakdowns, and economic instability. It was founded in 2006 in **Totnes, UK** (transitiontowntotnes.org), and is coordinated internationally by **The Transition Network** (transitionnetwork.org) and in the US by **Transition US** (transitionus.org).

- The **Permaculture Movement** (permaculture.org, permacultureglobal.org, permacultureglobal.org.uk, and many more) concentrates on the actual land-based practices through which thousands of communities are attempting to live sustainably and build cultures of such practice. One radical community experiment I have visited is Gaia Yoga Gardens on the Big Island of Hawaii (gaiayoga.org).

- **Integral City Meshworks** (integralcity.com) was founded by my friend Marilyn Hamilton in 2005. Now a constellation of communities of practice nurtures cities as "human hives." It connects the citizens, civic managers, civic society, and businesses of participating cities to energize relationships, unify visions, and develop eco-regional resilience strategies for wellbeing.

- **Compassionate Communities** are local organizations working to live and spread the Charter for Compassion (charterforcompassion.org), which bears witness to humanity's deep interdependence, sees through boundaries, eases conflicts, and serves an increasingly just economy and peaceful world. For example, where I live**, Compassionate California** (compassionatecalifornia.org) supports ten local "Compassionate Cities."

- The **Cool City Challenge** (coolcitychallenge.org) is a nonprofit initiative founded by *Social Change 2.0* author David Gershon, as a way for cities "to achieve dramatic carbon reduction, vibrant livability, and green prosperity" by linking neighbors and proactive governments.

- **Breakthrough Communities** (breakthroughcommunities.info) was founded by architect, planner, and veteran public servant Carl Anthony with scholar, nonprofit executive, and integral practitioner Paloma Pavel, PhD, to imagine and promote integrated solutions to environmental problems that intertwine with social and racial justice dynamics. They educate and organize communities to come together, plan, and advocate on behalf of their health and sustainability in a manner that can work for everyone.

- **Impact Hub Oakland** (oakland.impacthub.net), based in the San Francisco Bay Area, is one of the 80-plus Impact Hub Global Communities (see full description under Conscious Business). I mention it here because, as the Impact Hub I know best, it's the center of a dynamic local community of social entrepreneurs and activists, spawning dozens of initiatives that bring wholeness, in many forms, to the local community. Thus (like many Impact Hubs, no doubt) it relates not only to social entrepreneurship but to many aspects of tribal and community empowerment. Three of its founders, Lisa Chacon, Konda Mason, and Edward West, are integral practitioners and personal friends.

Climate and Ecology Activism

Thousands of organizations worldwide are engaging specific initiatives to raise awareness of our ecological predicament and to affect public policy as well as individual and organizational behavior. They are also gathering places for concerned citizens, and many are spawning serious communities of practice. Here I will list a few of the organizations I value with the briefest of descriptions. There are MANY others.

- **Bioneers** (bioneers.org), founded by Kenny Ausubel and Nina Simons, is best known through its annual National Bioneers Conference and local conferences, community networks, and media—including "Bioneers Radio," featured on national NPR stations. Their programs and conferences cover such themes as rights of nature, sustainability, permaculture, restorative food systems, and indigenous peoples' issues. It is an important meeting place for grassroots conscious ecologists.

- **350.org,** founded by Bill McKibben, is an international organization dedicated to building the global climate movement through online campaigns, grassroots organizing, and mass public actions aimed especially at the fossil-fuel infrastructure. Its ultimate goal is to reduce atmospheric carbon dioxide levels from the current 400+ parts per million to 350 parts per million.

- **Our Children's Trust** (ourchildrenstrust.org) advocates for the rights of young people to a stable climate and healthy atmosphere. Its programs help youth participate in science-based advocacy, public education, and civic engagement on behalf of the ongoing viability of Earth's natural systems. Its members have filed a major lawsuit seeking systemic, science-based emissions reductions and climate recovery policy at all levels of government.

- **The Post-Carbon Institute** (postcarbon.org) understands the interrelated ecological, economic, energy, and equity crises of the 21st century in many of the ways this book describes, and it convenes, educates and serves many of the activists who are leading the transition to a more resilient, equitable, and sustainable world.

- **Project Drawdown** (drawdown.org) involves an international coalition of scientists and researchers who offer bold solutions to climate change based on already existing technologies and practices. These solutions are described in the book *Drawdown: The Most Comprehensive Plan Ever Proposed to Reverse Global Warming,* edited by Paul Hawken. Each of the one hundred top solutions is described in terms of costs, benefits, and how much each can contribute to "drawing down" atmospheric carbon levels by 2050. The project and its findings are mentioned in chapter 1 of this book.

- **The Rocky Mountain Institute** (rmi.org) engages with businesses, communities, institutions, and entrepreneurs to accelerate the adoption of market-based and cost-effective approaches that shift fossil-fuel dependence to efficiency and renewables. Among its many initiatives are the transformation of Caribbean island economies to local, renewable energy, and helping China to surpass its emissions targets and dramatically reduce its fossil-fuel dependency. It has recently released *The Carbon-Free City Handbook*, a resource for city leaders containing twenty-two ready-to-implement solutions with proven success.

- **Shut It Down—Climate Direct Action** (shutitdown.today) is a website supporting acts of civil disobedience to slow climate change, such as the "valve turners," who had cut off the pipelines bringing tar sand oil into the USA in October 2016. They undertake and support actions that illustrate with moral clarity the urgency and magnitude of change needed to avert climate cataclysm.

- **New Dream** (newdream.org) seeks to change social norms around consumption and consumerism by empowering individuals, communities, and organizations to transform consumption habits to improve wellbeing for people and the planet. Their mission is closely linked to **The Story of Stuff** (storyofstuff.org), which began with a twenty-minute movie that went viral and has now become a movement to avoid plastic, microfibers, vinyl, and other destructive forms of consumerism.

- **Honor the Earth** (honorearth.org) seeks to develop financial and political resources for the survival of sustainable Native communities and to increase awareness of these issues generally. It partners with grassroots organizations to address climate-change issues and looks to convert to a more sustainable, land-based economics.

- **The Pachamama Alliance**, listed above under "Heart Intelligence," is a dynamic partnership between indigenous Amazonian Achuar people and North Americans, which promotes local empowerment and nature conservation in the Ecuadorian interior and education worldwide.

- The **largest and best-known environmental advocacy groups** play a key institutional role in affecting public policy and perceptions. The **Sierra Club** (sierraclub.org), founded by John Muir in 1892, is still a leading voice in promoting sustainable energy and climate-change solutions and is also a recreational organization whose local chapters sponsor many activities. The

National Resources Defense Council (nrdc.org) and **Environmental Defense Fund** (edf.org) have both long played a key role in the filing of legal actions in federal and state US courts. EDF also emphasizes the creation of economic incentives for the private sector. **Friends of the Earth International** (foei.org) is said to be the world's largest environmental network, and its US branch, **Friends of the Earth** (foe.org), is involved in policy analysis, activism, and litigation. **Greenpeace** (greenpeace.org), with offices in over forty countries, places emphasis on direct action as well as education and community. **Earth Island Institute** (earthisland.org) provides public education, sponsors many fledgling activist groups and projects worldwide through financing and organizational infrastructure, and publishes the award-winning *Earth Island Journal*. **Rainforest Action Network** (ran.org) has run many effective campaigns to halt environmentally destructive practices of corporations, especially as they relate to the manufacture of consumer products. The **World Wildlife Fund** (worldwildlife.org) works with habitat and endangered species preservation and maintenance of biodiversity.

- **Vandana Shiva** (vandanashiva.org) is an influential Indian scholar, environmental and anti-globalization activist, and food sovereignty advocate who has authored more than twenty books and influenced Indian agricultural policy. She argues for the wisdom of many traditional practices, advises the scientific committee of Spain's Socialist Party's think tank, and has been widely honored worldwide. Many activists stay tuned to her leadership on many cutting-edge issues.

- **Connect 4 Climate** (connect4climate.org) was founded by the World Bank and the governments of Italy and Germany and now has more than four hundred international partners working to raise awareness, promote commitment to action, and build coalitions to influence policy-makers and private businesses. It has spawned almost a dozen sub-initiatives including cities4climate, hack4climate, and youth4climate. Along with my friends

Raul Hernandez and Frank Marrero, I personally participated in preventing the clear-cutting of over 200 acres of coastal Redwood forests through an initiative called **Old-Growth Again** (foreverredwood.com/restoration-forestry/overview/).

Conscious Business

Countless small- and large-scale social entrepreneurs and corporate executives are working to make business a powerful force for environmental responsibility and positive social and economic change. Recognizing how profit and growth are central drivers of ecological destruction, they're redefining a "triple bottom line" approach (planet, people, profit) by which businesses can measure success. New legal and accounting mechanisms include corporate social responsibility reports, benefit corporations, the concept of "blended value" enterprises, and legal "B Corps," as well as new corporate governance practices. Here are some organizations that support this movement.

Many leading-edge experiments in transformational conversations have been refined by top consultants doing organizational and leadership development, conflict mediation, team building, and stakeholder harmonization. They are numerous and diverse. Among the most well known are **Otto Scharmer** (author of *Theory U* and *Presence*) and his U-Lab (ottoscharmer.com, presencing.com), **Peter Senge** (author of *The Fifth Discipline* and *The Necessary Revolution*) and the Society for Organizational Learning (solonline.org), **Bill Torbert** (author of *Action-Inquiry*) and **Fred Kofman** (author of *Conscious Business* and *Authentic Communication*). **Rob Evans**'s elegant Design Shop process integrates many of these principles (imaginal-labs.com). The edges of possibility are being explored by many skilled consultants including my longtime friends **Bert Parlee** (bertparlee.com), leadership expert **Barrett C. Brown** (apheno.com), **Grant Hunter** (syntropycenter.com), and **Adam B. Leonard** (now in-house at Google/Alphabet). **Werner Erhard, Michael Jensen** and their colleagues are making powerful pioneering contributions to the understanding and teaching of leadership (wernererhard.net leadership and beingaleader.net), which are described in chapter 6.

Some resources for social entrepreneurs and investors are:

- **The Impact Hub Global Community** (impacthub.net) supports and mobilizes one of the most effective connection tools of social entrepreneurship communities: urban co-working spaces. The Impact Hub global community includes more than eighty centers on five continents that offer co-working social entrepreneurs the resources, inspiration, services, events, and opportunities for collaboration and networking, as well as many additional community resources (see Impact Hub Oakland above for more details).

- **SOCAP (Social Capital Markets)** (socialcapitalmarkets.net) is a network of investors, entrepreneurs, and social impact leaders who bring together ideas and capital to address the world's toughest challenges through market-based solutions. Its conferences are a key gathering place for social entrepreneurs worldwide.

- For over thirty years, the **Social Venture Network** (svn.org) has worked "to support and empower diverse, innovative leaders who leverage business to serve the greater good." Bringing together investors, communities, and the environment, SVN has given birth to many initiatives, including Businesses for Social Responsibility (below).

- **Businesses for Social Responsibility—BSR** (bsr.org)—is a global nonprofit business network dedicated to sustainability. It has offices on three continents and 250 large corporate members. BSR helps its members upgrade their practices and those of their supply chains, especially regarding environment, energy, climate, ecosystems, water, social justice, women's and LBGT issues.

- **The Hult Prize** (hultprize.org) is an enormous engine for the launch of for-good, for-profit startups emerging from universities. With over 2,500 staff and volunteers around the world, it has deployed more than $50M of capital since 2009 and mobilized more than one million young people to re-think the future of business as it continues to breed disruptive innovation on college and university campuses across one hundred-plus countries.

- **The Laudato Si Challenge** (laudatosichallenge.org) is a global initiative partnering with the Vatican in response to Pope Francis's encyclical calling for "integral ecology." It identifies, funds, and mentors startups to achieve viability to grow breakthrough solutions to humanity's boldest challenges relating to energy, food, water, urban challenges, human potential, conservation, and industry and finance.

- **Game Changers** (gamechangers.co) finds, ranks, connects, and supports the top for-benefit businesses in the world. It shares their stories, organizes trainings, and aims to catalyze the creation of new for-benefit businesses worldwide.

- **Conscious Capitalism** (consciouscapitalism.org), founded by Whole Foods founder John Mackey, believes in free-enterprise capitalism as "the most powerful system for social cooperation and human progress ever conceived," and aims to direct it towards the goal of creating "financial, intellectual, social, cultural, emotional, spiritual, physical and ecological wealth."

- **Teal Organizations** as described in Frederick LaLoux's important book, *Reinventing Organizations,* are going beyond top-down "command and control" management and opening new possibilities for *how* organizations can operate to maximize personal responsibility, human cooperation, and synergy. Cited examples include Buurtzorg, Morningstar Company, Zappo's, and Holocracy One. But the innovations these organizations exemplify are spontaneously emerging in many organizations all over the world, often facilitated by sophisticated consultants and coaches.

- **Living Goods** (livinggoods.org) supports networks of "Avon-like" entrepreneurs in the developing world who deliver life-changing products door to door—including nutritious foods, water filters, and treatments for such life-threatening illnesses, such as malaria and diarrhea. It creates livelihoods for enterprising individuals as well as seriously addressing individual and public health issues, concentrating on areas where child deaths are most likely (e.g., Uganda, Kenya, Myanmar).

- **Juma Ventures** (juma.org) takes at-risk youth across America and places them in socially engaging jobs that teach leadership skills, thus reducing recidivism and creating resources for successful careers. It owns twenty-plus social enterprise operations and serves low-income youth in nine US cities.

- **Acumen Fund** (acumen.org) invests philanthropic dollars into proven change makers. Thus it aims to transform philanthropy by bringing sustainable solutions to poverty, creating access to basic services, and moving toward equality of opportunity.

- **Echoing Green** (echoing green.org) provides seed funding and leadership development to support visionaries around the world who are transforming their communities through economic development, gender equity, and environmental sustainability. Its seven hundred-plus innovators have launched hundreds of programs and initiatives.

Growth Centers and Conscious Conference Communities

Esalen Institute (esalen.org) is a retreat center and intentional community founded in 1962 by Michael Murphy and Richard Price at the Murphy family's beautiful hot springs resort on the bluffs of the Big Sur coast. It has offered workshops and programs focusing on humanistic alternative education and played a key role in birthing the human potential movement through innovative encounter groups, a focus on mind-body connections, and ongoing experimentation in personal awareness. It also sponsored major research and service projects including US-Soviet "Track II" citizen diplomacy and original meta-research documenting the proven effects of meditation, as well as hosting catalytic invitation-only meetings. It is now reimagining its role and, with its expertise in convening conversations that matter, I expect it may be hosting many of the conversations I see emerging in the time ahead.

Omega Institute (omega.org) is a nonprofit educational retreat center in Rhinebeck, New York that was founded in 1977 by Elizabeth Lesser and Stephan Rechtschaffen, inspired by Sufi teacher Pir Vilayat Inayat Khan. It now offers classes to over 25,000 people a year. Its mission is to "provide hope and healing for individuals and society" through "innovative educational experiences that awaken the best in the human spirit." Omega's workshops, conferences, and retreats aim to create dialogues that connect science, spirituality, and creativity; integrate modern medicine and natural healing; and build the groundwork for new traditions and lifestyles.

The Kripalu Center for Yoga and Health (kripalu.org) was founded by Amrit Desai in 1974 and dedicated to his teacher Kripalu. It operates a health and yoga retreat in Stockbridge, MA, in a large former Jesuit seminary. It can accommodate over 650 overnight guests and may be the largest residential facility for holistic health and education in America. It is dedicated to empowering people and communities to realize their full potential through the transformative wisdom and practice of yoga.

Spirit Rock Meditation Center (spiritrock.org), located in rural western Marin County north of San Francisco, offers many programs ranging from weekly meditation events to drop-in classes to silent residential retreats lasting from a few days to a year or more. Although emphasizing profoundly transformative silent Buddhist vipassana practice and retreats, like its sister center, the Insight Meditation Society of Barre, MA (dharma. org), Spirit Rock's approach is ecumenical, with presentations and programs offered by spiritual leaders of many traditions. In addition to explicitly spiritual themes, programs are offered in such areas as relationships and family, community, movement and music, and the natural world. Online classes are also offered.

1440 Multiversity (1440.org) opened in May 2017, offering weekend and five-day workshops and trainings at its state-of-the-art seventy-five-acre campus, nestled in the redwoods of Scotts Valley, CA, between Santa Cruz and San Jose. Named by founders Scott and Joanie Kriens for the number of minutes in a day, it is designed to be a beautiful and nurturing physical location where people of all walks of life can come together in community—to explore, learn, reflect, connect, and reenergize. It supports integration of the emotional, relational, and spiritual dimensions of people's lives to assist in better connecting people to themselves and others.

The Institute of Noetic Sciences (noetic.org) was founded by astronaut Edgar Mitchell to support individual and collective transformation through consciousness research, transformative learning, and engaging a global community in the realization of human potential. It conducts, advances, and broadens the science of the wholeness that connects human beings, reaching new understandings about the nature of reality and our extended capacities. It also creates real-world tools that empower people to apply conscious awareness in their personal lives, and in healthcare, education, and business. At its Petaluma, CA campus, and its annual conferences, it hosts a community of explorers and change agents who are working together to make a difference in the world. Its goal is to create a shift in consciousness worldwide—where people recognize that they are all part of an interconnected whole and are inspired to take action to help humanity and the planet thrive.

Wisdom 2.0 (wisdom2conference.com) is an events company founded by Soren Gordhamer, also the author of a book by the same name. It addresses the great challenge of not only living connected to one another through technology, but to do so in ways that are beneficial to our own well-being, effective in our work, and useful to the world. Its flagship event attracts very well-known C-level executives from Silicon Valley's leading firms as well as scientists and meditation teachers. It is held in February every year in the San Francisco Bay Area and brings together over 2,500 people from twenty-four countries, and it also holds smaller meet-ups, gatherings, and retreats.

The Science and Nonduality Conference (or **SAND,** scienceand-nonduality.org) is an annual conference where leading scientists, philosophers, and spiritual teachers gather to explore a new understanding, rooted in radical wholeness, of who human beings really are, both as individuals and a society. It holds annual conferences that attract hundreds of leading-edge thinkers and practitioners both in the San Francisco Bay Area and Europe, and it also sponsors smaller events.

Integral Transformative Practice International (itp-international. org), founded by George Leonard and Michael Murphy, serves as a hub for communications, education, and research relating to integral practices involving body, mind, and spirit—and creating a society that advances love, deep feeling, and creativity. Ongoing programs and classes are held in California and various US cities.

The Mind and Life Institute (mindandlife.org) has since 1987 convened a series of dialogues between the Dalai Lama and various western scientists on the nature of mind, mindfulness, and the nature of reality, spawning a great body of influential research integrating science with contemplative practice. The Institute has given birth to numerous programs and continues to sponsor dialogues, conferences, and symposia.

The Wellspring Institute for Neuroscience and Contemplative Wisdom (wisebrain.org/wellspring-institute), whose board I serve on, is a nonprofit organization offering skillful means for changing the brain that contribute to individual and global transformation. It utilizes discoveries and methods found where psychology, neurology, and contemplative practice intersect. It addresses a wide range of needs and provides a spectrum of programs and services. It publishes *The Wise Brain Bulletin* six times a year.

Non-Local Communities of Practice

Sounds True (soundstrue.com) was founded by Tami Simon in 1985. It is now a multimedia publishing company with a library of more than 1,500 titles featuring some of the leading teachers and visionaries of our time, and an ever-expanding family of customers from across the world who sometimes come together in online and in-person community events. Sounds True exists to inspire, support, and serve personal transformation and spiritual awakening.

The Shift Network (theshiftnetwork.com) was founded by Stephen Dinan and offers transformative educational programs with over a hundred teachers (including Terry Patten) that have educated and inspired over a hundred thousand people, spread new ideas and practices, and connected global citizens called to create a better world into a planetary network. It is dedicated to supporting a transformational cultural shift through education, lobbying, activism, and philanthropy.

Evolving Wisdom (evolvingwisdom.com) serves the evolution of consciousness and culture by building and nurturing large-scale state-of-the-art global transformative learning communities, including major courses taught by founders Craig Hamilton (the International Integral Enlightenment Community of Direct Awakening) and Claire Zammit (the International Feminine Power Community), as well as Terry Patten, Jean Houston, Neale Donald Walsh, Lynne Twist, and Ariel Ford.

Transpartisan Initiatives

While some attempts at transpartisanship in the USA (such as No Labels) are well known, a wide variety of transpartisan initiatives are advancing on many different fronts.

- **Living Room Conversations** (livingroomconversations.org), founded by a lifelong Democrat and a lifelong Republican, provides proven tools and networks to people who want to engage honest productive conversations that link them with people across various social divides. Most of these conversations reweave connections among people on two or more sides of America's current dividing lines of cultural polarization.

- *The Transpartisan Review* (transpartisanreview.com), edited by A. Lawrence Chickering and James S. Turner, is a recently inaugurated digital journal of politics, society, and culture. It explores the apparent disintegration of the traditional political, social, and cultural order from a transpartisan point of view and looks at the deeper social and cultural forces in play in our political system.

- The **Institute for Cultural Evolution (ICE)** (culturalevolution.org) is the first avowedly integral think tank in the United States. Founded by integral philosophers Steve McIntosh and Carter Phipps, ICE looks to find ways that both the left and right can get past political gridlock and enact a dialectic that gets past the destructive dead-ends of our culture wars. ICE is discussed in detail in chapter 8.

- The **Bridge Alliance** (bridgealliance.us) is a diverse coalition of more than eighty civic action organizations committed to revitalizing the democratic process in America. It provides infrastructure and investment for its member organizations to connect and collaborate on projects that further shared goals to generate a collective impact on elections, governance, policy, and civic life.

- **Undivide Us, and the practice of "Undebate"** (undivide-us.com), implements ways to reunite the United States through a powerful dialogue-based, five-step method (called the "undebate method") for collaborative problem solving and by providing a framework to help identify biases and cultivate empathy.

- **Civil Conversations** (civilconversationsproject.org) was created by podcaster Krista Tippett "to renew common life in a fractured and tender world." It convenes public conversations and publishes a starter guide to better conversations across divides.

- **Converge** (convergeforimpact.com) has led the creation of multi-stakeholder collaborations, partnerships, and networks in diverse fields such as urban revitalization, health care, and environmental conservation. It brings its experience and expertise in systems and design thinking and in organizational and network strategy.

- **All Sides Now** (allsides.com) is a unique news site that displays reports on current events from the left, right, and center, designed to free people from filter bubbles so they can better understand the world and each other. It employs multi-partisan technologies fueled by patented crowd-driven data. Founded by lifelong Republican John Gable, it intends to ameliorate the national security threat of excessive polarization.

- **Better Angels** (better-angels.org) is a citizens' movement aimed to reduce political polarization and gridlock in the US by bringing liberals and conservatives together for workshops and teaching skills for bridging the partisan divide.

- **Village Square Conversations** (tlh.villagesquare.us) is a US non-profit, membership organization whose mission is to build dynamic, constructive civil discourse across political divides in one's hometown, state, and nation, reviving the spirit of the town hall across America, and fostering debate that is both vigorous and civil.

International transpartisan initiatives include well-known efforts like **The Elders** (theelders.org), an independent group of world-famous global leaders working together to promote the shared interests of humanity and small creative initiatives like **SimPol** (simpol.org), which promotes "simultaneous policy implementation" to enable individual nations to express leadership and build momentum toward addressing global problems. It is described in chapter 8.

Partisan Political Activism (USA)

From the very rich and broad world of progressive activism, addressing issues of economic, political, gender, and racial justice, I list only a very few, very general progressive initiatives here, including some that partner with the Democratic Party. It must be said that there is also a great need for principled, responsible conservative activists to reform the current pathologies of the Republican Party and refresh its viability.

Meanwhile, many good people are working around the system through conservative churches and charities, as well as innovative charitable initiatives like **Stand Together** (stand-together.org), which finds successful grassroots programs and helps them scale.

Some conservatives are partnering with people on the left to foster honest conversations across boundaries, such as John Gable, founder of All Sides Now, who partnered with Joan Blades, cofounder of moveon.org to create **Living Room Conversations**.

- *The Indivisible Guide* (indivisibleguide.com/guide) presents step-by-step guidelines and advice on using tactics of proven effectiveness to create progressive change in American politics. The guide includes chapters on grassroots advocacy, how to make your congressional representatives listen and act, how to mobilize your fellow constituents, and how to make sure your congressional members speak for you.

- **Our Revolution** (ourrevolution.com), founded by Bernie Sanders, is dedicated to working both within and around the current system to empower large numbers of individuals to make the American political system more responsive to working families. Its three stated goals are to revitalize American democracy, empower progressive leaders, and elevate the political consciousness.

- **The Action Network** (actionnetwork.org) is a nonprofit organization that makes available online tools expressly for progressive activists—including tools for fundraising, mass mailings, collaboration with other individuals/organizations, etc. It is designed for groups of all sizes, with pricing structures to match, including free intuitive tools.

- **Represent Us** (represent.us) is a nonpartisan initiative focusing on political corruption in the U.S. It works to oppose and expose the most fundamental expression of fragmentation in politics, creating a ground for restoring wholeness. Countless movements in other countries focus on opposing corruption all over the world.

Exploring Our Stories

The **Great Transition Stories** project described in chapter 7 intends to gather, understand, and share the great, simple, emotionally powerful stories that describe our human journey and call higher human potentials from us. This project was conceived and directed by Duane Elgin (duaneelgin.com) in partnership with Lynnaea Lumbard (newstories. org) and Jeff Vander Clute. They are most fully expressed at the Great Transition Stories wiki (greattransitionstories.org).

Mythopoetic Storytelling is a catalyst for facing our world, and several resources for contacting ancient and new stories are worth sharing. The **Mosaic Multicultural Foundation** (mosaicvoices.org) was founded by storyteller, author, and scholar of mythology, anthropology, and psychology **Michael Meade**, whose books, blog posts, and podcasts, combine hypnotic storytelling and street-savvy perceptiveness and connect them to the stories we are living today. **Martin Shaw** (drmartinshaw. com)—founder of **The Westcountry School of Myth** (schoolofmyth. com)—is a mythologist, author, and "one of the greatest storytellers we have" according to Robert Bly. He resurrects ancient fairy tales like the tale of the lindwurm's bride recounted in chapter 7, and delivers them as initiations for facing the mysterious challenges of our time. **The Great Mother and New Father Conference** (greatmotherconference.org) was begun in 1975 by Robert Bly. Its website says "Story has a way of getting into the nervous system of the entire conference over the week. It brushes elbows with ritual, influences the food we eat and when we eat it, supports the work of poetry, activism, and art..." **The Dark Mountain**

Project (dark-mountain.net) is "a network of writers, artists, and think-ers who have stopped believing the stories our civilization tells itself." They feel that the world is entering an age of ecological collapse, mate-rial contraction, and social and political unraveling, and they want their cultural responses to play a crucial role in coming to terms with this real-ity rather than denying it. The project's Dark Mountain Manifesto lays down the gauntlet, and now the project publishes regular anthologies of "uncivilized" writing in carefully crafted, three-hundred-page hardcover books that showcase radical essays, fiction, non-fiction, poetry, art, "and various uncategorizable things."

Understanding Our Ecological Predicament— Facing the Darkness

My denial of our ecological predicament was punctured when I reviewed the evidence, as interpreted primarily by climate scientists like James Hansen, Michael Mann, and Kevin Anderson, and by expert journalists like Bill McKibben and Katherine Kolbert. And my sobriety has been deepened by deep study of the intelligent conversa-tions going on among ecologists who have projected current trends and concluded that it is too late to avert civilization-level disasters. Although I don't share their certainty of collapse, one can outgrow deni-alism and gain gravitas by listening openly, honestly, and carefully to their perspectives.

- My friends **Michael Dowd and Connie Barlow** (thegreatstory.org) exited their conventional lives and partnered in a life of full-time evolutionary evangelism almost a decade ago. Since then, they have crisscrossed America in their van, recently focusing exclu-sively on our climate emergency. Their **Deep Sustainability** web page (thegreatstory.org/sustainability-audios.html) includes links to articles and books, as well as an extensive library of audio files of Michael reading dozens of books (by authors ranging from William Catton to Richard Heinberg to John Michael Greer) that clarify and explore the implacable nature of Earth's bio-logical and geological limits. It is their expectation that we are entering a post-industrial "eco-technic" future that retains scien-tific knowledge but in many ways resembles the pre-industrial past. Michael was the Virgil who guided my descent into an unblinking apprehension of the enormity and intractability of our ecological predicament.

- **Carolyn Baker** (carolynbaker.net) is a psychologist, futurist, community organizer, and environmental activist, who concluded some years ago that industrial civilization is already in the process of collapse and set about trying to help people navigate the enormous psychological and spiritual adjustment to that reality. Through her webinars, podcasts, live workshops, books, and articles, as well as one-on-one life coaching, Carolyn creates "islands of sanity" among people preparing for the dire consequences of the collapse of industrial civilization and abrupt climate change. She also publishes a comprehensive Daily News Digest.

- **John Michael Greer** (ecosophia.net) is acknowledged as the Archdruid of two American Druidic organizations and had long authored the widely read weekly blog, **The Archdruid Report**, as well as more than thirty books on a wide range of subjects, including peak oil and the future of industrial society. He sneers at techno-optimism as his books discuss *The Ecotechnic Future* and *A Dark Age America*, and he recommends we *Collapse Now and Avoid the Rush.*

- Radical environmentalist **Derrick Jensen** (derrickjensen.org) is a coauthor of *Deep Green Resistance* and the author of *Endgame, The Culture of Make Believe, A Language Older than Words*, and many other books. He is widely published in many general circulation publications. A scholarly, soulful visionary and radical activist committed to "the non-human world," he advocates radical and mostly (but not absolutely) nonviolent direct action.

- I end this section on a much more hopeful note with the **Inspiring Transition Initiative** (inspiringtransition.net), an open community that recognizes the grim severity of our global ecological emergency and the necessity for whole-system change to transition to a life-sustaining society. Convener Andrew Gaines and his friends have definitely *not* given up, though, and they work to equip others to become "citizen educators" but not with any centralized direction. Their website provides ready-to-use tools, including sample emails, guerrilla marketing, presentations, workshops, and focused "Kitchen Table Conversations."

Communities of Spiritual Practice and Inner Work

"Communities of practice" are central to the vision of this book. For these communities to make a critical social difference they must embody new higher ways of being and behaving, and that requires profound transformative practice. The majority of the most dedicated communities of practice are spiritual communities. And as we embrace new forms of practice, our experiments will necessarily draw upon this legacy.

These are primarily Buddhist, Hindu, Christian, and evolutionary communities of practice, but useful resources also include Jewish and Islamic communities, as well as those of any and all and no religions. There are more and more authentic teachers and schools of "direct awakening" and dedicated personal growth and development. There is also a growing movement of "interspirituality," not only as a philosophy but as a lived experience. In churches, synagogues, study groups, ashrams, sanghas, schools, and seminaries, we can find many of our richest current communities of practice.

Here I have space to mention only some of the communities of practice that have served me personally. Each of these is of course imperfect, while yet authentically related to something unblemished. I mention them here because I believe they sincerely try to engage genuine practice and transformation. Since I'm limiting this discussion to communities and teachers I have experienced personally, it should *not* be regarded as anything more than my own sharing of what I've known and benefited from. Thus, in this subsection (unlike other subsections of this Resources section), I'm not producing a list of specific resources as such, (the full universe of spiritual practice communities is too vast) but only hinting at some of the types of useful resources available.

I was raised in **The York Center Community Co-operative**, an intentional interracial community founded by members of The Church of the Brethren (one of America's three peace churches) as "a witness for peace and brotherhood." It was a wonderful community in which to grow up, where I was generously mentored by many adult leaders and activists for peace and justice.

Even so, I had to go deep into serious spiritual practice in order to experience the awakenings in consciousness that are expressed in this book. All over the world, people in their chosen spiritual communities are practicing deeply and undergoing transformations that are expressing aspects of the new republic of the heart I'm describing here. Dynamic communities of practice also arise around schools that teach transformative psychotherapy, coaching, leadership, and organizational development.

I practice in the international *integral evolutionary* ecosystem, teaching, learning from, and sharing fellowship with many of the most intelligent and innovative thinkers I know. It is not a structured community of practice, and yet it provides a context for tremendous personal growth.

For the past four years I have helped my friend Thomas Hübl create and grow a dynamic international community of practice and inquiry, growing in spiritual and intuitive competence and leadership (thomashueblonline.com).

I am an occasional participant in the **Two Arrows Zen** (twoarrowszen.org) sangha led by my dear friends, Senseis Diane Musho Hamilton and Michael Mugaku Zimmerman.

I have also benefited tremendously from the meditation instruction of Daniel P. Brown and the **Great Pointing Out Way of Indo-Tibetan Buddhism** (pointingoutway.org).

I have benefited from and still feel deep kinship and grateful spiritual fellowship with Candice O'Denver and her **Balanced View** (balancedview.org) teachings of "short moments of open intelligence, repeated many times until benefit is pervasive at all times."

Saniel Bonder is one of my oldest friends, and his **Waking Down Community** is part of my extended spiritual family. His work is at sanielandlinda.com; the community he inspired has moved on, but I still feel close to the **Trillium Awakening** community (trilliumawakening.org), which was formerly called the Waking Down Teachers Association.

I also benefit from the spiritual fellowship of many teachers from the **Spirit Rock Center** (spiritrock.org) here in my local community, including Rick Hanson (rickhanson.net), James Baraz (awakeningjoy.com), Debra Chamberlin-Taylor, George Taylor, Wes Nisker (wesnisker.com), and Jack Kornfield (jackkornfield.com). I'm also blessed to practice with and learn from many teachers and students in the Diamond Heart work founded by A.H. Almaas (diamondapproach.org).

Gangaji (gangaji.org), who comes from the tradition of nondual Vedanta, was an important guide at a crucial time in my sadhana, and I will always be grateful for her clarity and graciousness.

The living earth and particular natural places give me essential sacred community and guidance. Ecopsychologist Bill Plotkin, the author of *Soulcraft,* has helped that relationship clarify and deepen. The **Animas Valley Institute** he founded (animas.org) offers nature-based journeys of soul initiation that facilitate visionary leadership for cultural regeneration.

Now that I teach, much of my practice takes the form of engaging a universal integral practice with my own students, and with the larger communities of evolutionaries who find value in my contributions.

But I continue to deeply draw on my spiritual "family of origin"—the sangha that developed around the incomparably potent teachings and spiritual transmission of **Adi Da Samraj.** I found my way to him when I was twenty-two and lived immersed in practice in his ashram until I was thirty-seven (from 1973 to 1988), and my life will forever be grounded in the essential "Way of the Heart" that he communicated during those years. His brilliant teachings and uniquely powerful, uncompromising, bright spiritual transmission has given unending wondrous initiatory gifts and a spiritual education for which I will always be grateful. He was a famously defiant and difficult man, and the gathering of his devotees is aging, and yet those who drink his wisdom transmission deeply and wisely can receive a supremely potent dose of divine consciousness and love. Many videos of him can be found on YouTube. My favorite websites are beezone.com and adidaupclose.com; his official institutional website is adidam.org.

NOTES

1   Paul Hawken, ed., *Drawdown: The Most Comprehensive Plan Ever Proposed to Reverse Global Warming* (New York: Penguin Books, 2017).

2   Malcolm Gladwell, *The Tipping Point: How Little Things Can Make a Big Difference* (New York: Little, Brown & Co., 2000), 12.

3   Johan Rockstrom et al, "A Safe Operating Space for Humanity," *Nature* 461 (September 24, 2009), 472–75. (Link at www.nature.com/news/specials /planeteryboundaries/index.html#.feature.)

4   Geoffrey West, *Scale: The Universal Laws of Growth, Innovation, Sustainability, and the Pace of Life in Organisms, Cities, Economies, and Companies* (New York: Penguin Press, 2017), 426.

5   Peter Russell, "Blind Spot: The Unforeseen End of Accelerating Change," www.peterrussell.com/blindspot/blindspot.php (last revised June 29, 2017).

6   Ilya Prigogine, letter to Bertrand Schneider (originally published as part of the proceedings of the World Symposium on Network Media, March 1–5, 1999, Poitiers, France—organized by UNESCO and the Foundation of the Club of Rome), *First Monday*, 4, no. 8 (August 2, 1999); journals.uic.edu/ojs/index .php/fm/article/view/687/597.

7   National Academy of Science, National Academy of Engineering, and Institute of Medicine, *Population Summit of the World's Scientific Academies* (Washington, DC: National Academy of Sciences Press, 1993), 13.

8   Jeffrey Conklin, *Dialogue Mapping: Building Shared Understanding of Wicked Problems* (Chichester, England: Wiley Publishing, 2006).

9   Alan Watkins and Ken Wilber, *Wicked and Wise: How to Solve the World's Toughest Problems* (Chatham, Kent, England: Urbane Publications, 2015).

10 Kelly Levin, Benjamin Cashore, Steven Bernstein, and Graeme Auld, "Overcoming the Tragedy of Super Wicked Problems: Constraining Our Future Selves to Ameliorate Global Climate Change," *Policy Sciences* 45, May 2012, 123–52.

11 Ibid.

12 Nassim Nicholas Taleb, *The Black Swan: The Impact of the Highly Improbable* (New York: Random House, 2006).

13 Ibid., 8.

14 See Horst W. J. Rittel and Melvin M. Webber, "Dilemmas in a General Theory of Planning," *Policy Sciences* 4 (1973): 155–69.

15 Geoffrey West, *Scale* (see full citation above).

16 Charles T. Tart, *Waking Up: Overcoming the Obstacles to Human Potential* (Boston: Shambhala, 1986). "Consensus trance" is defined on pages 85–86 and is discussed in detail in chapter 10 and elsewhere.

17 Chuang Tzu, "Discussion on Making All Things Equal," in Burton Watson, trans., *Chuang Tzu* (New York: Columbia University Press, 1996), 43.

18 See James Hillman, *The Force of Character: And the Lasting Life* (New York: Random House/Ballantine, 1999).

19 George Leonard, *Mastery: The Keys to Success and Long-Term Fulfillment* (New York: Dutton, 1992), 27ff.

20 Howard Gardner, *Extraordinary Minds: Portraits of Four Exceptional Individuals and an Examination of our Own Extraordinariness* (New York: Perseus/BasicBooks, 1997), 117.

21 https://w2.vatican.va/content/francesco/en/homilies/2013/documents/papa-francesco_20130319_omelia-inizio-pontificato.html

22 Marianne Williamson talk, "Spiritual Politics," http://interspirit.net/spirit/spirit.cfm?ref=100373 (retrieved December 3, 2015).

23 This phraseology for wholeness was first used by Nicholas of Cusa in his classic work *De Docta Ignorantia*, written in 1440.

24 Holmes Rolston III, *Three Big Bangs: Matter-Energy, Life, Mind* (New York: Columbia University Press, 2010). See references throughout book.

25 Wilber, following Arthur Koestler, distinguishes between a hierarchy and a holarchy. Whereas hierarchy, by its definition, has an absolute top and bottom, a holarchy describes the dynamic relationships among *holons,* which are both wholes and parts. So in a holarchy there is no final top or bottom, or even normative (better/worse) relationships among the levels.

26 See Ken Wilber, *Sex, Ecology, Spirituality* (Boston: Shambhala, 1995).

27 For a compact summary of AQAL theory, see chapter 5 (pages 67–125) of Ken Wilber, Terry Patten, Adam Leonard, and Marco Morelli, *Integral Life Practice: A 21st-Century Blueprint for Physical Health, Emotional Balance, Mental Clarity, and Spiritual Awakening* (Boston: Integral Books, 2008).

28 *Integral Ecology: Uniting Multiple Perspectives on the Natural World,* by Sean Esbjörn-Hargens and Michael E. Zimmerman (Boston: Integral Books, 2009), conducts a rigorous and revelatory integral study of an enormous range of distinct approaches to understanding ecology, and points to what each perspective reveals. The authors account for, but do not advocate, a radical ecological approach.

29 Scientists at the Social Cognitive Networks Academic Research Center (SCNARC) at Rensselaer Polytechnic Institute conducted this research, described at: https://phys.org/news/2011-07-minority-scientists-ideas.html.

30 Donald O. Hebb, *The Organization of Behavior* (New York: Wiley & Sons, 1949).

31 Pierre Teilhard de Chardin, *Toward the Future* (Boston: Mariner Books, 2002), 86–87. Written in 1934.

32 *Integral Life Practice* was referenced in full in the AQAL note above.

33 Michael P. Mrazek, Benjamin W. Mooneyham, Kaita L. Mrazek, and Jonathan W. Schooler, "Pushing the Limits: Cognitive, Affective, and Neural Plasticity Revealed by an Intensive Multifaceted Intervention," March 18, 2016, http://journal.frontiersin.org/article/10.3389/fnhum.2016.00117/full.

34 Werner H. Erhard and Michael C. Jensen, "The Four Ways of Being that Create the Foundation for Great Leadership, a Great Organization, and a Great Personal Life," Nov. 22, 2013, Harvard Business School NOM Unit Working Paper No. 14-027; Barbados Group Working Paper No. 13-03. (Harvard Business School Negotiation, Organizations and Markets Unit Research Paper Series.)

35 Chris Argyris, "Teaching Smart People How to Learn," *Harvard Business Review* (1991), 99–109.

36 Erhard and Jensen, "Four Ways of Being" (referenced above).

37 Terry Patten, "Integral Soul Work: The Integral Marriage of Spirit, Soul, and Social Activism," *Journal of Integral Theory and Practice* 10, no. 1 (June 2015), 134–45.

38 Purpose Guides Institute, "What Scientific Studies Show Purpose Gives You," www.purposeguides.org/discover-your-purpose/.

39 When this transparent clarity blossoms and stabilizes it is often obvious that very few others are awake to this same freedom. There is an obvious and enormous difference between the free one (me) and the unfree ones (almost everybody else). And many schools and traditions of awakening acknowledge this difference in consciousness by bestowing honorific titles and differentiated roles in hierarchies of maturity (which are often accompanied by practices and responsibilities that ground and further mature those who

have awakened and those they serve). Outside of such traditions, those who awaken spontaneously often identify themselves as "enlightened" at this point. And this identification is usually a subtle form of egoic delusion and makes people, at least temporarily, spiritually arrogant and immune to feedback. But the thrust of transcendental spirituality ultimately delivers a realization of wholeness and unity, and wakes you up to the fact that this life is not and could not ever be primarily about "you," "your enlightenment," or any kind of personal fulfillment of any human individual.

40 Described in an unpublished talk by Adi Da Samraj given at the Mountain of Attention Sanctuary (Lake County, California), August 14, 1979.

41 This account is excerpted from an interview with Duane Elgin by Elizabeth Debold for *evolve magazin,* a German-language quarterly, May 2015.

42 See www.greattransitionstories.org/wiki/Main_Page, a project created by Duane Elgin, Lynnaea Lumbard, and Jeff Vander Clute.

43 When I was six years old, my parents moved our family from Chicago to the York Center Community Co-operative, a 70-acre cornfield that was purchased by members of the nearby Church of the Brethren (one of America's three peace churches) and converted into a cooperatively-owned interracial community as "a witness for peace and brotherhood." There I was generously mentored by my "co-op aunts and uncles"—a varied mix of fierce individuals, including conscientious objectors, Japanese-Americans who had been interned during WWII, civil rights leaders, labor organizers, and in-the-system political activists.

44 Michael Meade, *The Genius Myth* (Seattle: Greenfire Press, 2016). Source based on my correspondence with author.

45 Daniel Pellerin translation of "Schopenhauer as Educator"—excerpt quoted from Maria Popova's Brainpickings site: www.brainpickings.org/2015/09 /30/nietzsche-find-yourself-schopenhauer-as-educator/.

46 See Joanne Hunt, "Transcending and Including Our Current Way of Being: An Introduction to Integral Coaching," *Journal of Integral Theory and Practice* 4, no. 1 (2009), 1–20.

47 See https://pocketproject.org.

48 Sam Keen, introduction to the 1973 edition of Ernest Becker, *The Denial of Death* (New York: The Free Press, 1973), xiii.

49 "Answering the Call of the Mycelium Warrior," March 8, 2016, http:// fantasticfungi.com/mycelium-warrior (accessed May 1, 2017).

50 Ibid.

51 See http://arts.brookes.ac.uk/staff/shelleysacks.html.

52 Vimala Thakar, *The Mystery of Silence* (Holland: The Vimala Thakar Foundation, 1977).

53 Charles Eisenstein, "The Election: Of Hate, Grief, and a New Story," November 10, 2016 blog entry, https://charleseisenstein.net/essays/hategriefandanewstory.

54 Adi Da Samraj, *Not-Two Is Peace*, 3rd ed. (Middletown, CA: The Dawn). Horse Press, 2009).

55 Paul Hawken, *Blessed Unrest: How the Largest Social Movement in History Is Restoring Grace, Justice, and Beauty to the World* (New York: Penguin, 2007), 4.

56 John Kania and Mark Kramer, "Collective Impact," *Stanford Social Innovation Review,* Winter 2011, https://ssir.org/articles/entry/collective_impact.

57 Ibid.

58 A. Lawrence Chickering and James S. Turner, *Voice of the People: The Transpartisan Imperative in American Life* (Goleta, CA: da Vinci Press, 2008).

59 As pointed out in the previous chapter, tribes, ethnic groups, religions, races, and nations have shared interiors and collective "souls." The souls of nations and peoples are essential dimensions of human character. Recent events make it clear that they will violently resist being homogenized into a single world culture. And yet we live together on a single globe, and many of us have lost a sense of our original tribal identities and become global citizens. We are members, in effect, of new global tribe(s). Others of us are dual citizens, of both our global and our original tribes. The polarity between nationalism and globalism is complex—something we are all just beginning to learn to navigate.

60 Integral politics is international and diverse. Although this discussion refers to universal principles, I and most of my readers are most deeply familiar with U.S. politics, and many references here are to the particular political dynamics of the U.S. These references are also appropriate because the U.S. is the world's most politically powerful and consequential nation.

61 John T. Kesler, *A Call for an Integral Political Movement* (2017)—from my review of a prepublication draft. Also see Part One of this work, "Why Maturity Matters in Our Political Leadership," posted on Kesler's site at https://johnkesler.com/why-maturity-matters.

62 See Robb Smith, "Inside the Great Release," (August 31, 2017), http://integrallife.com; and "The Great Divide" (August 11, 2016) and "Thriving in the Transformational Era" (March 11, 2016) at Robb Smith's website, www.robbsmith.com (which includes many of his blogposts).

63 See Jonathan Haidt, *The Righteous Mind: Why Good People Are Divided by Politics and Religion* (New York: Random House, 2012).

64 Ken Wilber, *Trump and a Post-Truth World* (Boston: Shambhala, 2017).

65 See Chickering and Turner, *Voice of the People.*

66 www.transpartisanreview.com

67 www.bridgealliance.us

68 David Brooks, "Startling Adult Friendships," September 18, 2014, www.nytimes.com/2014/09/19/opinion/david-brooks-there-are-social-and-political-benefits-to-having-friends.html.

69 Steve McIntosh, "Why Centrism Fails and How We Can Better Achieve Political Cooperation" (The Institute for Cultural Evolution, July 2016), www.culturalevolution.org/docs/ICE-Why-Centrism-Fails.pdf (retrieved April 3, 2017).

70 Ibid.

71 Andrew Harvey, *The Hope: A Guide to Sacred Activism* (Carlsbad, CA: Hay House, 2009), 125.

72 There is profound happiness in engagement, so we need not disconnect from the truth Campbell points to either.

73 David Bohm suggested that the world's crisis could best be addressed by deep open dialogue that could liberate the limiting structures of thought that were creating it; he proposed some basic practices, and engaged a series of public dialogues with Jiddu Krishnamurti, spawning "Bohmian dialogue."

74 See Terry Patten, "Why 'We' Matters: Transformational Potentials of Evolutionary Subjectivity." In O. Gunnlaugson and M. Brabant, eds., *Cohering the Integral We Space: Engaging Collective Emergence, Wisdom and Healing in Groups* (Occidental, CA: Integral Publishing House, 2016).

75 *The Technium* ("Scenius, or Communal Genius") on Kevin Kelley's website: http://kk.org/thetechnium/scenius-or-comm (accessed May 3, 2017).

76 Ibid.

77 The earliest we-space experiments took place around Ken Wilber, who allocated an entire quadrant (the lower left) to intersubjective practice, and created Integral Institute seminars where higher intersubjective spaces were regularly convened and facilitated, especially through Genpo Roshi's "Big Mind" process as transmitted by him and by Diane Musho Hamilton. Some important early work on collective awakening came from the Enlighten-Next spiritual community, founded by Andrew Cohen, and, upon the community's demise, has produced exciting offshoots through the work of Craig Hamilton, Jeff Carreira, Thomas Steininger, and Elizabeth Debold.

Olen Gunnlaugson brought methodological clarity and self-awareness to the fact that a whole field is emerging, drawing from previous dialogue practices, especially from Francisco Varela and Otto Scharmer. This greater experiment spread through the whole integral evolutionary mainstream via integral conferences, both theoretical and practice-oriented. Then Decker Cunov and a whole community devoted to "Circling" (a dynamic, open-ended, intersubjective practice) attracted a whole generation of integral practitioners. Robert MacNaughton built perhaps the largest of all communities of integral we-space practice at Jeff Salzman's Boulder Integral Center, where he has, with Diane Hamilton and myself, been offering "The Integral Living Room" in a forum where people have "the best conversations of our lives." Spiritual teacher Thomas Hübl taught people to access subtle information fields and engage in transparent communication and the birthing of a new "we." Patricia Albere developed the Evolutionary Collective, which involved long-term commitment and community. Dustin Diperna, Christina Vickory, and others developed WE Practice. Sean Wilkinson, John Thompson, Jordan Allen, and Philip Watson are now spreading and evolving Circling in Europe and Latin America. I have worked with most of these people and conducted original experiments in integral rhetorical praxis and soul work. This list is undoubtedly leaving out many important additional experiments. Michael Brabant and Olen Gunnlaugson coedited *Cohering the Integral We Space,* an anthology of writings expressing different schools, and convened online community exploration of the field. Conferences have been held in both the U.S. and Europe.

78 Bill Kauth and Zoe Alowan, *We Need Each Other: Building Gift Community* (Ashland, OR: Silver Light Publications, 2011).

79 Terry Patten, "Enacting an Integral Revolution: How Can We Have Truly Radical Conversations in a Time of Global Crisis?" *Journal of Integral Theory and Practice* 8, nos. 3 and 4 (December 2013).

80 The former name of their intersubjective practice was "Evolutionary Dialogue."

81 Thomas Steininger and Elizabeth Debold, "Emerge Dialogue Process: The Intersection of the Higher We and Dialogue Process," in Olen Gunnlaugson and Michael Brabant, *Cohering the Integral We Space: Engaging Collective Emergence, Wisdom, and Healing in Groups* (Occidental, CA: Integral Publishing House, 2016), 269–94.

82 In this enormous global project, which has already begun and which will occupy us for decades, we are working a process whose potential is to discover how to honor and learn from people of every racial, ethnic, gender, religious, and worldview classification, without failing to honor progress,

tradition, or the unique role of our new, universalist global tribe. Our task is to find ways to hear one another without giving up our own experience, interests, and unique perspectives—ways that allow us to coexist and cooperatively enact effective approaches to our challenges amidst a whole new order of cultural collisions.

INDEX

ABOUT THE AUTHOR

Terry Patten speaks and consults internationally as a community organizer, philosopher, and teacher. Over the last fifteen years he has devoted his efforts to the integral project of evolving consciousness through practice and facing, examining, and healing our global crisis through the marriage of spirit and activism. With Ken Wilber and a core team at the Integral Institute, Patten cowrote *Integral Life Practice*, which distills ancient and modern practices into a contemporary transformational lifestyle. As creator and host of the online series Beyond Awakening, he has explored the big questions of our time with some of our most prominent and dynamic thought leaders. He founded and leads Bay Area Integral, which gathers and supports an integral community in the San Francisco Bay Area; he led a team at the Heart-Math Institute that developed its first heart-rate variability monitor; and he founded the catalog company Tools For Exploration, which defined the field of consciousness technologies. Patten is also a social entrepreneur involved in supporting restorative redwood forestry, innovating new technological alternatives to fossil fuels, and creating new currencies for a sustainable economy.

About North Atlantic Books

North Atlantic Books (NAB) is an independent, nonprofit publisher committed to a bold exploration of the relationships between mind, body, spirit, and nature. Founded in 1974, NAB aims to nurture a holistic view of the arts, sciences, humanities, and healing. To make a donation or to learn more about our books, authors, events, and newsletter, please visit www.northatlanticbooks.com.

North Atlantic Books is the publishing arm of the Society for the Study of Native Arts and Sciences, a 501(c)(3) nonprofit educational organization that promotes cross-cultural perspectives linking scientific, social, and artistic fields. To learn how you can support us, please visit our website.